Investor Protection

A. C. PAGE
Professor of Public Law, University of Dundee

R. B. FERGUSON
Deputy Director, Securities and Investments Board, London

WEIDENFELD AND NICOLSON
London

To
Michael and Rebecca Page
and
David and Andrew Ferguson

George Weidenfeld and Nicolson Ltd
Orion House, 5 Upper St Martin's Lane,
London, WC2H 9EA

ISBN 0 297 82131 8 cased
ISBN 0 297 82132 6 paperback

Photoset by Deltatype Ltd, Ellesmere Port, Cheshire
Printed in Great Britain by
Butler & Tanner Ltd, Frome and London

INVESTOR PROTECTION

This be

CHAR

LAW IN CONTEXT

Editors: Robert Stevens (Covington & Burling, London)
William Twining (University College, London) and
Christopher McCrudden (Lincoln College, Oxford)

PUBLISHED TITLES INCLUDE:

Atiyah's Accidents, Compensation and the Law (Fourth Edition), Peter Cane
Karl Llewellyn and the Realist Movement (reissue), William Twining
Cases and Materials on the English Legal System (Fifth Edition), Michael Zander
How to do Things with Rules (Third Edition), William Twining and David
  Miers
Evidence, Proof and Probability (Second Edition), Richard Eggleston
Family Law and Social Policy (Second Edition), John Eekelaar
Labour Law (Second Edition), Paul Davies and Mark Freedland
The Law Making Process (Third Edition), Michael Zander
An Introduction to Law (Third Edition), Phil Harris
Law and Administration, Carol Harlow and Richard Rawlings
Legal Foundations of the Welfare State, Ross Cranston
British Government and the Constitution (Second Edition), Colin Turpin
Sexual Divisions in Law, Katherine O'Donovan
The Law of Contract, Hugh Collins
Regulation and Public Law, Robert Baldwin and Christopher McCrudden
Freedom of Information, Patrick Birkinshaw
Remedies in Contract and Tort, Donald Harris
Trusts Law, Graham Moffat and Michael Chesterman
Courts and Administrators, Michael Detmold
Consumer Protection, Iain Ramsay
Subjects, Citizens, Aliens and Others, Ann Dummett and Andrew Nicol
New Directions in European Community Law, Francis Snyder
Languages of Law, Peter Goodrich
Reconstructing Criminal Law, Nicola Lacey, Celia Wells and Dirk Meure
Analysis of Evidence, Terence Anderson and William Twining
International Business Taxation, Sol Picciotto
Sentencing and Criminal Justice, Andrew Ashworth

CONTENTS

PART II – INVESTMENT MEDIA AND INSTITUTIONS

PREFACE

We have written *Investor Protection* with two main types of reader in mind: first, students of investor protection, regulation and compliance, company law and consumer protection – in other words, those whose courses are concerned with the role of regulation in the savings and investment industry; secondly, compliance practitioners, financial services lawyers, regulators and financial journalists – in short, those with a professional interest in the business of regulation.

The book is designed to give an overview of the legal and regulatory arrangements for investor protection in the United Kingdom. 'Investor protection' is often spoken of as if its scope could be equated with that of the Financial Services Act, but we have taken a broader view. The modern financial system offers a wide range of alternative (and competing) savings and investment vehicles for ordinary people – e.g. National Savings products, bank and building society accounts, endowment policies, unit trusts, investment trusts, personal pensions, company pensions, stocks and shares, and managed portfolios – and provision for investor protection is made in various branches of legislation. The question this raises is whether it is sensible to treat investor protection as a subject in its own right, susceptible to coherent overall treatment, rather than as a collection of separate and unconnected topics – the protection of policyholders, of depositors, of the clients of businesses regulated under the Financial Services Act, and so on. This book embodies our view that there is enough common ground among these topics to make possible an exposition of investor protection viewed as a legal subject in its own right. As we argue in Chapter 1, the necessary degree of unity comes from the fact that similar concerns and similar policies tend to underlie the various sets of rules designed for the protection of savers and investors, and similar legal and regulatory devices are often employed to realise these policies.

A book which takes as its subject investor protection defined in this broad sense has a lot of ground to cover – some of it shifting sand. Our approach has been to strike a balance between breadth and detail. There is a great deal of systematic legal exposition in this book, but we have not felt obliged to refer to each and every clause in the applicable legislation. Throughout we have tried to focus on the legal mainstream and to relate the regulatory arrangements in place to the concerns which have prompted them and the policies they reflect. Thus we offer an account of the law of investor protection in the context of its economic background and purposes.

We have, of course, been trying to hit a moving target. The requirements introduced under the Financial Services Act have been particularly labile, but the prospects are good that the Core Rules made in 1991 will indeed provide a core of stability. Our text reflects the law as it stood on 1 January 1992, and in several areas it has been possible to absorb later developments – for example the Investment Advertisement Exemption Orders and the Occupational Pension Schemes (Investment of Scheme's Resources) Regulations issued in March 1992.

The idea for *Investor Protection* was developed when both authors were in the Department of Law at Dundee University. As a result, however, of Bob Ferguson's move to the Securities and Investments Board in 1987, responsibility for the initial drafting of the text was redivided; Alan Page was thus responsible for most of Parts I and II, Bob Ferguson for most of Part III. We are grateful to those who have made suggestions – in particular to Martin Loughlin, Andrew Kennon, Colette Bowe and Jane Welch. Our thanks also go to Fiona Walker, who prepared the tables of legal sources, to Marion McGregor and Pat Mowle, who typed the manuscript, and to Ian Melville.

Finally, we wish to record that we have written as private individuals. The views expressed by us must not be attributed to the University of Dundee or to the Securities and Investments Board.

Alan Page
Bob Ferguson
April 1992

Part I
GENERAL

I
The Concept of Investor Protection

Our primary aim in this introductory chapter is to explain what we mean by the term 'investor protection'. Although the term is used increasingly in the United Kingdom, particularly since the Financial Services Act 1986, it cannot yet be said to have acquired a sufficiently clear meaning to free us from the need to explain our understanding of it. We also want to provide a justification of investor protection as a subject worthy of study in its own right, and to outline the relationship between investor protection, as we have defined it, and other branches of the law. Our task, in short, is to locate investor protection on the legal map. We begin by looking at investment and related concepts.

INVESTMENT

When the term investment is used we tend to think immediately of company shares and government stocks; remembering that property is – or was – 'a good investment' we might also think of the ownership of land and property; and depending on how sophisticated is our knowledge of investment we might go on to think of unit trusts, pension schemes, life assurance policies, futures, options and an almost endless list of other media. We are unlikely, on the other hand, to think of backing horses or gaming in casinos which we would describe instead as gambling. And yet investors in, for example, commodities are frequently likened to gamblers, and we can bet on the future movement of the FT-SE 100 index at the bookmakers as well as on the stock-market. What is it, therefore, that makes shares, for example, an investment, and what, if anything, marks investment off from other activities such as gambling?

Drawing clear conceptual distinctions between investment and cognate terms such as saving, speculating and gambling is far from easy. The basic idea of investment is, however, straightforward. To invest, in everyday usage, simply means to lay out something (usually money, but it could be labour or expertise) in the expectation of a return. Where money is laid out, the return expected may take the form of a once-and-for-all capital gain or else a periodic return or income. It is in this sense that we talk of shares or property as investments. So long, therefore, as what is acquired is done so with a view to gain, it is, in terms of everyday usage, an investment regardless of whether it is securities, land, commodities or goods.

The more specialised usage of economics imparts a different meaning to the term. Economists use the term 'real' or 'productive' investment to denote spending by industry on capital goods. Whereas our investor is a capital *supplier*, the economist's investor is a capital *user*, the capital used, or investment, representing a contribution to the productive process. Economists also draw a distinction between real investment and 'financial' or 'personal' investment; here investment is being used in its everyday sense, albeit to denote the acquisition of financial claims only and not physical goods by individuals.

Neither of these approaches provides a satisfactory basis for a *legal* definition of investment. In particular, if motive is treated as the key, the result is likely to be uncertainty as to what is and what is not an investment. The motive with which an asset is acquired may not be apparent, and the same asset may be acquired with different motives.[1] The characteristic legislative response to this problem in the United Kingdom has been to eschew general definitions of investment in favour of stipulating what are investments for the purpose of the legislation in question. This is the approach adopted in the Financial Services Act which devotes fifteen pages of the first schedule to the definition of 'investment' and 'investment business'.[2]

Investment and saving

The counterpart of the economist's capital user is the capital supplier or *saver*. In economic terms a saver is someone whose income exceeds his consumption and who thus has money available to advance to others. Capital users and suppliers seldom come together directly; more commonly they are linked by a financial institution which collects savings and then lends them on. Long-term savings are typically collected by insurance companies and pension schemes; short-term savings by banks and building societies.

Bank and building society savings and deposit accounts are not investments for the purposes of the Financial Services Act. Other than in economic terms, however, it is difficult to draw a clear distinction between saving and investment. One traditional approach treats the distinction between the two as a matter of risk. The Financial Services Act White Paper, for example, asserted that: 'Investment – as distinct from saving with a bank or building

---

[1] Compare the treatment of money on deposit in *Price* v. *Newton* [1905] 2 Ch.55, with *O'Sullivan* v. *Robbins* [1937] 1 Ch.118.
[2] See, further, Chapter 15.

society – necessarily entails taking deliberately considered risks.'[1] However, we need only think of the collapse of a bank – BCCI for example – or a building society to spot the weakness in this approach. While it can be argued plausibly that savers attach greater importance to safety than do, for example, investors in shares, it does not follow that savings are risk-free; as we shall see, savings can be risky, and there are some forms of investment which come close to being risk-free. For practical purposes, therefore, investment and saving are effectively indistinguishable. Only by putting our savings under the mattress or burying them in the garden is it possible for us to save without investing.

Investment, speculation and gambling

Speculation is usually thought of as occupying a position midway between investment and gambling. It has strong affinities with gambling, but is said to be distinguishable from it by virtue of the fact that, like investment, it takes place on markets rather than at the bookmakers or on the racecourse; it occurs in relation to what are sometimes described as naturally occurring risks rather than artificially created ones. Given, however, that we can bet on the movement of the FT-SE 100 index at the bookmakers as well as on the Stock Exchange, or invest our savings in premium bonds with the chance of a tax-free prize, it is difficult to see this distinction itself as other than somewhat artificial.

An alternative approach treats the distinction between investment, speculation and gambling as a matter of time and risk. Gambling is thus supposed to be very quick and very risky, speculation takes longer and is less risky, and investment is long-term and the least risky of all. The weaknesses of this approach are again fairly obvious. A bet on the winner of the next World Cup is long-term, but it is still a bet. And there may be less risk for an experienced player in a game of backgammon than there would be in an investment in shares.

The reason why it is difficult to draw a satisfactory distinction is not because we cannot invest without gambling – we can – but rather because the three transactions are economically very similar. Gambling is customarily defined as the placing of something of value at risk in relation to an uncertain event. We lay out money and get, not a good or service immediately, but a monetary return later if an uncertain event occurs.[2] But these three elements – money, risk and uncertainty – are equally common to investment and speculation. Like the gambler, the investor, other than the investor in property over which he obtains exclusive control, does not get a good or service in return for his investment, and what he does get may turn out, depending on future events, to be as worthless or as valuable as, for example, his betting slip.

[1] Para.1.7.
[2] Downie, 'Gambling and the gamblers', in *The World of Monetary Risk* (1980), pp.17–19.

Where investment, speculation and gambling do differ is in the way in which they are regarded by society. Investment, most obviously in the economist's sense of real investment, is regarded with approval and as something to be encouraged; its connotations are almost entirely positive. Speculation has rather less positive connotations. In *Ironmonger* v. *Dyne*, Scrutton L.J. described currency speculators as 'beneath contempt',[1] a sentiment which has been echoed many times since. Such positive connotations as it does possess derive mainly from the fact that it takes place on markets: economists, for example, defend speculation as essential to ensuring their liquidity and hence their efficient functioning. Gambling, finally, is viewed with disapproval; its connotations are almost entirely negative.

These varying connotations are carried over into the law which extends its protection to investors and speculators but not to gamblers. By virtue of the gaming legislation, gambling transactions are null and void and hence unenforceable;[2] speculative as well as investment transactions, on the other hand, are treated as valid and enforceable.[3] Although it may be difficult, therefore, to distinguish between investment and speculation on the one hand and gambling on the other, the difficulty is nevertheless one which the courts have had to face. Their response, formulated in a series of cases at the end of the last century and in the early years of this, was to draw a parallel distinction between *real* contracts and *fictitious* ones. The essence of a real contract, which was enforceable, was that the parties intended that delivery of the shares, currency or other investments which formed the subject of the contract should take place. If, on the other hand, there was no intention that delivery should take place, there being instead an understanding that the contract should be settled by the payment of the difference between the price of the investments at a certain date and their price at some future date, the contract was treated as a fictitious one and as unenforceable.[4]

One consequence of this amalgam of statute and case law was to cast doubt on the validity of contracts such as options and futures contracts where the parties normally do not intend that delivery should take place but that differences only should be accounted for. This doubt has now been removed by the Financial Services Act, Schedule 1, which provides that no regard is to be had to the gaming legislation or the common law of Scotland in determining whether anything constitutes an investment or the carrying on of investment business for the purposes of that Schedule.[5] The Act also ensures the

---

[1] (1928) 44 T.L.R. 497.

[2] Gaming Act 1845, s.18. In Scotland, where the Act does not apply, they are unenforceable at common law.

[3] *Universal Stock Exchange* v. *Strachan* [1896] A.C. 166; for Scotland, see *Shaw* v. *Caledonian Railway Co.* (1890) 17 R. 466.

[4] *Universal Stock Exchange* v. *Strachan* [1896] A.C. 166. For a fuller survey, albeit one involving a rather strained reading of the cases, see Chaikin and Moher, 'Commodity futures contracts and the Gaming Act' [1986] *Lloyd's Maritime and Commercial Law Quarterly* 390.

[5] Sch. 1, para.33.

enforceability of any contract the making or performance of which by either party constitutes dealing in investments.[1]

Investment and trade

Investment and trading are usually thought of as distinct. Distinguishing the two, however, is again difficult. One context in which the distinction has nevertheless had to be drawn is taxation, trading profits being liable to income tax, investment profits to capital gains tax. The Royal Commission on the Taxation of Profits and Income concluded that no single fixed rule should be applied in determining whether a transaction was 'an adventure in the nature of trade', but that each case should be decided according to its own circumstances.[2] Transactions are therefore examined to see whether they bear any of a number of 'badges of trade', the implication, if they bear sufficient badges, being that they are embarked upon for the purpose of trade and not investment. Factors taken into account include: the subject matter of the transaction; the length of period of ownership; the frequency or number of similar transactions; whether or not any work was done on the subject matter of the transaction; the circumstances responsible for its realisation; and the motive with which it was entered into.[3] For example, an intention to resell immediately or in the short term is indicative of a trading transaction; conversely, an intention to hold on to the asset suggests an investment transaction.

Another context in which the distinction is important is the Financial Services Act which excludes, from the definition of investments, futures contracts made for 'commercial' rather than 'investment' purposes. Again no attempt is made to draw a hard and fast line between these forward delivery contracts, which are excluded, and futures contracts designed to allocate the risk of price fluctuations, which are not. (As well as providing a means of covering or hedging the risk that the price will move unfavourably between the time the contract is entered into and the time it is to be performed, these contracts provide a means of speculating on movements in the price of the underlying assets.) Instead the Act supplies a number of criteria, some of which are conclusive, others merely indicative, of the purpose for which the contract is made. Thus contracts made or traded on a recognised investment exchange are to be regarded as made for investment purposes, as are off-exchange contracts which simulate such contracts. On the other hand, a contract is made for commercial purposes if delivery is to be made within seven days.[4]

---

[1] s.63; *City Index Ltd.* v. *Leslie* [1991] 3 All E.R. 180.   [2] Cmd. 9474 (1955), para.116.

[3] *ibid.*; and see *Marson* v. *Morton* [1986] 1 W.L.R. 1343.

[4] Sch. 1, para.8; see further Chapter 15 below.

Investment and insurance

If investment and gambling are economically similar, then the difference between insurance and investment must be the same as that between insurance and gambling. Unfortunately, this does not take us very far, because insurance and gambling are also closely related. The conventional way of distinguishing them is to say that insurance is about avoiding risks, gambling about taking them; we lay out money with a view to avoiding a loss rather than making a gain.[1]

On this analysis, insurance is to be distinguished from investment by virtue of the fact that it is about risk-aversion rather than risk-taking. But as well as providing a means of protection, life assurance also constitutes an important medium for saving and investment. 'The fact of the matter is that life assurance . . . has traditionally been a medium for saving and investment as well as a means of helping the policyholder to make financial provision for his dependants, and that life companies place considerable emphasis in their promotional material on this investment aspect.'[2] Hence rights under long-term insurance contracts, other than pure protection policies, are investments for the purposes of the Financial Services Act.[3]

INVESTOR PROTECTION AND THE LAW

Until about the middle of the nineteenth century, the development of capitalism in the United Kingdom took place within a framework characterised by and large by the *immediate* ownership of resources by individuals; the paradigmatic investor was the owner-manager. In this context the law afforded protection to investors primarily by recognising and enforcing property rights. Participation in the enterprise of others might be enjoyed through the device of partnership, or by constituting the relationship of creditor and debtor; hence the importance of the development and rationalisation of these branches of law as well as the law of property.

The major development which has occurred since the middle of the last century has been the growth of *intermediated* property and credit relations. It is in this context that legal measures emerge to protect the investor, not as a property owner or as creditor, but in a variety of other guises. The intermediation of *credit* relations is largely the achievement of the bank and the building society, by virtue of which the ultimate supplier of credit is divorced from its ultimate recipient and transformed into a depositor or shareholder, who may be protected as such. The central factor in the intermediation of

---

[1] Legally, the requirement of an insurable interest serves to distinguish insurance contracts from wagering contracts: see *MacGillivray and Parkington on Insurance Law* (8th edn, 1988), Chapter 1.

[2] *Linked Life Assurance: Report of the Committee on Property Bonds and Equity-Linked Life Assurance*, Cmnd. 5281 (1973), para.71.

[3] Sch.1, para.10.

property relations is, of course, the rise of the registered company over the last 100 years or so from a comparatively minor position to become the predominant business form. The interpolation of the corporate form between the investor and the assets of the business divests him of legal ownership of them; so if the investor is to be protected, it must be as a shareholder or debenture holder.

The ascendancy of the registered company is not, however, the end of the story. The process of intermediation has been carried a stage further by the growing popularity of various forms of indirect investment such as unit trusts, life assurance policies and pension schemes. Modern surveys of shareholdings in companies listed on the Stock Exchange indicate the growth in importance of institutional investors (and hence of indirect investment). Between 1963 and 1990 the proportion of shares held by unit trusts grew from 1.3 per cent to 6.1 per cent; by insurance companies from 10 per cent to 20.4 per cent; and by pension funds from 6.4 per cent to 31.4 per cent.[1] In addition, institutional investors account for more than 40 per cent of market holdings of national debt and are the largest investors in commercial property.[2] This expansion of indirect investment means that investor protection comes to include the protection of the investor *qua* unit-holder, life policyholder, pension scheme beneficiary, etc.

This trend towards indirect investment has not been reversed or halted by the policy of widening share ownership which has been pursued in the United Kingdom since 1983. Although privatisation of public sector assets, in combination with personal equity plans (PEPs) and employee share schemes, has brought about a dramatic increase in the number of individual shareholders – from an estimated three million in 1979 to nearly eleven million a decade later – the proportion of shares quoted on the Stock Exchange held by individuals has continued to fall – from 28.9 per cent in 1981 to only 21.1 per cent in 1989.[3]

PEPs are one of the instruments which have been employed in the promotion of wider share ownership. Their history illustrates in microcosm the history of individual investment in the United Kingdom. They were introduced by the Finance Act 1986 to encourage, by means of tax reliefs, direct investment by individuals in UK companies. But in response to the criticism that they would tempt to invest in shares people for whom pooled investments would be more suitable, the requirements governing the investment of plan subscriptions have been relaxed to allow an element of investment in authorised unit trusts or investment trust companies. What began as a vehicle for investment in equities has thus become a vehicle for investment in unit

[1] *Economic Trends*, October 1991.

[2] Richardson, 'The provision of pensions' (1983) 23 *Bank of England Quarterly Bulletin* 502.

[3] London Stock Exchange, Quality of Markets Quarterly Review: Autumn 1991, *Stock Exchange Quarterly* (Autumn 1991).

trusts and investment trusts. This is, of course, contrary to the original purpose of encouraging direct investment, but is not necessarily contrary to the interests of investors for whom collective savings vehicles such as unit trusts possess advantages in terms of risk spreading (a survey in 1988 found that 56 per cent of individual shareholders held shares in only one quoted company) and professional management, which may make them a more suitable form of investment for investors of limited means than direct investment in shares.

The upshot of this growth in indirect investment is that the investor protection function of modern law is spread over several branches of the law, from the law of property to the law of pensions, each of which has its own history. There is no formal unity overall; instead, each type of investment has its own distinctive legal characteristics – a bank account involves the relationship of creditor and debtor, occupational pension scheme membership the relationship of beneficiary and trustee, and so on. Moreover, from an economic point of view, different legal packages tend to have different financial properties; they vary in their riskiness, their liquidity, i.e. the ease and speed with which they may be turned into cash, and their susceptibility to loss of value due to inflation. In view of this legal and economic heterogeneity, it might be doubted whether it is feasible to advance any generalisations about investor protection as such. It is therefore to the scope and attendant logic of our book that we now turn.

SCOPE AND LOGIC OF INVESTOR PROTECTION

Our concern in this book is with investor protection in the context of *intermediated* property and credit relations. We thus exclude investor protection in the context of the *immediate* ownership of resources by individuals, and hence investments such as property and 'collectibles', i.e. works of art, coins, manuscripts etc., from the scope of our concern. With these investments, the investor obtains, at least in theory, direct personal control over his investment. By contrast, the investor in the vehicles of investment with which we are concerned does not; he is required to put his faith in others. But even if we exclude property and direct credit relations from the scope of our concern, we are still left with a picture of considerable diversity. How then can a book on investor protection be justified, bearing in mind that the various branches of the law we have mentioned have traditionally been taught and written about separately?

The economic justification for our book can be stated briefly. It is that direct share ownership – the traditional focus of legal scholarship – constitutes only one among a wide range of *competing* savings and investment media, so that instead of there being separate markets for deposit accounts, life policies, unit trusts and so on, there is what is in effect a single market for personal investment: 'all investment markets [are] connected by a seamless web, in the sense that all investment markets are in competition with each other to look after the pound in the consumer's pocket.'[1] It is this element of competition between investment media, creating this unified market, which makes the modern personal investor as likely to be a pension scheme beneficiary, life policyholder, unit-holder etc., as a shareholder, and which provides the underlying economic rationale for our book.

The legal justification for our book is more complex. Table 1 below identifies, for a number of investments, the legal relationship(s) involved. Clearly there is diversity, but there is more unity than might be supposed in the sense that the same relationships, the same building blocks, recur across the whole field – the relationship of creditor and debtor, trustee and beneficiary, shareholder/member and corporation and, in the context of intermediaries, that of principal and agent. Moreover, this unity is increased by the parallels which exist between these building blocks. Thus the concept of the fiduciary duty is common to both the law of trusts and the law of agency.[2]

Table 1

INVESTMENT	LEGAL RELATIONSHIP
bank account	creditor/debtor
building society account	creditor/debtor; shareholder/corporation
unit trusts	beneficiary/trustee
government stocks	creditor/debtor
company shares	shareholder/corporation
life assurance policy	creditor/debtor; member/corporation
occupational pension scheme	beneficiary/trustee

However, it is only when we take into account the effect on these relationships of legislative interventions that the unity of investor protection becomes most fully apparent. The result of successive legislative interventions,

---

[1] Weinberg, 'The Consumer and the Revolution in Personal Finance' (1988) 136 *RSA Journal* 475 at p. 479.

[2] See further Chapter 2 below.

as we shall see, is that as we move from one investment to another, and from one investment relationship to another, we find the same legal devices keep cropping up, the same policies and principles being applied. What this suggests in turn is that the needs of investors are not as diverse as the legal forms their investments may take, and that legislators have tended to respond to investors' needs irrespective of the legal classification of their investments.

In the following chapters we explore thoroughly the considerations which lie behind investor protection regulation. At this early juncture it is sufficient to identify three pervasive themes in accounts of investor protection measures. The first is the concern that, in the financial system, the bankruptcy of one company may start a chain reaction leading to the bankruptcy of many other financial companies and, in the final analysis, to what is called 'systemic failure' – a general breakdown of the financial system. This so-called risk of contagion is held to justify 'prudential regulation' – that is, regulation designed to ensure that financial companies do not take risks recklessly, and that they have enough capital.

The second theme is that a free market cannot work efficiently unless it is competitive, and a market cannot function competitively unless buyers are in a position to make an *informed* choice between different products and services. Buyers need information about price, quality, risks etc. So much investor protection regulation is concerned with ensuring that there is full and proper disclosure of information about investment products and services. In this way, the argument goes, savers and investors can make informed choices and the market will operate in a competitive way.

A third reason for regulating financial markets is to ensure that savers and investors have sufficient confidence in the honesty and integrity of financial companies to entrust their money to them. People must be encouraged to save so as to make capital available for investment in productive resources. People must also be encouraged to save so that they will not become a burden on the state when they are old. But people will not entrust their savings to banks, building societies, insurance companies etc., if they are afraid that their money will then be stolen, or gambled away, or not invested in accordance with their wishes. Much regulatory effort is directed, therefore, to ensuring that only honest and competent people can run financial companies, that money is invested in accordance with savers' expectations, and that money managers tailor their decisions to the needs and circumstances of their customers.

As we shall see, none of these arguments is unproblematic; but their recurrence in relation to the regulation of different sectors of the savings and investment industry, and their influence on the character of the regulatory controls in each sector, contributes to the overall coherence of investor protection as a phenomenon.

To sum up: each type of investment has its own legal rules; moreover, each investment has its own financial properties. But to an appreciable extent, the same policy concerns and the same legal devices and arrangements are to be found throughout the field. This gives investor protection the unity upon which our book is premised.

The 'law' of investor protection

There is no reason why the job of investor protection must be done exclusively by *state* law. A part in investor protection may also be played by 'private legal systems',[1] a possibility which is specially important in connection with United Kingdom experience. Indeed, the neglect by traditional legal scholarship of these private legal systems has been one of the factors which arguably has hindered the emergence of a concept of investor protection along the lines we have canvassed. Accordingly, when we speak in this book of the role of the 'law' or the 'legal system' in investor protection, we have in mind not only state law but also the rules of various self-regulatory bodies whether or not these rules enjoy a statutory or contractual basis.

Investor protection and company law

Investor protection, as we have defined it, is not coextensive with shareholder protection in company law. At the same time, company law does fall logically within its scope; a great deal of company law is concerned with the protection of the investor *qua* shareholder and debenture holder. Given, however, that company law is a well-developed subject in its own right, we have concluded, in working out the practical scope of our book, that it would be wasteful to duplicate the content of company law texts here. Accordingly, we exclude direct investment in companies, and concentrate on the legal arrangements for the protection of investors making use of financial institutions and investment intermediaries.

Investor protection and securities regulation

Unlike several other countries, including the United States, the United Kingdom does not draw a distinction between the law of company organisation and that of securities regulation. In this country the law relating to the distribution of securities and insider dealing forms part of company law. Our observations in respect of company law are thus equally applicable to securities regulation: investor protection is broader than securities regulation, and insofar as the latter is treated as part of company law, we do not cover it here.

[1] Evan, 'Public and Private Legal Systems' in Evan (ed.), *Law and Sociology* (1962), p. 165.

Investor protection and consumer protection

Given that investment represents deferred consumption, it is tempting to see investor protection as the other side of the coin from consumer protection. Any attempt to draw a distinction along these lines, however, would be misconceived. The investors with whom we are concerned in this book are also consumers – of financial services, namely the services of advisers, brokers, dealers, managers etc. There are, therefore, strong affinities between investor protection and consumer protection.

STRUCTURE OF THIS BOOK

Our book is divided into three parts. In the remainder of Part I we deal with matters general to investor protection. We concentrate in particular on the rationales for investor protection, the legal devices commonly employed, the forms and institutions of investor protection, and enforcement. Against this general background, we examine in Part II the protective arrangements in force in respect of investment-creating institutions other than companies. The institutions which we examine may be divided into deposit-taking institutions, i.e. banks and building societies, and institutions which collect longer-term savings, i.e. insurance companies and friendly societies, collective investment schemes and occupational pension schemes. In Part III, finally, we examine the regimes governing investment intermediaries and marketing of investments.

2
Investor Protection and the Law of the Land

Leaving aside the rules and codes of conduct of various self-regulatory bodies, the legal protection of investors is in the main a function of the specialised statutes which have been passed to regulate specific investment relationships. However, these statutes by no means constitute the only source of law with a bearing on investor protection. The general law of the land is also capable of affording protection to investors, and as a rule the specialised regulatory statutes do not exclude its application to investment relationships. The purpose of this chapter is to review the more important applications of the general law to the enterprise of investor protection.

AGENCY

Looking at it from the investor's point of view, the main application of the law of agency is to relationships between investors and investment intermediaries. Where an intermediary (e.g. a stockbroker or insurance broker) holds himself out as acting on the investor's behalf he becomes the agent of the investor, who is thereby afforded the protections associated with the principal-agent relationship. But not all intermediaries are the agents of investors: where an intermediary holds himself out as representing an investment institution the intermediary will not normally be regarded as the investor's agent. Where an intermediary is the agent of the investor he assumes certain obligations to his client. In the first place he must exercise due skill, care and diligence with a view to securing the best bargain for his client. Secondly, since the investor puts his faith in his agent (in other words, the relationship is one involving trust), the intermediary owes fiduciary duties (sometimes called duties of loyalty) to his client. These have been conveniently summarised as follows:
  (i)   to act at all time[s] in the best interests of the client;
  (ii) to disclose all material facts to the client;
  (iii) not, without the fully informed consent of the client

    (a) to place himself in a position where his duty to the client conflicts with his [own] interest or his duty to another client; or

    (b) to deal as a principal with the client;

(iv) not to make a secret profit, whether or not it is at the expense of the client.[1]

The law of agency and the conduct of business rules

From our point of view the obligations imposed by the law of agency are important not only in their own right as a possible source of investor protection, but also as a formative influence upon the content of the conduct of business rules laid down by the Securities and Investments Board (SIB) and other bodies within the framework of the Financial Services Act.[2] On the face of it conduct of business rules which 'draw substantially on the law of agency'[3] might be thought redundant as an unnecessary duplication of the common law. In fact this is not so: the common law of agency is weakened by limitations for which conduct of business rules can compensate.

First, enforcement of the law of agency rests entirely on private initiative – that is, on civil actions pursued by wronged clients.[4] Such a system of enforcement can work only to the extent that clients become aware that they have been wronged, and have the resources and determination to pursue their remedies.[5] The conduct of business rules, on the other hand, are civilly enforceable not only at the suit of persons adversely affected by their breach but also at the instance of SIB.[6] The conduct of business rules are administratively enforceable as well: their breach may lead directly or indirectly to loss of authorisation to carry on investment business.[7]

Secondly, the law of agency has failed to realise its full potential in certain investment contexts. With respect to stockbroking, for example, an attempt to apply the agent's duty of skill, care and diligence to investment advice given by brokers was frustrated in *Schweder* v. *Walton*.[8] There the court, proceeding on the basis of the distinction between contractual (i.e. remunerated) and non-contractual (i.e. gratuitous) agency, took the view that stockbrokers are employed merely to execute (in return for commission) orders given to them and that advice proffered in between orders is gratuitous; accordingly such advice need not be formulated with reasonable care as long as it is given bona fide.

---

[1] Stock Exchange, *Conflicts of Interest and their Regulation* (November 1984), para. 2.1.

[2] See Chapter 17.

[3] SIB/MIBOC, *Regulation of Investment Business: The New Framework* (1985), para. 3.30.

[4] For a brief summary of the available remedies see G. H. L. Fridman, *The Law of Agency* (6th edn, 1990), pp. 182–4.

[5] See further Chapter 7.   [6] FSA, s.61.   [7] See further Chapter 16.

[8] (1910) 27 T.L.R. 89.

This analysis of the stockbroker/client relationship as a series of separate transactions rather than as a continuing agency relationship is narrow and somewhat unrealistic inasmuch as the provision of investment advice is a normal incident of the service provided by stockbrokers, and it may be that it could be bypassed by means of an imposition of tortious liability.[1] Even so, the case law furnishes us with little guidance as to what particular precautions a stockbroker should take before offering advice. The uncertainty and poverty of the common law in this respect may be contrasted with the way in which the conduct of business rules elaborate the duty of care into 'know your customer' and 'suitability' duties, and differentiate between the various categories of customer to whom these duties are or are not owed.[2] One virtue of conduct of business rules, then, is that they are a vehicle for the development and clarification of principles which at common law exist only in inchoate form.

Again, some softening of agency principles has traditionally been a feature of the life assurance industry. It has always been the practice among insurance intermediaries not to disclose to clients the commission paid by the insurance company. Some derogation from mainstream agency principles was apparently legitimised by *Great Western Insurance Company of New York* v. *Cunliffe*,[3] where it was said:

> If a person employs another . . . to do certain work for him, as his agent with other persons, and does not choose to ask him what his charge will be, and in fact knows that he is to be remunerated, not by him, but by the other persons . . . he must allow the ordinary amount which agents are in the habit of charging.[4]

However, this was said in a context (shipping reinsurance) far removed from that of the modern relationship between intermediaries and their private investment clients. In any event, even if it covers commission paid according to a customary scale, it furnishes no legal justification for the non-disclosure of special incentive payments.[5] In this situation again conduct of business rules can, even if they do not utterly vindicate mainstream agency principles, at least bring insurance industry practices more closely into line with those principles.

A third reason for bolstering the common law with conduct of business rules is that the protective value of the law of agency standing on its own is diminished by how readily at common law the client's rights, or indeed the whole character of the relationship between investor and intermediary, can be contractually redefined.[6] The conduct of business rules not only affirm,

---

[1] But see *Briggs* v. *Gunner* [1979] N.L.J. 116; see generally the discussion in Scherer, 'The Stockbrokers' Duty of Care in the US and UK (2)', (1985) 6 *Company Lawyer*, 164.

[2] See further Chapter 17. [3] (1874) 9 Ch. App. 525; followed in *Baring* v. *Stanton* (1876) 3 Ch.D.502.

[4] (1874) 9 Ch. App. at p. 540.

[5] See, further, O'Neill, 'Insurance Brokers and their Commission' [1978] *Journal of Business Law* 339 at pp. 344–6.

[6] Cf. for America, Harvey B. Bines, *The Law of Investment Management* (1978), para. 1.01(1)(b).

develop and elaborate the protections of the law of agency, they also seek to ensure that an investor entitled to those protections will not be held to have waived them or signed them away. This is done by the imposition of rules which apply across the board to transactions and relationships with investors (save sometimes those with 'execution-only' status), and by confining contracting-out to those deemed capable of looking after their own interests, i.e. to 'non-private' and 'experienced' customers only.[1]

TRUSTS

As a legal form within which investment may be undertaken the trust has several applications. Unit trusts, as their name implies, are constituted under a trust deed. Occupational pension schemes too are generally constituted under the law of trusts with the result that pension funds are trust funds. But the investments of a unit trust are managed not by the corporate trustees but by a management company, and the assets of pension schemes are in practice commonly invested by fund managers. There is also a variety of private trusts, such as family trusts, constituted by testamentary or other instruments under which funds are invested. In these, professional trustees such as solicitors, banks and trust corporations often play a prominent role.

As a protective device the trust offers two main advantages. First, trust funds are earmarked for the beneficiaries of the trust and insulated against the eventuality of the trustees' insolvency. The creditors of trustees have no claim upon trust funds. So, for example, if an employer becomes insolvent the pension scheme assets are beyond the reach of the employer's creditors.

Secondly, trustees owe to the beneficiaries of the trust fiduciary duties broadly parallel to those owed by an agent to his client.[2] Thus it is the duty of trustees

... to exercise their powers in the best interests of the present and future beneficiaries of the trust, holding the scales impartially between different classes of beneficiaries. This duty of the trustees towards their beneficiaries is paramount. They must, of course, obey the law; but subject to that, they must put the interests of their beneficiaries first. When the purpose of the trust is to provide financial benefits for the beneficiaries ... the best interests of the beneficiaries are normally their best financial interests. In the case of a power of investment ... the power must be exercised so as to yield the best return for the beneficiaries, judged in relation to the risks of the investments in question. ...[3]

Moreover, trustees must not put themselves in a position where their duty and interests conflict, or retain profits derived from the trust, except insofar as authorised by the trust instrument. In addition, trustees owe a duty of care to their beneficiaries; this duty of care is encapsulated in the 'prudent man rule'.

---

[1] For a statement of the underlying thinking, see SIB/MIBOC, *op. cit.*, paras. 3.30–3.32.

[2] Above, p. 15.   [3] Sir Robert Megarry V-C in *Cowan* v. *Scargill* [1984] 2 All E.R. 750 at p. 760.

The prudent man rule

According to the modern version of the prudent man rule, it is incumbent upon a trustee to conduct the business of the trust with the same care as an 'ordinary prudent man of business' would conduct his own.[1] This duty, however, is subject to a qualification in that

> . . . care must be taken not to lose sight of the fact that the business of the trustee, and the business which the ordinary prudent man is supposed to be conducting for himself is the business of investing money for the benefit of persons who are to enjoy it at some future time, and not for the sole benefit of the person entitled to the present income. The duty of the trustee is not to take such care only as a prudent man would take if he had only himself to consider; the duty rather is to take such care as an ordinary prudent man would take if he were minded to make an investment for the benefit of other people for whom he felt morally bound to provide.[2]

This qualification, which in effect raises the standard of care required of a trustee, was of course enunciated in the context of a family trust. While it seems perfectly applicable to occupational pension schemes, it is doubtful whether it is apposite in the case of unit trusts where the unit-holder is both present and ultimate beneficiary and the prospective investor can choose between 'growth' and 'income' trusts. In any event the qualification means only that speculative or hazardous investments are to be avoided; the trustee may take a 'prudent degree of risk' and cannot be held liable for a mere 'error in judgement', eventuating in a loss on an investment.[3] Unless he is an investment expert the trustee is not expected to rely exclusively on his own judgement in taking investment decisions: the obligation imposed by the prudent man rule includes a duty to 'seek advice on matters which the trustee does not understand . . . and on receiving that advice to act with the same degree of prudence'.[4] Professional advice is not to be rejected unless an ordinary prudent man would reject it.

These common law principles have been reinforced by section 6(1) of the Trustee Investments Act 1961 by virtue of which a trustee exercising his powers of investment must have regard

(a) to the need for diversification of the trust, insofar as is appropriate to the circumstances of the trust;

(b) to the suitability to the trust of investments of the description of investment proposed and of the investment proposed as an investment of that description.

---

[1] *In re Speight* (1883) 22 Ch. D. 727 at pp. 739,762; *Bartlett* v. *Barclays Trust Co. (No.1)* [1980] Ch. 515 at p. 531. In America, the *locus classicus* of the prudent man rule is *Harvard College* v. *Amory*, 26 Mass. 446 (1830); see Shettuck, 'The Development of the Prudent Man Rule for Fiduciary Investment in the United States in the Twentieth Century', 12 *Ohio St. L. J.* 491 (1951).

[2] Lindley L.J. in *In re Whitely* (1886) 33 Ch. D. 347 at p. 355.

[3] *Learoyd* v. *Whitely* (1887) 12 App. Cas. 727 at p. 733; Brightman L.J. in *Bartlett* v. *Barclays Trust Co. (No.1)* [1980] Ch. 515 at p. 531; Lopes L.J. in *In re Chapman* [1896] 2 Ch. 763 at p. 778.

[4] Sir Robert Megarry V-C in *Cowan* v. *Scargill* [1984] 2 All E.R. 750 at p. 762.

The prudent man rule was developed with amateur trustees in mind, and it is arguable that professional trustees ought to be held to a higher standard. This view was vigorously espoused by Brightman L.J. in the comparatively recent case of *Bartlett* v. *Barclays Bank Trust Co. (No.1)*:

> I am of opinion that a higher duty of care is plainly due from someone like a trust corporation which carries on a specialised business of trust management. A trust corporation holds itself out in its advertising literature as being above ordinary mortals. With a specialist staff of trained trust officers and managers, with ready access to financial information and professional advice, dealing with and solving trust problems day after day, the trust corporation holds itself out, and rightly, as capable of providing an expertise which it would be unrealistic to expect and unjust to demand from the ordinary prudent man or woman who accepts, probably unpaid and sometimes reluctantly from a sense of family duty, the burdens of a trusteeship. Just as, under the law of contract, a professional person possessed of a particular skill is liable for breach of contract if he neglects to use the skill and experience which he professes, so I think that a professional corporate trustee is liable for breach of trust if loss is caused to the trust fund because it neglects to exercise the special care and skill which it professes to have.[1]

The concrete implications of this view have yet to be elaborated.

At common law there is nothing to stop a trust deed excluding the trustee's liability for breach of the duty of care under the prudent man rule (or indeed for breach of trust generally). In respect of authorised unit trusts, however, section 84 of the Financial Services Act makes void any trust deed provision 'in so far as it would have the effect of exempting the . . . trustee from liability for any failure to exercise due care and diligence in the discharge of his functions'.[2]

The Trustee Investments Act

In the late eighteenth and early nineteenth centuries the courts held that the only investments that trustees might prudently make (in the absence of special authorisation in the trust instrument) were in mortgages and government stock, these being regarded as safer than other forms of investments. With the maturation of commerce and the financial system in the nineteenth century this position gradually came to be seen as unduly restrictive, and a series of statutes was passed which slowly extended trustees' powers of investment.[3] Nevertheless the legislation continued to favour British government stock, and in this way, arguably, to stimulate artificially demand for it. The Trustee Investments Act 1961 superseded the earlier legislation and took the trend towards relaxation of its restrictions further by empowering trustees to undertake a certain amount of investment in ordinary company shares.

[1] [1980] Ch. 515 at p. 534.   [2] Cf. Companies Act 1985, s.192.
[3] George W. Keeton, *Modern Developments in the Law of Trusts* (1971), Chapter 5; Grosh, 'Trustee Investment:

In its historical context, therefore, the Trustee Investments Act 1961 was a liberalising measure. Viewed in the light of present-day conditions, however, the Act can be criticised for imposing on trustees restrictions which are capable of damaging the interests of their beneficiaries. The strategy of the legislation is to confine those trustees whose decisions it governs to a 'legal list' of investments beyond the bounds of which they must not go. Under the Act permitted investments are divided into two classes – narrower-range investments and wider-range investments. Narrower-range investments include National Savings products, government and local authority stock, UK corporate debentures, building society deposits, and mortgages. Wider-range investments include ordinary company shares quoted on the Stock Exchange and unit trusts.[1] Broadly speaking, trustees are empowered to invest half the trust fund in wider-range investments, the remaining half being confined to the narrower-range.[2] Trustees making investments under the 1961 Act are also bound (with one or two exceptions) to obtain and consider proper advice (i.e. the advice of a person who is reasonably believed by the trustee to be qualified by his ability in and practical experience of financial matters) as to whether the investments are suitable to the trust and satisfactory having regard to the need for diversification.[3]

The trouble with the Trustee Investments Act is that its 'legal list' approach denies trustees the latitude in investment decision-making that they need to safeguard the interests of their beneficiaries during a period of pronounced economic fluctuations. In the course of the last two decades real interest rates have been negative at one point, unprecedentedly high at another; share prices have risen, plummeted and risen again. In these conditions trustees need investment powers more flexible than those conferred by the 1961 Act:

> The Act has proved to be tiresome, cumbrous and expensive in operation with the result that its provisions are now seen to be inadequate. Furthermore, careful investment in equities is perhaps more likely in the long run to protect and benefit both income and capital beneficiaries than is investment in fixed-interest securities.[4]

Accordingly, the Law Reform Committee in its 1982 report recommended that the trustee investments legislation should be reformed by simply affirming the trustee's duty to exercise due care and skill and by providing that this duty would be fulfilled either by investment in a statutory list of 'safe' investments or by taking professional advice. 'Safety' would be identified with what are currently narrower-range investments with the addition of unit trusts and

English Law and the American Prudent Man Rule', (1974) 23 *International and Comparative Law Quarterly* 748, pp. 751–2.

[1] Trustee Investments Act 1961, Sch.1 as amended.   [2] ss.1,2.

[3] Investments in National Savings products and the like are excepted by virtue of s.6(2) and Sch.1, Part I. A trustee qualified to advise his fellow trustees need not himself seek advice, nor need a qualified officer or servant (e.g. of a trust corporation): s.6(6).

[4] Law Reform Committee, 23rd Report, *The Powers and Duties of Trustees*, Cmnd. 8733 (1982), para. 3.17.

investment trusts. The Law Reform Committee rejected the more radical idea of doing away with the legal list altogether and relying exclusively on the prudent man rule on the grounds that this might create difficulties especially for smaller trusts: 'the law should continue to provide some guidance and indeed protection for trustees'.[1]

Legislative implementation of the Law Reform Committee's proposals is unlikely to be regarded as a matter of urgency because, in practice, the Trustee Investments Act does not do a great deal of harm. The investment powers conferred by the Act are in addition to, and not in derogation from, powers conferred by the trust instrument,[2] and 'in the vast majority of cases'[3] modern trust deeds give powers of investment much wider than those set out in the Act.[4] As a rule, therefore, the Act serves only to constrain investment under some older trusts, and where this constraint has harmful effects the trustees may ask the court to give them wider investment powers.[5] Thus in *Mason* v. *Farbrother*, [6] the trustees of the Co-op pension fund (established in 1929) succeeded in getting for themselves the wide powers of investment regarded as necessary for a modern pension fund in an inflationary age.[7] It does not follow, however, that the statutory list in the Trustee Investments Act is wholly devoid of practical importance. There are still trusts, particularly small ones, that are bound by it. And some friendly societies are confined to the list, along with certain other investments specified by statute.[8]

Trust accounts

An investor whose funds are in the hands of an intermediary prior to their investment or after the realisation of an investment runs the risk that the intermediary will become insolvent during that time. Upon such an occurrence the investor is not automatically entitled to a refund of his monies. Under the law of insolvency he is merely an ordinary creditor with a claim based on contract. Accordingly his funds fall to be treated as part of the assets of the insolvent intermediary to be distributed among the creditors generally, and his claim to repayment, like that of his fellow investors, ranks behind the claims of the secured creditors and those with a statutory preference. The trust device, by enabling investors to base their claims on property rather than contract, furnishes them with a means of securing a position stronger than that

---

[1] *Ibid.*, paras. 3.20,3.21. In America many states have repealed their legal lists altogether: see Grosh, 'Trustee Investment', p. 750 n. 4, pp. 754–7.

[2] Trustee Investments Act 1961, s.3(1).

[3] Law Reform Committee, *Powers and Duties of Trustees*, para. 3.16.

[4] See, e. g., Young, 'Trustee Investment Standards and Responsibilities in England – Past and Present' (1976) 11 *Real Property, Probate and Trust J.* 711 at p. 719.

[5] Under the Trustee Act 1925, s.57(1).   [6] [1983] 2 All E.R. 1078.

[7] For the relevant principles, see *Trustees of the British Museum* v. *A.-G.* [1984] 1 All E.R. 337.

[8] Friendly Societies Act 1974, s.46(1); see Chapter 11.

of the ordinary creditor. If investors' funds are held on trust by the
intermediary and paid into a 'client account' they are thereby segregated from
the assets available to creditors generally and preserved exclusively for the
investors.

The creation of client accounts is a transparent device to get round the law
of insolvency, but in *Re Kayford Ltd.* the legal efficacy of the voluntary
unilateral use of a client account for customer prepayments by a company in
financial difficulties was judicially acknowledged. 'One is concerned here',
said Megarry J., 'with the question not of preferring creditors but of
preventing those who pay money from becoming creditors, by making them
beneficiaries under a trust.'[1] Notwithstanding the distinction drawn by
Megarry J., the correctness of this decision has been questioned because of its
doubtful compatibility with the general policy of insolvency legislation.[2]
However, in the particular context of investor protection, the use of client
accounts is required by legislation,[3] and this statutory endorsement must put
beyond question their legal efficacy for investors.

NEGLIGENCE

The wide scope of the modern tort of negligence is such that there are several
situations in which the law of negligence might conceivably be brought to bear
in order to secure compensation for an investor who has suffered financial loss.
Here we shall consider the possible applications of the law to investment
advisers, to auditors, and indeed to regulatory authorities themselves. It is
important to bear in mind, however, that while the cumulative implications of
recent decisions on negligence for investor protection are potentially far-
reaching, the extent to which that potential can be realised depends on just
how the abstract principles of the modern law of negligence are to be applied in
concrete investment situations – a question on which there is comparatively
little authority.

Investment advisers

That liability may be incurred for loss occasioned by reliance upon investment
advice negligently given by a professional investment adviser is clear by virtue
of the *Hedley Byrne* decision.[4] Liability may, however, be avoided by dint of a

---

1 [1975] 1 All E.R. 604 at p. 606.
2 See, e.g. Goodhart and Jones, 'The Infiltration of Equitable Doctrine into English Commercial Law',
(1980) 43 *Modern Law Review* 489 at pp. 492–501; but cf. *Carreras Ltd.* v. *Freeman Mathews Ltd.* [1985] Ch. 207.
3 e.g. FSA, s.55.
4 *Hedley Byrne & Co. Ltd.* v. *Heller & Partners Ltd.* [1964] A.C. 465. The thesis advanced by Foster J. in *Briggs* v.
Gunner (1979) NLJ 116 that the *Hedley Byrne* case has not imposed upon stockbrokers a duty to take reasonable
care in giving investment advice, is untenable: see Scherer, 'The Stockbrokers' Duty of Care in the US and UK
(2)' (1985) 6 *Company Lawyer* 164 at pp. 169–71.

suitably worded disclaimer, provided that this does not fall foul of the Unfair Contract Terms Act 1977.[1] In any event a distinction must be drawn between bad advice (i.e. advice formulated without reasonable care) and bad results. Losing money as a result of following investment advice by no means necessarily implies that one's adviser has been careless. Thus, in *Stafford* v. *Conti Commodity Services Ltd.* a claim by the client of commodity brokers that his rate of success was so poor (only 10 out of 46 transactions were profitable) that an inference of negligence must be drawn was firmly rejected on the footing that 'losses in the ordinary course of things do occur even if proper care is used when one is dealing with the transactions on the commodities futures market'.[2] The Court of Appeal reached a similar conclusion in *Merrill Lynch Futures Inc.* v. *York House Trading Ltd.*,[3] observing that futures markets are 'unpredictable, volatile and extremely risky' places where even experienced persons sometimes lose vast sums of money; accordingly the unsuccessfulness of a deal could not by itself raise the inference that the advice to enter into it was necessarily negligent. Conceivably the result might be otherwise if the aggrieved investor could point to a long series of disastrous results in a more stable market.

The remedy in tort for negligent advice coexists, where there is a contractual nexus, with a remedy in contract.[4] Contractual liability for negligent advice is illustrated by the 1908 case of an investor who wrote to the city editor of a newspaper asking how he might invest a substantial sum of money fairly safely, and also for the name of a 'good stockbroker'. He was given the name of an 'outside broker' (i.e. one who was not a member of the Stock Exchange) who promptly embezzled the money he entrusted to him. In those days outside brokers were not regulated at all. It turned out that this particular one was an undischarged bankrupt, a fact which the city editor could readily have ascertained had he bothered to make proper enquiries. In these circumstances the court held that the investor could recover his loss from the newspaper: there was a contract between them (the consideration being his willingness to allow his letter to be published in the newspaper) and the editor had failed to take reasonable care in nominating the broker.[5]

Auditors

That the law of tort imposes a duty on auditors to take reasonable care in the discharge of their functions is beyond doubt.[6] What has been in doubt is how wide is the circle of investors to whom this duty of care is owed, but in *Caparo*

---

[1] s.2.   [2] [1981] 1 All E.R. 691, *per* Mocatta J. at p. 698.

[3] *The Times*, May 24, 1984, C.A.

[4] The contractual duty of care is legislatively restated in the Supply of Goods and Services Act 1982, s.13.

[5] *De la Bere* v. *Pearson Ltd.* [1908] 1 K.B. 280.

[6] See the dissenting judgment of Denning L.J. in *Candler* v. *Crane, Christmas & Co.* [1951] 2 K.B. 164, approved by the House of Lords in *Hedley Byrne & Co. Ltd.* v. *Heller & Partners Ltd.* [1964] A.C. 465.

Industries v. *Dickman*[1] the House of Lords held that, as regards its annual accounts, the liability of a company's auditors was confined to the company itself and did not extend to members of the public contemplating investment in the company in reliance upon those accounts. To hold otherwise, it was argued, would be, in the classic words of Cardozo C.J., to 'expose accountants to a liability in an indeterminate amount for an indeterminate time to an indeterminate class'.[2] The position is different, however, where, in the course of a bid for a company, express representations are made with the intention that they should be relied upon by the bidder. In such a case the directors of the target company and its financial advisers owe the bidder a duty of care not to be negligent in making representations which might mislead him.[3]

Regulatory authorities

The law does not confer any blanket immunity from actions for negligence on the authorities responsible for the regulation of investment markets, institutions and intermediaries, and such actions have occasionally been pursued. In particular, before the passage of the Lloyd's Act 1982, the Corporation of Lloyd's was sued for alleged regulatory negligence by underwriting members who had invested in the Sasse syndicate and had incurred substantial losses; Lloyd's met the bulk of their claim in an out-of-court settlement.[4] The collapse of the Savings and Investment Bank on the Isle of Man also gave rise to a claim founded on averments of negligence in supervision on the part of the island's banking regulators.

Such actions raise policy issues comparable in some respects to those encountered in the context of auditors' negligence. On the one hand, it may be urged that an investor who suffers loss as a result of a regulatory body's carelessness has a moral claim to compensation from the body whose negligence has damnified him, and that potential liability for negligence will encourage regulators to discharge their functions with reasonable care. On the other hand, there is again the spectre of open-ended liability to an indefinitely large number of investors. As is the case in relation to auditors, however, the courts have shown themselves generally unwilling to accept that regulators owe investors a duty of care in negligence. In *Yun Kun Yeu* v. *Attorney General of Hong Kong*[5] the Privy Council held that the Hong Kong banking supervisor did not owe the depositors of a failed institution a duty to take reasonable care to

---

[1] [1990] 2 W.L.R. 358.
[2] *Ultamares Corp.* v. *Touche, Niven and Co.*, 255 NY 170 (1931) at p. 179, quoted at p. 368 *per* Lord Bridge of Harwich. The court also rejected (at pp. 377–8) the suggestion that it was any part of the statutory purpose of an audit to assist in the making of informed investment decisions, a claim which is difficult to reconcile with, for example, the requirement that audited accounts be registered and thereby made accessible to the public at large.
[3] *Morgan Crucible Co. plc* v. *Hill Samuel Bank Ltd.* [1991] 1 All E.R. 148.
[4] See Godfrey Hodgson, *Lloyd's of London: A Reputation at Risk* (1984), pp. 270–83.
[5] [1987] 3 W.L.R. 776.

prevent them suffering financial loss by reason of the fraudulent or improvident conduct of the institution's affairs. And in *Davis* v. *Radcliffe*,[1] which arose out of the collapse of the Isle of Man Savings and Investment Bank, the Privy Council followed its earlier decision in holding that the relationship between the depositors and the supervisor was not such that it would be 'just and reasonable' to impose a liability in negligence on the supervisor for the loss suffered by the depositors.

In both cases the Privy Council drew attention to the adverse consequences that might flow from the imposition of a duty of care on regulators. In the Hong Kong case the court noted (but did not rest its decision on the observation) that there would be reason to apprehend that the imposition of a duty of care would have 'a seriously inhibiting effect' on the work of a supervisor:

A sound judgment would be less likely to be exercised if the commissioner were to be constantly looking over his shoulder at the prospect of claims against him, and his activities would be likely to be conducted in a detrimentally defensive frame of mind. In the result, the effectiveness of his functions would be at risk of diminution. Consciousness of liability could lead to distortions of judgment.[2]

And in the Isle of Man case it was commented that the 'very nature' of the regulatory task 'with its emphasis on the broader public interest, is one which militates strongly against the imposition a duty of care being imposed [*sic*] upon such an agency in favour of any particular section of the public.'[3]

These public policy considerations also find their expression in statute which in certain cases confers immunity from suit on regulators. Under the Financial Services Act the Securities and Investments Board and the SROs are not liable in damages for anything done or omitted in the discharge (or purported discharge) of their functions unless their act or omission is shown to have been in bad faith, and the Bank of England enjoys an identical immunity in respect of the discharge of its functions under the Banking Act.[4] The immunity conferred on regulators under the Financial Services Act was explicitly premised, as was that conferred on the Bank of England by the Banking Act, on the proposition that regulators should not be inhibited in the performance of their tasks by fear of liability; the quality and effectiveness of regulation would suffer, it was argued, were supervisors to have the threat of actions for damages hanging over their heads when taking difficult decisions.[5] It is also relevant to the grant of immunity under the Financial Services Act

---

[1] [1990] 1 W.L.R. 821.   [2] At p. 789, *per* Lord Keith of Kinkel.
[3] At p. 826, *per* Lord Goff of Chieveley.
[4] FSA, s. 187; BA, s. 1 (4). A similar immunity is conferred upon the London Stock Exchange in its statutory capacity as the 'competent authority' responsible for the official listing of securities: FSA s. 187(4). See also the Lloyd's Act 1982, s. 14; Special Report from the Select Committee of the House of Lords on the Lloyd's Bill, HL 187 (1982).
[5] HC Debs. Standing Committee E, 1986, cols. 406–7.

that a substantial award in damages would undoubtedly bankrupt a private regulator such as FIMBRA.

CRIMINAL LAW

Many criminal prohibitions of general application confer protection on investors in one context or another. Here we shall confine ourselves to those major criminal laws which are most likely to bear upon defalcations by investment intermediaries or persons occupying positions of responsibility in investment institutions.

Theft

A person is guilty of theft (maximum penalty: ten years imprisonment)[1] if in the words of the Theft Act 1968, 'he dishonestly appropriates property belonging to another with the intention of permanently depriving the other of it'.[2]

A distinctive characteristic of the phenomenon whose legal aspects are addressed in this book – intermediated investment – is that the investor commonly relinquishes legal ownership of his investment, becoming (for example) a creditor, or a beneficiary of a trust. Nevertheless, a misappropriator of investments or investment monies will not always be in a position to maintain that what he appropriated was his own property rather than property 'belonging to another'. The legal analysis of course depends on the circumstances of the investor. Money deposited with a bank or a building society plainly belongs to the deposit-taking institution in question. Where legal ownership of investments is vested in trustees, as in the case of a pension fund or a family trust, a misappropriation by the trustees will be regarded as the appropriation of property belonging to another (i.e. the beneficiaries) by virtue of s.5(2) of the 1968 Act, which provides that where property is subject to a trust, the persons to whom it belongs are to be regarded as including 'any person having a right to enforce the trust'.[3]

Again, where monies are paid over to an intermediary who is the investor's agent (e.g. a stockbroker or investment manager), pending their investment or retained after the realisation of an investment, there will normally be an obligation (under the applicable set of clients' money regulations or rules) to pay them into a client account. If this obligation is honoured a trust is created, and s.5(2) is once more applicable. If, however, this obligation is disregarded, s.5(3) comes into play. The intermediary is a person who receives property 'from or on account of another', and who is (thanks to the relevant clients'

---

[1] Theft Act 1968, s.7.   [2] Theft Act 1968, s.1(1).

[3] Section 5(1), according to which property is to be regarded as belonging to any person 'having in it any proprietary right or interest', also appears to be applicable.

money regulations or rules) under an obligation to the other to retain and deal with that property or its proceeds in a particular way and, accordingly, the property or proceeds are to be regarded as belonging to the investor. Where what is in issue is an intermediary's handling of a client's investments (rather than money), the intermediary will normally be under an obligation to register the investments in the name of the client or his nominee, or to hold the investment in such a way that the client's ownership is apparent. If this obligation is satisfied the investments in question are clearly identified as 'property belonging to another'. If it is not, s.5(3) may well again be applicable.

It is important to recognise the limitations associated with the concept of 'appropriation'. Appropriation is defined in the legislation as 'any assumption . . . of the rights of an owner'.[1] According to the House of Lords,[2] appropriation necessarily involves some adverse interference with the owner's rights or some usurpation of them. On this view[3] there is no appropriation if one deals with property in a manner which has been authorised by the owner but which unbeknownst to him confers some secret benefit upon oneself. Thus the controller of a bank or an insurance company who makes secret profits for himself out of dealings with corporate property for which he has authority apparently does not commit theft.[4] Nor does the intermediary who does likewise with an investor's property commit theft.[5]

Other offences

Various other statutory offences have obvious implications for investment firms or transactions. Under section 15 of the Theft Act 1968 obtaining property by deception is an offence (maximum penalty: ten years imprisonment) which might be committed, for example, where an investor parts with money on the strength of a deceptive prospectus, advertisement or statement.[6] False accounting is an offence (maximum penalty: seven years imprisonment) under section 17 of the same Act.[7]

---

[1] Theft Act 1968, s.3(1).   [2] *Morris* [1984] A.C. 320.

[3] A broader conception of appropriation might be based on *Lawrence* v. *Metropolitan Police Commissioner* [1972] A.C. 629, which was followed in *Dobson* v. *General Accident Fire and Life Corp. plc* [1989] 3 All E.R. 927. The narrower *Morris* approach was preferred in *R.* v. *Gomez* [1991] 3 All E.R. 394.

[4] *Tarling (No.1)* v. *Government of Singapore* (1980) 70 Cr. App. R. 77 involved allegations of persons in a fiduciary capacity making a secret profit at the expense of their companies. According to Lord Wilberforce (at p. 110): 'Breach of fiduciary duty, exorbitant profit making, secrecy, failure to comply with the law as to company accounts . . . are one thing; theft and fraud are others.'

[5] For discussion of the difficulties of the concept of appropriation, see L. H. Leigh, *The Control of Corporate Fraud* (1982), pp. 75–7; and the articles by Sullivan [1983] *Crim. L.R.* 512; Dine [1984] *Crim. L.R.* 397; and von Nessen [1986] *Crim. L.R.* 154.

[6] The causal nexus between the deception and the obtaining is established if it is found that the victim would not have parted with his property had he known the truth: *M.P.C.* v. *Charles* [1977] A.C. 177; *Lambie* [1982] A.C. 449.

[7] See Leigh, *op. cit.*, pp. 82–3.

The companies legislation makes it an offence (maximum penalty: seven years imprisonment)[1] if any business of a company is carried on with intent to defraud creditors, or for any fraudulent purpose, or to be knowingly a party to the carrying on of the business in that manner.[2] The Prevention of Corruption Act 1906 prohibits (maximum penalty: two years imprisonment) any agent from corruptly accepting any gift or consideration as an inducement or reward for doing (or forbearing to do) any act in relation to his principal's affairs, or for showing (or forbearing to show) favour or disfavour to any person in relation to his principal's affairs.[3] This seems particularly relevant to independent insurance and unit trust intermediaries, since intermediaries involved in the sale of such investments derive their income not from the investors whose agents they are but from the insurance companies and unit trust management companies to whom they bring business. The crucial question is under what circumstances it can be said that an inducement has been accepted 'corruptly'. Now that the conduct of business rules laid down by the Securities and Investments Board and the other FSA regulators ban the acceptance of 'overriders' and 'benefits in kind' by intermediaries, the view might be taken that the acceptance (by someone apprised of the demands of the rules) of such inducements is corrupt and therefore an offence under the 1906 Act.

The question of dishonesty

A common element in the Theft Act offences noted above is that the establishment of guilt depends on proof that the accused has acted 'dishonestly'. This requires that the jury be satisfied (i) that what the accused did was dishonest 'according to the ordinary standards of reasonable and honest people', and (ii) that the accused himself must have realised that what he was doing was by those standards dishonest.[4] This second criterion means that an investment practitioner accused of a crime of dishonesty falls to be judged 'on his perception of standards operating within the community at large and not those [perhaps more permissive] of his particular milieu'.[5] Even so, the invocation of the 'current standards of ordinary decent people'[6] is problematic whenever 'the context of the case is a specialised one, involving intricate financial activities or dealings in a specialised market'. As Griew says: 'It is neither reasonable nor rational to expect ordinary people to judge as "dishonest" or "not dishonest" conduct of which, for want of relevant experience, they cannot appreciate the contextual flavour.'[7] The larger issue is of course whether jury trial is appropriate in such cases at all.[8]

[1] Companies Act 1985, Sch.24.   [2] Companies Act 1985, s.458; Leigh, *op. cit.*, pp. 142–5.
[3] s.1(1).   [4] *Ghosh* [1982] Q.B. 1053 at p.1064.
[5] Sullivan, 'Fraud and the Efficacy of the Criminal Law' [1985] *Crim. L.R.* 616 at p. 625, n. 66.
[6] *Feely* [1973] Q.B. 530 at pp. 537–8.
[7] Griew, 'Dishonesty: The Objections to Feely and Ghosh' [1985] *Crim. L.R.* 341 at p. 345.
[8] This is discussed in Chapter 7.

INVESTOR PROTECTION AND SCOTS LAW

Civil law

In its bearing upon the protection of investors the civil law of Scotland does not proceed upon markedly different principles from those applicable in England. The principles of the law of negligence relevant to investor protection are as much Scots as English in character. Moreover, an agent owes his principal the same fiduciary obligations and the same duty of care, though in Scotland as in England it is arguable that the courts have sometimes held back from giving full expression to agency principles. In *Cleland* v. *Brownlie, Watson and Beckett*[1] Lord President Robertson came close to enunciating 'know your customer' and 'adequate research' doctrines:

> For an agent to bring an investment under the notice of a client is of course to a certain extent a recommendation. . . . If besides thus introducing an investment an agent expresses a favourable opinion of it, he will be liable, if his opinion was either not honest or given when he had no adequate information entitling him to give an opinion at all. But then it is necessary to bear in mind that all this has to be considered in relation to the client in question, and to the kind of investment which he is known to desire.[2]

But this dictum did not bear fruit in subsequent cases.[3]

The fiduciary obligations of a trustee under Scots law are comparable to those under English law, and the prudent man rule is part of Scots law.[4] The Trustee Investments Act 1961 applies to Scotland, and the Scottish court like the English is now prepared to consider applications by trustees for powers wider than those conferred by the 1961 Act.[5] With respect to client accounts, however, the Financial Services Act prescribes, not that clients' money shall be held on trust, but that it should be held by the investment firm 'as agent for the person who is entitled to call for it'.[6] This provision is designed to get round the difficulties, real or imaginary, posed by an old Scots Act, the Blank Bonds and Trusts Act 1696.[7]

Criminal law

The criminal law of Scotland has not undergone a series of statutory reforms and restatements such as have shaped modern English criminal law, and

---

[1] (1892) 20 R. 152.   [2] At p. 162.   [3] e.g. *Johnstone* v. *Thorburn* (1901) 3 F. 497.

[4] *Maclean* v. *Soady's Tr.* (1888) 15 R. 966 at p. 985; *Rae* v. *Meek* (1889) 14 App. Cas. 558 at p. 569; *Hutton* v. *Annan* (1898) 25 R. (H.L.) 23; *Buchanan* v. *Eaton* 1911 S.C. (H.L.) 40.

[5] *Henderson, Petitioner* 1981 S.L.T. (Notes) 40; cf. *Inglis and Others, Petitioners* 1965 S.L.T. 326.

[6] FSA, s.55(5).

[7] See Office of Fair Trading, *The Protection of Consumer Prepayments: A Discussion Paper* (October 1984), para. 6.13; Estate Agents Act 1979, s.13(2). But contrast *Newton's Executrix* v. *Meiklejohn's Judicial Factor* 1959 S.L.T. 72; Solicitors (Scotland) Accounts Rules 1981, r.2(1).

remains essentially a common law system. Moreover, the Scottish judiciary tends to favour broad and open-ended definitions of the common law crimes, and to subordinate technical to moral considerations. Scots criminal law is therefore quite different in its formal structure from its English counterpart, and this is reflected in those crimes which bear most directly upon the interests of investors.

The crime of breach of trust and embezzlement seems almost tailor-made to deal with defalcations at the expense of investors. A charge of breach of trust is particularly apposite where someone with a 'power of administration' over a fund or a portfolio appropriates (i.e. applies to his own use and purpose) money for which he is liable to account to someone else.[1] Such a power of administration is vested, for example, in trustees and investment managers. More generally, it is arguable that any misappropriation of monies in breach of a fiduciary obligation is criminal if done with *mens rea* – i.e., in this context, 'some element of bad faith, some corrupt motive, some guilty knowledge, some fraudulent intent'.[2]

The breadth of breach of trust and embezzlement is such that there has been no need to expand the concept of theft along the lines laid out in section 5 of the Theft Act 1968.[3] Theft involves (*inter alia*) an appropriation of property belonging to another in the ordinary sense, and thus misappropriation by a trustee of trust property is not theft.[4]

The notion of fraud in Scots criminal law also evinces striking latitude. Broadly speaking, fraud is committed by bringing about some definite practical result by means of false pretences.[5] This is certainly wide enough to cover the situation where funds are obtained by means of a misrepresentation in an advertisement or an offer document.

---

[1] G.H. Gordon, *The Criminal Law of Scotland* (2nd edn, 1978), para. 17–22.

[2] *H.M. Adv.* v. *City of Glasgow Bank Directors* (1879) 4 Couper 161, *per* Lord Justice-Clerk Moncrieff at p. 187; see also *H.M. Adv.* v. *Lawrence* (1872) 2 Couper 168; *H.M. Adv.* v. *Laing* (1891) 2 White 572.

[3] Above, p. 27. [4] Gordon, *op. cit.*, para. 14–49.

[5] J. H. A. Macdonald, *A Practical Treatise on the Criminal Law of Scotland* (5th edn 1948, by J. Walker and D. J. Stevenson), p. 52; *Adcock* v. *Archibald* 1925 J.C. 58.

3
Competition, Regulation and Public Policy

In 1972, in a report on the future of London as an international financial centre, the Inter-Bank Research Organisation offered the following summary of the principles on which a competitive financial system should in theory be based:

Financial institutions from the public and private sectors alike will provide most efficiently the financial services needed by government, corporations and companies, and individual customers, if they are permitted and compelled to operate in an open and competitive environment. They are also likely to initiate most readily in such an environment the kind of new services needed by their customers in the future. They must, of course, be regulated to protect the public interest, but in such ways as will detract as little as possible from their ability to compete fairly and openly with one another.[1]

Although this summary does not specifically address the issue, it neatly encapsulates the three main tenets of current public policy on investor protection. The first of these tenets is that the needs of investors are best met by the market: '*Market forces* provide the best means of ensuring that an industry meets the needs of its customers.'[2] The second is that although, as we saw in the last chapter, the market's legal counterpart – the general law of the land – affords investors a measure of protection, that protection is insufficient. Regulation is therefore needed to ensure that investors are protected. 'In all developed countries proper regulation to protect the interests of investors is seen as a necessary element in the healthy development of financial services.'[3] The final tenet is that this protective regulation should go no further than is strictly necessary for the protection of investors. 'The Government . . . intend that the regulation of the financial services industry should be no more than the minimum necessary to protect the investor.'[4]

Our main concern in this chapter is with the second of these tenets – the

---

[1] *The Future of London as an International Financial Centre* (1973), para. 96.
[2] FSA White Paper, para. 3.2(i).   [3] *Ibid.*, para. 1.2.   [4] *Ibid.*, para. 1.5.

need for protection going beyond that afforded by the general law of the land. A striking feature of current public policy in this regard is its failure to spell out in any detail why exactly it is that, in the words of the Financial Services Act White Paper, '*caveat emptor* alone is not enough'.[1] To the extent that any justification is offered for the provision of protective regulations, it is commonly couched in terms of the need to maintain or restore the *confidence* of investors. One of the Government's stated objectives in designing a new framework for investor protection, for example, was that the system of regulation should 'inspire confidence in issuers and investors by ensuring that the financial services sector is, and is seen to be, a "clean" place to do business'.[2] And Gower, on whose recommendations the investment business regime is substantially based, argued that what was required was regulation 'to protect reasonable people from being made fools of. That degree of protection is essential if members of the public are to have the justified confidence to invest. . . .'[3] The problem with such psychological justifications, however, is that they can be invoked to justify any and every measure of investor protection – from the most liberal to the most paternalistic. They do very little, therefore, to enhance our understanding of the rationales underlying particular measures.

What we want to do in this chapter, therefore, is to go behind the language of confidence and, by implication, of fools and their money being soon parted, with a view to identifying and making explicit the specific rationales which may be adduced in support of particular measures. Doing so has the principal benefit for us of providing us with a framework within which to examine systematically what would otherwise have all the appearance of an impenetrable mass of rules. It is also an essential preliminary to any attempt to evaluate the appropriateness of particular measures, as well as to any assessment of whether the third tenet of current public policy – regulation should not exceed the minimum necessary – is in fact satisfied (always assuming that such an assessment is practicable).

COMPETITION

When market forces are described as the best means of ensuring that investors' needs are met, what is meant is that investors' preferences are more likely to be satisfied when firms *compete with one another* for their business. Relying on market forces means relying on competition, which is seen as being capable of generating benefits for investors 'in terms of price, innovation and quality and variety of service'.[4] Its ability to generate those benefits is a function of the pressure it exerts on firms to provide the products and services their customers want. As the Governor of the Bank of England suggested in discussing the

[1] *Ibid.*, para. 3.4.   [2] *Ibid.*, para. 3.1.   [3] *Report*, Part I, para. 1.16, emphasis removed.
[4] Wilson Report, para. 1071.

extent to which increased competition could play a part in promoting investors' interests:

> In an environment in which financial intermediaries are in direct and open competition, the pressures on them, above all to ensure that their product is both what their clients want and competitively priced, could themselves serve to strengthen the position of the client compared with a situation in which competition is less, or at any rate less overt, and there is consequently less freedom of choice.[1]

It is possible, therefore, to view competition as the market's equivalent of regulation, working to increase investors' freedom of choice by restricting investment firms' own freedom of action – by, in short, subjecting them to the 'discipline of the market'.

The benefits associated with competition do not flow automatically from any degree of competition however slight. Economists contend that those benefits will be most fully realised in markets which most closely approximate the ideal of perfect competition, that is in markets in which there are numerous fully informed buyers and sellers acting independently of one another. Under such conditions business will gravitate towards the more efficient, and the less efficient will be driven out of business. Conversely, in markets where these conditions do not obtain – where there is a lack of competition – this will not happen, and the advantages associated with competition will not be realised, to the overall detriment of investors.

Although competition is regarded as being in the interests generally of investors, the question that needs to be addressed is whether it has any bearing on investor protection, the interest of investors with which we are primarily concerned. A possible answer might be that, since in a competitive market-place firms with a high reputation may expect to fare better than their rivals, competition contributes to investor protection by reinforcing firms' concern with their reputation, this concern constituting one reason why firms honour investors' expectations. The difficulty with this answer, however, is that it is manifestly not the case that all firms are equally concerned to protect their reputation. It was for this reason that the City Capital Markets Committee commented that experience suggested that very little reliance could be placed upon competition alone to protect the interests of investors. 'Persons who engage in fraud', it wrote, '*expect* to be uncovered eventually; they just plan to be beyond the reach of the law before that happens. To them the maintenance of high standards of conduct in order to compete in reputation with other practitioners is irrelevant.'[2]

---

[1] 'Changing boundaries in financial services' (1984) 24 *Bank of England Quarterly Bulletin*, 40 at p. 44.

[2] Comments on the Financial Services White Paper (February 1985), p. 8. See also Goodhart, 'The Costs of Regulation', in Seldon (ed.), *Financial Regulation – or Over Regulation?* (1988), pp. 25–6.

REGULATION

Current public policy asserts that investor protection regulation is necessary. The question is why is it necessary, bearing in mind that regulation restricts competition,[1] and hence the benefits it may be expected to generate for investors. Two kinds of possible justification suggest themselves. One, which is suggested by the Government's stipulation that regulation 'must stimulate competition and encourage innovation',[2] is that its rationale is essentially economic. The argument here is that regulation is a response to specific instances of what economists term 'market failure', in other words, circumstances which prevent markets from working in accordance with the ideal model outlined above. We examine this possibility under three headings: the prevention of dishonesty, informational problems and the risk of systemic failure. The other, contrary possibility is that its rationale has nothing to do with a desire to improve the functioning of markets *per se*. We examine this possibility under the heading of paternalism.

Prevention of dishonesty

As the title of the precursor to the Financial Services Act 1986 indicates – Prevention of Fraud (Investments) Act 1958 (this Act was itself preceded by the Prevention of Fraud (Investments) Act 1939) – the prevention of fraud and sharp practice of all sorts has long been a pervasive concern of investor protection legislation. Not even the most avid proponent of the free market and *caveat emptor* would object to legal sanctions against fraud. For fraud is objectionable not only on moral grounds, but also from an economic point of view, in that it derogates from the voluntariness of investment transactions and thereby leads to an inefficient allocation of resources. The question is whether there need be legal safeguards against fraud other than those afforded by the general civil and criminal law.

In support of such safeguards there are two main arguments. The first is that the conception of fraud embodied in the general law will not necessarily be wide enough to encompass satisfactorily the kinds of sharp practice that are encountered in the context of investment. It was anxieties on this score that prompted the enactment, in the Prevention of Fraud (Investments) Acts, of a special offence of fraudulently inducing persons to invest money, variants of which now appear in several modern statutes.[3]

---

1 'Restriction of competition – in the sense of restrictions on the freedom of any person freely to provide any service – is inherent in any system of regulation': *The SIB's Application for Designated Agency Status under the Terms of the Financial Services Act* (February 1987), para. 25.

2 FSA White Paper, para. 3.1(ii).

3 PFI Act 1939, s.12; PFI Act 1958, s.13; see below, p. 301. The 1939 legislation covered *misleading* as well as false representations, *promises* and *forecasts* as well as statements, and *dishonest concealment* of material

The second argument is that 'prevention is better than cure'.[1] In Gower's words, 'it is better to stop someone who ought not to be engaged in investment business from engaging in it than to wait until his . . . lack of probity has caused losses to investors'.[2] This argument suggests the need for administrative controls to exclude from investment business those with a propensity to act dishonestly, and to ensure that investment business is conducted in such a way that opportunities for dishonesty are minimised. Of course, the ordinary criminal law performs a deterrent as well as a retributive function; and to be sure, the civil law is concerned with deterrence as well as compensation. But in the context of investment, as elsewhere, both the civil and criminal law have weaknesses as methods of preventing dishonesty[3] which can be offset by administrative prophylaxis.

It is this argument which underlies, in part at least, many of the licensing arrangements upon which specific regimes are based. It is not one, however, which commands universal support. Proponents of the free market argue that licensing is excessively restrictive, and that protection could be provided in a competitively less damaging way by requiring investment businesses to be insured against the risk of dishonesty. How practicable a proposition this is is not altogether clear. Goodhart, for example, acknowledges that the provision of insurance on the scale required would probably require governmental intervention. Moreover, unless the insurance premiums were priced so as to accurately reflect the risk posed by individual firms, which is difficult if not impossible, the result would be the creation of a moral hazard, whereby the behaviour insured against would be encouraged, since the cost would be borne elsewhere, and this in turn would need to be countered by some form of supervision.[4]

Informational problems

Informational problems provide another recurring theme of investor protection legislation. They take two main forms. The first is the straightforward problem of an insufficiency of information. Information is an example of what economists term a public good. Like lighthouses or defence, it will tend to be under-provided because suppliers cannot capture all the benefits to themselves of its provision; once it is made public it is impossible to prevent 'free-riding' on the efforts of others without paying for its provision. It does not follow that every information failure should be remedied; at some point the costs of providing the information will outweigh the benefits to be expected.[5]

facts, at a time when it was at least doubtful whether the Larceny Act 1916 did so: see HC Debs. 5th ser., vol. 340, col. 1383 (Nov. 21, 1938).

[1] FSA White Paper, para. 3.2(iii).   [2] *Report*, Part I, para. 10.14.   [3] See further Chapter 7.
[4] *Op. cit.*, pp. 28–9.
[5] Beales, Craswell and Salop, 'The Efficient Regulation of Consumer Information' (1981) 24 *Journal of Law and Economics* 491 at p. 512.

But in some cases at least, the argument runs, intervention to compel disclosure is justified as furnishing investors with the information which they require if they are to make the informed calculations of risk and return from which an efficient allocation of resources will emerge. 'If market forces are to operate properly it is essential that . . . as much information as possible is disclosed about the investments and services on offer to the customer.'[1]

The second type of problem concerns the evaluation of information. Investments and investment services are examples of what economists term experience goods; unlike search goods such as clothing their quality cannot be ascertained in advance.[2] As Gower observed, 'it is in the nature of investments that their risk cannot be adequately assessed on the basis of existing information about them, since the risk depends too on the probity and skill of those who will in future be managing the investment or undertaking in which the investment is made'.[3] The Wilson Committee commented to the same effect: 'By their nature financial services are often more difficult than other goods and services to test at the time of purchase. Some are used relatively rarely, and the benefits may be deferred and have to be taken largely on trust. This is most obviously true in the case of life assurance where the intervening period can be very long indeed.'[4] Only experience will tell, therefore, whether the investor has been sold a pup.

These observations lead to two arguments. The first is that the principle of *caveat emptor* should be rejected. As Pennington explains: 'The notion of the early common law, that the buyer must make his own inquiries and the seller need not volunteer information − the notion of *caveat emptor* − was sensible only when applied to things whose qualities and defects could be discovered by a physical inspection which the buyer was as competent to undertake as the seller.'[5]

The second argument is to the effect that some assurance of minimum quality should be provided, thus relieving the investor of the need to choose between undertaking an expensive search for information and the risk of making a potentially disastrous choice. McMahon, for example, argues,

problems arise where it is inherently difficult for the individual consumer to assess the good or service he is buying − or where the learning process for the society may be judged too costly or difficult. Thus we have safety regulations for cars and some food and drugs. Similarly there seems to be a case for laying down minimum standards or guidelines for some activities where an individual would find it hard to assess for himself the risk of loss in a particular transaction and where, at the same time, the cost of being wrong might be relatively severe. These criteria taken together might suggest that there was a relatively weak case for serious supervision of say the mail order industry but a strong case in respect of life assurance and banks.[6]

1 FSA White Paper, para. 3.2(i).
2 Nelson, 'Information and Consumer Behaviour' (1970) 78 *Journal of Political Economy* 311.
3 *Disc. Doc.*, para. 2.01. 4 Para. 1079.
5 *The Investor and the Law* (1966), p. 158; see also Gower, *Disc. Doc.*, para. 7.01.
6 'The Business of Financial Supervision' (1984) 24 *Bank of England Quarterly Bulletin* 46 at p. 48.

As regards the form an assurance of minimum quality should take, McMahon suggests that because of 'the difficulty and costliness of presenting and assessing a full array of factual information about financial institutions', it may be more efficient for a supervisor 'to make his own judgments on the basis of qualitative assessments which he then transfers to the markets in the form of a seal of approval, a licence or a recognition'.[1] The trouble with this suggestion is that it disregards the analytical distinction (by no means always observed in statutory terminology) between certification or accreditation on the one hand, and licensing or authorisation on the other. Certification evidences conformity to certain standards on the part of the accredited practitioner or firm without debarring the uncertificated from carrying on the business in question. Under a system of licensing or authorisation, by contrast, the unauthorised are prohibited from engaging in the relevant activity, or are at any rate subjected to additional legal constraints.[2] In effect, therefore, the conditions of authorisation become mandatory requirements, limiting the business's freedom of action and the investor's freedom of choice.

Plainly, if the object is simply to provide an assurance that certain minimum standards are met, certification is all that is necessary. In the sphere of investor protection, however, systems of authorisation coupled with a criminal prohibition of unauthorised activity are much more common than mere accreditation, which suggests that the rationale for such systems does not lie solely in the provision of information about standards. In favour of licensing as a means of communicating information about standards, however, it may be argued that it has the merits of being clear-cut and easily understood in contrast to a distinction between certified and uncertified firms, the significance of which investors may fail to grasp readily.

That investors may indeed fail to grasp the significance of a distinction between certified and uncertified firms is suggested by the example of the Insurance Brokers (Registration) Act 1977. This legislation was enacted as part of an attempt to raise standards among insurance intermediaries. It sought to achieve this purpose by reserving the appellation 'insurance broker' to intermediaries registered with the Insurance Brokers Registration Council established by the Act, the idea being that brokers would be induced to submit to regulation by the prospect of losing the right to describe themselves as brokers. Members of the public, however, proved largely insensitive to the connotations of the word 'broker', and thousands of intermediaries were able to side-step the requirements imposed on brokers by the simple expedient of labelling themselves as 'advisers' or 'consultants'.

---

[1] *Loc. cit.*

[2] Friedman, *Capitalism and Freedom* (1962), pp. 144–9; Cranston, *Consumers and the Law* (2nd edn, 1984), pp. 371–2.

Systemic failure

The risk of systemic failure – of a complete collapse of the financial system – constitutes a separate economic rationale for the *prudential* regulation of financial institutions, i.e. for regulation designed to curb excessive risk-taking on the part of institutions.[1] The argument is that the failure of one institution may cast doubt on the soundness of others and lead through panic to widespread financial failure.

> Some financial activities cannot be allowed to default because of the readiness with which financial panic can spread. This consideration underlines the essential difference between industrial competition and financial competition: the former may well be in the national interest even if it leads to the survival only of the fittest, but in the financial sector the failure even of the unfit may create crisis.[2]

Safeguards are needed, therefore, in the form of measures to control the risks institutions may incur, coupled with a preparedness on the part of the central bank to act as lender of last resort to the system, thereby preventing an uncontrollable panic from emerging.

Historically this risk has been most closely identified with deposit-taking institutions such as banks which tend to be linked together by long chains of transactions and whose depositors can withdraw their funds at short notice. The 'risk of contagion'[3] is less apparent in relation to institutions whose investors are locked in for longer periods such as insurance companies and pension schemes, and less apparent still in relation to intermediaries such as advisers. However, the growing links between banks and other financial institutions has enlarged the range of institutions whose failure may, through their impact on the banking system, have implications for the financial system as a whole.

Paternalism

Some aspects of modern investor protection regimes undoubtedly can be justified as a response to market imperfections. Thus capital adequacy requirements can be justified as a response to the risk of systemic failure; disclosure requirements as a response to information failures; and entry controls, too, can perhaps be justified as a response to a combination of dishonesty and information failure. But not every aspect of modern regimes can be justified in these terms. Compensation arrangements in their existing

---

[1] Prudential regulation is to be contrasted with *protective* regulation, which aims at the protection of investors. The two types of regulation are closely related, prudential regulation forming an important component of the overall protection of investors.

[2] Llewellyn, 'The Changing Structure of the UK Financial System', *The Three Banks Review*, No. 145 (March 1985), 19 at p. 33.

[3] McMahon, *op. cit.*, p. 49.

form seem particularly difficult to fit into the trinity of dishonesty, informational problems and systemic failure (although they are perhaps justifiable as a response to the difficulty which investors may experience in evaluating information), as do many aspects of portfolio regulation.

The question thus arises of the extent to which this state of affairs has a paternalistic rationale.[1] Wealthy investors, the argument goes, are likely to have the sophistication needed to make an informed choice among potential investments (and if they are unsophisticated they can purchase expert advice); wealthy investors, moreover, can afford to take the rough with the smooth. On the other hand, the 'small man' who wishes to invest his savings (perhaps to provide for old age) may be unable to identify in an unregulated market what he 'really' needs, may be tempted to seek high returns without fully appreciating the high risks entailed, and cannot afford to lose his nest egg.

> If these frauds were practised only at the expense of the well-to-do – that is to say, of the foolish young man who has come into a large sum of money or the wealthy man who wishes to make a little more – your Lordships and people generally might say that with their education, their bringing-up and their knowledge of the world and so on they should know better and would have to stand the racket. But, as a rule, the victims of these frauds are people of a very different class – widows, spinsters, pensioners, retired professional men living on their savings, clergymen with perhaps poor livings and large families – all these form so to speak the happy hunting-ground of the fraudulent share-pusher. . . .[2]

A thorough-going paternalistic solution to this problem might well require high-risk investments (and perhaps gambling also) to be made the exclusive domain of the wealthy. In fact, of course, protective arrangements in the United Kingdom stop far short of such a smothering approach. A compromise between paternalism and freedom of choice is effected by regulating certain investment media (for example, building societies) so that they are comparatively safe and generally known to be so, while putting hurdles in the way of the promotion of high-risk investments to the general public. Those who invest in, say, building societies are held to have opted for a safe haven, and regulation is designed to ensure that this expectation will not be disappointed.

The minimum necessary?

The third tenet of public policy we identified was that regulation should go no further than is necessary for the protection of investors. The difficulty with this tenet is that, although it is possible to identify a number of rationales for investor protection regulation, we have no way of knowing just how far-reaching measures of investor protection need to be in order to achieve their

---

[1] See generally Kleinig, *Paternalism* (1983), esp. Chapter 7; McMahon, *op. cit.*, 48–9; Clark, 'The Soundness of Financial Intermediaries' (1976) 86 *Yale Law Journal* 3 at pp. 18–23.

[2] HL Debs. 5th ser. vol. 111 cols. 970–1 (February 28, 1939).

purpose, and hence no basis on which to establish whether this particular tenet of current public policy is in fact satisfied. This difficulty is, of course, no bar to arguing that current investor protection regulation does go further than is 'necessary', but the fact remains that the proposition itself is not one that is susceptible of proof.

The criticism that investor protection regulation goes further than is necessary is one which may be made of any system of investor protection that goes beyond simple reliance on the general law of the land. An extreme version of this criticism treats regulation generally as unwarranted on the grounds that it restricts and distorts competition, and also that it generally fails to achieve its objectives. A less extreme version accepts the need for some degree of regulation but sees regulatory systems as tending inevitably towards over-regulation. Goodhart, for example, argues, in relation to the investment business regime established by the Financial Services Act, that the omission of any mention of the costs of protection from Gower's terms of reference meant that

the likelihood always was that the associated costs would be given little weight in the formulation of the legislation. Moreover, the incentive for regulators, especially when they do not bear the burden of the costs themselves, is to impose such comprehensive regulations that they will not personally be likely to be held responsible for failures and failings during their own term of office. Since success for a regulator, when the costs of regulation are not fully taken into account, can be measured by the absence of newsworthy failures, the incentive will often be for over-regulation.[1]

Whether the architects of the investment business regime were as cavalier in their disregard of its costs as this suggests is questionable. In formulating his recommendations Gower did not attempt any sort of cost-benefit analysis, 'partly because I am not competent to undertake it and partly because I am sceptical about its practicability'.[2] But in his discussion document he acknowledged that 'It would be self-defeating to introduce regulations which are so stringent that they cannot be complied with without expense or labour wholly disproportionate to the value of the protection which they afford. The likely effect would be to drive out the scrupulous, who would be unwilling to continue in breach of the regulations, and leave matters in the hands of the unscrupulous.'[3] In his subsequent report he rejected the criticism that he favoured 'regulating for the sake of regulation. On the contrary I fully accept that regulation should be reduced to the minimum necessary adequately to protect investors . . .'[4] Elsewhere he had written, echoing the reports of successive company law amendment committees, 'No system can wholly protect fools from their own folly or from the knavery of others, and the advantages of trying to do so as fully as possible have to be weighed against the

---

[1] *op. cit.*, p.31.   [2] *Report*, Part I, para. 1.16.   [3] *Disc. Doc.*, para. 7.01(e).
[4] *Report*, Part I, para. 1.13.

disadvantages of imposing fetters on business conducted honestly and efficiently.'[1]

There is in any event no agreement as to what the costs and benefits of the system are. Lomax, on whom Goodhart relies for his estimate of the system's direct costs, confines his estimate of its benefits to the reduction of losses incurred through fraud and sharp practice. On this basis he concludes that the system's costs are 'substantially greater than any identified losses suffered by investors in public "scandals" in recent years'; moreover, they have been increased, by implication needlessly, as a result of 'a massive overkill of the supervisory structure'.[2] But against this it can be argued that the benefits which the system seeks to realise are not confined to the reduction of fraud and sharp practice but extend, for example, to improved decision-making as a result of the tackling of informational problems, and that, to the extent that they are realised, they too ought to be taken into account in any calculus of the costs and benefits of the system overall.

THE INTERNATIONAL DIMENSION

States, like firms, may value a reputation for securing effective investor protection on the theory that such a reputation is good for business. But if this reputation is achieved at the expense of regulation which is more burdensome than that encountered elsewhere, it may have the undesired consequence of diverting business to other centres. Concern for the protection of investors is matched, therefore, in the United Kingdom by concern to maintain the international competitiveness of the financial services industry, and in particular London's position as a leading international financial centre. 'It would be lamentable', wrote Gower, 'if our regulations were so strict in comparison with those of other countries that London ceases to be the world's centre for financial services as it still is. If the constraints imposed here are unduly severe, market makers will move elsewhere.'[3]

In the context of the Financial Services Act this concern has been a significant factor in the differential treatment of private investors, on the one hand, and 'professionals' on the other – the latter being left to a far greater extent to negotiate the content of their contracts and relationships according to their own commercial judgement. Thus, for example, many of the Core Conduct of Business Rules do not apply where 'non-private customers' are concerned, and even more do not apply to dealings with 'market counterparties';[4] professionals fall outside the Client Money Regulations (unless they contract in);[5] and they can be freely 'cold-called'.[6] Money market institutions

[1] *Gower's Principles of Modern Company Law* (4th edn, 1979), p. 494. The reports echoed are those of the Greene Committee (Cmd. 2657 (1926), para. 9), the Cohen Committee (Cmd. 6659 (1945), para. 5) and the Jenkins Committee (Cmnd. 1749 (1962), para. 11).

[2] *London Markets After the Financial Services Act* (1987), p. 198.   [3] *Disc. Doc.*, para. 7.01.

[4] See below, pp. 269–71.   [5] Financial Services (Client Money) Regulations 1991, reg. 2.02.

[6] See below, p. 317.

are exempt from the Act's authorisation requirement as respects their wholesale business,[1] and there is special provision for 'stabilisation' of issues as practised on the Eurobond market.[2] And the right of civil action conferred by section 62 of the Act is largely reserved for private investors.[3] Viewed cumulatively, these arrangements (along with others not mentioned here) create a 'light' regime for dealings between professionals, thereby reducing the risk of international firms seeking a more congenial regulatory environment elsewhere.

However, the growing internationalisation of financial services and markets and the sometimes intense competition between countries to attract business on the basis of a lower level of regulation than is to be found elsewhere, raises fears of successive cycles of 'competitive deregulation', or of 'competition in laxity', as a result of which regulation is eventually driven down to the lowest common denominator with a consequent heightening of prudential risk and a diminution in the protection afforded to investors.[4] This risk is one that ultimately can only be tackled by the international harmonisation of regulation. Outside the European Community, however, progress towards this goal has been painfully slow, being confined mainly to the adoption of the Group of Ten countries of minimum capital adequacy standards for banks,[5] the adoption by IOSCO of a set of international conduct of business principles,[6] and the fostering of co-operation and mutual trust between national regulatory authorities.[7]

Within the European Community the emphasis has been on the liberalisation of financial services in the context of the completion of the 'single market'.[8] Liberalisation has been sought, not on the basis of a single set of rules directly applicable throughout the Community, but on the basis of the 'mutual recognition' of national systems of regulation, in particular those relating to banking, insurance and investment services. This in turn requires some degree of harmonisation of national standards relating to authorisation, capital adequacy and so on. Once national systems conforming to agreed minimum standards are in place, a company authorised to do business in one Member State (its 'home state') will be able to provide services in other Member States (on a cross-border or branch basis) without the need for further authorisation (the concept of a 'single licence'). In providing those services the company will

---

[1] See below, p. 242.   [2] See below, pp. 286–7.   [3] See below, p. 268.

[4] Edwards, 'Financial Institutions and Regulation in the 21st Century: After the Crash?' in Verheirstraeten (ed.), *Competition and Regulation in Financial Markets* (1981), p. 1.

[5] Basle Committee on Banking Regulations and Supervisory Practices, *International Convergence of Capital Measurement and Capital Standards* (July 1988).

[6] Resolution of the International Organisation of Securities Commissions, *International Conduct of Business Principles* (1990).

[7] See, e.g., the Memorandum of Understanding between the UK and the US on Securities and Futures (1986) 25 I.L.M. 1431.

[8] Commission of the European Communities, *Completing the Internal Market* (1985), paras. 101–7, *Sixth Report of the Commission to the Council and the European Parliament*, COM (91) 237, 19 June 1991.

be subject to the supervision of its home state regulator, with whom 'host state' regulators will therefore have to liaise. The principle of 'home state control' is not universally applicable, however, so that host states will be able to insist, for example, on compliance with local conduct of business rules, providing that they are genuinely intended for the protection of investors and are not simply a disguised restriction on trade.[1]

Liberalisation in trade in financial services has also been sought unilaterally by means of reciprocity provisions. These are provisions aimed at securing access for domestic financial firms to foreign markets. Section 183 of the Financial Services Act empowers the DTI and the Treasury to serve notices on firms connected with overseas countries disqualifying them from, or restricting them in, carrying on investment, insurance or banking business in the United Kingdom. This power may be exercised wherever it appears that the country with which they are connected prevents, by law or governmental action, United Kingdom investment, insurance or banking firms from carrying on business in that country on terms as favourable as those afforded to firms connected with that country in the United Kingdom, and if it is adjudged in the national interest to do so.[2] In addition, the Banking Act 1987 makes provision for the refusal by the Bank of England, at the direction of the Treasury, of its consent to the acquisition of a controlling shareholding in an authorised institution on grounds of lack of reciprocity.[3] These powers have never been formally invoked, but the threat of their exercise has been used, in combination with a refusal to consider an application for authorisation under the banking legislation, to secure access for UK firms to the Tokyo Stock Exchange.

[1] Case 205/84 *Commission* v. *Federal Republic of Germany* [1986] E.C.R. 3955. See further, Chapters. 8, 10 and 16; and Key and Scott, *International Trade in Banking Services: A Conceptual Framework* (1991).

[2] Section 91 of the Banking Act 1987 makes it plain that disqualified or restricted firms need not be carrying on the same kind of business as those discriminated against – thus discrimination against, say, UK investment firms in Japan may lead to the disqualification or restriction of Japanese banks in the UK.

[3] s.23.

4
Disclosure

In this and the following chapter we turn our attention to the various devices commonly employed in modern investor protection. One such device makes provision for the disclosure of financial and other kinds of information to investors about investment products, the status and methods of remuneration of investment firms, the terms upon which they conduct business, any interests which they may have in transactions, and so on. In addition, a number of cognate devices are utilised: provision is made for cooling-off periods to be provided and for risk warnings to be included in promotional and other material. And some investments have voting rights attached to them. It is with these various devices that we are concerned in this chapter. We begin by examining the rationales for *compelling* the disclosure of information.

RATIONALES FOR DISCLOSURE

The modern rationale for compelling disclosure stresses its role in fostering the efficient functioning of markets through providing investors with the information which they require in order to arrive at informed decisions. The original rationale for disclosure concentrated on specific examples of the kinds of information failure which may prevent markets from working in accordance with the model of ideal competition outlined earlier.[1] Chief among these were false claims: insisting on the disclosure of material information, it was argued, would put a stop to the promotion of manifestly fraudulent schemes. 'Publicity is all that is necessary. Show up the roguery and it is harmless,' said Gladstone in introducing the first companies legislation.[2]

Almost as much emphasis was placed on the prophylactic effects of disclosure on sharp practice. If the disclosure of material information were to

---

[1] See above, pp. 36–7 and generally Beales, Craswell and Salop, 'The Efficient Regulation of Consumer Information' (1981) 24 *Journal of Law and Economics* 491.

[2] Hansard LXXV [1844] 277.

be compelled, it was argued, individuals would be discouraged from engaging in practices which, although not legally prohibited, would be unlikely to withstand scrutiny were their details to be made public. The most often quoted articulation of this argument was that of Brandeis: 'Publicity is justly commended as a remedy for social and industrial diseases. Sunlight is said to be the best of disinfectants; electric light the most efficient policeman.'[1] According to Seligman, this argument was influential in the enactment of the United States securities laws:

To the proponents of the 1933 and 1934 securities laws, prevention of excessive insider or underwriter compensation was nearly as important a justification for these acts as the prevention of fraud. Insider conflicts of interest, self-dealing, waste or unfair transactions, it was argued, were less likely to occur if insiders realised that the material details of such transactions would have to be disclosed.[2]

For their proponents, modern disclosure requirements have two principal virtues. First, they provide investors with the means to protect themselves. Armed with the requisite information the investor 'need only act in accordance with what he sees to be his own best interests. Once informed, he can protect himself without resort to law, without relying on the co-operation of others.'[3] This assumes, of course, that the investor has a choice. Where he has no choice (as was the case, for example, with occupational pension schemes before 1988) the argument is obviously less compelling. 'Something more than disclosure must be relied upon where the recipient is already deeply committed – he may find it easy to refuse to buy a security, less easy to reform his union or change his job.'[4] But where the investor has a choice disclosure gives him the means to protect himself. Whether in fact he does so is, to the proponents of disclosure, immaterial. Disclosure does not take away from the investor 'his inalienable right to make a fool of himself. It simply attempt[s] to prevent others from making a fool of him.'[5]

The second virtue claimed for disclosure is that, apart from the need to comply with the obligation itself, freedom of business action is left unimpaired. It thus combines investor protection with the maximum freedom of enterprise: '. . . the ultimate purpose of disclosure is to render possible freedom of contract and to keep as wide as possible the scope for experimentation in financial affairs. The alternative is inevitably the imposition of rigid legislative restrictions on business behaviour; ultimately the choice is between freedom with publicity, on the one hand, and suspicion leading to legal restriction of action, on the other.'[6] As a corollary, disclosure has the additional virtue of

[1] *Other People's Money* (1914), p. 92.

[2] 'The Historical Need for a Mandatory Corporate Disclosure System' (1983) 9 *Journal of Corporation Law* 1 at p. 45.

[3] 'Disclosure as a Legislative Device' (1963) 76 *Harvard Law Review* 1273 at pp. 1292–3.

[4] *Ibid.*, p. 1278.

[5] Loss, *Fundamentals of Securities Regulation* (1983), p. 36. Exactly the same claim is made of substantive regulation; see above, p. 41.

[6] Rose, *Disclosure in Company Accounts* (1963), p. 8.

freeing government from the burden of determining the bounds of permissible conduct: 'information remedies allow consumers to protect themselves according to personal preferences rather than place on regulators the difficult task of compromising diverse preferences with a common standard.'[1]

These claims have not gone unchallenged. Proponents of the free market question the need to compel the disclosure of information, and in particular whether its benefits are at all commensurate with the costs involved. In a competitive market, they argue, it is in the interests of producers and intermediaries to disclose information about the investments and services which they offer; so too investors have an incentive to pay for information in order to lower the cost or improve the quality of their choices. 'Thus, one might argue that the overall richness and competitiveness of information markets imply that it is *never* efficient to mandate the generation or dissemination of currently undisclosed information.'[2] The main theoretical counter to this argument, as we have seen, is that market failures may prevent an efficient quantity and quality of information from being produced. Indeed, according to Beales, Craswell and Salop, 'As long as information is not perfectly free or products perfectly simple, there are almost certain to be some forms of market imperfections present.'[3] Corrective intervention may therefore be justified.

This debate has been most vigorously pursued over the last 25 years in relation to the United States Securities and Exchange Commission's system of mandatory disclosure. Critics of mandatory disclosure argue that it produces few discernible benefits at disproportionate cost.[4] Its most prominent defender, Seligman, counters that this claim ignores or underestimates the evidence of fraud, excessive underwriters' and insiders' compensation and the need for public confidence in the securities market which in his view led to the system's introduction.[5] More recently, the debate has entered a 'post-revisionist' phase involving a more cautious assessment of the system's strengths and weaknesses. The federal securities laws 'ain't necessarily broke', the post-revisionists argue, 'so let's be careful about fixing them'.[6]

This debate has had no direct counterpart in the United Kingdom. Not that disclosure requirements in the United Kingdom have not been attacked as excessively burdensome.[7] And criticism of the costs entailed in complying with them, particularly for privatised undertakings with many thousands of small shareholders, has led to listed companies being empowered to offer share-

---

[1] Beales, Craswell and Salop, *op. cit.*, p. 513.   [2] Beales, Craswell and Salop, *op. cit.* p. 502.

[3] *Ibid.*, p. 503.

[4] See, for example, Stigler, 'Public Regulation of the Securities Market' (1964) 37 *Journal of Business*, 117; Benston, *Corporate Financial Disclosure in the UK and USA* (1976); and Manne, *Insider Trading and the Stock Market* (1966).

[5] *Op. cit.*

[6] Coffee, 'Market Failure and the Economic Case for a Mandatory Disclosure System' (1984) 70 *Virginia Law Review* 717 at p. 753.

[7] See, in this vein, Sealy, 'The Disclosure Philosophy and Company Law Reform' (1981) 2 *Company Lawyer* 51; *Company Law and Commercial Reality* (1984).

holders the option of receiving summary financial statements rather than full annual report and accounts.[1] But there has been nothing approaching the scale of the debate in the United States, nor indeed any account taken in the legal literature of the developments in financial theory, agency theory and the theory of the firm upon which much of that debate is based.[2]

The assumption that investors are rational and capable of looking after their own interests has also been challenged. A contrary view insists that investors are essentially irrational and in need of protection from themselves. This paternalist argument has been employed in the context of disclosure to radically different ends. One end to which it has been employed has been to justify going beyond disclosure and imposing substantive restrictions on freedom of business action.[3] But it has also been used to justify secrecy and the withholding of information (in effect, reliance upon the principle of *caveat emptor*). Thus, the reports of early company law amendment committees subordinated disclosure to the maintenance by companies of a substantial measure of confidentiality in the conduct of their financial affairs.

Traces of this argument survive in the freedom accorded merchant banks to make transfers to and from hidden reserves before disclosing their annual profits. The case for granting banks generally this freedom was set out by the Jenkins Committee.

It is that confidence in the stability of banks is an asset of national importance as lack of confidence may induce depositors both at home and abroad to withdraw their deposits which form the essential working capital of the banking system; that banks are subject to very large fluctuations in the value of their investments and to periodical losses on lendings which can be out of all proportion to the profits of a single year; and that full disclosure of these fluctuations and losses in the annual accounts might well lead to loss of confidence on the part of depositors and the general public.

There were, the Committee pointed out, corresponding disadvantages. 'Shareholders in banking companies are deprived of information they need in order to judge the value of their shares, and to exercise intelligent control over the board of directors: and the right to conceal the size of, and transfers to and from, inner reserves can be used to conceal weaknesses as well as strength.' Nevertheless, the Committee was 'not prepared wholly to discount the possibility of risk if full disclosure were statutorily imposed upon the banks.'[4]

Nor is it necessarily a fatal objection to disclosure that not all investors are capable of evaluating the information disclosed. The investor need not rely on

---

[1] Companies Act 1985, s.251, inserted by Companies Act 1989, s.15; there have also been proposals for the simplification and relaxation of accounting requirements for small companies: DTI, *Accounting and Audit Requirements for Small Firms: A Consultative Document* (1985).

[2] There is a vast legal literature in the United States; for a review, see Gordon and Kornhauser, 'Efficient Markets, Costly Information and Securities Research' (1985) 60 *New York University Law Review* 761.

[3] See below, Chapter 5.

[4] *Report of the Company Law Committee*, Cmnd. 1749 (1962), paras. 401 and 403–4; see now the Companies Act 1985, ss.255–255B and Sch. 9.

capable of evaluating the information disclosed. The investor need not rely on his own expertise; he may (indeed, frequently does) rely on the services of intermediaries whose expertise includes the analysis of information. While this brings with it its own problems (how do we evaluate intermediaries?), the image of the small investor struggling on his own to understand a mass of complicated information, which tends to underlie some criticisms of disclosure, is a misleading one. As Coffee points out:

> Easy as it is today to criticise the original premise of the federal securities laws – i.e., that mandatory disclosure would enable the small investor to identify and invest in higher quality and lower risk securities – such criticism does not take us very far because its target has shifted. The securities markets have evolved significantly since the 1930s, and one of the most important developments is the appearance of the professional securities analyst.[1]

But where required disclosures *are* aimed at the individual investor, rather than intermediaries, it is clearly essential that they should be capable of being readily understood and that attention should not be diverted from them by burying them beneath a mass of other information.[2]

COGNATE DEVICES

Registration

Disclosure is sometimes allied with registration. Like disclosure, registration is a device for making information available. Instead of (or in addition to) being supplied to investors directly, however, the information is filed or deposited at a central point where it is open to inspection by the public at large. It is therefore of obvious utility where potential users of the information cannot all be identified in advance. Thus companies are obliged to file prescribed information which is open to inspection at the appropriate Companies House, and similar arrangements exist in respect of building societies and insurance companies.[3]

Other benefits may be sought by means of registration apart from the making of information available. The Social Security Act 1985, for example, made provision for the registration of occupational pension schemes.[4] The Government argued that the benefits of a system of registration would include helping to secure the widest possible compliance with disclosure requirements, giving employees better access to such information in the face of uncooperative or dilatory employers and acting as a more powerful deterrent

---

[1] *Op. cit.*, p. 723.
[2] Whitford, 'The Functions of Disclosure Regulation in Consumer Transactions' (1973) *Wisconsin Law Review* 400.
[3] Companies Act 1985, s.709; BSA, s.106; ICA, s.65.   [4] s.3 and Sch. 2.

to fraud or negligence than disclosure on its own in that access to the information would not be confined to members.[1] However, the system was never implemented because of the scale of the task involved.[2]

A clear distinction used to be drawn between registration on the one hand, and certification and licensing on the other. Whereas certification and licensing both connoted official approval, the distinguishing feature of registration was that it did not. The Bodkin Committee thus favoured the registration of dealers in securities but rejected their licensing on the ground that it 'would imply governmental approval and control'.[3] However, this usage is no longer observed; registration in relation to the Insurance Brokers Registration Council, for example, means accreditation or certification rather than mere entry on an official list.[4] It was presumably because the distinction is no longer familiar that the Occupational Pensions Board, while favouring the registration of occupational pension schemes, opposed the registration of financial information, arguing that it 'would create the clear but erroneous expectation among scheme members that the Board were monitoring the solvency of their scheme on an individual basis'.[5]

Like any investor protection requirement, registration is vulnerable to non-compliance. The more dependent investors are for their protection on registration alone, the more serious non-compliance is. An investigation by the Committee of Public Accounts of the reliability of the companies register found 'massive avoidance' by companies of their obligation to file annual returns and accounts. In 1983 over 40 per cent of companies had failed to do so. The DTI, the Committee concluded, had 'clearly failed' to ensure that the registers afforded the protection to the public that Parliament had intended.[6] Failure on this scale is of itself sufficient to justify Sealy's view that: 'There is far more myth than truth in the law's perennial assumption that those who deal with limited companies get any real protection or help from the information which a search of the registers will yield for them.'[7] Companies House has since become a 'Next Steps Agency' with an initial target for the two years to April 1991 of a 10 per cent reduction in the proportion of companies not filing their annual return and accounts, so that by June 1991 the compliance rate would be increased to 83 per cent. The actual compliance rate achieved was 77 per cent.

---

[1] DHSS, *Greater Security or the Rights and Expectations of Members of Occupational Pension Schemes* (1984), para.28.

[2] See below, p. 216

[3] *Report of a Departmental Committee on Sharepushing*, Cmnd. 5539 (1937), para. 71.

[4] As to the distinction between certification and licensing, see above, p. 38.

[5] Cmnd. 5904 (1975), para. 68.

[6] *Reliability of Companies Register*, Thirty-Sixth Report from the Committee of Public Accounts (1983–84; HC 511), paras. 3 and 18; and see in a different context, *Monitoring and Control of Charities in England and Wales*, Sixteenth Report from the Committee of Public Accounts (1987–8; HC 116).

[7] *Company Law and Commercial Reality* (1984), pp. 25–6.

Audit

Investor protection commonly makes provision for accounts and other financial statements supplied to investors to be audited.[1] The explanatory foreword to the auditing standards and guidelines issued by the Auditing Practices Board (formerly the Auditing Practices Committee) of the Consultative Committee of Accountancy Bodies defines an audit as 'the independent examination of, and expression of opinion on, the financial statements of an enterprise by an appointed auditor in pursuance of that appointment and in compliance with any relevant statutory obligation'. The conventional statutory obligation imposed on auditors is to check that financial statements have been properly prepared and that they give 'a true and fair view', in other words to check that they are not misleading. An unqualified report thus provides 'not so much an independent source of information as some guarantee of the accuracy of other sources'; a qualified report, on the other hand, 'should be treated as a red light'.[2]

How valuable a safeguard is this in practice? The recent rash of sometimes spectacular company failures has provoked renewed criticism of the performance by auditors of their role.[3] Particular criticism has been directed to their alleged failure to detect fraud and other financial irregularities. Auditors reject this criticism as misplaced, arguing that the primary responsibility for the prevention and detection of fraud, irregularities or errors rests not with them but with the management of client firms.[4] The auditor's role, they insist, is that of a 'watchdog' rather than a 'bloodhound',[5] his responsibility being confined to planning, performing and evaluating his audit work so that he has a reasonable expectation of detecting material misstatements which might impair the truth or fairness of the view given by financial statements.[6] An unqualified report does not, therefore, warrant that fraud has not occurred, only that no fraud has been uncovered which an auditor acting with the skill and care that a reasonably competent auditor would employ in the circumstances would be expected to uncover, or else that any fraud which has been uncovered does not impair the truth and fairness of the view given by the financial statements. Auditors accept that users of financial statements have higher expectations; not surprisingly, however, given the increased potential liability to which they would be exposed, they have resisted any suggestion

---

[1] See, e.g., Companies Act 1985, s.235; BSA, ss.78–9; Financial Services (Regulated Schemes) Regs. 1991, reg. 7.05; Occupational Pension Schemes (Disclosure of Information) Regs. 1986, SI 1986/1046, reg. 7. The relationship between auditors and regulators is considered below, p. 117.

[2] *Gower's Principles of Modern Company Law* (4th edn, 1979), p. 519.

[3] See, earlier, Savage, 'Auditors: a Critical Review of their Role' (1983) 4 *Company Lawyer* 187.

[4] Auditing Practices Committee, *The auditor's responsibility in relation to fraud, other irregularities and errors* (1990), para. 8.

[5] *Re Kingston Cotton Mill Co. (No. 2)* [1896] 2 Ch. 279 at 288, *per* Lopes L.J.

[6] *The auditor's responsibility in relation to fraud etc.*, para. 9.

that their responsibility for the detection of fraud should be extended beyond its existing apparent limits.

A second point of concern is the independence of auditors from management who normally appoint them and fix their remuneration. Company law provides a number of formal safeguards of the auditor's independence. Thus, an auditor who is removed from office has the right to speak at any general meeting of the company at which it is proposed to fill the vacancy,[1] and an auditor who resigns is required to state whether there are circumstances connected with his resignation which should be brought to the notice of members or creditors.[2] Where there are such circumstances, the auditor has the right to require the directors to convene an extraordinary general meeting to receive and consider the statement.[3] The effectiveness of these safeguards against the application of client pressure has been questioned, and various reforms have been proposed, including the compulsory rotation of auditors and the appointment of audit committees with non-executive directors among their membership. Only in relation to banks, however, has there been any move towards implementing the latter of these proposals.[4]

Auditors are also subject to professional self-regulation in the performance of their audit work within the overall framework provided by Part II of the Companies Act 1989. One of the main purposes of this legislation is to secure, in implementation the Eighth Company Law Directive,[5] that company audits are carried out 'properly and with integrity and with a proper degree of independence'.[6] Eligibility for appointment as a company auditor is accordingly confined to members of recognised supervisory bodies who are eligible for appointment under the rules of the body of which they are a member.[7] The Act makes it a condition of the recognition of a supervisory body that it have adequate rules and practices designed to ensure, *inter alia*, that company audit work is conducted properly and with integrity and that persons are not appointed company auditor in circumstances in which they have any interest likely to conflict with the proper conduct of an audit.[8] The Act also prohibits the appointment of a person connected with a company as its auditor.[9]

One factor which may compromise an auditor's independence is the provision to a client of ancillary services such as management consultancy and tax planning. Among the means of tackling this potential conflict of interests which were canvassed when the implementation of the Eighth Company Law Directive was under discussion, was the introduction of an outright ban on the provision of non-audit services.[10] But the less restrictive alternative has been

[1] Companies Act 1985, s.391(4).   [2] s.394.   [3] s.392A.   [4] See below, pp. 131–2.

[5] Dir. 84/253/EEC, OJ 1984 L126/20, obliging Member States to, *inter alia*, ensure that statutory audits are carried out with professional integrity and that there are appropriate safeguards in national law to protect auditors' independence.

[6] s.24.   [7] s.25; the right to audit may be more narrowly restricted: see e.g. BSA, Sch. 11, para. 5.

[8] Sch. 11, para. 7.   [9] s.27.   [10] DTI, *Regulation of Auditors* (1986).

preferred of requiring client firms to disclose the amount of any fees paid to auditors in respect of non-audit services, leaving the investor to judge whether or not the auditor's report may have been influenced by the lucrativeness of other services provided.[1]

Finally, the relative indeterminacy of the concept of a true and fair view affords ample scope for divergences of opinion as to whether or not financial statements match the required statutory standard. It was in an effort to reduce such divergences that the Consultative Committee of Accountancy Bodies set up the Accounting Standards Committee in 1970, in the aftermath of a number of accounting scandals, to develop definitive standards of financial reporting. In this endeavour the ASC was less than successful. It had no power to issue standards in its own right (proposed standards required ratification by each of the six accountancy bodies), and although indirect legal and non-legal support was afforded to its standards in a variety of ways, it also lacked power to compel companies to observe what were in the final analysis standards laid down by and for accountants. It has therefore been replaced by a more elaborate system for setting and securing compliance with accounting standards which seeks to combine the perceived benefits of non-statutory standard-setting[2] with statutory powers of enforcement.

At the heart of this system, which is based on the recommendation of the Dearing Report,[3] is a new representative body – the Financial Reporting Council – whose membership is drawn from a wide range of affected interests and whose principal task is 'to promote good financial reporting'. It is flanked by an Accounting Standards Board which, in contrast to its predecessor, has power to issue accounting standards on its own authority, and a Financial Reporting Review Panel with power to apply to the court for a declaration that a company's annual accounts do not comply with the statutory requirements, and for an order requiring revised accounts to be prepared.[4] If the court finds that a company's accounts are defective, it may order the costs of the application and any reasonable expenses incurred in the preparation of revised accounts to be borne by the directors who were party to the approval of the defective accounts.[5]

Risk warnings

A risk warning, as the name indicates, is a device to foster consideration of risks by investors, the idea being by warning the investor of the risks associated with a particular product to induce him to stop and reflect before making what

[1] Companies Act 1985 (Disclosure of Remuneration for Non-Audit Work), Regs. 1991, SI 1991/2128.

[2] As to which see below, pp. 79–80. [3] *The Making of Accounting Standards* (1988).

[4] Companies Act 1985, s.245B(1).

[5] s.245B(4). As to the legal status of accounting standards, see Companies Act 1985, Sch. 1, para. 7; *Lloyd Cheyham and Co. Ltd.* v. *Littlejohn and Co. Ltd.* [1987] BCLC 303; and Ferguson, 'The Legal Status of Non-Statutory Codes of Practice' [1988] *Journal of Business Law* 12.

might otherwise be a hasty and ill-informed decision. Risk warnings are widely employed in investor protection. Before recommending a transaction to a private customer, or acting as a discretionary manager for him, an investment firm is required to take 'reasonable steps' to enable him to understand the nature of the risks involved; in other words, it must warn him of the risks involved.[1] Persons considering investing in high-risk investments, i.e. futures, contracts for differences and options, must in addition be supplied with one or more written risk disclosure statements, warning them that the risk of loss in these investments can be substantial, drawing their attention to matters of which they should be aware and enjoining them to consider carefully their suitability in the light of their personal circumstances and financial resources.[2] Advertisements and published recommendations, too, must include appropriate warnings of the risks involved in acquiring or holding the investments to which they relate, so that if, for example, the investment is not readily realisable, the investor's attention must be drawn to this fact.[3]

Two concerns have been expressed in relation to risk warnings. One is that warnings are not always sufficiently sensitive to the nature of the risks presented by a particular product.[4] The other, which may be a partial reflection of the same phenomenon, is that investors will respond irrationally to them. Investors may thus ignore the warning, feeling that if the risks were so great the investment would be banned. And even if they pay heed to it initially, they may come to discount it, a phenomenon known as 'wear out'.[5] Alternatively, they may refuse to have anything to do with the investment. 'In neither case', Breyer points out, 'is the choice based on a meaningful assessment of risk.'[6] As we have seen, however, this fear is immaterial to proponents of disclosure: what matters is that investors have been warned, thereby placing them in a position to protect themselves.

Cooling-off periods

A cooling-off period is one during which an investor may unilaterally withdraw from a transaction. Whereas risk warnings enjoin the investor to stop and reflect before making a decision, a cooling-off period gives him the opportunity to consider the information with which he has been supplied and, if he so chooses, to change his mind. 'The policy of ensuring that the investor is provided with sufficient information to enable him to make an informed investment decision is complemented by giving the investor time to assimilate

---

[1] Core rule 10. [2] SIB CBRs (1990), 4.15–4.16.

[3] SIB CBRs (1990), 7.22 and 8.09; see also Banking Act 1987 (Advertisements) Regs. 1988 SI 1988/645,reg. 6 ('controlled advertisements' must state that deposits are not covered by the Deposit Protection Scheme under the Banking Act 1987).

[4] SIB, *Regulation of Marketing of Investment Products and Services* (1990), para. 9.21.

[5] Beales, Craswell and Salop, *op. cit.* p. 530. [6] *Regulation and its Reform* (1982), p. 163.

that information and to act in a properly considered way before he is irrevocably committed to the transaction.'[1]

In investor protection particular importance has attached to the provision of cooling-off opportunities as a means of mitigating the effects of high-pressure selling. High-pressure selling is sometimes found to be associated in particular with the practice of 'cold-calling', i.e. the pushing of investments through unsolicited calls on investors, but pressure-selling can occur without cold-calling, and vice versa. For this reason, in the cooling-off provisions which have emerged under the FSA regime (for life assurance, unit trusts, PEPs and BES funds), the general pattern is to require a cooling-off period to be given whenever a sale is prompted by personal advice from an inter-mediary, but not when no intermediary has been involved (e.g. because the investor has responded to a mailshot).[2]

INVESTOR CONTROL

One of the advantages claimed for disclosure, as we have seen, is that it enables investors to protect themselves. One way in which investors may protect themselves is by not buying or getting out (sometimes referred to as exit). They may also seek to protect themselves by combining with other investors to apply pressure (sometimes referred to as voice) in an effort to force those on whom the obligation to disclose rests to modify their conduct, and disclosure requirements may be imposed to facilitate this. One consequence of such disclosure in the context of investor protection may be to discourage conduct of a kind which it is thought would be unlikely to withstand public scrutiny.[3]

Group pressure may be institutionalised through the conferral of voting rights on investors. Thus, provision is made for the managers of companies and some other undertakings to be elected (and removed from office) by investors, they must also account to investors for their stewardship of the assets under their control, and on some decisions investors have the final say. Disclosure is clearly an essential element of such systems of investor control; as Rose observes in relation to companies, 'any significant degree of control, even if exercised only by critical questioning at company meetings, requires the provision of adequate information to shareholders; disclosure is a necessary, if not a sufficient, condition of effective vigilance'.[4]

How effective, however, are voting rights? Where the numbers involved are small, voting rights may be highly effective. In large companies, however, with many thousands of shareholders, control is commonly regarded as being

[1] *Regulation of the Marketing of Investment Products and Services*, para. 6.5.

[2] See below, pp. 316–18. Despite this growth in the importance of cooling-off opportunities in the protection of investors there has been little published research on their effectiveness; for an attempted evaluation, see Whitford, *op. cit.* p. 463; see also Sher, 'The Cooling-Off Period in Door-to-Door Sales' (1968) 15 *University of California Los Angeles Law Review* 717.

[3] See above, pp. 45–6. [4] *Op. cit.*, p. 9.

divorced from ownership; instead of being exercised by shareholders, it is seen as residing in the hands of management who are able, through the proxy voting system and other methods, to insulate themselves from the preferences of shareholders.[1] '. . . for practical purposes the management of almost all large quoted companies may be regarded as a self-perpetuating oligarchy free from effective intervention on the part of shareholders.'[2] In such companies, the argument runs, voting rights are of dubious value.

For small investors in large companies with widely dispersed shareholdings voting rights undoubtedly are of limited value. It would be wrong, however, to exaggerate the extent of the 'managerial revolution'. Although the once prevailing pattern of direct family control of large companies through majority ownership has declined, it has tended to give way to control by major shareholders (often financial institutions) who between them own a sufficient proportion of their shares to enable them, if they so choose, to exercise a decisive influence over corporate strategy.[3] For these shareholders voting rights are important, and the importance which institutional shareholders attach to them is reflected, among other ways, in the establishment by them of investment protection committees through which the exercise of their voting rights may be co-ordinated.[4]

This qualification does not apply to mutual institutions such as building societies and some insurance companies which have no outside shareholders, but which are instead owned by the beneficiaries of their operations, their depositors, policyholders and so on. In such institutions investor control is substantially weaker. Not only are the incentives for individual investors to intervene normally limited by the size of their stake, but against these must be set the costs involved as well as the sheer difficulty of co-ordinating the exercise of what may be many thousands of single votes. Indeed, so great are the obstacles to the exercise of investor control that investors in mutual institutions are effectively disenfranchised.[5]

There is thus a gap of varying proportions between the theory of investor control and its practice; in some cases investors are able to exercise control, in others they are not. In assessing the significance of this gap from the viewpoint of investor protection (the qualification is important in that owner control may embrace wider concerns than the protection of investments), the availability of 'exit' as an alternative to 'voice' should be borne in mind. While resort to voice may be expensive and its results at best uncertain, exit may provide a relatively inexpensive and more certain alternative. Thus it has been argued forcefully that: 'a building society shareholder, who thinks his money is being

[1] Following Berle and Means, *The Modern Corporation and Private Property* (1932).

[2] Hadden, *Company Law and Capitalism* (2nd edn, 1977), p. 81.

[3] Scott, *Corporations, Classes and Capitalism* (1979), pp. 43–74.

[4] See the Wilson Report, paras. 252–3. Such control as is exercised tends to be exercised informally, rather than formally through voting: Scott, *op. cit.*, p. 93. The two are of course linked.

[5] Scott, *op. cit.*, pp. 81–2.

mismanaged, can and should quietly withdraw his money . . .; the last thing he should do is to start alerting his fellow investors and requisitioning meetings of them. Democratic principles are no doubt very fine in their proper place, but for the individual investor it is better to get his money back.'[1]

The availability of exit has been one of the factors which has diminished the incentive to make voting rights effective. It is not, however, uniformly available. Policyholders in an insurance company, or shareholders in an unquoted company with no market for its shares, do not enjoy the flexibility of the building society shareholder or the shareholder of a listed company who can withdraw his money or sell his shares. And even where exit is available not all investors may be able to protect themselves to the same extent. A sudden rush of withdrawals from a building society may precipitate its collapse, and increased selling of shares may drive down their price.

The issue of control addressed by voting rights therefore remains, although the context in which it arises has in many cases changed. In relation to mutual institutions, for example, regulation has come largely to replace owner control and to perform essentially the same function; the issue in relation to these institutions has thus been transformed from one of the effectiveness of voting rights as an instrument of control to one of the effectiveness of the various regulatory arrangements to which they are subject. On this basis the question of the effectiveness of voting rights is of mainly theoretical interest. Nevertheless, there has been a general reluctance to accept that voting rights allied to disclosure have no part to play in the control of mutual institutions. '. . . it cannot be healthy,' commented the Chief Registrar, 'for there to be such a wide gap between a [building] society's constitution on paper and in practice.'[2]

The same reluctance is evident in relation to companies; as Loss observes, there is in securities regulation 'something of the idea that corporations ought to be run on the "town meeting" principle – a concept that, for all its naivete, cannot be easily abandoned without an agonising reappraisal of the major premise of Anglo-American corporation law to the effect that management is accountable to the owners of the enterprise.'[3] Unlike mutual institutions, however, companies generally are not regulated for the protection of their investors and creditors. Are we therefore to conclude of them, as did the Cohen Committee, that the control exercised by shareholders is merely 'illusory', or, as did the Jenkins Committee, that it is only 'theoretically desirable'?[4] The

[1] Wurtzburg and Mills, *Building Society Law* (14th edn, 1976), p. 9.

[2] Registry of Friendly Societies, *Report of the Chief Registrar 1981–1982* (1983), p. 16. The issue has been more widely discussed in the United States: see e.g. Anderson, 'Policyholder Control of a Mutual Life Insurance Company' (1973) 22 *Cleveland State Law Review* 439; 'Mutual Funds and their Advisors: Strengthening Disclosure and Shareholder Control' (1974) 83 *Yale Law Journal* 1475; Long, 'Governance of Mutual Insurance Companies: A Call for Reform' (1980) 29 *Drake Law Review* 693.

[3] *Op. cit.*, p. 7.

[4] *Report of the Committee on Company Law Amendment*, Cmnd. 6659 (1945), para. 7; *Report of the Company Law Committee, op. cit.*, para. 14.

changing pattern of control of large companies noted above suggests not. While the value of voting rights to small shareholders should not be overestimated, they are important to major shareholders (as well as to those who benefit indirectly from their actions), in that they enable those who have amassed sufficient votes to gain control. In the final analysis, the significance of voting rights is precisely that they enable control to be transferred. Voting is thus 'neither pointless nor, given its point, a failure'.[1]

---

[1] Easterbrook and Fischel, 'Voting in Corporate Law' (1983) 26 *Journal of Law and Economics* 395 at p.398.

5
Beyond Disclosure

Investor protection in the United Kingdom goes much further than the mere imposition of disclosure requirements and the utilisation of cognate devices. Disclosure devices are designed to make possible an assessment of the risks entailed by a particular investment and to foster consideration of those risks. In contrast, this chapter deals with devices whose function is to *limit* the level of risk to which an investor is exposed in connection with a particular investment.[1] Such devices vary greatly in form. There are controls over market entry in the form of authorisation or licensing requirements for firms or individuals. There are capital, solvency and liquidity requirements. There are controls over where investment institutions may invest their funds. There are special powers to intervene in the affairs of investment firms and institutions. There is provision for the operation of compensation schemes. And there are special facilities for savers and investors provided by the state itself.

RATIONALES AND CONSEQUENCES OF GOING BEYOND DISCLOSURE

Disclosure, as we have seen, combines freedom of decision-making with individual responsibility. Regulatory authorities are wont to maintain that the realisation of these values remains unimpaired by a policy of going beyond disclosure. In practice that is not so: freedom of decision-making is curtailed and the responsibility for the protection of investors is borne by government as well as by individual investors. The justification for this assumption of responsibility by government we have already examined. Partly, it is justified on the basis of the paternalist argument that investors, or some investors at least, need protection from themselves. It is also partly justified as a response to market imperfections, notably fraud and sharp practice, information failure

---

[1] Cf. Clark, 'The Soundness of Financial Intermediaries' (1976) 86 *Yale Law Journal* 3.

(in particular, the difficulties investors may experience in evaluating information), and the risk of a complete collapse of the financial system.[1] There are, however, certain drawbacks which may be associated with going beyond disclosure. One drawback is that regulation may fail to achieve its objectives; for example, the assurance regulation is designed to provide may prove to be unwarranted. Going beyond disclosure was for a long time opposed for this reason. The Greene Committee, for example, argued that dealers in securities should not be licensed because if a dealer were able to so describe himself it 'would undoubtedly give to any person with whom he dealt a false sense of security'.[2] In the event their fear turned out to be wholly justified. As Gower pointed out:

Among the unsophisticated investing public . . . the fact that the firm has been licensed by the Department of Trade [under the now repealed Prevention of Fraud (Investments) Act] is regarded as a Government guarantee of respectability and reliability. Under the Conduct of Business Rules the fact that the firm has been granted this misleading tag has to be stated on the documents that clients receive and the fact that firms are forbidden from adding anything which implies that licensing denotes Governmental approval is ineffectual to correct the implication of respectability resulting from the description.[3]

One solution to this problem would be to fall back on disclosure. For example, one reason why evaluation of the merits of new issues has never been attempted is because it risks acting as a rubber stamp giving investors a false sense of security. Another solution, consistent with a policy of going beyond disclosure, would be to guarantee investors' expectations. To a degree this has been done,[4] but guarantees illustrate in its most extreme form a second problem associated with going beyond disclosure, namely that they may induce investors to take more risks, to exercise less care, than they would in an unregulated market. Worse still, from the viewpoint of regulators, they may act in the belief, sometimes justified, that they will be relieved of any adverse consequences of their decisions. As McMahon explains:

The fact that the institutions concerned are regulated or supervised may be taken, even if inappropriately, as in some sense meaning that they have been given an official seal of approval. Some may then wish to draw a further inference that the supervisory authorities carry some responsibility towards those members of the public that have put their trust in, and their money, with the institutions. There may grow up the belief that either the authorities will not allow the institutions to fail or that if they fail, the depositors or policyholders will be 'bailed out'.[5]

One way in which regulatory authorities have sought to minimise this 'moral

---

[1] See above, pp. 35–40.

[2] *Report of the Company Law Amendment Committee*, Cmnd. 2657 (1926), para. 49.

[3] *Disc. Doc.*, para. 5.10.   [4] See below, pp. 71–4.

[5] 'The business of financial supervision', (1984) 24 *Bank of England Quarterly Bulletin* 46 at p. 48.

hazard' is by urging investors not to relax their vigilance. SIB's literature, for example, contains the following risk warning: 'All investment carries some degree of risk, whether relating to business or general economic conditions. The existence of SIB no more removes the need for investors to pay attention to where they place their money than the existence of the highway code removes the need to look before crossing the road.'[1] But there are limits to the extent one can reasonably expect investors to beware, where regulation is a response to the difficulty of evaluating information in the first place. We can judge with our own eyes and ears the risks involved in crossing the road; we cannot by the same means as readily assess the risks involved in placing our money.

Even if it is unrealistic to expect investors to be fully aware, regulators have nevertheless sought to insist that going beyond disclosure does not relieve investors of responsibility for their own decisions: 'No regulatory system can, or should, relieve the investor of responsibility and care in deciding how to invest his money. If he makes a foolish decision . . . he cannot look to any regulator to make good the losses arising from his own misjudgement.'[2] To the same effect, the White Paper, *Banking Supervision*, insisted: 'Depositors can never altogether shrug off their own responsibilities, given that they take their own decisions on where to place their funds.'[3] Since the incentive for investors to exercise discretion and judgement would be destroyed if regulators made good their losses, it could hardly be suggested otherwise. But short of statutory immunity regulators cannot disclaim all responsibility for the negligent exercise or non-exercise of the powers entrusted to them. And even if they are not legally liable, investors may argue that they are under a moral obligation to compensate them where things have gone wrong.[4]

The problem of moral hazard also arises in relation to investment firms and institutions who may be tempted to play fast and loose with the rules in the belief that any gains will accrue to them with any losses falling elsewhere. One response to this problem has been regulation. It was because the Bank of England found itself as lender of last resort to the banking system that it first began to regulate banks; faced with a potentially unlimited liability it sought to control the behaviour of those who might trigger that liability.[5] Regulatory authorities have also insisted that their supervisory role does not detract from the responsibility of management for the running of firms; they have therefore resisted the notion that they will step in to rescue them should things go wrong. 'Management decisions in banks must be taken by the directors and managers. When those decisions prove to be wrong, it is always they and the shareholders who should suffer the consequences. Managers' jobs are at risk,

---

1 *Financial Services – A Guide to the New Regulatory System* (1987), p. 5.
2 *Financial Services Act White Paper*, para. 3.3.   3 Cmnd. 9695 (1985), para. 3.4.
4 As to the legal liability of regulatory authorities, see above, pp. 25–7.
5 See below, pp. 123–4.

and shareholders lose their money. In a free enterprise system, this is as it should be.'[1] In practice, however, matters may work out differently.[2]

AUTHORISATION

Control over market entry in the UK characteristically takes the form of prohibitions against carrying on the kinds of business in question (deposit-taking, insurance, investment) without authorisation.[3] Contravention of these prohibitions is criminal, the maximum penalty being imprisonment for two years.[4] By engendering the need for authorisation to be obtained and retained, these provisions are the keystone of a framework within which other requirements – statutory or discretionary – such as the fit and proper person requirement may be imposed on those whose activities fall within the scope of the basic prohibitions. These requirements fall to be discussed in the following sections of this chapter.

The legal enforceability of contracts effected by businesses lacking the requisite authorisation is a complicated question. The paramount policy consideration is that legislation whose purpose is to protect depositors, policyholders or other investors should not be used to deprive innocent investors of the benefits of their contracts. This policy is reflected in the banking and building societies legislation through provisions to the effect that the taking of money in contravention of the basic prohibitions does not affect any civil liability in respect of the money taken.[5] But in the *Bedford Insurance* case Parker J. felt constrained to hold, in the absence of a corresponding provision in the insurance legislation then applicable, that an insurance contract effected by an unauthorised insurer was void *ab initio*.[6] This decision was heavily criticised for jeopardising the interests of policyholders, and in *Stewart* v. *Oriental Fire and Marine Insurance Co. Ltd.* Leggat J. declined to follow it, holding instead that 'as a matter of commercial practicality contracts of insurance such as these should not . . . be rendered unenforceable by an innocent insured.'[7] When it came to the enactment of the financial services legislation, therefore, it was necessary to incorporate an express provision in order to side-step this conflict of authority. Not surprisingly, the *Bedford* approach is rejected in section 5 of the Financial Services Act, the broad effect

---

[1] *Banking Supervision*, para. 3.2. 'This fundamental tenet of the supervisors' creed', McMahon recalls, 'was put most succinctly by the former Chairman of the Federal Reserve System, Dr Arthur Burns, when, being asked by a bank what the Federal Reserve would do in the event of a banking collapse, he replied that he would be glad to discuss that question with their successors as management.' *op. cit.*, p. 49.

[2] See below, p. 74.   [3] BA, s.3(1); ICA, s.2(1); FSA, s.3.

[4] BA, s.3(2); ICA, s.14(1), (3); FSA, s.4(1).   [5] BA, s.3(3); BSA, s.9(11).

[6] *Bedford Insurance Co. Ltd.* v. *Institute de Resseguros do Brasil* [1985] Q.B. 966.

[7] [1985] Q.B. 988 at 1008. Leggat J. applied his own precedent to what was assumed for the sake of argument to be a deposit-taking transaction in *SCF Finance Co. Ltd.* v. *Masri (No. 2)* [1986] 1 All E.R. 40 (affirmed [1987] 1 All E.R. 176 (C.A.)).

of which is to prevent the enforcement of an 'investment agreement' by an unauthorised business, while allowing its enforcement by the investor.[1]

For a system based on authorisation to function effectively, the regulatory authority needs to be furnished with such information as is necessary to enable it to decide whether an applicant satisfies the criteria for the conferral of authorisation. The more wide-ranging and open-ended these criteria become, the greater the volume of information to be furnished by the applicant. Where regulation is concerned with honesty, competence and solvency the applicant will typically be required to submit a mass of biographical information about key staff (embracing such matters as criminal record, financial standing, training and experience), and financial information about the business, along with a 'business plan' or 'business profile' setting out the business's intentions regarding future activities and development.[2]

Since the bulk of a regulator's information is supplied by the businesses regulated, it is crucial that this information should be reliable. There are several mechanisms whose function it is to foster the reliability of information furnished. First, the various regulatory statutes make it a criminal offence knowingly or recklessly to furnish in connection with an application for authorisation information which is false or misleading in a material particular.[3] Secondly, there are commonly requirements that information be verified – for example, by a solicitor, auditor or actuary – prior to its submission to the regulatory authority.[4] And thirdly, in relation to authorised businesses, regulatory authorities generally have a power to do random checks which may, among other things, throw light on the quality of the information with which they have been furnished.[5]

There would be little point in maintaining elaborate controls over market entry if these controls could simply be avoided by taking over an already authorised firm. To guard against this possibility, changes of control may be subjected to the need for prior approval. The Banking Act, for example, makes the acquisition of controlling shareholders in UK incorporated institutions conditional upon the Bank of England's consent, and the Bank has power to object to proposed changes of control on prudential grounds. A person who becomes or remains a controller after a notice of objection has been served may be stripped of control and, at the discretion of the court, of ownership of the institution.[6]

---

[1] A parallel provision governs non-investment insurance contracts: s.132. The position at common law was resolved in favour of the *Bedford* view by the Court of Appeal in *Phoenix General Insurance Co. of Greece SA* v. *Havalon Insurance Co. Ltd.* [1987] 2 W.L.R. 512; see also *Re Cavalier Insurance* [1989] 2 Lloyd's Rep. 430 (assured entitled to recover premiums despite illegality).

[2] BA, s.8(2); BSA, s.9(8), Sch. 3, para. 2; FSA, s.26(2); ICA, s.5(1).

[3] BA, s.94(2); BSA, Sch. 3, para. 3(2) (para. 3(1) makes the offence one of strict liability in relation to the building society itself); FSA, s.200(1). The ICA, s.14(2), covers false but not misleading information.

[4] BA, s.8(5); FSA. s. 26(5); Insurance Companies Regs. SI 1981/1654, reg. 29, Sch. 4.

[5] See further Chapter 7.   [6] BA, ss.21–7; see also ICA, ss.60–4.

THE 'FIT AND PROPER' TEST

The fit and proper persons test is a fundamental feature of modern investor protection legislation. The broad thrust of the legislation is to apply the test to those who run the business in question. In the case of the legislation on banks, building societies and insurance companies this is done directly by enumerating the categories of persons who are subject to the test – for example, directors, controllers and managers. In the case of the financial services legislation it is done by requiring that the *applicant* – whether corporate entity, partnership or sole trader – itself be a fit and proper person, and adding that there may be taken into account any matter relating to the applicant business's directors, controllers, employees, associates or tied agents.[1]

Most investor protection legislation refrains from spelling out the qualities which must be evinced in order to pass the fit and proper test; only in the banking legislation is there a statement of the matters to which regard is to be had in applying the test.[2] To a certain extent the phrase must take its colour from the context of its application. In the case of individuals the question is always whether the individual is fit and proper to hold the particular post held by him:[3] thus one might be fit and proper to hold one office but unfit (say because of lack of relevant experience) to hold another. In the case of businesses seeking authorisation under the Financial Services Act the question is whether the applicant is fit and proper to provide the particular services described in its business profile.[4] Fitness to function as a life insurance intermediary does not imply fitness to become a futures broker.

Notwithstanding the relativity of the fit and proper test, there are standard factors to which regard will be had in the course of its application in any investment context.

(i) *Reputation and character.* What is sought in this respect is generally summarised by means of such words as honesty, probity and integrity.[5] The view is likely to be taken that a fit and proper person is not only honest in his transactions with investors but also open in his dealings with the regulatory authority. In the context of the supervision of insurance companies, for

---

[1] BA, Sch. 3, para. 1; BSA, ss.9(4) (b), 41(6) (c), 44(4) (c); ICA, ss.7(3), 8(2), 9(5); FSA, s.27(2), (3). Some of these terms are elaborately defined: see BA, s.105; BSA, s.119; ICA, s.7(4)–(8); FSA, s.207(1), (5), (6). Note, for example, that control of 15% of voting power makes one a controller: BA, s.105(3); ICA, s.7(4) (c) (ii) as amended by the FSA, s.134; FSA, s.207(5).

[2] BA, Sch. 3, para. 1; see also PFI Act, s.5 (now repealed). The advantage of a statutory definition from the viewpoint of supervisory authorities is that it puts beyond doubt their power to have regard to matters which the courts might otherwise treat as irrelevant; its disadvantage is that matters not specifically mentioned might be treated as irrelevant.

[3] BA, Sch.3, para.1(1); BSA, ss.9(4) (b), 41(6) (c); ICA, ss.7(3), 8(2), 9(5).   [4] s.27(2).

[5] Criminal convictions are of obvious relevance in this connection. The policy of helping the rehabilitation of offenders by allowing a veil to be drawn over 'spent' convictions is subordinated to the informational needs of financial supervisors by virtue of the Rehabilitation of Offenders Act 1974 (Exceptions) Order 1975 (SI 1975/1023), art. 4, Sch. 1, Part III, para. 3, the Banking Act, s.95(4) and the Financial Services Act, s.189(4).

example, the DTI has said that they 'must be able to have full confidence that they can rely on the good faith of those controlling them'.[1] Moreover, aspects of character other than honesty may be relevant. Someone who is reckless or imprudent in his approach to business, or who lacks the motivation to apply himself diligently, might be regarded as unfit.[2]

(ii) *Competence*. Since the fit and proper test is designed to protect investors from the inept as well as the crooked – the charlatan as well as the rogue – the skills, knowledge and experience of the person under scrutiny are relevant factors.[3] Possession of appropriate formal qualifications may be regarded as evidence of competence, but by and large the investment industry has traditionally placed more stress on experience and know-how than on formal tests of competence. In his discussion document, Gower argued in favour of more formal testing:

> It is often argued that education, training and the passing of examinations cannot ensure that the person concerned will prove to be a competent practitioner; and that is true. It is further suggested as a corollary, that hence no educational qualification is needed or practicable. This corollary . . . is demonstrably untrue. What education and training can do is to ensure that an applicant for admission has an opportunity of acquiring the knowledge without which he cannot hope to be a competent practitioner, and what an examination can do is to ensure that he has acquired an essential minimum knowledge and the ability to apply it with a modicum of sound judgement.[4]

In fact, the long-term trend is probably towards the 'professionalisation' of those involved in the investment industry along the lines favoured by Gower, but the practical difficulties are considerable.[5] Where formal tests of competence are imposed, passing them tends to be a requirement additional to passing the fit and proper test; the competence dimension of the fit and proper persons criterion is not entirely extinguished because it is always possible that a person with the right qualifications will turn out to be incompetent in practice.

(iii) *Solvency*. The financial standing of persons subject to the fit and proper test is relevant above all to their ability to meet their commitments. It is also a matter of interest insofar as it may throw light on their prudence or indeed honesty, or on their ability to withstand financial temptation. Under the Financial Services Act as originally conceived financial resources requirements for investment businesses were to have been imposed by means of the fit

---

[1] Annual Report of the Parliamentary Commissioner for Administration for 1976 (1976–7; HC 116), Appx. B, para. 24; see also SIB, Principle 10, reproduced below in the Appendix, and the report and conclusions of the Financial Services Tribunal in the matter of Noble Warren Investments Ltd. (May 1989).

[2] BA, Sch.3, para. 1(2); Bank of England, *Statement of principles* (1988) (issued pursuant to s.16 of the Act), para. 2.40.

[3] *Kaplan* v. *UK* (1981) 21 ECHR 5 at para. 24; BA, Sch. 3, para. 1(2), Bank of England, *Statement of principles*, para. 2.35.

[4] para. 9.18.   [5] SIB, *Training and Competence in the Financial Services Industry*, CP 40 (1990).

and proper person test (or under the conduct of business rules), but arguments about whether the test was broad enough to embrace their financial standing led the Government to amend the draft legislation to put the SIB's power to impose financial resources requirements on them beyond doubt.[1] The solvency of firms and institutions is discussed below as a separate matter.

(iv) *The interests of investors.* It must not be forgotten that the fit and proper test exists in order to protect the interests of present and future investors; the protection of their interests, the Bank of England states, is 'the key consideration'.[2] In the final analysis, therefore, anything for which a person is responsible that damages or threatens to damage the interests of investors may, depending on the circumstances, give rise to the inference that he is not fit and proper. An apparently venial sin might prove to be mortal when viewed in the context of past failings.[3]

The consequences of an administrative determination of unfitness are serious. Under the insurance, banking and building societies legislation a finding that a person is unfit to be a director, controller or manager does not formally disqualify him or entail his dismissal; rather it means that the employing institution is liable to lose or forgo authorisation, or to suffer administrative intervention in its affairs.[4] In practice, however, the unfit individual is likely to be dismissed in order to obviate these consequences. Under the financial services legislation a finding of unfitness can attach directly to the business itself with the same legal consequences (loss or denial of authorisation, liability to administrative intervention).[5] In addition, however, any individual who is not a fit and proper person to be employed in connection with investment business may be made the subject of a disqualification direction under section 59 of the Act whose effect is to debar him from employment by any investment business. In fact SIB has never exercised its power to disqualify individuals, preferring to rely instead on the screening procedures of the SROs.[6]

FINANCIAL REGULATION

Standard economic theory treats bankruptcy as part and parcel of a healthy process of economic evolution in a market economy, which allows resources to be transferred to more productive uses, and hence as something which the state should not intervene to prevent artificially.[7] However, whereas this

[1] FSA, s.49.   [2] *Statement of principles*, para. 2.34; BA, Sch. 3, para. 2.
[3] *Statement of principles*, para. 2.40.   [4] ICA, ss.7–9, 11, 37; BA, ss.9, 11, 12; BSA, ss.9,41–4.
[5] FSA, ss.27,28,64.
[6] The reason is that the making of a single disqualification direction by SIB would force investment businesses to check the SIB register each time they employed someone, thus generating tens of thousands of enquiries each year. This would be the combined effect of FSA, s.103(1), (2) with s.59(6).
[7] Burton, *Picking Losers. . . ?* (1983), pp. 21–4.

theory is commonly applied to ordinary industrial and commercial firms, it is not rigorously applied to financial firms, partly because of the systemic consequences their failure may entail.[1] Such firms may therefore be subject to financial regulation in the form of requirements to maintain assets in a specified amount and form, breach of which exposes them to the risk of administrative intervention.

Two types of financial resources requirements are commonly encountered in investor protection. The first are capital adequacy or solvency requirements of the kind applied to banks, building societies, insurance companies and some investment firms, whose broad purpose is to ensure that the firms have sufficient assets to enable them to survive the occurrence of the kinds of risks, for example of borrowers defaulting, or of unfavourable price movements, to which they are exposed. In relation to building societies, for example, their purpose is 'to give an institution the financial strength to ride out a change in circumstances which significantly affects its business, to give it time to adjust as necessary to those circumstances and to maintain public confidence while it is so doing'.[2] Likewise, in relation to insurance companies, the 'essential purposes' of requiring an excess of assets over liabilities are 'to provide a safety margin in case the value placed on those liabilities proves to be too low, and to provide a "breathing space" before actual insolvency is reached, to enable the Department to intervene for the purpose either of ensuring that suitable remedial measures are taken to avoid actual insolvency or of minimising the losses if winding-up is unavoidable'.[3] The second type of requirement are *liquidity* requirements of the kind applied to banks and building societies (which typically borrow short and lend long) and which are designed to enable the firms to which they apply to meet claims as they fall due.

Capital adequacy and liquidity requirements are to be distinguished from initial or minimum capital requirements whereby banks and building societies, for example, are required to have net assets in excess of a specified sum in order to obtain authorisation. The principal rationale for the imposition of such requirements appears to be to deter 'men of straw' and 'fly-by-night operators'.[4] Like all financial requirements they operate to discourage entry and competition between firms. A balance needs to be struck, therefore, between the deterrence of applicants whose intentions are less than serious and the restriction of competition. Where precisely that balance is to be struck is a matter of judgement. 'There can be no scientific computation of a figure which would be sufficiently high to serve as an effective deterrent while not being so high as to act as an undue hindrance to competition.'[5]

---

[1] For a discussion of the rationales of financial regulation, see Franks and Mayer, *Risk, Regulation and Investor Protection: The Case of Investment Management* (1989).

[2] Chief Registrar of Friendly Societies, *Building Societies Act 1986: Capital Adequacy* (August 1986), para. 4.2.

[3] *Linked Life Assurance: Report of the Committee on Property Bonds and Equity-Linked Life Assurance*, Cmnd. 5281 (1973), para. 90.

[4] *Linked Life Assurance*, para. 113.   [5] *Ibid.*, para. 114.

PORTFOLIO REGULATION

The need to meet financial resources requirements may exert a strong influence on the way in which institutions invest their funds. The Friendly Societies (Long Term Insurance Business) Regulations 1987, for example, stipulate that for the purpose of calculating the solvency of societies to which they apply, some assets are to be left out of account altogether, and others may be taken into account only within specified limits.[1] Those assets are therefore unlikely to feature prominently in a society's portfolio. Apart from the need to meet the requirements themselves, however, financial regulation does not involve any restriction of institutions' freedom to invest their funds as they see fit. This is in contrast to portfolio regulation which does involve the imposition of direct restrictions on powers of investment.

A common theme of such restrictions is the avoidance of riskier classes of investments. Thus, whereas (after 1 January 1993) at least 75 per cent of a building society's assets must take the form of class 1 assets (that is, advances to individuals fully secured by a first mortgage on land), not more than 15 per cent may take the form of class 3 assets, that is, unsecured loans.[2] Another theme is risk-spreading: the basic rule in relation to authorised unit trusts classified as securities funds, for example, is that not more than 5 per cent in value of the property of the fund can be invested in the securities of a single issuer.[3] And a third theme is the avoidance of conflicts of interests: for example, securities funds are prohibited from acquiring more than 10 per cent of the voting shares in a company, a restriction designed to ensure that the interests of unit-holders remain paramount.[4]

Investment powers may of course be restricted for reasons other than those of investor protection. The confinement of building societies for much of their history to mortgage lending has had as much to do with ensuring a ready supply of housing finance as with the protection of investors. So too the prominence of government securities in lists of permitted investments has had a great deal to do with ensuring a ready market for government debt. Not that, in terms of safety at least, the pursuit of these aims has necessarily run contrary to the interests of investors: land and government debt have traditionally been regarded as being among the safest forms of investment.

The more difficult question raised by existing techniques of portfolio regulation is not whether they can reduce the level of risk to which investors are exposed, but whether they allow investors to achieve the maximum rate of return consistent with a specified level of risk. It seems unlikely that they do, especially where – as in the case of the 'legal list' approach adopted in the Trustee Investments Act 1961 – they risk denying investment managers the flexibility they need in order to respond to changing economic conditions.[5]

[1] SI 1987/2132.
[2] BSA, s.20; Building Societies (Limits on Commercial Assets) Order 1988, SI 1988/1142.
[3] Financial Services (Regulated Schemes) Regs. 1991, reg. 5.10.   [4] *Ibid.*, reg. 5.14.
[5] See above, pp.20–22; and Clark, *op. cit.*, pp. 50–8.

POWERS OF INTERVENTION

A feature of modern investor protection regulation is the possession by regulatory authorities of far-reaching and broadly-grounded powers of intervention. Under the Financial Services Act, for example, S I B has power to restrict the kind or extent of business (including non-investment business) directly authorised firms may undertake, as well as power to freeze their assets, to require them to be vested in an approved trustee and to require them to be maintained in the UK.[1] So too under the Banking Act, the Bank of England has power to restrict an institution's authorisation, by imposing conditions on it, as well as power to revoke its authorisation outright.[2]

Powers of intervention are analytically distinguishable from powers of enforcement (although the same powers may serve both purposes). Their essential purpose is the protection of investors rather than the punishment of offenders. They fall to be exercised, therefore, whenever to do so appears 'desirable' or 'expedient' for the protection of investors, and not merely when specific breaches of regulatory requirements have been uncovered. Indeed, their exercise may be quite unconnected with any breach of requirements as, for example, where a bank's authorisation is restricted in response to a sudden external threat, unconnected with the institution's conduct, such as a natural catastrophe or the imposition by a government of a debt moratorium.[3]

The exercise of powers of intervention where there is uncertainty about an institution's soundness may pose a considerable dilemma for regulators. If they exercise their powers, existing investors will face disruption and they will be accused of harassing business which is being legitimately conducted; moreover, if the fact of their intervention becomes publicly known, they may induce such a loss of confidence as to lead to the firm's collapse. If, on the other hand, they do not intervene, and the firm collapses, they will almost certainly face claims from investors that they should have intervened to prevent losses from occurring. This dilemma was graphically illustrated by the collapse of Vehicle and General where, as the report of the tribunal appointed to inquire into its collapse explained:

> the increasing size of the Group led to an increasing fear that if statutory action were taken, and this became public knowledge, there might well be a smash of unprecedented proportions in the insurance market, and, amongst other unfortunate consequences, this might cause considerable damage to the high reputation of British insurance at home and abroad. Those considerations unfortunately prevailed over those which should have pointed in the opposite direction – that the main purpose of the Department's functions was to protect the public against the failure of insurance companies, and that the larger the Group's insurance business was allowed to grow, the greater the number of persons who would suffer if it collapsed.[4]

[1] ss.64–8. [2] s.12; see also BSA, ss.42–3 and ICA, ss.37–45.

[3] *Statement of principles*, para. 4.7; see also *R.* v. *Chief Registrar of Friendly Societies ex p. New Cross Building Society* [1984] 2 All E.R. 27.

[4] Report of the Tribunal appointed to inquire into certain issues in relation to the circumstances leading up to the cessation of trading by the Vehicle and General Company Limited (HL 80, HC 133, 1971–2) para. 169.

One way in which regulators have traditionally tried to resolve this dilemma is by keeping secret the fact of their intervention.[1] In evidence to the Treasury and Civil Service Committee, the Governor of the Bank of England explained that there were cases in which the Bank intervened to 'preserve banking institutions in the interests of depositors' about which the public did not hear 'because the whole purpose of our preservation actions is that they should remain in confidence and the bank should be strengthened and there should be no intermediate period in which the bank in difficulty or under supervisory discipline should be known to be in that state'.[2] 'Doing good by stealth' is nevertheless open to the objection that it deprives investors of material information; potential investors in particular would be unlikely to invest if they knew that the authorities harboured doubts about a firm's soundness. To warn them off, however, may simply precipitate the firm's collapse and deny existing investors the chance of rescue. As the Governor of the Bank of England put it: 'A hint from the Bank of England that somebody on our list may not be quite pukka would be the kiss of death to the future of a bank.'[3]

Hadden suggests in relation to company inspections that this problem is one largely of regulators' own making. 'It is only the fact that the Department has consistently used its formal powers only at the last possible moment which has encouraged the deduction that any company subjected to an inspection must be near to insolvency. A more active policy of intervention as soon as there is any reasonable doubt as to a company's financial state might well have bred a rather different public expectation.'[4] This may be so, but to intervene where there were no doubts about a firm's soundness, which is what would be required to dissipate the public's expectation, would be to waste resources as well as to expose the authorities to the criticism that they were engaged in the unwarranted harassment of legitimate business activities. This particular regulatory dilemma is not, therefore, one which is easily resolved.

Regulatory authorities also have power to petition the court for firms to be compulsorily wound up.[5] The court may grant a petition if the firm is unable to pay its debts, or if in its opinion it is 'just and equitable' to do so. (There are additional grounds upon which petitions may be granted in the cases of insurance companies and building societies.) What is just and equitable in the context of investment firms was considered at some length by the Court of Appeal in *Re Walter L Jacob and Co. Ltd.*[6] In the Court's judgment it was in the public interest that a firm which had misled members of the public into buying shares of dubious value and restricted marketability should be wound up. 'The

[1] *Bank of England: First Report of the Select Committee on the Nationalised Industries* (1969–70; HC 258), paras.91–4; *R* v. *Chief Registrar of Friendly Societies ex p. New Cross Building Society* [1984] 2 All E.R. 27 at 31–2.

[2] *Banking Supervision and BCCI* 1990–1, HC 636–i, p. 2.   [3] *Ibid..*, p. 6.

[4] *Company Law and Capitalism* (2nd edn, 1977), pp. 408–9.

[5] BA, s.92; BSA, s.89; FSA, ss.72–4; ICA, s.54; note also Companies Act 1985, s.440 (Secretary of State may petition where it appears expedient in the public interest).

[6] (1988) December 12 (unreported).

public interest requires that individuals and companies who deal in securities with the public should maintain at least the generally accepted minimum standards of commercial behaviour, and that those who, for whatever reason, fall below those standards should have their activities stopped.'[1] The Court's assessment of where the public interest lay was not altered by the fact that the firm had stopped dealing in securities:

. . . it would offend ordinary notions of what is just and equitable that, by ceasing to trade on becoming aware that the net is closing around it, a company which has misconducted itself on the securities market can thereby enable itself to remain in being despite its previous history . . . by winding up such a company the court will be expressing, in a meaningful way, its disapproval of such misconduct. Moreover, in addition to being a fitting outcome for the company itself, such a course has the further benefit of spelling out to others that the court will not hesitate to wind up companies whose standards of dealing with the investing public are unacceptable.[2]

COMPENSATION SCHEMES

Compensation schemes for investors exist because of the acknowledged fallibility of regulatory arrangements, however efficient, designed to prevent insolvencies among investment institutions and intermediaries. In the words of the Wilson Report: 'No system of regulation can be totally effective in preventing failures altogether, particularly where institutions are permitted to compete fairly freely among themselves.'[3] Accordingly, the argument goes, compensation schemes are necessary to provide a 'safety net' for investors.[4] The cost of providing such a safety net is normally met by levies on firms operating in the relevant sector of the investment industry.

Critics of compensation schemes have made two main points, which reflect the philosophy of free enterprise and individual responsibility. The first is that compensation schemes, where they cover all firms carrying on a particular kind of business, attenuate competition between them in that 'they reduce the extent to which they can compete with each other in terms of the security they offer their customers'. Worse still, by exacting levies from healthy firms to compensate the customers of failed firms, they require sound businesses to 'underwrite the activities of their less sound competitors'.[5] The conventional response to this criticism is that such schemes benefit even sound firms by enhancing public confidence in the investment medium or kind of intermediary in question, and thereby increase public readiness to invest in the medium or through the intermediaries covered by the scheme. As Templeman

---

[1] 27–8. [2] 31–2. [3] para. 1089.
[4] *Ibid.*; Department of Trade, *Report on the Policyholders Protection Act 1975* (1980–1; HC 363), paras. 11–12; Gower, *Report*, Part 1, para. 6.31.
[5] Wilson Report, para. 1090.

J. observed in sanctioning the participation of leading building societies in a scheme to compensate investors in the Grays Building Society:

> It is unthinkable that the Grays Building Society's investors, who shared in the general belief – passionately held and publicised by the building society industry – that building society investors are safe, should be left to bear the present loss. . . . If £8 million is withdrawn for the purpose of indemnifying the Grays Building Society's investors, the amount will be much less than the withdrawal which would take place from the building societies if the Grays Building Society's investors were inflicted with the loss of £8 million.[1]

The second criticism that has been made is that compensation schemes reduce the incentive for investors to be 'discerning', that is, to discriminate between firms by reference to their financial soundness.[2] However, the force of this criticism is reduced when, as is commonly the case, the 'safety net' affords only partial compensation. Besides, it is questionable whether discernment can be realistically expected. Clark suspects that 'most ordinary people, even if supplied regularly and quickly with financial statements, would be unable to assess properly the risk of financial failure of the intermediaries [or institutions] without a great deal of effort'.[3]

The idea that compensation schemes are a necessary and integral component of investor protection has only recently gained general acceptance. Compensation schemes themselves are, of course, nothing new. The Law Societies set up theirs (for the benefit of solicitors' clients in general, not just investment clients) in the 1940s.[4] The Stock Exchange established its compensation fund in 1950. These bodies presumably saw their schemes as a means of enhancing the credibility of their self-regulation and of providing an incentive for doing business with their members. The Policyholders Protection Act 1975 was a new departure, in that the government of the day, reacting to recent insurance company collapses, foisted upon a reluctant industry a scheme (covering general as well as life insurance policyholders) involving the involuntary participation of all insurance companies. (The parallels with the Air Travel Reserve Fund Act 1975 are obvious.) The 1975 Act has in some respects provided a model for subsequent developments. The Banking Act 1979 provided for compulsory participation in a compensation scheme for bank depositors, a provision that has been maintained by the Banking Act 1987, while the Building Societies Act 1986 makes provision for a similar scheme for building society savers. The view that compensation schemes are a *sine qua non* of adequate investor protection has also prevailed in relation to FSA investment businesses. According to SIB: 'A scheme to give reasonable compensation to investors when the firm with which they are dealing cannot meet its obligations is an essential part of any system of investor protection',[5]

---

[1] *Halifax Building Society* v. *Registry of Friendly Societies* [1978] 1 W.L.R. 1544 at 1546–7.
[2] The Stock Exchange, *Membership and the Constitution* (1985), App. 6, para. 2.   [3] *Op. cit.*, p. 93.
[4] Monopolies Commission, *Professional Services*, Part II, Cmnd. 4463-I (1970), App. 14, Annex B.
[5] SIB/MIBOC, *Regulation of Investment Business: The New Framework* (1985), para. 1.34.

and indeed the Financial Services Act calls for 'the best provision that can reasonably be made' in this respect.[1]

Implicit in this line of development seems to be the idea that compensation schemes are appropriate in two contexts, first, in relation to ostensibly 'safe' investments, such as bank deposits, building society savings and traditional life assurance policies. In this connection the argument must be that the investor's choice of investment shows him to have opted for security, so that he must be protected against loss in order to avoid the disappointment of his legitimate expectations. Secondly, compensation schemes have come to be seen as apposite in relation to investment firms functioning as money managers or intermediaries, regardless of the magnitude of the risk presented by the ultimate investment made through the firm. In this second case we are concerned with loss occasioned by the failure of the firm to fulfil its obligations, for example, to account for client money. It is certainly arguable, where an investor entrusts his affairs to an investment firm precisely in order to be able to rely less on his own judgement and more on the expertise of the intermediary, that the object of the exercise would be defeated if the absence of a compensation scheme forced the investor to make an assessment of the risk presented by the intermediary instead.[2] Where, on the other hand, the investor is prepared to run risks having made his own evaluation of them, and the investment firm is merely a means of access to the chosen market, it is less apparent why the soundness of the intermediary should not be regarded as a risk to be evaluated like any other.

A feature common to all four statutory compensation schemes is that they limit the compensation payable to a specified proportion of the amount lost, or disregard losses in excess of a specified sum, or both. Under the Policyholders Protection Act compensation is limited to 90 per cent of the value of the policy. Under the Banking Act the depositor recoups only 75 per cent of his loss, and losses in excess of £20,000 do not come into the reckoning. The largest sum that can be recovered is therefore £15,000. Under the Building Societies Act the proportion recoverable is set at 90 per cent with losses in excess of £20,000 again being ignored. The largest sum that can be recovered is therefore £18,000. Under the Investors Compensation Scheme the limit of compensation is £48,000 per customer, the ceiling for 100 per cent compensation being set at £30,000.

An obvious function of such limitations is that they reduce the potential cost of operating the schemes. In addition, they represent a concession to the ethos of individual responsibility associated with the disclosure philosophy: even the small investor is left with a residual incentive to give some thought to the soundness of the institution or firm to which he proposes to hand over his money.[3] At the same time, these limitations leave scope for particular self-

[1] Sch. 8, para. 10.
[2] Cf. Clark, 'The Four Stages of Capitalism', (1981) 94 *Harvard Law Rev.* 561 at p. 571.
[3] Report on the Policyholders Protection Act 1975, para. 13; Wilson Report, para. 1091.

regulatory bodies or groups of firms to devise schemes offering fuller compensation upon the default of one of their members than is provided for by statute. In this way there can still be a measure of competition on security between firms which are members of different associations or even of the same association. For example, the relative generosity of the Stock Exchange scheme was designed to encourage investors to bring their substantial transactions to the Stock Exchange rather than elsewhere, and the Building Societies Act permits societies to enter into voluntary arrangements for the payment of more generous compensation than is available under the statutory scheme.[1]

If the alternative to compensation schemes is to leave the customers of an insolvent investment business ranking as ordinary creditors in a liquidation, there can be no doubt that such schemes, notwithstanding the partial compensation they offer, afford investors a significant degree of comfort. But experience has shown that, particularly in the case of deposit-taking institutions, there are sometimes other alternatives more advantageous to the investor, such as the rescue of the insolvent institution (as occurred with the launch of the Bank of England 'lifeboat' in response to the secondary banking crisis of 1973–5) or a 'transfer of engagements' to a healthy institution (as happened with the Grays Building Society in 1978).

Insofar as a compensation scheme has the effect of displacing these alternatives, it actually increases the risk to which the investor is exposed. So, for example, the Chief Registrar of Friendly Societies believed the non-statutory compensation scheme introduced by the Building Societies Association in 1982 to have ended

> the presumption that had been generated by the rescue of investors in the Grays and some other societies that the collectivity of societies would assure investors in any building society which got into difficulties of 100 per cent recovery. That presumption had become inappropriate with the greater competition between societies: investors ought to have some incentive to have regard to the financial strength of societies in which they are considering investing.[2]

However, the availability of a compensation scheme does not in practice preclude the possibility of a rescue for an insolvent institution or its investors. Particularly in the case of a large institution – one which is 'too big to fail' – regulatory authorities may still feel impelled to arrange a full-scale rescue to avoid a shock to the financial system and to sustain public confidence.

STATE FACILITIES

The Department for National Savings administers a wide range of savings and

---

[1] Stock Exchange, *Membership and the Constitution* (1985), App. 6, para. 20; BSA, s.31.

[2] Registry of Friendly Societies, *Report of the Chief Registrar 1981–82*, 22.

investment facilities. 'National Savings' currently comprise Treasury securities, including savings certificates, the yearly plan savings scheme, save as you earn contracts, income bonds, capital bonds and premium bonds, as well as the ordinary and investment account facilities offered by the National Savings Bank. Historically, two aims have been sought through their provision. One has been to help finance the government's borrowing requirement. The other has been to ensure that suitable facilities are available for meeting the needs of small unsophisticated savers – persons of modest means – and in this way to help foster the savings habit and a sense of personal financial responsibility. The National Savings Bank's predecessor, the Post Office Savings Bank, for example, was established in 1861 'with the express purpose of promoting working-class thrift by providing a secure alternative to [trustee savings banks] which offered a limited service, often open only a few hours a week, and which had been subject to a number of financial scandals involving the defalcations of officers.'[1]

From the standpoint of investor protection, the most important feature of National Savings facilities is the fact that they carry a government guarantee. National Savings Treasury securities are issued under the authority of the National Loans Act 1968, which provides for liabilities 'to be charged on and paid out of the National Loan Fund with recourse to the Consolidated Fund'.[2] The former is the fund through which all government borrowings and most of its lending is channelled, the latter the fund into which the receipts of taxation are paid. Insofar as liabilities cannot be met from repayments on lending or further borrowing, the shortfall must therefore be made good out of taxation:[3] '. . . in the last analysis, to be a charge on the Consolidated Fund is to have a guarantee of payment out of taxation'.[4] For their part, National Savings Bank account holders enjoy, by virtue of similar provisions, the same 'direct security of the State' as was given, in the words of its preamble, by the Post Office Savings Bank Act 1861 to their predecessors with the Post Office Savings Bank.[5]

The extent to which meeting the needs of the unsophisticated continues to form part of the rationale for the provision of National Savings facilities is unclear. The Radcliffe Committee thought it 'right that action in relation to [National Savings] should be strongly coloured by the need on social grounds to encourage thrift in the broad mass of the people'.[6] Without, in their own words, attempting 'to moralise on the question of saving,' the Page Committee, which undertook the last review of National Savings, were

[1] Johnson, *Saving and Spending* (1985), 89.   [2] s.12(4); see also National Debt Act 1972, s.8(1).
[3] See, too, National Loans Act 1968, s.19(1) and the Consolidated Fund Act 1816, s.1 of which makes the service of the national debt a prior charge on the Consolidated Fund.
[4] Pliatzky, *Getting and Spending* (1984), p. 232.
[5] Post Office Savings Bank Act 1861, 24 Vict. c.14; see now National Savings Bank Act 1971, ss.20, 25 and Finance Act 1980, s.120.
[6] *Report of the Committee on the Working of the Monetary System*, Cmnd. 8276 (1959), para. 601.

prepared 'to accept that a citizen who is financially responsible will tend to be a better citizen than one who relies completely on the community to look after him in times of hardship and misfortune . . . a provident citizen may be regarded as an important social asset'.[1] It followed, the Committee concluded, that there was a 'social need', for the meeting of which the state retained 'overall responsibility', to ensure the availability of a range of investment facilities. However, these facilities did not have to be provided by the state itself: they could be provided equally well by institutions under its close supervision and control (as was the case with trustee savings banks until 1976).[2]

One reason why the state continues to provide facilities itself is because of the potential contribution they may make to the funding of its own activities. Their importance in this respect was underlined by the setting of targets between 1981 and 1985 for the contribution to be made by National Savings to the financing of the public sector borrowing requirement, but as the public sector has moved into surplus in recent years their role in this respect has been revised.[3] Notwithstanding the diminished emphasis placed on National Savings as a source of government borrowing, there remains a potential conflict between the state's interest as borrower and the interests of National Savings holders: '. . . the Government will wish to obtain finance in the cheapest possible way, which may conflict with the objective of offering a "fair deal" to the small and unsophisticated saver.'[4] The risk, of course, is that any conflict will be resolved in favour of the state to the detriment of savers. Such was most obviously the case with inflation before the introduction of the first issues of index-linked retirement certificates and save as you earn contracts in 1975. As the Page Committee explained, 'inflation has operated like a tax from which the Government as debtor has received great advantage'.[5]

The Page Committee recommended that those who had been hardest hit by the effects of inflation – 'the small and unsophisticated saver who has responded to appeals to his patriotism and to assurances that his capital will be absolutely safe' – should be offered protection through the issue of an index-linked security.[6] When index-linking was first introduced in 1975 it was this argument upon which the greatest emphasis was placed. As their popular description – granny bonds – made clear, index-linked retirement certificates were confined to persons of national retirement age. But after 1980, when greater emphasis was placed on the contribution to be made by National Savings to the financing of the public sector borrowing requirement, the purpose of their provision became more firmly linked to the state's economic objective. One result of this has been that index-linking has become more

---

[1] *Report of the Committee to Review National Savings*, Cmnd. 5273 (1973), para. 5.   [2] *Ibid.*, paras. 23–4.
[3] National Savings, *Annual Report 1987–88*, p. 5.
[4] *Report of the Committee to Review National Savings*, para. 30.   [5] *Ibid.*
[6] *Ibid.*, para. 570, 580.

widespread. The age restriction on index-linked certificates was twice reduced before being removed entirely in 1981, and a range of other facilities, including index-linked stocks, has been made available.

6
Forms and Institutions

A system of investor protection may be organised according to one of two basic principles. The first principle is the *institutional* principle which, on the assumption that the kinds of business they carry on are broadly similar, concentrates on the different kinds of institutions – banks, building societies and so on – engaged in the provision of financial services, and allocates responsibility for the supervision of each kind of institution to a separate authority. The other is the *functional* principle, which focuses on the different kinds of business carried on – investment business, deposit-taking business, insurance business and so on – without regard to the kinds of institution by which they are carried on, responsibility for the regulation of each kind of business again being allocated to a separate authority. Both principles have their drawbacks. The weakness of the institutional principle is that it is ill-suited to an era in which the boundaries between different kinds of financial institution have become progressively more and more blurred. The weakness of the functional principle is that, in the case of institutions carrying on more than one kind of business, it may give rise to problems of co-ordination between regulatory authorities and competitive handicaps as a result of the need for such institutions to satisfy different and possibly conflicting regulatory requirements.

The United Kingdom system of investor protection is constructed along broadly functional lines with responsibility for the regulation of each kind of business being entrusted to a separate authority. Thus deposit-taking business is mainly regulated by the Bank of England, insurance business by the DTI and so on. However, the functional principle is not universally applied. The regulation of the non-investment business activities of building societies and friendly societies, for example, is organised along institutional rather than functional lines, while the responsibility of recognised professional bodies for the regulation of the investment business activities of their members is likewise an example of the application of the institutional principle.

In this chapter we examine the functions and status of the main authorities –

public and private – involved in modern investor protection, the extent of ministerial and other controls exercisable over them, their relationships with one another, and the opportunities for public scrutiny and for redress that exist in respect of their activities. We begin by examining the forms and types of regulation employed in modern investor protection.

STATUTORY AND NON-STATUTORY REGULATION

The foundations of modern investor protection are for the most part statutory. Banks, building societies, insurance companies and investment businesses, for example, are all regulated on the basis of statute. Within the overall framework provided by statute, however, significant elements of non-statutory regulation sometimes occur. The regulation by self-regulating organisations of the conduct of their members, for example, is non-statutory. So, too, is the regulation of the conduct of takeovers and mergers.

Non-statutory regulation normally proceeds on the basis of consent. Firms agree to submit to it – instead of being forced to do so – usually in order to gain or preserve some benefit to themselves, whether in the form of membership of an association or the exercise of a discretion in their favour. Investment businesses thus join self-regulating organisations, and in so doing undertake to observe their rules, because membership confers authorisation to carry on investment business.[1] So, too, money market institutions seek admission to a list maintained by the Bank of England, and in so doing undertake to observe the London Code of Conduct, because admission to this list exempts them from the need to be authorised in respect of transactions in the wholesale money markets.[2]

Non-statutory regulation is not, however, always consensual. The threat to withhold a benefit may be employed in the same way as the threat of legal sanctions to force firms to submit to regulation. The City Code, for example, purports to apply to everyone involved in takeovers and mergers – not just to those who, through their membership of the various organisations represented on the Panel, may be deemed to have consented to be bound by its rules. The Panel seeks to enforce the Code, among other ways, by threatening to withdraw the facilities of the securities markets from those who do not conduct themselves according to its provisions. In such cases non-statutory regulation is distinguishable from its statutory counterpart by reason only of its lack of formal legal status and the nature of the sanctions deployed in its support.

Non-statutory regulation is widely regarded as possessing a number of

[1] FSA, s.7(1).
[2] s.43; Bank of England, *The regulation of the wholesale markets in sterling, foreign exchange and bullion* (April 1988).

advantages over statutory regulation. There is no single satisfactory statement of these advantages, but the following are among the advantages commonly ascribed to non-statutory regulation. First, it is said to be capable of generating and maintaining higher standards than the mere 'minimum standards' said to be attainable by statutory means, presumably because obligations are normally voluntarily assumed rather than imposed. Secondly, non-statutory regulation is typically expressed in the form of a mixture of general principles and subsidiary rules, rather than in the form of detailed rules, which firms are expected to observe in their spirit as well as their letter. This combination of principles and rules is said to allow the legislative project to be kept within manageable bounds, to allow the underlying purpose of obligations to be made plain and to discourage conduct at or near the margin of unlawfulness. Non-statutory regulation thus denies firms and their advisers the freedom 'to exercise their ingenuity in so ordering their affairs to avoid the application of inconvenient or prohibitory norms'.[1] Systems which rely on law and specific regulation as the 'sole guide' to behaviour in commercial affairs, by contrast, may lead to any conduct being regarded as permissible so long as it satisfies the legal requirements.[2]

Thirdly, non-statutory regulation is claimed to be more readily adaptable to changing circumstances or new developments; new cases can be decided by reference to the general principles on which systems are based, and the rules themselves can be changed quickly and with a minimum of formality. Statutory regulation, by contrast, is said to be slow and difficult to change. Fourthly, non-statutory regulation is said to be quicker and more flexible in its application to individual cases; the rules can be interpreted and applied in a practical, common-sense (less legalistic) manner, taking into account their spirit as well as their letter. Statutory regulation, on the other hand, is said to invite the inflexible application of the rules without regard to their underlying purpose. Finally, non-statutory regulation is said to be less vulnerable to challenge in the courts; 'unnecessary and expensive litigation' can therefore be avoided.[3] It thus combines certainty of effect with the avoidance of tactical litigation.[4]

Whether or not non-statutory systems have always realised these advantages is open to question. Nor is it by any means self-evident that statutory regulation should, for example, be less adaptable or flexible, or command a lesser degree of support, than non-statutory regulation; or indeed that firms should prefer a non-statutory system of regulation which on the face of it offers them less certainty – in the form of detailed rules – and grants regulators greater discretion than might be thought acceptable under a

[1] Wilson Report, Second Stage Evidence, Panel on Take-overs and Mergers.
[2] *Ibid.*, Bank of England, para. 23; see, however, pp. 266–9 (SIB's rulebook).
[3] *Ibid*, the Stock Exchange, para. 70.
[4] *Annual Report of the Panel on Take-overs and Mergers* (1991), p. 6.

statutory regime. Nevertheless, the belief that non-statutory regulation does possess these advantages, and that because of them it is more effective and less inhibiting of competition and innovation than statutory regulation is a widespread one. The Wilson Committee, for example, reported that the supposedly less formalised approach to regulation in the United Kingdom was widely believed to have considerable advantages in terms of the range and cost of financial services provided in this country, and of the competitive edge shown by domestic institutions overseas.[1] And the Panel has consistently declined direct statutory backing for its rules on the theory that this would diminish the flexibility with which they are applied.

The principal weakness of the non-statutory approach to regulation, however, is that it is only practicable where regulators control benefits on the basis of which firms may be either induced or compelled to submit to regulation. To be an effective substitute for legal coercion, the benefits offered, or the denial of which is threatened, must be exclusive; i.e. they must be unobtainable in any other way. Moreover, they must exceed the costs entailed by submission, otherwise firms may simply decline to submit; and the benefits must continue to exceed the costs, otherwise firms may simply defect. Regulators, however, seldom control benefits which meet these requirements. As a result the practical scope for non-statutory regulation is limited. Non-statutory regulation of the insurance industry, for example, has never been possible because, as the Wilson Committee pointed out, membership of the British Insurance Association (as it then was), or of any other representative body, offers insufficient in the way of commercial advantage to induce all insurers to join.[2] The former Stock Exchange, by contrast, was able to act as an effective regulatory body, but only because it controlled access to a near-monopoly market; those who sought access to that market had no choice, therefore, but to undertake to observe its rules.

Statutory regulation, on the other hand, does not suffer from this limitation. Its great strength is that it can be universally applied as a matter of direct legal obligation; firms have no choice but to submit to regulation (statutory or non-statutory) if they are to avoid the penalties for acting illegally. Using the threat of legal sanctions to force firms to submit to regulation may mean, however, that the advantages associated with non-statutory regulation are forgone: firms may exploit loopholes in the rules in preference to complying with their spirit; regulation may lag behind current practices; innovation may be stifled by the rigid and mechanistic application of the rules;[3] and regulators may find themselves entrammelled in questions of *vires*.[4] Regulators have made strenuous efforts to avoid these consequences. But if the only way in which

---

[1] para. 1072.   [2] para. 1101.   [3] For an example, see Gower, *Disc. Doc.*, para. 6.02.

[4] For an example, see *Report of the Committee set up to Consider the System of Banking Supervision*, Cmnd. 9550 (1985), para. 3.6.

regulation can be applied to firms is by invoking the threat of legal penalties, they may be unavoidable.

GOVERNMENTAL AND SELF-REGULATION

The term 'governmental regulation' requires little by way of explanation. It is regulation carried on by governmental authorities, whether in the exercise of statutory or non-statutory powers. The majority of the regulatory authorities involved in investor protection are governmental in character, the powers they exercise deriving mainly from statute, although they may be non-statutory. The Bank of England, for example, relied for a long time on its 'traditional powers' as the central bank of the United Kingdom in the regulation of banking and the wholesale money markets, and the latter continue to be regulated on a non-statutory basis.

Self-regulation, on the other hand, denotes the regulation by a voluntary association of the conduct of its members, again in the exercise of statutory or, as is more common, non-statutory powers. It is collective rather than individual in character, and hence it is not to be confused with the integrity, honour and self-discipline of individual firms.[1] While the desire of individual firms to maintain their reputation may be of inestimable value to those with whom they have dealings, it cannot be counted as part of the overall regulatory structure. Self-regulation is also regulatory rather than non-regulatory: there are many associations whose activities do not extend to the regulation of their members' conduct but are instead restricted to the provision of common services and the representation of their members' interests. Those that do regulate their members' conduct spontaneously – without being encouraged to do so by government – do so because their members, recognising that their individual reputations are bound up with that of the association as a whole, have a common interest in acting to maintain their collective reputation. Their ability to do so depends in turn on the importance of the benefits – social as well as economic – which membership confers. The more important the benefits, the greater the likelihood that firms will subscribe and the more effective a sanction their withdrawal is; the less significant the benefits, the less the likelihood that firms will subscribe and the weaker a sanction their threatened withdrawal is.

Self-regulation has a long history in the financial sphere in the United Kingdom – the old Stock Exchange and Lloyd's being the best known examples – though whether it is the 'traditional' or 'predominant' method of financial regulation, as is often claimed,[2] is open to serious doubt in view of the equally long and much more broadly based tradition of governmental regulation (statutory or non-statutory) of banks, building societies, insurance

[1] *Cf.* Walker, 'Regulation in Financial Markets' (1983) 23 *Bank of England Quarterly Bulletin*, p. 499.
[2] See, e.g. the Bank of England's evidence to the Wilson Committee, Second Stage Evidence, para.8.

companies, friendly societies, unit trusts and so on. Recent years have witnessed, however, a considerable extension of the practical scope of financial self-regulation, mainly as a result of the introduction by the Financial Services Act of a new and more comprehensive framework for the regulation of investment business, based on the principle of 'self-regulation subject to governmental surveillance'.[1]

It is no exaggeration to see the investment business regime as the culmination of the enormous efforts that have been devoted by government and the financial community alike over the last two decades and more to building a belief in the self-regulatory mechanism and its continued place in the protection of investors. Their motives have to some extent been different. For government, self-regulation has offered the prospect of avoiding a task it does not relish and which it is ill-equipped to undertake.[2] For the financial community, self-regulation has offered the prospect of maintaining a greater measure of autonomy than they would enjoy were they to be subject to direct governmental regulation. More important than either of these factors, however, has been the belief, common to both, that self-regulation possesses the self-same advantages as are conventionally ascribed to non-statutory regulation – notwithstanding the fact that it may be statutory.[3] High standards, compliance with the spirit as well as the letter of the rules, adaptability and flexibility in their formulation and application, and speed and finality in regulatory decision-making are thus among the prime virtues that proponents of self-regulation typically ascribe to it over its governmental counterpart.

Additional advantages are seen as stemming from the involvement of practitioners in the formulation and application of rules. Chief among these advantages are greater expertise in the matters to be regulated, enhanced commitment to the observance of the rules, and more effective enforcement. Again, there is no inherent reason why governmental regulation should not be expert, or command a high level of support, or be effectively enforced, but the belief that self-regulation, like non-statutory regulation, is more effective and less inhibiting of competition and innovation than its counterpart, is again a widespread one, which has exercised a persistent influence on the design of regulatory regimes.

Reliance upon practitioners does, however, carry with it one obvious danger, which is that the interests of practitioners may take precedence over the interests of investors; self-protection, in other words, may prevail over investor protection. As the Financial Services Act White Paper acknowledged,

[1] Gower, *Report*, Part 1, para. 2.03.
[2] Cabinet Office and HM Treasury, *Non Departmental Public Bodies: A Guide for Departments* (2nd edn, 1985), para. 2.4.
[3] Although self-regulation may be statutory, advocates of self-regulation generally treat self-regulation and non-statutory regulation as synonymous; see e.g. the Bank of England's evidence to the Wilson Committee in which self-regulation is treated as a distinct species of non-statutory regulation: para. 5.

'it is a risk of regulation by practitioner-based organisations that they may degenerate into cosy clubs or cartels.'[1] Among the 'inherent limitations in allowing an industry to regulate itself', a 1973 Senate Securities Sub-Committee Report included:

> The natural lack of enthusiasm for regulation on the part of the group to be regulated, the temptation to use a facade of industry regulation as a shield to ward off more meaningful regulation, the tendency for businessmen to use collective action to advance their interests through the imposition of purely anti-competitive restraints as opposed to those justified by regulatory needs, and a resistance to changes in the regulatory pattern because of vested economic interests in its preservation.[2]

Because of this danger it has become accepted that, if self-regulation is to be employed in the protection of investors, it has to be subject to a measure of external supervision and control. 'Even if it were practical,' the Wilson Committee observed, 'we do not regard it as acceptable that the regulation of financial institutions, particularly those as important as the Stock Exchange and Lloyd's, should be left entirely to the institutions themselves.'[3] Not surprisingly, this idea has been bitterly resisted by self-regulatory communities. The effect of its application, however, has been to render modern financial self-regulation – or 'practitioner-based regulation' – materially different from its historical predecessor. From being essentially autonomous organisations, modern self-regulating organisations have, with important exceptions, been transformed into organisations whose freedom of action is more closely circumscribed than was that of their predecessors.[4]

GOVERNMENTAL AUTHORITIES

The Department of Trade and Industry

The DTI is responsible for the administration of the Companies Acts, for the supervision of insurance companies under the Insurance Companies Act, and for the investment business regime established by the Financial Services Act. The majority of its functions under the Financial Services Act have been transferred to a 'designated agency' – SIB – some subject to a reservation that they are exercisable concurrently by the DTI.[5] Others cannot be transferred and are therefore exercisable solely by it.[6] The DTI is a conventional central

[1] para. 5.8; the self-regulatory 'tradition' in the United Kingdom is arguably as much one of restrictive practices as it is one of investor protection.

[2] Quoted in Seligman, 'The Historical Need for a Mandatory Corporate Disclosure System' (1983) 9 *Journal of Corporation Law* 1, at pp. 55–6.

[3] para. 1108.   [4] See below, pp. 92–6.

[5] Financial Services Act 1986 (Delegation) Order 1987, SI 1987/942; Financial Services Act 1986 (Delegation) (No. 2) Order 1988 SI 1988/738; Companies Act 1989 (Commencement No.3, Transistional Provisions and Transfer of Functions under the Financial Services Act 1986) Order 1990, SI 1990/354; Financial Services Act 1986 (Delegation) Order 1991 SI 1991/200.

[6] Financial Services Act 1986, s. 114(5)–(6).

government department staffed by civil servants and headed by a minister responsible to Parliament.

The Bank of England

The Bank of England is the central bank of the United Kingdom. Its core purposes, according to its annual report, are to maintain the value of the currency and the integrity of the financial system, and to promote the efficiency of financial markets.[1] Its responsibility for maintaining the integrity of the financial system embraces specific responsibilities in relation to the regulation of banks and the wholesale money markets as well as 'a more diffuse responsibility as guardian of the good order of the financial system as a whole'.[2]

Unlike the DTI, the Bank is not a part of central government. It is a separate legal entity, incorporated by Royal Charter in 1694 and taken into public ownership by the Bank of England Act 1946. The Governor and court of directors of the Bank are appointed by the Crown,[3] and the Treasury has the power, which it has never exercised, to give the Bank directions in the national interest.[4] The Treasury does not, however, control its financing, which is met from its own banking operations.[5]

The importance attached to the Bank's responsibility for banking supervision is underlined by the Banking Act 1987, section 1(1) of which imposes on it the duty generally to supervise the institutions authorised by it in the exercise of the powers conferred on it by the Act.[6] The legal, as opposed to political, significance of this provision, which had no equivalent in the legislation the Act replaces, is diminished, however, by the almost complete immunity from liability in damages which the Act confers upon the Bank in respect of the discharge of its functions under it; only in the unlikely event that bad faith can be shown will the Bank be liable.[7] This immunity does not extend, however, to judicial review and the possibility of an individual seeking, for example, a declaration that the Bank is acting in breach of its statutory duty cannot, therefore, be ruled out.[8]

Whether, in view of the Bank's other responsibilities, banking supervision should be entrusted to a separate authority is a moot point. Critics of the Bank argue that its other responsibilities, many of which depend for their successful

[1] Report and Accounts 1991, p. 9.   [2] Wilson Report, para. 1260.
[3] Bank of England Act 1946, s.2.   [4] s.4(1).
[5] The Treasury has no direct investor protection responsibilities of its own, but it exercises varying degrees of control over the Bank, the Building Societies Commission and the Registry of Friendly Societies.
[6] The Act also obliges the Bank to keep under review the operation of the Act and developments in the field of banking which appear to it to be relevant to the exercise of its powers and the discharge of its duties: s.1(2).
[7] s.1(4); see above, pp. 26–7.
[8] See in a different context, *Minories Finance Ltd.* v. *Arthur Young (a firm) Bank of England (a third party)* [1989] 2 All E.R. 105.

execution on the active co-operation of the banking sector, mean that it will be more inclined to take a lenient view of prudential lapses than would an authority charged solely with the task of supervision.[1] When the introduction of banking legislation was first discussed, a section of opinion within the Bank also favoured hiving off responsibility to a separate authority, not on the grounds that it would necessarily be any more effective, but that it would provide a buffer between the Bank and the banking sector, thereby distancing it from responsibility should conflicts arise or lapses occur – as was in fact to happen with Johnson Matthey Bankers.[2] In the wake of the Johnson Matthey scandal, however, the Government rejected radical change in the organisation of banking supervision on the grounds that the possible advantages would not outweigh the inevitable loss of continuity and administrative upheaval.[3] Clearly, also, such a change would have been seen as a massive blow to the Bank's prestige.

The main legacy of the review of the organisation of banking supervision carried out in the aftermath of the Johnson Matthey scandal was the setting up, in response to criticisms of the lack of commercial banking experience of the Bank's supervisory staff, of an advisory committee – the misleadingly named Board of Banking Supervision – as a forum for the provision of 'expert, practitioner-based' advice to the Bank on all matters concerning banking supervision. The Board consists of three *ex officio* members (the Governor, the Deputy Governor and the executive director of the Bank responsible for banking supervision) and six independent members appointed jointly by the Chancellor of the Exchequer and the Governor,[4] the duty of the independent members being to advise the *ex officio* members on the exercise by the Bank of its functions under the Act and on related matters.[5] The *ex officio* members are not obliged to follow the advice of the independent members, but should they decline to do so they must inform the Chancellor.[6] The Board thus provides a means of alerting the Treasury to differences of opinion between the Bank and the banking community, as represented by its independent members, as well as of increasing the influence of practitioners on the conduct of banking supervision.

Beyond its statutory responsibility for banking supervision (and its non-statutory responsibility for the supervision of the wholesale money markets), the Bank also lays claim to a general non-statutory responsibility for ensuring 'the good order of the financial system as a whole', a responsibility more recently defined as one of ensuring 'proper conduct in the financial services industry'.[7] The origins of this self-imposed responsibility are difficult to identify with precision. It was not listed among the functions of the Bank by

---

[1] See e.g. HC Debs. Standing Cttee E, cols. 712–13 (March 11, 1986).
[2] Fay, *Portrait of an Old Lady* (1987), p. 90.
[3] HM Treasury, *Banking Supervision*, Cmnd. 9695 (1985), para. 5.4.   [4] BA, s.2(2).   [5] s.2(3).
[6] s.2(5).   [7] *Financial Times*, July 27, 1989.

the Radcliffe Committee on the Working of the Monetary System in 1959.[1] Since then, however, it has become much more prominent – Gower described the Bank as having 'a finger in every pie except insurance',[2] and it has been accompanied by a greater readiness on its part to promote change.

In carrying out this responsibility the Bank relied for a long time (as it did in banking supervision, and it continues to do in the wholesale markets) on the voluntary acceptance of its authority, reinforced by such sanctions as it had at its disposal in the shape of its ability to grant and withhold benefits on a selective basis. The potency of this mixture has undergone a marked decline, causing some commentators to dismiss the Bank's claim to inherent 'discretionary' powers of control[3] as an elaborate fiction designed to conceal a lack of any real power. 'The discretionary powers of the Bank are usable only if not challenged. The emperor has no clothes, but this does not matter so long as everybody acts as if the emperor has clothes.'[4] One consequence of replacing the non-statutory system of banking supervision by one based on statute, however, has been to increase the Bank's capacity to enforce its own conception of proper standards of conduct through the exploitation of the latitude afforded it by the statutory provisions. Thus, in the case of Morgan Grenfell, for example, the Bank was able to use the threat of the exercise of its powers under the Banking Act to secure the removal of key figures in the scandal.[5]

The Radcliffe Committee said of the relationship between the Bank and government that it was 'not easy to describe in formal language with any great precision';[6] in similar vein the Wilson Committee described the relationship as 'a mixture of statute and convention which, like other working relationships, is unlikely ever to remain static'.[7] The history of the relationship generally, however, has been one of the increasing subordination of the Bank to government, the clearest illustration of this being the formulation and execution of monetary policy, where the setting of interest rates and the management of the gilt-edged market, which were previously regarded as part of 'the affairs of the Bank', and hence, under section 4(2) of Bank of England Act, as matters for the Bank, subject to any direction it might be given by the Treasury, are now firmly controlled by the Treasury.[8] However, this trend has not been as readily apparent in the fields of prudential regulation and investor protection, although the Johnson Matthey affair has led the Treasury to

---

[1] Cmnd. 827 (1959). [2] *Disc. Doc.*, para. 3.33.

[3] In its evidence to the Wilson Committee the Bank identified its 'traditional powers as the central bank of the United Kingdom in controlling and supervising generally the banking system and money markets' as a distinctive species of non-statutory regulation: Second Stage Evidence, para. 4.

[4] Gemmill, 'Regulating Futures Markets: A Review in the Context of British and American Practice' in Streit (ed.), *Futures Markets: Modelling, Managing and Monitoring Futures Trading* (1983), 295 at p. 298.

[5] Fay, *op. cit.*, pp. 186–7; see also p. 131.

[6] *Report of the Committee on the Working of the Monetary System*, Cmnd. 827 (1959), para. 761.

[7] para. 1263.

[8] Moran, 'Monetary Policy and the Machinery of Government' (1981) 59 *Public Administration* 47.

increase its capacity to monitor the Bank's activities in the field of banking supervision through the Board of Banking Supervision. Moreover, the vesting of functions directly in a separate legal entity, with a substantial measure of financial autonomy and no provision for ministerial control or direction over their exercise, makes the assertion of political control more difficult. Consequently, the Bank appears to enjoy a greater measure of freedom to act independently of government in investor protection than it does in monetary policy.[1]

The Building Societies Commission

The Building Societies Commission is responsible for the supervision of building societies under the Building Societies Act 1986. Before the Commission assumed responsibility for their supervision, building societies were supervised by the Registry of Friendly Societies, a non-ministerial department headed by a single office holder – the Chief Registrar of Friendly Societies. The primary rationale for allocating the task to a Commission rather than a single office-holder is that it makes it possible to involve outsiders directly in its administration. (In contrast to the Board of Banking Supervision practitioners are here involved in an executive rather than advisory capacity.) Like the Bank of England, the Commission is a separate legal entity, incorporated by statute rather than by Royal Charter.[2] It consists of a chairman, a deputy chairman and five other members, all appointed by the Treasury.[3] The present chairman (First Commissioner) is also the Chief Registrar and the Commission is served by the Registry. Its financing and staffing, unlike those of the Bank of England, are also controlled by the Treasury.

The general functions of the Commission are prescribed by the Building Societies Act 1986. They are to promote the protection by each building society of the investments of its shareholders and depositors; to promote the financial stability of building societies generally; to secure that the principal purpose of building societies remains that of raising, primarily from their members, funds for making advances to members secured upon land for residential use; to administer the system of regulation of building societies; and to advise and make recommendations to the Treasury or other government

---

[1] When the Bank was first taken into public ownership its independence from government was seen as an advantage in the organisation of the latter's dealings with financial institutions: 'Clearly that independence is not to be exercised on major issues of policy. . . . But on day-to-day relations with other financial institutions, there is everything to be said for viewing the Bank as a Public Corporation, subject to control on policy but not to interference in the running of the machine. . . . Moreover, the more it is permitted "independence" on unessentials the easier it will be for the Bank to maintain its intimate relations with other parts of the financial system and with City interests . . . [its] independence must . . . now be clearly qualified on issues of policy, but we have much to gain by leaving it formally undisturbed on the interior management and interior relations.' Treasury Minute of 2 August 1945, quoted in Chester; *The Nationalisation of British Industry, 1945–51* (1975), p. 880.

[2] BSA, s.1(1).   [3] s.1(2).

departments on any matter relating to building societies.[1] No provision is made for ministerial control or direction of the Commission in the exercise of those functions.

The Registry of Friendly Societies

The Registry of Friendly Societies is responsible for the supervision of friendly societies under the Friendly Societies Acts. Unlike the DTI or the Treasury, it is a non-ministerial department, that is, a department headed (in this case) by a single office-holder – the Chief Registrar – who is appointed by the Treasury.[2] The legal significance of this status derives from the fact that the powers it exercises are vested in the Chief Registrar rather than, as is normal practice in relation to government departments, in ministers; in the absence of specific provision to the contrary, therefore, the Chief Registrar is not subject to ministerial control or direction in their exercise. As well as appointing the Chief Registrar, the Treasury controls staffing and financing of the Registry.

The Occupational Pensions Board

The Occupational Pensions Board was set up by the Social Security Act 1973, *inter alia*, to administer the contracting-out provisions of the reserve pension scheme introduced by the Act. The reserve pension scheme was not proceeded with by the incoming Labour Government, but the OPB was retained to oversee the contracting-out arrangements in respect of its replacement – the state earnings-related pension scheme (SERPS) – which was introduced by the Social Security Pensions Act 1975.

In addition to its responsibilities in relation to contracting-out by means of occupational pensions schemes and (under the Social Security Act 1986) personal pension schemes, the Board is responsible for various other matters including the policing of the preservation requirements of the Social Security Act 1973 and the equal access provisions of the Social Security Pensions Act 1975. It is also responsible for advising the Secretary of State for Social Security on matters relating to occupational pension schemes.[3] Like the Bank of England and the Building Societies Commission, the Board is a separate legal entity, incorporated by statute, and consisting of a chairman, a deputy chairman and ten other members, all appointed by the Secretary of State for Social Security, one of the ordinary members being appointed after consultation with organisations representative of employers and another being appointed after consultation with organisations representative of employed persons.[4] Its staffing and expenses are met by the Department of Social Security.

[1] s.1(4). [2] Friendly Societies Act 1974, s.2(4). [3] SSA 1973, s.66(1). [4] s.66(2).

The overall pattern

The overall pattern of governmental organisation in relation to investor protection reflects the influence of a number of factors. One is tradition. If the tasks of supervising insurance companies, friendly societies and banks were being allocated for the first time, it is unlikely that they would be allocated to their present holders. A second is the importance attached to involving representatives of affected interests – practitioners – in their administration either in an advisory (Board of Banking Supervision) or an executive (Building Societies Commission, Occupational Pensions Board) capacity. The last is the parallel emphasis on insulating the administration of supervisory functions from the political process by vesting them in separate legal entities with no provision for ministerial control or direction over their exercise, which is designed to increase the confidence of affected interests in the impartiality of their administration as well as to distance government from responsibility for day-to-day decision-making.[1]

The last two factors point to an emerging pattern of 'arm's length' supervision based on the allocation of responsibility for the protection of investors to a number of non-departmental public bodies, the membership of whose governing bodies includes representatives of affected interests and which enjoy a substantial measure of *de jure* and *de facto* independence from ministers in the exercise of the particular tasks entrusted to them. From here it is but a short step to entrusting responsibility for the protection of investors to 'practitioner-based' organisations with a similar degree of independence from ministers, but which, unlike the bodies so far examined, do not form part of the official machinery of government.

NON-GOVERNMENTAL AUTHORITIES

The Securities and Investments Board

Five principal groups of functions have been transferred to SIB.[2] First, it was given responsibility for setting up a new and comprehensive system for the regulation of investment business, based on the recognition and subsequent monitoring and supervision of self-regulating organisations, professional bodies, investment exchanges and clearing houses. Secondly, it has been given extensive legislative functions; these were at first confined to the making of rules and regulations but, in order to facilitate the introduction of a new style of rulebooks as part of the 'new settlement', they have been extended to include the issue of statements of principle, the designation of rules to apply directly to members of self-regulating organisations and the issue of codes of practice.[3]

[1] See below, pp. 90–100.   [2] See above, p. 84.
[3] As to the new settlement, see below, pp. 228–9.

Thirdly, it has been given powers to authorise and regulate the carrying on of investment business by firms that choose to be regulated in respect of that business by it rather than by a self-regulating organisation or professional body. Fourthly, it has been given wide powers of enforcement and intervention, including powers to seek injunctions and restitution orders, to issue disqualification directions, to discipline directly regulated firms, and powers to institute criminal proceedings. Finally, it has been given responsibility for authorising and recognising collective investment schemes, and for otherwise administering the provisions of the Act relating to such schemes.

SIB was set up as a registered company limited by guarantee[1] for the express purpose of securing the transfer to it of the Secretary of State's main functions under Part I of the Financial Services Act, as the sole designated agency, rather than by the legislation itself (which merely identified it as the body to which the Secretary of State's functions were to be first transferred).[2] The reasons for establishing SIB as a private company, rather than as a non-departmental public body along lines similar to those of the Building Societies Commission, were partly symbolic – it underlined the commitment of the industry to regulating itself, while at the same time enabling the Government to avoid the charge that it was a Securities and Exchange Commission in all but name. It also had the more tangible advantage of freeing SIB from the financial constraints to which a public sector body would be subject.[3] Notwithstanding this advantage, the proposed transfer of far-reaching statutory powers to a private company, set up and financed by the industry it was intended to regulate, attracted persistent criticism when the legislation was before Parliament.[4] Unprecedented though such a transfer was – as the Government freely conceded[5] – there is no inherent reason why – given the necessary vigour in their exercise – a private company should prove any less (or more) effective a vehicle for the exercise of regulatory powers than a public authority.[6]

The Act laid down a number of requirements which SIB had to meet as a condition of the transfer of functions to it, and which it must continue to meet as an implied condition of their retention. First, its constitution must provide for its chairman and the other members of its governing body to be appointed (and liable to removal from office) by the Secretary of State and the Governor of the Bank of England acting jointly,[7] thereby giving government the same

---

[1] The Financial Services Act exempts it from the requirements of the Companies Act relating to the use of 'limited' as part of its name: Sch. 9, para. 2.

[2] s.114(2).   [3] The Board finances its activities through levies imposed on the industry: ss.112–13.

[4] Earlier, in discussing whether the former Council for the Securities Industry could be converted into the regulatory authority, Gower expressed the view that: 'The Government clearly could not abdicate in favour of a purely private body representative of the constituency that it was supposed to regulate in the public interest.' *Report*, Part I, para. 3.15. For his views on the Board, see *Report*, Part II, paras. 2.06–2.09.

[5] FSA White Paper, para. 5.7.   [6] As to its accountability, see below, p. 100.

[7] Sch. 7, para. 1(2).

control over its membership as it possesses over the membership of a public authority. Its membership is drawn mainly from the investment industry, but it must also include an independent element.[1] Secondly, its rulebook must afford investors 'an adequate level of protection', and comply with the principles set out in Schedule 8 to the Act.[2] It is obliged to consult publicly on its proposed rules,[3] and it must also have satisfactory arrangements for taking into account, in framing rules, both the costs of complying with them, and any other controls applying to the firms concerned.[4] Thirdly, its overall impact on competition must not exceed that necessary for the protection of investors.[5] Compliance with this principle is monitored by the Director General of Fair Trading.[6] And, finally, it must have a satisfactory system for monitoring and enforcing compliance with the obligations imposed upon persons regulated by it,[7] effective arrangements for the investigation of complaints,[8] and be able and willing to promote and maintain high standards of integrity and fair dealing in the carrying on of investment business.[9]

Notwithstanding the differences in its status and methods of financing, SIB's position in relation to the Secretary of State is broadly comparable to that of a non-departmental public body. Should it cease to meet the conditions governing the retention of transferred functions, the Secretary of State may resume those functions in whole or in part,[10] a power which Gower likened to 'a nuclear deterrent which could hardly be used and which, if used, would initially make matters worse [since] the Department itself would be ill-equipped to undertake the regulatory role'.[11] Short of the resumption of transferred functions, and the possible statutory conversion of SIB into a body more akin to the Securities and Exchange Commission, the Secretary of State's powers over the Board are confined to altering, with the agreement of the Governor of the Bank, its composition,[12] and to forcing it to change its rules, but only where their anti-competitive effects are adjudged excessive,[13] or in order to comply with the United Kingdom's Community or international obligations;[14] he has no power to force rule changes on the ground that they are required for the protection of investors. SIB therefore enjoys a large measure of autonomy from government in the exercise of the functions transferred.

Recognised self-regulating organisations (SROs)

Although SIB has power to authorise and regulate investment businesses, the

[1] para. 1(3).   [2] s.114(9)(b); see below, pp. 227–9.   [3] Sch. 8, para. 12.
[4] Sch. 7, para. 2A, inserted by the Companies Act 1989, s.204(4).   [5] s.121(2).
[6] s.122(4)–(6).   [7] Sch. 7, para. 3.   [8] para. 4.   [9] para. 5.
[10] s.115(2); provision is also made for their resumption by agreement: s.115(1).
[11] *Report*, Part II, para. 2.06.
[12] Sch. 7, para. 1. Any successor governing body must have the same practitioner-based character as its predecessor.
[13] s.121(3)(b).   [14] s.192(1).

system of regulation introduced by the Financial Services Act was intended to operate, so far as possible, in accordance with the principle of self-regulation subject to governmental surveillance. To this end the Act made provision for the 'recognition' of self-regulating organisations.[1] The Act defines a self-regulating organisation as a body 'which regulates the carrying on of investment business of any kind by enforcing rules which are binding on persons carrying on business of that kind either because they are members of that body or because they are otherwise subject to its control'.[2] The advantage of recognition for such a body is that its members are thereby authorised to carry on investment business.[3]

SIB's primary aim in approaching the task of recognition was to achieve a comprehensive system of SROs capable of providing authorisation to all potential investment businesses. At the same time, it sought to avoid an excessive proliferation of SROs, which would make the task of their supervision more difficult, as well as give rise to obvious problems of overlap and duplication of effort. To this end, the legislation empowered it to refuse recognition to an applicant when an organisation covering the same kind of investment business was already in existence and was recognised or to be recognised.[4] In practice the application of this 'need' test was tempered by the need to make the structure of SROs attractive to the largest possible number of firms, thereby making it more likely that they would seek authorisation through membership of an SRO rather than directly from SIB itself.[5]

Five SROs were initially recognised by SIB, which number has been reduced to four as a result of the merger in 1991 of the AFBD and TSA. They are:

(1) the Financial Intermediaries, Managers and Brokers Regulatory Association (FIMBRA), which is primarily concerned with the regulation of retail investment business by independent investment intermediaries;

(2) the Investment Management Regulatory Organisation (IMRO), which is primarily concerned with the regulation of investment management (including pension fund management), the operation and trusteeship of collective investment schemes, the management of investment trusts' investments and advice to corporate customers;

(3) the Securities and Futures Authority (SFA), formed by the merger of the Securities Association (TSA) and the Association of Futures Brokers and Dealers (AFBD), which is primarily concerned with the regulation of investment business involving securities and derivatives, together with ancillary investment management and advice; and

[1] s.10. [2] s.8(1). [3] s.7(1). [4] s.10(4).

[5] 'If the principle of self-regulation is to play the part envisaged by the creators of the system, the various regulating units in the self-regulating tier must be ones with which their respective memberships can identify. The fewer the regulators the more difficult would genuine self-regulation be to achieve': Vile, 'The SIB/SRO Structure: Its Advantages and State of Health' in MacLachan (ed.), *Life After Big Bang* (1987), p. 40.

(4) the Life Assurance and Unit Trust Regulatory Organisation (Lautro), which is primarily concerned with the marketing of life policies and units in regulated collective investment schemes by life offices, friendly societies and operators of regulated schemes and by their marketing associates.

As a condition of their recognition, SROs must satisfy an extensive series of requirements, designed for the most part to ensure that they regulate their members effectively, and in particular that investors receive no less a standard of protection in respect of their members than they receive in respect of directly authorised firms. The membership of the governing body of each SRO must include a sufficient number of persons independent of the organisation and its members to secure a proper balance between the interests of the organisation or its members and the interests of the public.[1] Their membership requirements must ensure that their members are 'fit and proper' persons to carry on the kinds of investment business with which they are concerned,[2] and each SRO must have a 'scope' rule preventing its members from carrying on, without separate authorisation or exemption, kinds of investment business not regulated by the organisation.[3] They must also meet the same requirements as SIB in relation to the monitoring and enforcement of compliance by their members with the obligations imposed upon them, the investigation of complaints and the promotion and maintenance of standards.[4]

As regards their rulebooks, the legislation as originally enacted stipulated that they should afford investors protection 'at least equivalent' to that afforded by SIB's rulebook (the 'principle of equivalence').[5] During the implementation of the Act, however, the principle of equivalence was heavily criticised for promoting rigidity at the expense of the flexibility of response to changing circumstances and new developments which was regarded as one of the prime virtues of the original scheme.[6] It has therefore been replaced by a new test of 'adequacy', in terms of which SROs are required to have rules governing the carrying on of investment business by their members which, together with the statements of principle, rules, regulations and codes of practice to which their members are subject, are such as to afford an adequate level of protection for investors, which test is designed to allow SROs a greater

---

[1] FSA, Sch. 2, para. 5; it must also secure a proper balance between the interests of the different members of the organisation.

[2] Sch. 2, para. 1.

[3] s.10(3). The 'scope' rule also provides a means of reducing overlap between SROs.

[4] Sch. 2, paras. 4, 6 and 7.

[5] Sch. 2, para. 3; this paragraph also required an organisation, so far as practicable, to have powers over its members corresponding to the Board's powers of intervention, together with rules enabling it to prevent a member from resigning to avoid investigation, discipline or the use of these powers.

[6] 'Regulation by properly-run SROs, with rules and enforcement capabilities equivalent to those of the Board, should promote high regulatory standards while at the same time ensuring that the system as a whole responds flexibly to the needs of different and often rapidly changing markets': SIB/MIBOC, *Regulation of Investment Business: The New Framework* (1985), para. 9.

measure of freedom to tailor their rules to the circumstances of their members.[1] SROs are also required to have satisfactory arrangements for taking into account, in framing rules, the costs for firms of complying with those rules and any other controls to which they are subject.[2]

Responsibility for ensuring that these requirements are met rests with SIB, which acts in this respect as a buffer between the SROs and the political process. Should they cease to be met, SIB has a number of formal sanctions at its disposal, the most drastic of which is the withdrawal of an SRO's recognition, thereby depriving its members of their authorisation to carry on investment business (unless they are separately authorised or exempted).[3] As less drastic alternatives, it may restrict the kinds of investment business an SRO's members are authorised to undertake by virtue of their membership of the organisation,[4] or seek a compliance order from the courts directing it to comply with any requirement of which it is in breach.[5] Safeguards are provided. A recognition order may not be revoked, or a restriction order made, without notice being given and an opportunity afforded for representations to be made. But these safeguards may be dispensed with if this is considered essential in the interests of investors.

These provisions seek to strike a balance between two conflicting considerations. On the one hand they are designed to preserve sufficient incentive for practitioners to regulate themselves through a suitably comprehensive structure of SROs. On the other hand they are designed to put the authority of SIB beyond doubt, thereby ensuring, to paraphrase the words of SIB's first chairman, that the SRO tail is not allowed to wag the SIB dog.[6] Particular importance in this regard has been attached to the power to alter an SRO's rules. Such a power was written into the legislation as originally enacted in response to criticism that without it SIB's position would be too weak, but SIB now has power, under section 63A of the Act, to 'designate' rules and regulations so as to apply to SRO members, and it has therefore been repealed.[7]

SROs are also subject to a special regime for the scrutiny of their impact on competition. Should an SRO's impact on competition exceed that necessary for the protection of investors, the Secretary of State, who retains control, may

---

[1] Companies Act 1989, s.203(1), replacing FSA, Sch. 2, para. 3(1),(2). SROs may elect whether to comply with the test of equivalence or the test of adequacy for a transistional period: The Companies Act 1989 (Commencement No 3) (Transitional Provisions and Transfer of Functions under the Financial Services Act 1986) Order 1990, SI 1990/354.

[2] Sch. 2, para. 3A, inserted by Companies Act 1989, s.204(1).

[3] FSA, s.11.

[4] s.13(2).

[5] s.12.

[6] 'The Role of the Securities and Investments Board' (October 1985).

[7] FSA, s.13(1), repealed by Companies Act 1989, Sched. 23, para. 1.

either himself revoke its recognition or, through SIB, cause it to take appropriate remedial action.[1] He also has power, exercisable again through SIB, to cause an SRO to take, or to refrain from taking, any action within its powers in order to comply with the UK's Community or international obligations.[2]

Recognised professional bodies (RPBs)

The Financial Services Act made provision for the recognition of professional bodies in an effort to avoid the enormous problems that would have been created by the need to make separate arrangements for the regulation of the investment business activities of their members. Recognition has the advantage for a professional body that it enables it to authorise its members to carry on investment business, provided it is not their main business, through the device of certification.[3] In return, professional bodies are obliged to extend the scope of their existing regulation to embrace the investment business activities of certified members.

Nine professional bodies have been recognised by SIB: the Law Society; the Law Society of Scotland; the Law Society of Northern Ireland; the Institute of Chartered Accountants in England and Wales; the Institute of Chartered Accountants of Scotland; the Institute of Chartered Accountants in Ireland; the Chartered Association of Certified Accountants; the Institute of Actuaries; and the Insurance Brokers Registration Council.

Membership of a professional body was not envisaged 'as a soft option or an easy route to authorisation'.[4] The requirements which professional bodies must satisfy as a condition of their recognition closely follow those applying to SROs and are directed to the same purpose of ensuring that they provide no less a level of protection than is provided by SIB. Certification must be confined to members whose main business is the practice of their profession;[5] members whose main business is investment business must therefore obtain authorisation through membership of an SRO or directly from SIB. They must have a scope rule imposing 'acceptable limits' on the kinds of investment business which may be carried on by persons certified by them, and the circumstances in which they may carry on such business, a requirement which is intended to reinforce the restriction of certification to persons whose main business is the practice of their profession.[6] Their rulebooks must provide an 'adequate level' of protection for investors (in place of the earlier requirement of equivalence).[7] And they must have adequate arrangements for enforcing

---

[1] s.120(4).   [2] s.192.   [3] s.15(1).   [4] SIB/MIBOC, *op. cit.*, para. 2.20.

[5] Sch. 3, para. 2(3). Carrying on a business consisting wholly or mainly of investment business is not the practice of a profession: s.16(1).

[6] s.18(3).

[7] Sch. 3, para. 3 as replaced by the Companies Act 1989, s.203(2). Para. 3A, which was inserted by s.204(1) of the Companies Act, requires them to have satisfactory arrangements for taking into account, in

their rules, together with effective arrangements for the investigation of complaints in relation to investment business done by their members.[1] Should an RPB cease to meet these requirements, SIB may either withdraw its recognition, subject to the same safeguards as are laid down in respect of the withdrawal of recognition from an SRO,[2] or seek a compliance order against it;[3] it has no power to restrict the kinds of investment business certified persons may undertake.

Recognised investment exchanges (RIEs)

An investment exchange is a body that provides a market within which transactions in investments can be effected. Investment exchanges do not have to be recognised under the Financial Services Act, but recognition confers two main benefits on an exchange. First, it exempts it from the need to be authorised to carry on investment business.[4] Secondly, it increases the attractiveness of an exchange to potential users in that, under SIB's conduct of business rules, transactions which are *not* effected through the facilities of a recognised exchange attract additional requirements for the protection of investors which are intended to offset the absence of those protections provided by a recognised exchange.[5]

Six exchanges are currently recognised by SIB: the London Stock Exchange (LSE), which operates and regulates markets in UK and foreign equities, gilt-edged and fixed interest stock, and traditional options; the London International Financial Futures Exchange (LIFFE), which operates and regulates markets in financial futures and options; the London Futures and Options Exchange (London FOX), which operates and regulates markets in futures and options contracts in cocoa, coffee, sugar and, following its merger with the Baltic Futures Exchange, freight, meat, potatoes, grain and soyabean meal; the London Metal Exchange (LME), which operates and regulates markets in futures and options contracts in various non-ferrous metals and silver; the International Petroleum Exchange of London (IPE), which operates and regulates trading in futures contracts in gas oil, gasoline, heavy fuel oil and crude oil and options contracts in gas oil; and OM London Limited (OML), which provides a linked market place with OM Stockholm Fondkommission AB for trading in futures and options in Swedish stocks and a Swedish index.

As a condition of their recognition, RIEs must satisfy the same requirements as SROs and RPBs in relation to the monitoring and enforcement of obligations, the investigation of complaints and the promotion and maintenance of standards.[6] In addition they must have sufficient financial

framing their rules, the costs for firms of complying with those rules and any other controls to which they are subject.

[1] Sch. 3, para. 4–5.   [2] s.19.   [3] s.20.   [4] s.36(1).   [5] Core rule 31.
[6] FSA, Sch. 4, paras. 3–5.

resources for the proper performance of their functions,[1] and their rules and practices must ensure that business conducted by means of their facilities is conducted in an orderly manner and so as to provide 'proper protection' to investors. In particular, they must limit dealings to investments in which there is a proper market, secure proper information for determining the current value of investments, and have arrangements for ensuring the performance of transactions and for recording them.[2] They must also have 'default rules' which, in the event of a member of the Exchange appearing to be unable to meet his obligations, enable action to be taken in respect of unsettled 'market contracts' to which he is a party.[3] Should these requirements cease to be met, SIB may either withdraw an RIE's recognition or seek a compliance order against it.[4]

RIEs are also subject to the same competition regime as SROs. Should the Director General of Fair Trading report that an RIE's impact on competition exceeds that necessary for the protection of investors, the Secretary of State may either revoke its recognition or, through SIB, cause it to take appropriate remedial action.[5] The Secretary of State also has power, exercisable through SIB, to cause an RIE to take, or to refrain from taking, any action within its powers in order to comply with the UK's Community or international obligations.[6]

Overseas investment exchanges

The Act also makes provision for the recognition (by the Secretary of State) of overseas exchanges.[7] Two overseas exchanges have been recognised: the National Association of Securities Dealers Automated Quotations System (NASDAQ), and the Sydney Futures Exchange. In addition, SIB has drawn up a list of 'designated' overseas exchanges, which do not require authorisation, but which are considered to afford investors protection equivalent to that provided by recognised exchanges. Transactions on such exchanges are treated for the purpose of the Board's conduct of business rules as though they had been effected on a recognised exchange.

Recognised clearing houses (RCHs)

An RIE is required to have arrangements for ensuring the performance of transactions on the exchange. These arrangements may be made by the exchange itself or through a clearing house recognised for this purpose under section 39 of the Act. Two clearing houses have been recognised: the International Commodities Clearing House, and the GAFTA Clearing House. Provision is also made for the recognition of overseas clearing houses.[8]

[1] para. 1.   [2] para. 2.   [3] Companies Act 1989, Sch. 21, Part 1.   [4] s.37(7)–(8).
[5] s.120(4).   [6] s.192.   [7] s.40.   [8] s.40.

CO-ORDINATION

The dispersal of responsibility for investor protection among so many regulatory authorities creates an obvious need for the co-ordination of their activities in order to avoid problems of duplication, confusion and oversight. This need is especially great in the case of firms or groups of firms whose activities are supervised by more than one regulator where it has been addressed by the establishment of an informal 'college' of regulators and by the nomination of one regulator as the 'lead regulator' for each firm or group. In the case of a single firm, the lead regulator is responsible for monitoring the firm's financial position on behalf of the other regulators; in the case of a group of firms, the lead regulator is responsible for promoting the exchange of information, in an effort to ensure that no part of the group escapes supervision, and co-ordinating any necessary remedial action. Lead regulator arrangements have also been entered into with overseas authorities in respect of UK branches of overseas institutions. These are extra-statutory arrangements, but their implementation – and the fostering of co-operation generally – has required the creation of 'gateways' through which information may be freely exchanged between regulators.[1]

PUBLIC SCRUTINY

The United Kingdom theory of responsible government assumes the exercise of powers by ministers who in turn are accountable for their exercise to Parliament. This position obtains to only a limited extent in investor protection where the majority of powers are exercised by bodies which are at one or more removes from direct ministerial control. This has two major consequences. First, it means that ministers are distanced from direct responsibility for the exercise of those powers. Secondly, in the absence of any alternative theory of accountability, it means that their exercise is subject to less scrutiny than would be the case if they were entrusted to ministers.

The main vehicle by which Parliament and the public are informed about the activities of governmental authorities (other than government departments for which ministers are accountable through the normal processes of inquiry and debate) is the annual report which each authority (with the exception of the Occupational Pensions Board) is obliged to produce and which the responsible minister lays before Parliament.[2] As 'associated public bodies', their expenditure, administration and policy may also be examined by the appropriate departmental select committee; such examination is, however, infrequent. Finally, ministers remain accountable for the exercise (or

1 FSA, ss.179–82, BSA, ss.53–4, BA, ss.82–7.
2 BA, ss.1(3), 2(6); BSA, s.4; Friendly Societies Act 1974, s.6; SSA 1973, s.66(6) (from time to time); the Secretary of State for Trade and Industry also lays a report before Parliament on the exercise of his functions under the Insurance Companies Act (s.98) and the Companies Act (s.729), but not the Financial Services Act.

non-exercise) of their own powers in relation to authorities, for example, their powers to appoint and dismiss the members of their governing bodies. However, only general matters may be raised by this means: questions about particular acts or matters of day-to-day administration are treated as matters for the body concerned.

The opportunities for the parliamentary scrutiny of the activities of non-governmental authorities are more limited. Only SIB is obliged to report annually through the Secretary of State to Parliament.[1] Neither it nor the bodies recognised by it are associated public bodies which means that, in theory, they are not subject to select committee scrutiny (although SIB appears to welcome such scrutiny). And although the Secretary of State's powers provide a hook upon which questions may be hung, the line so far taken in response to questions about such matters as the resources devoted by SROs to investigating the credentials of applicants for membership, and the training and qualifications of their staff, has been that these are matters for SIB and the SROs rather than the Secretary of State.[2] As a result the operation of the investment business regime is largely shielded from parliamentary scrutiny.

REDRESS

Appeals

Modern investor protection legislation commonly provides a right of appeal against decisions involving the refusal, suspension or revocation of a licence or other form of authorisation. Rights of appeal are provided by the banking, building societies, financial services and friendly societies legislation.[3] Under the pensions legislation there is no right of appeal as such, but the OPB is empowered to 'review' its decisions on the application of interested persons.[4] Only under the insurance companies legislation is there no provision for appeal.

In the past, attitudes towards the provision of appeals have varied. When licensing of dealers in securities was first introduced in 1939, it was accepted as axiomatic that those who were denied the freedom to pursue their chosen occupation should be provided with some means of redress: 'if these wide powers are to be given to the Board of Trade, there must be some tribunal to whom an applicant who is aggrieved either by refusal of a licence or by the revocation of a licence should be able to appeal.'[5] Persons aggrieved by the proposed refusal or revocation of a licence were therefore given the right to have their case referred to a tribunal of inquiry whose recommendation, if

---

[1] FSA, s.117(1),(2).   [2] See, e.g. HC Debs. vol. 143, cols. 259w, 567w and vol. 145 cols. 332–3w.

[3] BA, s.27; BSA, s.46; FSA, s.97, Sch. 2, para. 2 requires SROs' admission, expulsion and disciplinary procedures to include adequate provision for appeals; Friendly Societies Act, ss.16, 92.

[4] SSA 1973, s.67(2).   [5] Hansard 5th ser. HC Debs. vol. 340, col. 1378 Nov. 21, 1938.

favourable, was binding on the Department.[1] When, however, the insurance companies legislation was amended in 1973, in the wake of the collapse of Vehicle and General, a proposal that there should be a right of appeal against a finding that a person was not fit to be a director, controller or manager of an insurance company was rejected on the ground that it would prejudice the attainment of the central purpose of the legislation, which was the protection of the public against 'the charlatan and the rogue'.[2] It is difficult to identify any objective basis on which to distinguish these two cases. If the provision of a right of appeal might prejudice the attainment of the purpose of the insurance companies legislation, then so too might it prejudice the attainment of the purpose of any other investor protection legislation. Yet notwithstanding this risk, rights of appeal have been provided under the subsequent banking, building societies and financial services legislation.

The provision of rights of appeal by subsequent enactments is attributable to two main factors. One is the widespread feeling that the lack of any provision for appeal, whether against the refusal of a licence or membership of a self-regulating organisation, is of itself objectionable. 'In this day and age', argued Gower, 'it is just not acceptable . . . that people can be excluded from bodies, which are not mere social clubs but agencies on which their livelihood depends, without a right to seek to persuade an independent arbiter that they were wrongly excluded.'[3] The second is the recognition that in the absence of any provision for appeal, aggrieved investment firms are likely to have recourse to alternative means of redress, in particular judicial review of administrative action,[4] with consequences for the attainment of regulatory objectives which are potentially every bit as serious as those of a successful appeal. Rather than incur this risk, the architects of regulatory systems have preferred to establish special machinery for the settlement of disputes arising out of the powers conferred, which in accordance with general principles of administrative law must first be exhausted before recourse will be permitted to the supervisory jurisdiction of the superior courts.

One factor which has influenced the choice of bodies to which appeals may lie has been the desire to distance decisions from direct ministerial responsibility. Under the Banking Act 1979, the right of appeal lay to the Chancellor of the Exchequer (who was obliged to refer the matter to a tribunal but was not bound by its findings), but this procedure has been replaced by one under which the appeal, like those under the building societies and financial services legislation, lies to a specially constituted tribunal. The aim of distancing

---

[1] PFI Act 1939, s.6.

[2] It was also argued, somewhat disingenuously in view of the example of the PFI Act, that the question of fitness was not 'a justiciable issue of any kind', but 'a subjective judgment made by an instructed person upon a question of experience': HL Debs, vol. 340, col. 904 (22nd March 1973), *per* Hailsham L.C.).

[3] *Report*, Part 1, para. 6.23.

[4] Recourse has also been had to the European Commission of Human Rights: *Kaplan* v. *United Kingdom* (1982) 4 EHRR 64.

decisions from direct ministerial responsibility could of course be equally well achieved by the provision of an appeal to the courts, but the courts have found little favour as a means for settling disputes in this area; only under the friendly societies legislation does the appeal lie to the High Court (or Court of Session in Scotland).

Among the advantages commonly attributed to tribunals over courts are those of informality, speed, flexibility and expertise. Of particular importance in the financial field is expertise in the matter in hand. Each tribunal consists of a legally qualified chairman, appointed by the Lord Chancellor, and two other members, appointed by the relevant minister. In the case of banking one of the lay members must have experience of banking and the other experience of accountancy; in the case of building societies one of the lay members must have experience of the business of building societies or other financial institutions, and the other must have experience of accountancy; and in the case of financial services at least one of the lay members must have recent practical experience relevant to the case.[1]

The scope of appeals varies. Under the financial services legislation the appeal is in effect one on the merits, the task of the tribunal being to investigate each case and to make a report stating what would in its opinion be the 'appropriate decision' in the matter, which report is to be implemented by SIB 'forthwith'.[2] Given that the courses of action the tribunal may recommend are broadly commensurate with those open to SIB, this may lead to a decision which is more disadvantageous to the appellant than the proposed course of action against which the appeal is brought; for example, an appeal against a proposal to suspend a firm's authorisation may lead to its withdrawal. Under the banking and building societies legislation, by contrast, the appeal is confined to the legality of the authority's decision, the task of the tribunal being to determine 'whether, for the reasons adduced by the appellant, the decision was unlawful or not justified by the evidence on which it was based'.[3] The appellant does not, therefore, have the right to ask the tribunal to examine the merits of his case, a restriction justified on the grounds that a full rehearing would risk excessive duplication and delay.

An appeal on a point of law lies from these tribunals to the High Court (or Court of Session in Scotland), and from there to the Court of Appeal (or House of Lords in Scottish cases) with leave only.[4] If a decision by the banking or building societies tribunal is found to be wrong in law the matter must be remitted to the tribunal for a rehearing. An appeal on a point of law also lies to the High Court (Court of Session in Scotland) against a determination of the

---

[1] BA, s.28(2),(3); BSA, s.47(2),(3); FSA, s.96(2)–(4).

[2] FSA, s.98(1). The decision remains with SIB since it is SIB's proposed course of action that is referred to the tribunal.

[3] BA, s.29(1); BSA, s.47(4).   [4] BA, s.31; BSA, s.49; Tribunals and Inquiries Act 1971, s.13.

Occupational Pensions Board or a refusal by the Board to review a determination.[1]

Judicial review

Judicial review denotes the power of the superior courts – the High Court in England, the Court of Session in Scotland – to control administrative action on grounds of legality. The principal difference between judicial review and an ordinary right of appeal is that it is confined to the legality of decision-making, unlike an ordinary appeal which also lies to control its merits. But in the context of investor protection this distinction is largely irrelevant, since most appeals are also confined to the legality of regulatory decision-making.[2] Nevertheless, since judicial review is a remedy of last resort, any statutory remedies will normally have to be exhausted, even though they cover essentially the same ground, before recourse will be permitted to the supervisory jurisdiction of the superior courts.

Judicial review lies to control the activities of all the authorities involved in investor protection, not just those such as the Bank of England and SIB whose powers are statutory. In *R* v. *Panel on Take-overs and Mergers, ex parte Datafin plc*,[3] the Court of Appeal held that although the Panel possessed no statutory, prerogative or common law powers it was subject to judicial review; were it to be immune from review, the court argued, the 'immense power *de facto*' it exercised would be subject to no effective means of control.[4] What was decisive, in the court's view, was not the source of the Panel's power, but the fact that it was exercising a public function, which would otherwise have to be undertaken by government. On the same basis it would appear that self-regulating organisations, too, are amenable to review.[5]

Although the courts have therefore been prepared to extend the scope of judicial review to cover the activities of the various non-governmental authorities involved in investor protection, they have at the same time shown themselves to be acutely concerned both to avoid disrupting the functioning of

---

[1] SSA 1973, s.86(4). [2] See above, p. 102. [3] [1987] 2 WLR 699.

[4] 'Given that it is really unthinkable that . . . the panel should go on its way cocooned from the attention of the courts in defence of the citizenry, we sought to investigate whether it could conveniently be controlled by established forms of private law, e.g. torts such as actionable combinations in restraint of trade, and, to this end, pressed [counsel for the applicants] to draft a writ. Suffice it to say that the result was wholly unconvincing . . .' *per* Sir John Donaldson M.R. at p. 715. For a different view, see Falkner, 'Judicial Review of the Take-over Panel and Self-regulatory Organisations' [1987] 2 *Journal of International Business Law*, 103.

[5] *Bank of Scotland* v. *IMRO* 1989 SLT 432; *R* v. *FIMBRA, ex p. Cochrane, The Times*, June 23 1989; *R* v. *AFBD, ex p. Mordens Ltd, Financial Times*, July 11 1990; *R* v. *Lautro, ex p. Ross* [1992] 1 All E.R. 422. Since their powers over their members derive from contract, and judicial review does not lie to control the exercise of contractual powers, it could be argued that they are not amenable to review. Their raison d'être, however, is the performance of a public function – the regulation of their members' conduct – in exchange for recognition conferring authorisation upon their members to carry on investment business. See also *R* v. *Advertising Authority Ltd, ex parte The Insurance Service plc, Financial Times*, July 21, 1989.

financial markets, and to discourage resort to judicial review as a mere tactical ploy. In pursuance of these aims they have tended to subordinate considerations of strict legality to considerations of 'good public administration'. A case in point is *R* v. *Monopolies and Mergers Commission, ex parte Argyll Group plc*,[1] in which Argyll sought relief against a decision, made on the recommendation of the chairman of the Commission acting on his own, to set aside a reference to the Commission of the rival bid by Guinness for Distillers. The Court of Appeal held that the chairman had no power to act on his own, but declined to grant Argyll relief on the grounds that there was little doubt that the Commission would have reached the same decision as did its chairman and that to do so would be incompatible with the needs of 'good public administration'. In the financial field, the court explained, 'good public administration' was directed to substance rather than form; speed of decision-making; proper consideration of the public interest (against which Argyll's 'strong and legitimate interest in putting Guinness in baulk' was not 'of any great, or possibly any, weight'); and, lastly, decisiveness and finality ('The financial public has been entitled to rely upon the finality of the announced decision to set aside the reference . . . account must be taken of the probability that deals have been done in reliance upon the validity of the decisions now impugned').[2]

Essentially the same requirements of good administration were subsequently invoked by the Court of Appeal in the *Datafin* case as justification for its view that the relationship between the Panel and the courts should be 'historic rather than contemporaneous', with the courts allowing decisions to run their course and intervening, if at all, only retrospectively and by way of declaratory orders which would not affect the outcome of a takeover.[3] Essentially the same factors as are used to justify the adoption of different forms and types of regulation – the need for speed of decision-making and for decisiveness and finality – are thus being used to justify the adoption of a policy of judicial self-restraint, which may operate to deny individuals – the tactical litigant and the genuinely aggrieved alike – the same measure of protection against the abuse of power as obtains in other spheres of governmental activity.

The Parliamentary Commissioner for Administration

Aggrieved investors and firms may also complain, through an MP, to the Parliamentary Commissioner for Administration who is empowered to investigate complaints of injustice sustained in consequence of maladministration in connection with action taken by or on behalf of government

[1] [1986] 1 W.L.R. 763.   [2] *per* Sir John Donaldson M.R. at 774–5.
[3] [1987] 2 WLR, 699 at 718; see also *R* v. *Panel on Takeovers and Mergers, ex p. Guinness plc* [1989] 2 W.L.R. 863.

departments and other public bodies.[1] The PCA has no power to investigate matters in respect of which a legal remedy is available, but this restriction is flexibly applied.[2] Nor does he have power to make binding decisions, but his recommendations are in practice implemented.

The potential of the PCA as a means of redress in the financial field was amply demonstrated by the Barlow Clowes Affair where the Government agreed to pay an estimated £150–170 millions in compensation to some 18,000 investors whose losses the PCA attributed to maladministration by the DTI.[3] The PCA's utility as a means of redress is limited, however, by the paucity of bodies over which he has jurisdiction: only three authorities are subject to his jurisdiction: the DTI, the Building Societies Commission and the Registry of Friendly Societies. Moreover, the already limited use made of the PCA may be expected to decline still further as a result of the transfer of responsibility for the regulation of investment business – the most prolific source of complaints – from the DTI to SIB, which is not within the jurisdiction of the PCA.[4]

Barlow Clowes apart, complaints by investors and investment firms alike to the PCA have met with little success. In only one other reported case has an investor complained successfully to the PCA,[5] and there have been no reported cases of successful complaints by investment firms.[6].

[1] Parliamentary Commissioner Act 1967, s.5(1).   [2] s.5(2).

[3] PCA, First Report – Session 1989–90 *The Barlow Clowes Affair* (HC 76, 1989); see also *Observations by the Government on the Report of the PCA on Barlow Clowes* (HC 99, 1989).

[4] It could be argued that action taken by SIB is action taken 'on behalf of' the DTI, but since SIB cannot be made directly subject to his jurisdiction (by virtue of section 4(3) of the Parliamentary Commissioner Act) this argument is unlikely to be sustained.

[5] PCA, Fourth Report for Session 1985–6 (HC 536) Case No. C.591/83 (but for the Department's delay and ineffectiveness the complainant would probably not have suffered his financial losses). See also Fourth Report of the PCA 1975–6 (HC 485) (losses suffered as a result of the failure of the Nation Life Insurance Co. Ltd. not caused by maladministration on the part of the Department of Trade); PCA, First Report for Session 1983–4 (HC 44) Case No. C.912/81, C.471/82 (losses incurred as a result of the failure of Norton Warburg not caused by administrative failures on the part of the Department of Trade); PCA, Annual Report for 1987 (1986–7, HC 363), para. 56 (seven complaints rejected as revealing no *prima facie* evidence of maladministration; PCA, Fifth Report for Session 1990–1 (HC 657) Case No. C.438/89 (losses not caused by an alleged failure to regulate an investment business.)

[6] PCA, Second Report for Session 1976–7 (HC 116), Case No. C.618/V; Third Report for Session 1976–7 (HC 223), Case No. C.320/K.

7
Enforcement

If the protection of investors is to be secured, the rules for their protection need to possess two kinds of qualities. The first of these qualities is legitimacy, by which is meant that the subjects of the rules comply with their requirements because they believe they ought to act in accordance with 'the law' and not simply because of the threat of sanctions; compliance, in other words, is internally motivated rather than externally forced. Among regulatory authorities legitimacy is a highly prized quality, not least because it reduces the need for enforcement, and regulators therefore devote considerable efforts to securing the voluntary acceptance of the regimes they administer by those whose conduct is the object of regulation.

The second quality which the rules require is enforcement. As Weber observed: 'The inclination to forgo economic opportunity simply in order to act legally is obviously slight, unless circumvention of the formal law is strongly disapproved by a powerful convention, and such a situation is not likely to arise where the interests affected by a legal innovation (such as a new law) are widespread.'[1] The ability to apply sanctions to breaches of the rules is therefore no less important to the protection of investors. Across the field of investor protection responsibility for enforcement is divided to varying degrees between individual investors themselves, the police and prosecution authorities and regulatory authorities. In this chapter we concentrate on the part played by each in the overall enforcement of investor protection.

INVESTORS

Litigation

The role of investors in the enforcement process is essentially two-fold. First, by complaining they may alert regulatory authorities, and the police, to

[1] Rheinstein (ed.), *Max Weber on Law in Economy and Society* (1966), p. 38.

possible breaches of the law; much of the casework of these authorities is generated in this way. Second, they may themselves bring legal proceedings in an attempt to vindicate rights possessed by them which they regard as having been infringed. More often than not, however, investors fail to do so, either because they are insufficiently familiar with their rights, or because they lack the necessary resources and determination with which to pursue the legal remedies available to them. Civil actions by individual investors are not therefore commonly regarded as an effective means of protecting the majority of investors: '. . . given the expense of litigation, it is thoroughly unrealistic to assume that civil suits fully can protect small investors.'[1]

Civil actions by individual investors are in any event rare, but as the reference to 'small investors' in the sentence just quoted suggests, it would be wrong to suppose that the difficulties which stand in the way of individual enforcement affect all investors to the same extent. Implicit in the restriction of 'professional' investors' right of action under the Financial Services Act is the assumption that they will be less inhibited about pursuing civil remedies than their private counterparts whose right of action is left undisturbed.[2] Similarly, where several investors have all suffered the same wrong at the hands of a particular firm, a class action or some other form of representative proceedings may provide an individually less daunting means of seeking redress.

Redress for aggrieved investors nevertheless remains an important aim of investor protection.[3] One way in which the difficulties in the way of civil actions by investors may be mitigated is by giving financial regulators power to pursue remedies on their behalf. Provision to this effect is made by the banking and financial services legislation which gives regulators a right to intervene on behalf of investors in two sets of circumstances. First, where the basic prohibitions of the legislation have been contravened, proceedings may be brought with a view to obtaining a court order requiring the repayment of unlawfully accepted deposits or the unravelling of unlawfully entered-into transactions.[4] Second, where profits have accrued as a result of contraventions of those prohibitions (or as a result of the contravention of various other provisions in the case of the Financial Services Act) an order may be sought requiring those profits to be disgorged for distribution among investors.[5] SIB is also empowered to seek compensation for investors who have suffered loss or been otherwise adversely affected by contravention of various provisions.[6]

It is a feature of these provisions, however, that regulatory authorities cannot be compelled to intervene on investors' behalf. Moreover, the benefits to investors of their so doing is only one of the factors to be taken into account

---

[1] Seligman, 'The Historical Need for a Mandatory Corporate Disclosure System' (1983) 9 *Journal of Corporation Law* 56; Gower, *Disc. Doc*, para. 3.41.

[2] FSA, s.62A; see below, pp. 268–9.   [3] See e.g. FSA White Paper, para. 15.19.

[4] BA, s.48; FSA, s.6(2), cf. s.61(1).   [5] BA, s.49; FSA, ss.6(3)–(6), 61(3)–(6).

[6] FSA, ss.6(3)–(6), 61(3)–(6). The lack of any equivalent power under the banking legislation reflects the absence of any rules governing the conduct of deposit-taking business.

in deciding whether or not to institute proceedings. SIB lists among the factors to which regard might be had the deterrent effect of preventing firms from profiting from wrongdoing, the cost of obtaining court orders and the remedies otherwise available to investors.[1] The Bank of England has provided no indication of the factors it would take into account, but the banking legislation enjoins the court in deciding whether and on what terms to make an order to have specific regard to its effect on a firm's solvency and its ability to carry on its business in a manner satisfactory to its creditors.

Alternative procedures

Litigation is normally a last resort. Where alternative procedures for the investigation of complaints and the settlement of disputes are provided, their potential as a means of redress is likely to be explored before consideration is given to going to court. Alternative procedures for the settlement of disputes involving investors are not new: the Chief Registrar of Friendly Societies, for example, has long exercised jurisdiction to determine a range of disputes involving small savers and investors. The last decade, however, has witnessed a proliferation of alternative procedures, beginning with the establishment of the Insurance Ombudsman Bureau in 1981, and continuing through the establishment of parallel schemes for banks, building societies and investment businesses to the establishment of a scheme for occupational and personal pension schemes.

A number of factors, apart from recognition of the difficulties which stand in the way of legal proceedings, have played a part in the establishment of these procedures. Criticism of the adequacy of existing internal complaints procedures, in particular their lack of independence, allied to government pressure, was influential in the setting up, for example, of the insurance and banking ombudsmen schemes. Competitive considerations, too, have played a part: when the banks threatened to steal a march on the building societies by following the example of the insurance industry and establishing their own scheme, the building societies responded by abandoning their opposition to a scheme for building societies. And self-regulatory communities have long favoured extra-judicial mechanisms of dispute settlement as a means of keeping the courts out of their affairs; the Stock Exchange, for example, 'from its early days . . . considered complaints from clients against their members and enforced the same high standards as it did in dealings between members.'[2]

The legal form of these schemes varies: the pensions and building societies schemes are statutory, whereas the insurance and banking schemes are non-statutory; the investment business scheme, on the other hand, comprises a mixture of statutory and non-statutory elements. The most straightforward

---

[1] *SIB's Approach to its Regulatory Responsibilities* (1987), Section 24, para. 8.
[2] Morgan and Thomas, *The Stock Exchange: Its History and Functions* (1969), p. 166.

statutory provision is made by the Social Security Act 1990 which makes provision for the appointment by the Secretary of State of a Pensions Ombudsman with powers to investigate and determine disputes of fact and law as well as complaints of injustice sustained in consequence of maladministration by the trustees or managers of occupational or personal pension schemes.[1]

The Building Societies Act achieves the same result by indirect means: it requires authorised societies to be members of one or more 'recognised' schemes for the investigation of complaints, and lays down detailed requirements which schemes must satisfy in order to qualify for recognition by the Building Societies Commission.[2] Since only one scheme has been recognised – the Building Societies Ombudsman Scheme – membership of this scheme is effectively compulsory.

The provision made by the Financial Services Act in respect of investment businesses is also indirect, but much less specific. SIB is empowered to make provision under its conduct of business rules for arrangements for the settlement of disputes, and it is required to have effective arrangements for the investigation of complaints arising out of the conduct of investment business by authorised persons and against recognised bodies, which must make provision for the investigation of complaints in respect of authorised persons to be carried out in appropriate cases independently of SIB and those persons.[3] Recognised bodies, on the other hand, are simply required to have effective arrangements for investigating complaints against themselves and their members, which in the case of SROs and RPBs *may* make provision for the whole or part of that function to be performed by an independent body or person.[4] Instead of a single scheme, therefore, these provisions have generated a multiplicity of schemes, and with them a need for mechanisms to ensure that individual complaints find their way to the right destination.

The sheer diversity of the schemes in operation makes generalisation difficult. The principal feature they have in common, however, is that they all make provision for the submission of disputes to the determination of an independent third party, usually after any domestic complaints procedures have been exhausted, and usually with a ceiling on the amount of any award. Where schemes differ most obviously is in whether they employ arbitral or ombudsman techniques of dispute settlement. The essence of the ombudsman technique as it has been adapted to the financial services sector is two-fold. First, ombudsmen have greater flexibility than arbitrators in the way in which they handle disputes: they normally have powers of investigation, including powers to require the production of papers, and they can employ non-adjudicative means, i.e. negotiation, mediation and conciliation, as well as adjudicative means in the settlement of disputes. (Schemes based on

[1] s.12(1) and Sch. 3; see below, pp. 216–17. [2] BSA, s.83 and Sch. 12.
[3] s.48(2)(j), Sch. 7, para. 4. [4] Sch. 2, para. 6; Sch. 3, para. 5; Sch. 4, para.4.

arbitration may make separate provision for investigation and conciliation.) Secondly, their determinations are normally binding on firms, but not on investors who remain free to reject the determination and seek redress through the courts. Arbitral awards, on the other hand, are normally binding on both parties. (This distinction is not always observed. Under the pensions scheme the ombudsman's determination is binding on both parties. A building society, by contrast, may refuse to implement a determination, providing it is prepared to publicise its reasons for so doing.) In addition, ombudsmen usually have powers to go beyond the strict confines of the law in reaching a decision which is 'fair in all the circumstances of the case', though the precise relationship between legal and non-legal norms in determining fairness is not always clear.

Both statutory ombudsmen schemes make provision for an appeal to the courts on a point of law: a building society can require the ombudsman to state a case on a point of law for the opinion of the High Court (or Court of Session in Scotland), and the court can direct the ombudsman to reconsider the complaint;[1] and an appeal on a point of law lies to the High Court (or Court of Session) against any determination of a complaint or dispute by the Pensions Ombudsman.[2] An analogous result may be achieved by means of the 'test case' procedure incorporated in the non-statutory banking scheme, which allows a bank to remove a dispute from the ombudsman's jurisdiction which it believes either involves an issue with important consequences for its business, or the business of banks in general, or raises an important or novel point of law, providing it undertakes to pay the costs to the complainant of going to court, including the costs of any subsequent appeal by the bank (but not of any appeal by the complainant). There is no certainty under this procedure, however, that the case will reach court, since the onus remains on the complainant to institute proceedings, which he may be reluctant to do.

These schemes do not just provide a means for the settlement of disputes: individual complaints may reveal evidence of wrongdoing and the wider trends revealed by the pattern of disputes may indicate respects in which the applicable rules stand in need of revision. It is, however, against the standard of their effectiveness as a means for the settlement of disputes that schemes fall primarily to be judged. Their undoubted advantage in this respect is that they provide a cheaper (in ombudsman schemes, free) and more expeditious means of settling disputes, which in many cases are not worth the time and effort involved in going to court. Against this they have some obvious weaknesses. A major weakness of the insurance and banking schemes is that because membership is voluntary their coverage is incomplete. The investment business regime as a whole does not suffer from this weakness (although individual schemes are affected by it), but the piecemeal arrangements which

[1] BSA, s.84(5).   [2] SSPA, ss.59H(3), (4).

have resulted from SIB's lack of power to establish an industry-wide scheme have yet to fully meet the objectives SIB has set in terms of accessibility, efficient handling of information and consistency of standards of redress.[1] Overall, the chief weakness of the system is its sheer complexity, which threatens to negate the benefits its individual components are designed to achieve. This problem can only be satisfactorily resolved, however, if the existing industry-sponsored schemes are reorganised along essentially functional lines.

POLICE AND PROSECUTION AUTHORITIES

The police and prosecution authorities are the main authorities responsible for the enforcement of the criminal law. Several financial regulators – for example, the Bank of England and SIB – possess powers to prosecute offences arising out of the legislation they administer, but they typically deal with only the less serious offences created by that legislation. The more serious offences, including those forming part of the general law of the land, are normally handled by the police and prosecution authorities, upon whom the main responsibility for enforcing the criminal law therefore falls.

Criminal enforcement differs from administrative enforcement in a number of respects. First, it is essentially reactive rather than proactive in character. The police do not operate elaborate systems of surveillance of the kind maintained by regulatory authorities, but rely instead mainly on complaints – from investors, regulatory authorities and other participants – to bring possible offences to light. Secondly, the police and prosecution authorities have no powers to impose penalties on offenders, unlike regulators who have powers to impose penalties of an administrative nature on offenders as well as to institute criminal and civil proceedings. Finally, the imposition of criminal penalties is surrounded by elaborate procedural and evidential safeguards, which exert a much greater influence on the work of police and prosecution authorities than they do on regulatory authorities for whom criminal prosecutions constitute only a small part (at most) of their activities.

The 1980s witnessed an unprecedented degree of concern about the ability of the legal system in England and Wales to tackle effectively serious crimes of fraud. In 1983 a Fraud Trials Committee, chaired by Lord Roskill, was appointed by the Lord Chancellor and Home Secretary 'to consider in what ways the conduct of criminal proceedings in England and Wales arising from fraud can be improved and to consider what changes in existing law and procedure would be desirable to secure the just, expeditious and economical disposal of such proceedings'. The Committee's report, which was published three years later, did nothing to allay the concern then prevalent.

[1] *Report of the Securities and Investments Board 1989/90*, pp. 17–18.

The public no longer believes that the legal system in England and Wales is capable of bringing the perpetrators of serious frauds expeditiously and effectively to book. The overwhelming weight of the evidence laid before us suggests that the public is right. In relation to such crimes, and the skilful and determined criminals who commit them, the present legal system is archaic, cumbersome and unreliable. At every stage during investigation, preparation, committal, pre-trial review and trial, the present arrangements offer an open invitation to blatant delay and abuse. While petty frauds, clumsily committed, are likely to be detected and punished, it is all too likely that the largest and most cleverly executed crimes escape unpunished.[1]

Responsibility for remedying this state of affairs, the Committee insisted, lay with the Government which

has encouraged and continues to encourage ordinary families to invest their savings in the equity markets, particularly in the equities of formerly state-owned enterprises. If the Government cherishes the vision of an 'equity-owning democracy', then it also faces an inescapable duty to ensure that financial markets are honestly managed, and that transgressors in these markets are swiftly and effectively discovered, convicted and punished.[2]

Fraud is not tackled by the criminal law alone: one of the rationales of licensing requirements is the exclusion of potential offenders from the ranks of authorised firms.[3] Given this dual approach to the problem, it is arguable that a measure of ineffectiveness in the criminal law is tolerable, so long at least as preventive measures operate effectively to exclude potential rule-breakers, and that between these two approaches the emphasis ought to be on the prevention of misconduct in advance rather than its detection and punishment after the event.[4] It is also arguable, however, that there comes a point at which the apparent inability of the criminal law to punish misconduct threatens to undermine belief in the effectiveness of the regulatory system as a whole; it is for this reason, Levi points out, that many who 'do not believe that fraud is endemic or even common in Britain's financial institutions can see a long-term commercial advantage in competent state policing'.[5] Whether this point had been reached when the Roskill Committee reported in 1986 is open to question, but in a pre-election year the Government could not be seen to shirk the 'inescapable duty' which the Committee had identified, and legislation to implement the majority of its recommendations was swiftly enacted.

The major reform introduced by the subsequent Criminal Justice Act 1987 was the establishment of the Serious Fraud Office with powers to investigate and prosecute any suspected offence which appears to involve 'serious or complex fraud'.[6] The Office was set up in response to the Roskill Committee's criticism of the fragmented nature of the existing arrangements for investigating and prosecuting fraud, and of the lack of effective co-ordination and co-

---

[1] *Fraud Trials Committee Report* (1986), summary, para. 1.   [2] *Ibid.*   [3] See above, p. 36.
[4] See to this effect, Gower, *Report*, Part 1, para. 10.14; FSA White Paper, para. 15.21.
[5] *Regulating Fraud* (1987), p. 50.   [6] s.1.

operation between the various authorities involved. 'The very diversity of responsibilities between these organisations and the fragmented nature of the powers of investigation . . . act as a hindrance to the just, expeditious and economical disposal of criminal proceedings arising from fraud, in particular serious and complex fraud cases.'[1] In the Committee's view, this problem was exacerbated by 'a degree of institutional reluctance among the organisations concerned to work fully and effectively together'.[2]

In an earlier attempt to overcome this problem, a Fraud Investigation Group (FIG) was set up in 1985 within the then Department of the Director of Public Prosecutions, *inter alia*, to ensure that all the disciplines involved in the investigation and prosecution of offences worked closely together, and that investigations were concentrated on the major issues and major offenders so that there could be speedy investigation of offences likely to result in successful prosecution (or an early termination of investigations where no prospects of a successful prosecution were in sight).[3] The Roskill Committee considered FIG (which now forms part of the Crown Prosecution Service) 'a step in the right direction' insofar as it represented a move towards greater co-ordination and co-operation between separate organisations, but it raised for consideration the question of whether it should be taken a step further by the formation of 'a single unified organisation responsible for all the functions of detection, investigation and prosecution of serious fraud'.[4]

The Office is headed by a Director, in whom the powers it exercises are vested, who is appointed by the Attorney General and who is responsible to him (and through him to Parliament) for the exercise of those powers. It is staffed by lawyers (21) and accountants (19) who investigate cases in teams. Investigations may be conducted in conjunction with the police,[5] who do not form part of the formal establishment of the Office, but whose participation in the investigation of cases is secured through the device of 'co-location', which means essentially that they work in the same building but under a separate chain of command.[6]

The long-term aims of the Serious Fraud Office include economic benefit if its operation generates greater confidence in the City of London; a reduction in crime to the extent it deters fraud; and increased efficiency in the criminal justice system to the extent that it can introduce a novel, integrated approach to the handling of complex issues using several different disciplines working in teams.[7] Its immediate objectives are to ensure that a coherent approach is taken to the investigation of serious fraud; to concentrate resources on the essential issues involved in complex frauds; to increase the speed of

[1] *Fraud Trials Committee Report*, para. 2.1. [2] para. 2.47.
[3] *Fraud Trials Committee Report*, para. 2.27. [4] paras. 2.45–2.46.
[5] Criminal Justice Act s.1(4).
[6] Woods, 'The Serious Fraud Office' [1989] *Criminal Law Review* 175.
[7] SFO, *An Introduction to the Serious Fraud Office* (1989), para. 1.8.

investigations and of the institution of proceedings in important cases; to develop expertise in specialist areas of fraud; to use the new trial procedures for serious and complex fraud cases efficiently; to develop the presentation of evidence in complex fraud cases in new, more palatable and comprehensible forms; and to increase the proportion of successful prosecutions.[1]

The powers of the Office are restricted to cases which appear to its Director on reasonable grounds to involve serious or complex fraud.[2] The phrase 'serious or complex fraud' is not defined by the legislation and the Office has, therefore, a wide discretion in deciding which of the cases referred to it to accept for investigation and possible prosecution. Three criteria are paramount in the selection of cases: whether the facts or the law or both are of great complexity; whether the money lost or in serious danger of being lost exceeds £2 million; and whether there is great public interest or concern.[3] Applying these criteria, the Office aims to handle about 60 cases at any one time, selected from frauds discovered by the police and by regulatory authorities in the normal course of their business; frauds discovered as a result of investigations and enquiries under the companies, insurance companies, financial services, building societies and banking legislation; frauds committed in connection with financial and commodity exchanges and markets; frauds committed in the course of takeovers or mergers of companies and building societies; and frauds involving banking, the investment of money or management of funds subscribed directly or indirectly by members of the public, where the methods employed or the total sums at risk are such as to give rise to serious public concern.[4]

Section 2 of the Criminal Justice Act 1987 gives the SFO extensive powers of investigation, modelled on those possessed by the DTI under the Companies Acts, which may be used to investigate the affairs, or any aspect of the affairs, of 'any person'.[5] In the exercise of these powers, the Director, and any designated person, may require a person whose affairs are under investigation, or any other person whom he has reason to believe has relevant information, to answer questions and to produce documents.[6] Failure without reasonable excuse to comply with a requirement imposed in the exercise of these powers is a criminal offence.[7] Statements obtained in the exercise of these powers, in contrast to statements made in the exercise of the equivalent powers of regulatory authorities, are not admissible in evidence against the person making them, except on a prosecution for the offence of 'lying' to the SFO, or where, on a prosecution for an offence, a person makes a statement inconsistent with a statement made by him under section 2 questioning.[8] As well as making it an offence to fail without reasonable excuse to comply with a

---

[1] para. 1.9.   [2] Criminal Justice Act, s.1(2).

[3] *An Introduction to the Serious Fraud Office*, para. 1.12.   [4] para. 1.13.   [5] s.2(1).

[6] s.2(2),(3); provision is made for search warrants to be obtained where documents are not produced or where prior notice is not practicable or might seriously prejudice an investigation: s.2(4).

[7] s.2(13); as to the concept of 'reasonable excuse', see below, pp. 118–19.   [8] s.2(8).

requirement of the SFO, the Act also makes it an offence knowingly, or recklessly to deceive or mislead the SFO, and to falsify, conceal or destroy documents known or suspected to be relevant to a serious fraud investigation.[1]

The transposition of these powers from the regulatory to the criminal spheres has not been effected without controversy, even though they have been confined to the SFO and have not been conferred on the police as was recommended by the Roskill Committee, which saw no reason why the powers conferred, for example, by section 447 of the Companies Act (which empowers the DTI to require, on pain of criminal penalties, the production of documents and the provision of explanations of them) should be confined to the DTI.[2] Critics have accused the SFO of being too ready to invoke its section 2 powers, and in particular of using them for the purpose of mounting 'fishing expeditions'. In the one decided case that has arisen out of their exercise it was held that the SFO had no power to question witnesses about offences with which they had already been charged.[3] But it is difficult to see the scope for imposing greater constraints on the SFO without at the same time destroying the purpose for which its powers were conferred.[4]

The major recommendation of the Roskill Committee which was not implemented was its (majority) recommendation that in complex fraud cases trial by jury should be replaced by trial before a judge and two 'lay assessors' selected from a panel of persons with skill and expertise in business generally coupled with experience of complex business transactions.[5] The Committee's recommendation was founded on the proposition that in complex fraud cases jurors were 'out of their depth'.[6] Among other adverse consequences, this was said to cause prosecutors to prefer lesser charges or not to proceed with cases for fear that they would prove incomprehensible to a jury.[7] In the absence of research on jurors' comprehension of complex fraud trials, it is impossible to know whether jurors are genuinely out of their depths or merely baffled by the way in which cases are presented to them.[8] But on the face of it 'experts'

[1] ss.2(14),(16). [2] *Fraud Trials Committee Report*, para. 2.62.

[3] *R* v. *Director of the Serious Fraud Office, ex p. Smith, The Independent*, November 8, 1991.

[4] See also *Re Arrows Ltd.*, *Financial Times*, November 15, 1991. In *R* v. *Director of the Serious Fraud Office, exp. Nadir*, November 1, 1990 (unreported), leave was granted to apply for judicial review of the refusal by the director of the SFO to supply particulars of the matter under investigation, but the application was later withdrawn. By analogy with the approach adopted by the courts to the equivalent powers of regulatory authorities, the likelihood must be that the court would have held that the Director was under a duty to act fairly but that that duty did not extend to providing particulars of the matters under investigation: see below, pp. 119.

[5] Among the Committee's recommendations for the reform of rules of procedure and evidence which were implemented, were the introduction of a notice of transfer procedure by which committal proceedings may be avoided in serious or complex fraud cases (Criminal Justice Act 1987, ss.4–5), the introduction of preparatory hearings before a judge sitting alone for the purpose of clarifying and resolving issues that would otherwise fall to be considered in the absence of the jury at the trial (ss.7–10), and the relaxation of the rules governing the admissibility of documentary evidence (Criminal Justice Act 1988, Part II).

[6] *Fraud Trials Committee Report*, para. 8.35; in similar vein, see Gower, *Report*, Part 1, para. 10.23.

[7] *Fraud Trials Committee Report*, para. 8.36.

[8] If it is the latter then the improved methods of presentation which have been adopted as a result of the Committee's recommendations (at paras. 9.4–9.25) should help.

would seem to have a better chance of reaching the 'correct' decision than a jury selected at random with little or no experience of the milieu in which an alleged fraud was conducted; certainly the composition of tribunals in the financial field proceeds on this assumption.[1] But whether the decisions of experts would command the same degree of confidence as those of a jury is another matter. Although the Roskill Committee questioned whether public confidence in the jury was not misplaced, it did not address the question of whether the decisions of an expert tribunal would command the same degree of confidence, particularly if their decision was to acquit a defendant. It is this difficulty, as much as the political opposition a proposal for the abandonment of jury trial would encounter, which has left unresolved the deep-rooted conflict between 'rational', i.e. expert, and 'popular' models of decision-making highlighted by the Committee's recommendation.

REGULATORY AUTHORITIES

The investor protection regimes administered by the regulatory authorities introduced in the previous chapter are examples of what may be termed compliance strategies of social control.[2] The principal objective of such strategies is 'to secure conformity with law by means insuring compliance or by taking action to prevent potential law violations without the necessity to detect, process and penalise violations'.[3] Compliance strategies are to be contrasted with deterrent strategies of social control, of which the civil and criminal law are prime examples, whose principal objective by contrast is 'to secure conformity with law by detecting violations of the law, determining who is responsible for the violation, and penalising violators to deter violations in the future, either by those who are punished or by those who might do so were violations not punished'.[4] Whereas deterrent strategies are 'postmonitory', reacting to violations that have occurred, compliance strategies are 'premonitory, attending to conditions that induce conformity or to foreboding of harm'.[5]

Just as the regimes they administer proceed on the basis that prevention is better than cure,[6] such information as is available about the enforcement strategies pursued by individual regulators suggests that they too are weighted heavily towards compliance, i.e. the prevention of harm to investors, whether flowing from misconduct or otherwise, rather than towards deterrence, i.e. the penalising of offenders. SIB, for example, defines its enforcement objectives as

[1] See above, p. 102.

[2] Reiss, 'Selecting Strategies of Social Control over Organisational Life', in Hawkins and Thomas (eds.), *Enforcing Regulation* (1984).   [3] *Ibid.*   [4] *Ibid.*

[5] *Ibid*; see to similar effect, Hawkins, *Environment and Enforcement: Regulation and the Social Definition of Pollution* (1984), (sanctioning and compliance) and Summers, 'The Technique Element in Law', (1971) 59 *California Law Review* 733 (penal and regulatory); see also Braithwaite, Walker and Grabosky, 'An Enforcement Taxonomy of Regulatory Agencies', (1987) 9 *Law and Policy* 323.

[6] See above, p. 36.

being 'to achieve and maintain a "clean" UK investment industry, where both investors and participant firms are free from undue risks of malpractice or insolvency', and 'so far as investors or other firms do get caught up in malpractice or insolvency, to minimise their losses'.[1] One reason why a compliance strategy may commend itself to regulators is that it is likely to be more economical than a deterrent strategy; contested enforcement action in particular is massively expensive in terms of financial and human resources. Another reason is that it may appear to offer a better prospect of securing the co-operation of the regulated than a deterrent strategy which risks alienating the regulated as well as being expensive in terms of time and manpower to administer.[2]

The primary means by which compliance is sought is by monitoring financial and other information submitted by firms. The fact that this information is generated by firms renders monitoring inherently vulnerable to deception, despite penalties for the submission of information which is materially false or misleading, as was illustrated by the Johnson Matthey affair, where Johnson Matthey consistently misrepresented the level of its exposure to individual clients. Monitoring is therefore commonly supplemented by inspections on a routine as well as an *ad hoc* basis. In the case of building societies, for example, a system of inspections was instituted after the rescue of the Grays Building Society in 1978.

Another method by which the weaknesses of monitoring systems have been sought to be overcome is by enlisting the aid of auditors as 'whistleblowers' in the supervisory process. To this end auditors have been statutorily relieved of liability for breach of any duty, for example, of confidentiality, to which they may be subject in connection with communications made in good faith to regulatory authorities,[3] and professional guidance has been issued specifying the circumstances in which matters uncovered in the course of their audit work should be drawn to the attention of regulators.[4] Auditors have not welcomed this extension of their role, fearing that it will undermine their relationship with their clients, as well as widen the scope of their potential liability should they fail to report matters which it is later considered should have been reported. Their co-operation has been secured, however, by the assumption of reserve powers to impose a statutory duty to communicate, breach of which might result in the disqualification of an auditor, in the event that the professional guidance is adjudged unsatisfactory.[5]

---

[1] *Report of the Securities and Investments Board for 1989/90*, p. 15.

[2] Hawkins, 'Compliance Strategy, Prosecution Policy, and Aunt Sally', (1990) 30 *British Journal of Criminology* 444, at pp. 451–2. The observation that much regulatory enforcement appears to be weighted towards compliance does not exclude the possibility, exemplified by the DTI in relation to the Prevention of Fraud (Investments) Act, that some regulatory authorities may fail to pursue any credible strategy whatsoever.

[3] BA, s.47; BSA, s.82(8)–(9); FSA, s.109; ICA, s.21A.

[4] See below, pp. 136–7, 151–2, 170, and 225.

[5] BA, s.47(5); BSA, s.82(9); FSA, s.109(2); ICA, s.21A(2).

These attempts to strengthen the supervisory process have been accompanied by a greater emphasis on the responsibility of firms for compliance; it has become a truism of modern investor protection that compliance begins at the level of the firm. Firms are therefore commonly required to maintain 'adequate' internal systems of control, financial and otherwise, by means of which their compliance with regulatory obligations can be monitored by regulators (through the imposition of reporting requirements on auditors), as well as by firms themselves. SIB's principles for the conduct of investment business, for example, require investment firms to organise and control their internal affairs in a responsible manner, keeping proper records, and where they employ staff or are responsible for the conduct of investment business by others, to have adequate arrangements to ensure that they are suitable, adequately trained and properly supervised and that they have well-defined compliance procedures.[1] This 'compliance' principle is fleshed out by the core rules which require firms to take reasonable steps, including the establishment and maintenance of procedures, to ensure that their officers and employees (and officers and employees of their appointed representatives) act in conformity with, *inter alia*, their own and their employer's relevant responsibilities under the regulatory system.[2]

Financial regulators possess extensive powers of investigation modelled on those possessed by the DTI in respect of companies.[3] In the exercise of these powers they may require the production of documents and answers to questions (which may be used in evidence against the person giving them).[4] By analogy with the powers of inspectors under the companies legislation they have no power to insist on answers to questions,[5] but a failure 'without reasonable excuse' to answer questions is an offence, and it would appear that the concept of 'reasonable excuse' is not apt to cover a refusal by a person to answer on the ground that to do so might incriminate him.[6] In *Governor of the Bank of England* v. *Riley*[7] the Court of Appeal held that a person required to provide information under section 42 of the Banking Act 'is under a duty to provide that information and is not excused from so doing because the information would tend to show that he has indeed contravened that provision of the Act or any other provision of the criminal law'. Were the privilege against self-incrimination not to be displaced, the Court accepted, the provision in question would be effectively emasculated. Likewise, in *R* v. *Secretary of State for Trade and Industry, ex p. Wilson*[8] the Court of

---

[1] Principle 9 (international organisation).

[2] Core rule 34.1; as to what compliance with this obligation may involve at the level of the individual firm, see e.g. IMRO, *Compliance Standards and the Compliance Function* (June 1990).

[3] Companies Act 1985, ss.431–2, 447.   [4] See e.g. BA, s.41; BSA, s.55; ICA, s.44, and FSA, s.105.

[5] *McLelland, Pope and Langley Ltd* v. *Howard* [1968] 1 All E.R. 569.

[6] Save possibly, following *R* v. *Director of the Serious Fraud Office ex p. Smith*, (above, p. 115) in respect of matters with which he has already been charged.

[7] *The Times*, 1 November 1990, C.A.

[8] December 20, 1991 (unreported).

Appeal held that a person was not entitled to refuse to answer questions put to him by inspectors appointed under the Companies Acts on the ground that the purpose of the investigation was to discover whether a criminal offence had been committed.[1] As well as making it an offence to fail without reasonable excuse to comply with a requirement imposed in the exercise of these powers, the legislation also makes it an offence to make false or misleading statements (and to destroy, mutilate or falsify documents).

Again, by analogy with the powers conferred by the companies legislation, there are few restrictions on the exercise of these powers going beyond those implied by basic administrative law requirements of good faith and fairness. Thus, while regulatory authorities (and inspectors appointed by them) are under a duty to act fairly (the precise content of which is likely to vary depending on the context in which it is invoked), they are free to conduct their investigations as they see fit.[2] Nor are regulators under an obligation to disclose reasons for the exercise of their powers or to provide affected persons with an opportunity to make representations against their exercise.[3]

Regulators occupy an extremely powerful position in law in relation to the firms whose conduct they regulate. Unlike the police or prosecution authorities, they have the power to impose sanctions directly on firms. The ultimate sanction at their disposal usually takes the form of the withdrawal or revocation of a firm's licence or authorisation. Safeguards are provided against the abuse of regulators' powers of enforcement (and intervention), but they are less extensive than those which apply in the context of criminal or civil proceedings; there are no strict evidentiary rules, no burden of proof to be discharged, and the interposition of an appeals procedure between the regulator and the courts serves to shield the exercise of the regulator's discretion from immediate judicial scrutiny.[4] Accordingly, although regulators sometimes find it expedient to claim that they have no powers to act in the absence of 'conclusive proof', for example, such claims seldom accord with their position in law.

From a compliance perspective the primary significance of the various sanctions at regulators' disposal is that they provide a means whereby compliance or remedial action may be secured – through the threat of their imposition – rather than a means whereby regulatory infringements may be automatically penalised. They provide what SIB describes as 'statutory "muscle", the mere flexing of which can assist in dealing promptly and effectively with a number of cases without in fact having to resort to full legal process'.[5] For such strategy to work, however, firms need to believe that

---

[1] See also *R* v. *Harris* [1970] 3 All E.R. 743 and *R* v. *Secretary of State for Trade, ex p. Perestrello* [1980] 3 E.R. 28 (applicant not entitled to refuse to produce documents on the ground that an inspector is biased against him).

[2] *Re Pergammon Press Ltd.* [1970] 3 All E.R. 535, *Maxwell* v. *Department of Trade* [1974] 2 All E.R. 122.

[3] *Norwest Holt Ltd.* v. *Department of Trade* [1978] 3 All E.R. 280.   [4] See above, p. 101.

[5] *Report of the Securities and Investments Board 1989/90*, p. 22.

a regulator is prepared to formally invoke the sanctions at its disposal; at the very least, firms must not be confident that the regulator will take no action. The question is whether a belief in the preparedness of a regulator to take action can be generated by threats alone, or whether it requires an example to be made of offenders as well. The drawback on embarking on enforcement proceedings is that they are expensive in terms of financial and human resources, but unless a regulator is seen to take some action, the muscle afforded it by the powers at its disposal may quickly atrophy.

Part II

INVESTMENT MEDIA AND
INSTITUTIONS

8
Banks

BACKGROUND

The non-statutory system of banking regulation that evolved in the United Kingdom during the latter part of the nineteenth and early part of the twentieth centuries on the basis of the Bank of England's 'traditional powers' was institutional, rather than functional in character. Its subjects were those institutions that were 'recognised' as banks by the Bank of England and by their fellow members of the banking community. Outside this 'core' of recognised banks, however, there grew up during the 1950s and 1960s a 'fringe' of what were later termed secondary banks, which in common with recognised banks accepted deposits, including deposits from the public, but whose activities were not regulated by the Bank of England or by any other authority. In theory, a secondary bank could progress by means of a series of statutory and non-statutory recognitions to the status of a fully-fledged bank supervised by the Discount Office of the Bank, but this was a lengthy process which in its initial stages at least entailed few regulatory consequences. In the absence of the constraints to which recognised banks were subject, these secondary banks flourished.

An early attempt to close this gap by means of statutory powers was abandoned in 1958 because of 'their apparently daunting legislative complexity and perhaps also because the need for such powers was not sufficiently manifest'.[1] It was not closed until the onset of the secondary banking crisis in 1973 when the Bank found itself confronted 'with the imminent collapse of several deposit-taking institutions, and with the clear danger of a rapidly escalating crisis of confidence', which 'threatened other deposit-taking institutions and, if left unchecked, could have quickly passed into parts of the banking system proper'.[2] Its responsibility for the overall health of the

---

[1] Fforde, 'Competition, innovation and regulation in British banking' (1983) 23 *Bank of England Quarterly Bulletin* 364.

[2] 'The secondary banking crisis and the Bank of England's support operations' (1978) 18 *Bank of England Quarterly Bulletin* 230.

banking system having thus been engaged, the Bank responded by mounting a rescue operation with the assistance of the London and Scottish clearing banks (the 'lifeboat'), and by extending the scope of its supervisory arrangements to embrace the activities of all the significant deposit-taking institutions (other than building societies) outside the banking system.

This extension of the reach of the Bank's system of supervision was effected by non-statutory means. Doubts about the willingness of the secondary banks to submit to the Bank's authority once the crisis had passed, however, led the Bank to seek a more secure basis in statute for their supervision.

Despite the extent to which the enhanced supervisory arrangements had been accepted voluntarily by deposit-taking institutions it was concluded that it would be unwise to rely on the Bank's traditional authority being accepted comprehensively by all the institutions prospectively involved – particularly outside the City itself.[1]

A further reason for legislating was provided by the First Banking Co-ordination Directive which required Member States to have a system of prior authorisation for credit institutions.[2] Both needs were eventually met by the enactment of the Banking Act 1979 which placed the system of banking supervision on a statutory basis for the first time.

Although the Bank had thus been driven to seek statutory backing for its system of supervision, its conversion to the merits of statutory regulation was essentially confined to repairing the gap in its authority revealed by the secondary banking crisis. So far as recognised banks were concerned, it saw no reason to alter its existing informal approach to their supervision. It therefore promoted and secured the enactment of a two-tier system of authorisation, comprising a first tier of 'recognised banks', which would continue to be supervised in the same way as before, and a second tier of 'licensed deposit-takers' against whom the principal powers conferred by the legislation were directed. Although the Bank was later to deny that licensed deposit-taker status should be interpreted as a slur on an institution's standing, the distinction drawn in the legislation between the two types of institution reflected its basic belief that recognised banks could be relied upon to manage themselves more prudently and competently than institutions in the second tier.[3]

This belief was shattered by Johnson Matthey Bankers, a recognised bank (rather than a licensed deposit-taker) which the Bank felt compelled to rescue in 1984 in order to prevent 'unacceptable consequences for the banking system as a whole'.[4] Unlike the secondary banking crisis, from responsibility for which the Bank had successfully distanced itself, this was a failure of

---

[1] Cooke, 'Self-Regulation and Statute – The Evolution of Banking Supervision', in Gardener (ed.), *UK Banking Supervision Evolution, Practice and Issues* (1986), p. 90.

[2] Dir.77/780 EEC OJ L322/30.

[3] For the background to the two-tier system, see Fay, *Portrait of An Old Lady* (1987), pp. 86–92.

[4] Bank of England, *Report and accounts 1985*, p. 38.

supervision which fell squarely within the responsibility of the Bank. Worse than this, it was a failure whose origins were traceable in part to a system of supervision of the Bank's own devising. The Committee set up under the chairmanship of the Governor of the Bank to consider the system of banking supervision in the light of the problems which had arisen in Johnson Matthey Bankers, conceded that 'JMB's position as a recognised bank was a factor in the delay in the supervisors becoming aware of, and reacting to, its growing problems.'[1]

The Leigh-Pemberton Committee dismissed any suggestion that the existing system of supervision – whose special characteristics it identified as its flexible nature and the part played in it by the co-operation of the banks – was fundamentally flawed.[2] It did not, therefore, examine in any detail the possibility of changing to a different system involving, for example, the specification in statute of numerical prudential criteria or the adoption of a system of formal inspections in place of the existing system of informal supervisory interviews. Instead, it recommended a number of changes to the existing system and its accompanying legal framework, including the replacement of the two-tier system of authorisation by a unitary system with a single category of authorised institution, and the consequent extension to all institutions of its powers in relation to licensed deposit-takers. The Committee's recommendations were in the main followed in the subsequent White Paper, *Banking Supervision*,[3] which added the Government's own proposal for a Board of Banking Supervision 'to give more forceful direction to the task of bank supervision',[4] before being implemented by the Banking Act 1987. While materially strengthening the Bank's powers in relation to authorised institutions, the Act does not therefore signify any radical alteration in the Bank's approach to supervision which continues to be characterised by its emphasis on flexibility and co-operation.

THE SCOPE OF THE REGIME

The scope of the regime established by the Banking Act is delimited by the basic prohibition laid down in section 3(1):

> no person shall in the United Kingdom accept a deposit in the course of carrying on (whether there or elsewhere) a business which for the purposes of this Act is a deposit-taking business unless that person is an institution for the time being authorised. . . .

What is struck at by the Act, therefore, is the unauthorised acceptance of deposits in the United Kingdom in the course of carrying on a deposit-taking

---

[1] *Report of the Committee set up to Consider the System of Banking Supervision*, Cmnd. 9550 (1985), para. 3.3; see also Fay, *op. cit.*, p. 165.

[2] *Ibid.*, paras. 2.1–2.2.   [3] Cmnd. 9695 (1985).

[4] HC Debs. vol. 89, col. 159 17 Dec. 1985; see above, p. 86.

business in the United Kingdom or elsewhere. To gain a fuller understanding of the regime's scope we need to examine the various elements that make up this prohibition.

Deposit

The Act adopts an initially broad definition of the concepts of 'deposit' and 'deposit-taking business' which it then narrows through the provision of various exclusions. Flexibility is preserved through a power vested in the Treasury and exercisable in consultation with the Bank to amend the definitions by order.[1] The boundaries of the regime can thus be adjusted in the light of changing circumstances (including unfavourable judicial precedents) without the need for primary legislation.[2]

Section 5(1)(a) of the Act defines a deposit as 'a sum of money paid on terms under which it will be repaid . . . either on demand or at a time or in circumstances agreed . . .' A deposit is therefore a repayable sum of money. The fact that it may be repayable without interest or a premium is immaterial: what matters is that it is repayable.

Were the definition of deposit to be left at this it would cover many payments made in the course of ordinary commercial transactions which fall outside the scope of the Act's concerns. Excluded from the definition of deposit, therefore, are sums paid 'on terms referable to the provision of property or services or the giving of security' (s.5(1)(b)).

The scope of this exclusion is exhaustively defined by section 5(2) of the Act which excludes three types of payment:

(i)   The first type of payment excluded is money which 'is paid by way of advance or part payment under a contract for the sale, hire or other provision of property or services, *and* is repayable only in the event that the property or services is not or are not in fact sold, hired or otherwise provided' (s.5(2)(a)). The Bank of England interprets this provision as covering advance or part payment for *specific* items of property or service only and not, for example, credit balances maintained on behalf of customers in a shop budget account, which are held for the future purchase of unspecified goods, or monies placed with an investment manager for investment at his discretion, which are excluded from the scope of the regime by the Banking Act 1987 (Exempt Transactions) Regulations 1987.[3]

(ii)   The second type of payment excluded is money which 'is paid by way of

---

[1] s.7.

[2] The Banking Act 1987 (Meaning of Deposit) Order 1991 (SI 1991/1776) excludes from the definition of deposit for the purposes of the payment of compensation sums to which a person becomes entitled after a petition is presented for the winding up of an institution.

[3] See below, p. 129; Bank of England, *Banking Act 1987: Banking Supervision Guide* (1987).

security for the performance of a contract or by way of security in respect of loss which may result from the non-performance of a contract' (s.5(2)(b)). An example commonly given of money paid by way of security for the performance of a contract is a deposit payable at the time of exchange of contracts for house purchase.[1] In *SCF Finance Co. Ltd.* v. *Masri (No. 2)*[2] the Court of Appeal held that payments made by an investor to commodity brokers fell within the scope of the equivalent provision of the Banking Act 1979.[3] This provision, however, referred to sums paid 'by way of security for payment for the provision of property or services' rather than 'by way of security for the performance of a contract'. Whether such payments would now be treated as payable by way of security for the performance of a contract would depend on the terms of the contract, but regulatory interest in this question has been diminished by the Financial Services Act which makes separate provision for the regulation of the carrying on of investment as opposed to deposit-taking business.

(iii)   The third and final type of payment which is excluded is money which is paid 'by way of security for the delivery up or return of any property, whether in a particular state of repair or otherwise' (s.5(2)(c)). An example of money so paid is 'caution money' required by the landlord of furnished property.

Also excluded from the definition of deposits are sums paid by persons who are presumed not to require the protection of the Act either generally or in respect of particular payments. The former include sums paid by authorised institutions and moneylenders, the latter sums paid by one company to another at a time when one is a subsidiary of the other, or both are subsidiaries of another company, and sums paid by a person who at the time it is received is a 'close relative' of the person receiving it (s.5(3)).

Deposit-taking business

The Banking Act does not prohibit the acceptance of deposits without authorisation. What it prohibits is the acceptance of deposits in the course of carrying on a business which is a deposit-taking business without authorisation. This is a different matter. One can accept deposits without being in the business of deposit-taking. Accepting a loan from a friend does not require authorisation.

A business is a deposit-taking business for the purpose of the Act if 'in the course of the business money received by way of deposit is lent to others' (s.6(1)(a)), *or* 'any other activity of the business is financed, wholly or to any material extent, out of the capital of or interest on money received by way of deposit' (s.6(1)(b)). Excluded from the definition of deposit-taking business,

---

[1] See e.g. Penn, *Banking Supervision* (1989), p. 30.   [2] [1987] 1 All E.R. 175.   [3] s.1(6)(b).

however, is what may be termed, although the Act does not use the term, 'incidental deposit-taking', i.e. the acceptance of deposits by a person who 'does not hold himself out as accepting deposits on a day-to-day basis' *and* who accepts deposits 'only on particular occasions' (s.6(2)). In *SCF Finance Co. Ltd.* v. *Masri (No. 2)*,[1] the Court of Appeal held in relation to the equivalent provision in the Banking Act 1979 that commodity brokers who addressed periodic 'requests' to their clients for payments against the costs of trans-actions entered into on their behalf did not hold themselves out as accepting deposits on a day-to-day basis within the ordinary meaning of those words. Moreover, the fact that such requests were made frequently did not, in the court's view, make them any less particular for the purpose of obtaining the benefit of the exclusion. The legislation now provides, however, that in determining whether deposits are accepted 'only on particular occasions' regard is to be had 'to the *frequency* of those occasions and to any *characteristics distinguishing* them from each other' (s.6(4)). Where deposits are accepted frequently, therefore, with no variation in the circumstances in which they are accepted, it will be difficult to resist the conclusion that the business is a deposit-taking business, notwithstanding that it does not hold itself out as accepting deposits on a day-to-day basis.

Carrying on business

To fall within the scope of the prohibition, deposits must be accepted in the course of *carrying on a business* which for the purposes of the Act is a deposit-taking business. The concept of 'carrying on business' is common to the banking, insurance and investment business regimes.[2] Its broad purpose is to exclude from the scope of a regime's concerns that which is done for non-commercial reasons or on isolated occasions only. *Commercial motivation* thus constitutes an essential element of the carrying on of business; 'the expression . . . imports that . . . it is a business carried on for some pecuniary gain'.[3] The acceptance by a club of loans from its members for the purchase of premises, for example, is therefore unlikely to constitute the carrying on of a business. No less essential an element of the carrying on of business is *repetition* or *continuity*.[4] The isolated acceptance of deposits is thus unlikely to constitute the carrying on of a business, so long of course as the person accepting them does not hold himself out as accepting deposits on a day-to-day basis and deposits are accepted only on particular occasions (s.6(2)).

---

[1] [1987] 1 All E.R. 175.   [2] See below, pp. 163–4, 240.
[3] *Graham* v. *Lewis* (1888) 22 Q.B.D. 1 at 5, *per* Fry L.J.
[4] See e.g. *Smith* v. *Anderson* (1880) 15 Ch.D. 247 at 277–8.

The territorial dimension

The prohibition applies to the acceptance of deposits *in the United Kingdom*. The business in the course of which deposits are accepted, on the other hand, may be carried on in the United Kingdom *or elsewhere*. An institution which does not hold itself out as accepting deposits in the United Kingdom, and does so only on particular occasions, will therefore require authorisation if it is carrying on a deposit-taking business elsewhere, notwithstanding that it is not carrying on a deposit-taking business in the United Kingdom.

Exemptions

The Act exempts the Bank of England and the persons specified in Schedule 2 from the prohibition on accepting deposits without authorisation (s.4(1)). For our purposes the most important exemptions are those in favour of institutions whose activities are supervised under other regimes – that is, building societies, registered friendly societies and authorised insurance companies.

Provision is also made for the exemption by order of certain classes of transactions from the prohibition (s.4(4)–(6)). Transactions to which the prohibition does not apply include deposits accepted by practising solicitors in the course of their profession, pre-contract deposits accepted in the course of estate agency work, deposits accepted by companies on terms involving the issue of sterling debt securities or sterling commercial paper, and deposits accepted by authorised or exempted persons under the Financial Services Act. Several of these exemptions are qualified. That in respect of investment businesses, for example, is confined to the acceptance of deposits by firms, acting within the scope of their authorisation or exemption, 'in the course of or for the purpose of engaging in any dealing activity with or on behalf of the person by whom or on whose behalf the deposit is made or any service activity of that person'.[1]

UNLAWFUL DEPOSIT-TAKING

The Banking Act attaches a number of possible legal consequences to the contravention of section 3 – that is, to the acceptance of deposits in the United Kingdom in the course of carrying on a deposit-taking business without authorisation or exemption. First, unlawful deposit-taking is a criminal offence punishable with up to two years imprisonment or an unlimited fine or both (s.3(2)). It is not a defence for a person to prove that he took all reasonable precautions and exercised all due diligence to avoid the commission of the offence,[2] but in practice inadvertent contraventions are not

---

[1] Banking Act 1987 (Exempt Transactions) Regs. 1988, SI 1988/646. [2] Cf. FSA, s.4(2).

prosecuted. The Bank has wide powers to investigate illegal deposit-taking, including powers to require suspects and others who are believed to have information relevant to suspected breaches of the deposit-taking prohibition to produce documents and to answer questions.[1]

Secondly, the Bank may seek an injunction (interdict in Scotland) restraining a person from contravening (or continuing to contravene) the prohibition and from dissipating his assets – in order to preserve them for the benefit of depositors – while the suspected contravention is investigated (s.93). Finally, the Bank may apply to the court for an order requiring an unauthorised business (and any other person 'knowingly involved' in the contravention) to repay illegally accepted deposits, and for a disgorgement order requiring it to disgorge, for distribution among depositors, profits that have accrued as a result of contravention of the prohibition.[2] In deciding whether to grant either type of order, the court must have regard to its effect on the solvency of the person concerned and on his ability to carry on his business in a manner satisfactory to his creditors.[3] The power to seek repayment and disgorgement orders is without prejudice to the depositor's right to sue for recovery of illegally accepted deposits, liability in respect of which is preserved by section 3(3) of the Act.

AUTHORISATION

When the 1987 Act replaced the 1979 Act institutions that were already recognised or licensed under the 1979 Act were not required to seek fresh authorisation.[4] For institutions that were not previously recognised or licensed, authorisation is at the discretion of the Bank, subject to a right of appeal to a tribunal.[5] The paramount consideration in the exercise of the Bank's discretion is the interests of depositors. It will therefore refuse to grant an application 'if it considers for any reason that there is a significant threat to the interests of depositors', notwithstanding that the criteria for authorisation set out in the Act are fulfilled.[6]

Minimum criteria

Authorisation is restricted to applicants which fulfil the minimum criteria set out in Schedule 3 to the Act (s.9(2)). The six criteria set out in the Schedule are elaborated in a *Statement of principles* which the Bank was obliged to publish in accordance with section 16 of the Act. Their significance extends beyond the initial authorisation of applicants in that an authorised institution which fails to fulfil the criteria is liable to have its authorisation revoked (s.11(1)(a)).

---

[1] ss.42–3, see above, pp. 118–19.   [2] ss.48–9.   [3] ss.48(1), 49(2).   [4] Sch. 5, para. 2.
[5] ss.9(1), 27(1).   [6] *Banking Act 1987 Section 16: Statement of principles* (1988), para. 3(1).

They must therefore be satisfied by authorised institutions on a continuing basis.

(i) *'Fit and proper' persons.* Paragraph 1 of Schedule 3 provides that the applicant's directors, controllers and managers (as defined in section 105 of the Act) must be 'fit and proper' persons to hold their positions. In common with other investor protection legislation the Act does not define what is meant by a fit and proper person. It does, however, list four factors which must be taken into account in determining whether a person is fit and proper to hold his particular position: his *probity*, his *competence and soundness of judgement* for fulfilling the responsibilities of that position, his *diligence* in fulfilling those responsibilities and whether the *interests of depositors* are, or are likely to be, in any way threatened by his holding that position.[1] As well as identifying those factors which must be taken into account, the paragraph makes explicit the Bank's power to have regard to a person's 'previous conduct and activities in business or financial matters' in assessing his fitness and properness (para.1(3)). At first glance this provision seems superfluous, since it would be impossible to assess, say, a person's probity without taking into account his previous record. An examination of the examples contained in the paragraph of the kinds of matters which may be taken into account, however, makes clear the purpose of its inclusion. Apart from, for example, a person's criminal record and his record of compliance with statutory provisions designed for the protection of the public against financial loss due to dishonesty, incompetence or malpractice, they include any evidence that the person has 'engaged in any business practices appearing to the Bank to be deceitful or oppressive or otherwise improper (*whether unlawful or not*) or which otherwise reflect discredit on his method of conducting business' (para.1(3)(c)). The Bank is therefore given express licence to use the fit and proper person test in the enforcement of its conception of proper standards of conduct in the banking industry.[2]

(ii) *'Four-eyes'.* Paragraph 2 provides that at least two individuals must effectively direct the business of the institution. This criterion – commonly referred to as the four-eyes criterion – is not just a case of two heads being better than one: it is also intended to reduce the scope for dishonest or imprudent behaviour on the part of any one individual, each individual being expected to act as a check on the other. Both persons must therefore have 'sufficient experience and knowledge of the business and the necessary personal qualities to detect and resist any imprudence, dishonesty or other irregularities on the part of the other'.[3]

(iii) *Non-executive directors.* Paragraph 3 provides that each institution incorporated in the United Kingdom must have as many non-executive directors as the Bank considers appropriate in the light of its circumstances

---

[1] Sch. 3, para. 1(2).   [2] See above, p. 87.   [3] *Statement of principles*, para. 2–24.

and the nature and scale of its operations. The basis of this requirement is the Bank's policy that each institution should have an audit committee – normally composed mainly of non-executive directors – responsible for monitoring the performance of management with respect to such matters as accounts, records, audit arrangements and compliance.

(iv) *'Prudent manner'*. Paragraph 4 provides that the business of the institution must be conducted in a prudent manner. Subsumed under this broad requirement are specific requirements in relation to the institution's capital and liquidity, which are discussed below,[1] debt provision and records and systems of control.[2] These specific requirements are not exhaustive of the range of matters taken into account in determining whether an institution satisfies, or is likely to satisfy, the prudent manner criterion; paragraph 4 also incorporates a catch-all requirement – the 'general prudent conduct' requirement – under which are examined such matters as the institution's general strategy and objectives, its policies on lending and other exposures and its management arrangements.[3] It may thus fail to satisfy the prudent manner criterion, notwithstanding that it satisfies the various specific requirements that it entails.

(v) *'Integrity and skills'*. The fit and proper person test applies to those who run the deposit-taking business. The same requirements are in effect applied to the institution itself by paragraph 5 which provides that 'the business of the institution must be carried on with the integrity and professional skills appropriate to the nature and scale of its operations.' This paragraph is interpreted as requiring 'the observance by the *institution as a whole* of the highest professional, ethical and business standards, as befits the position of authorised institutions in the financial community'.[4] An institution may thus be adjudged not 'fit and proper' even though its directors, controllers and managers are fit and proper persons.

(vi) *Minimum net assets*. Paragraph 6, finally, provides that the institution must have authorised net assets of not less than £1 million at the time it is authorised. Unlike the capital adequacy requirement, which authorised institutions must continue to fulfil, this requirement only applies at the time of authorisation.

Normally, authorisation will depend on the Bank's evaluation of an applicant. In the case of an institution whose principal place of business is outside the United Kingdom, however, the Bank may treat the fit and proper persons, prudent manner and integrity and skills requirements as satisfied if the applicant's supervisory authority informs the Bank that it is satisfied with regard to the prudent management and overall financial soundness of the

---

[1] See below, pp. 134–6.   [2] para. 4(2)–(8).   [3] para. 4(9); *Statement of principles*, para. 2.23.
[4] *Banking Supervision Guide*, 11/6.

applicant *and* the Bank is satisfied as to the nature and scope of the supervision exercised by that authority (s.9(3)).

Applications must normally be determined within six months of the date of their receipt; where additional information is required this period is extended to a maximum of twelve months (s.10(6)). An institution whose application the Bank is minded to refuse must be told the reasons, and given an opportunity to make representations, which the Bank must take into account before reaching a decision.[1] If the Bank refuses the application, the applicant must be informed of the reasons and of its right of appeal (s.10(5)). The same safeguards are extended to persons whom the Bank adjudges not to be fit and proper.[2]

Changes of control

The Bank of England has long sought to influence the ownership and control of United Kingdom banks.[3] In the face of growing difficulty in exercising control on a purely informal basis[4] the Banking Act gave the Bank power for the first time to prevent the acquisition of controlling shareholdings in authorised institutions incorporated in the United Kingdom. The Act empowers the Bank to object to a person becoming a shareholder controller or an indirect controller (as defined in section 105 of the Act) of an authorised institution where it is not satisfied (i) that the person is a fit and proper person to become a controller, (ii) that the interests of depositors and potential depositors would not be threatened by the person becoming a controller, or (iii) that the schedule 3 criteria would continue to be fulfilled (s.22). The Bank is also empowered to object to an *existing* shareholder controller on the ground that he is not or is no longer a fit and proper person to become a controller (s.24). A person who becomes or continues to be a controller in the face of an objection by the Bank faces a number of penalties including the possible loss of his shareholding.

The purpose of these powers, which may have been used to remove the Fayeds from control of Harrods Bank, is prudential; they are designed to ensure that persons acquiring control of an authorised institution satisfy the same requirements of fitness and properness as those from whom control is obtained. The Bank's attitude towards take-overs, however, is not governed solely by prudential considerations. In an important gloss on the Banking Act's provisions, the Bank, while agreeing that banks should not be insulated from competition, has underlined its opposition to the take-over of banks,

---

[1] s.10(2), (4). [2] s.10(3)–(5).

[3] Sayers, *The Bank of England 1891–1944* (1976), ch. 10; see also (1972) 12 *Bank of England Quarterly Bulletin*, 452.

[4] See *Report of the Monopolies and Mergers Commission on the Proposed Mergers involving the Royal Bank of Scotland*, Cmnd. 8472 (1982), esp. ch. 8.

especially large banks, by non-financial firms and overseas institutions, insisting as regards the latter that:

it is of the highest importance that there should be a strong and continuing British presence in the banking system of the United Kingdom. It runs counter to commonsense to argue that the openness of the London market must be carried to the point where control of the core of our financial system – the payments mechanism, the supply of credit – may pass into the hands of institutions whose business aims and national interest lie elsewhere.[1]

The dividing line between law and policy in the Bank's statement is not made clear – perhaps intentionally – but it is doubtful whether this policy, resting as it appears to on considerations of national economic sovereignty, could be enforced on the basis of the provisions outlined. What is clear is that the Bank's commitment to competition in the market for ownership and control of UK banks is heavily qualified.

The Single Market

The Second Banking Co-ordination Directive[2] will have a profound effect on the system of authorisation under the Banking Act. Once it is implemented, which is to be by January 1, 1993, institutions authorised in other Member States will no longer require authorisation from the Bank to provide banking services on a cross-border, branch or services basis (the establishment of a subsidiary will continue to require authorisation) in the United Kingdom. Responsibility for ensuring the suitability of such institutions to accept deposits in the United Kingdom will therefore belong to their home state regulator rather than to the Bank of England, which will merely require to be notified of the provision of services on a branch or services basis. Such institutions will likewise be subject to the supervision of their home state regulator rather than the Bank of England in the provision of banking services in the United Kingdom. The Bank of England, however, will retain, pending further co-ordination of national standards, primary responsibility for the supervision of liquidity and position risk.

FINANCIAL REGULATION

'The crux of banking supervision is the setting and policing of safety margins.'[3] The two key aspects of a bank's business into which safety margins are built are its capital and its liquidity. Paragraph 4 of Schedule 3 to the Act provides that an institution shall not be regarded as conducting its business in a prudent manner unless it maintains *capital*[4] of an amount commensurate with the

---

[1] 'Ownership and control of UK banks' (1987) 27 *Bank of England Quarterly Bulletin* 525 at p. 526.

[2] Dir. 89/646/EEC OJ L386/1.

[3] Farrant and Hyde, *Report on Banking Supervision in the Isle of Man December 1982* (May 1990), para. 5.

[4] Capital is defined as net assets – that is, in relation to a body corporate, paid-up capital and reserves – together with other financial resources available to the institution of such nature and amount as are considered appropriate by the Bank. Such other financial resources are in practice constituted by subordinated loan stock issued by the institution.

nature and scale of its operations, and of an amount and nature sufficient to safeguard the interests of its depositors and potential depositors. In determining the sufficiency of an institution's capital regard is to be had to the nature and scale of its operations, the risks inherent in these operations and any other factors which appear to the Bank to be relevant.[1] Paragraph 4 also provides that an institution shall not be regarded as conducting its business in a prudent manner unless it maintains *adequate liquidity*; in determining the adequacy of an institution's liquidity regard is to be had to the relationship between its liquid assets and its actual and contingent liabilities, the times at which those liabilities will or may fall due and its assets mature and the same factors as are to be taken into account in determining the sufficiency of its capital (para.4(4)).

The Bank's approach to capital adequacy and liquidity is set out in a series of supervisory notices issued by the Banking Supervision Division after consultation with the banking community.[2] Its approach to *capital adequacy* is designed to ensure that all risks of loss to which institutions may be subject are taken into account in assessing their capital adequacy; these risks include: credit risk, foreign exchange risk, interest rate and position risk, operational risk, and contagion risk.[3] For individual institutions this involves analysing the various risks to which they are exposed on the basis of regular standardised returns submitted by them to the Bank. The results of this analysis are encapsulated in the form of a minimum capital ratio, or 'trigger ratio', which is set for each institution after discussion with its senior management. A higher 'target ratio' is also set for each institution in order to lessen the risk of its trigger ratio being breached. The Bank's approach to *liquidity* is designed to ensure that each institution is able to meet its obligations when they fall due. As with the setting of capital ratios, universally applicable liquidity ratios are eschewed in favour of individually agreed guidelines which reflect the circumstances of each institution. It is through this combination of open-ended statutory requirements and administrative discretion in their elaboration and application that the flexibility of the system of prudential supervision is maintained.

Compliance with capital and liquidity requirements is monitored by means of prudential returns which banks submit on a 'voluntary' basis. Returns are analysed and then informally discussed with the management of institutions, a practice which is founded on the belief that a system of informal supervisory interviews is at least as effective as a system of formal inspections in enabling the Bank to gauge the soundness of institutions. But whereas the majority of supervisory interviews used to take place at the Bank, a substantial proportion now take place on institutions' own premises. They have also been sup-

[1] Sch. 3, para. 4(2), (3).
[2] The relevant notices are listed in paras. 2.4 and 2.14, as amended, of the Bank's *Statement of principles*.
[3] These various risks are described in para. 2.10 of the Bank's *Statement of principles*.

plemented by an intensified programme of 'detailed on-the-spot reviews'. According to the Bank such visits do not necessarily indicate that it has particular concern about an institution; nor apparently does their increased use mean that it is looking to a system of formal inspections.[1]

The intensification of supervision in the wake of Johnson Matthey has been accompanied by the prescription of criminal penalties for the provision of false or misleading information: the Act makes it an offence for any person knowingly or recklessly to provide the Bank or any other person, for example, the parent of a banking subsidiary, with information which is false or misleading (s.94(1)). It is also an offence for an authorised (or former authorised) institution to *fail* to provide the Bank with information in its possession which it knows or has reasonable cause to believe is relevant to its supervision (s.94(3)).

A further check on the reliability of information furnished for supervisory purposes is provided by the appointment of 'reporting accountants' as surrogate inspectors. In the exercise of the powers conferred by section 39(1)(b) of the Act the Bank has required authorised institutions to appoint reporting accountants to examine and report on the accuracy of prudential returns as well as on the adequacy of their internal control systems. Regular trilateral meetings are held between the Bank, the management of institutions and their reporting accountants to discuss the scope of the checks to be undertaken and their results.[2]

Auditors and reporting accountants are also expected to act as 'whistle-blowers', ensuring that any matters of concern uncovered during the course of their work are brought to the attention of the Bank.[3] Guidance issued by the accountancy profession and approved by the Bank provides that auditors and reporting accountants should take the initiative in making an *ad hoc* report 'when they consider it expedient to do so in order to protect the interests of depositors because there has been a material loss or there exists a significant risk of such a loss'. This criterion is treated as being satisfied when there has been an adverse occurrence, or a change in the auditors' or reporting accountants' perception of an existing situation, which has given rise to a material loss or the reasonable probability of a material loss, and which is such that the interests of depositors might be better safeguarded if the Bank were aware of it.[4] The guidance provides that auditors and reporting accountants should normally ask the institution to draw matters about which they are concerned to the attention of the Bank, but that in exceptional circumstances –

---

[1] Bank of England, *Report and accounts 1986*, p. 44.

[2] Guidance note on accounting and other records and internal control systems and reporting accountants' reports thereon BSD/1987/2; Guidance note on reporting accountants' reports on Bank of England returns used for prudential purposes BSD/1987/3.

[3] See above, p. 117.

[4] Auditing Practices Committee, *Banks in the United Kingdom* (March 1989); the Bank of England's relationship with auditors and reporting accountants BSD/1987/4.

where it is in the interests of depositors that the management of the institution should not be given prior warning – the auditors or reporting accountants should report direct to the Bank.

PORTFOLIO REGULATION

A feature of the Banking Act is the absence of any direct restrictions on bank lending. In order to enable the Bank to monitor credit risk, i.e. the risk of default, however, there are special reporting arrangements for large exposures. Authorised institutions whose principal place of business is in the United Kingdom are required to report to the Bank transactions exposing them to the risk of incurring losses in excess of 10 per cent of their available capital resources, and to give *prior notice* of transactions which could result in their being exposed to the risk of incurring losses in excess of 25 per cent of those resurces.[1] A failure to report is a criminal offence (s.38(9)). The Bank's policy on large exposures provides that no exposure to a single party should exceed 10 per cent of an institution's capital base without 'thorough justification', and that no such exposure should exceed 25 per cent of its capital base other than in 'the most exceptional circumstances'. An institution which wishes to exceed these limits, and which can justify doing so, will normally be required to hold additional capital against the risk of default.[2]

INFORMATION AND INVESTIGATIONS

The Bank has wide powers to obtain information and to appoint investigators. Its information powers extend to such information, reports from reporting accountants and documents as it may reasonably require for the performance of its functions under the Act.[3] It may also obtain information and documents from connected persons.[4] Failure 'without reasonable excuse' to comply with a requirement imposed in the exercise of these powers is a criminal offence (s.39(11)). These powers have been used on a total of 25 occasions in the last five years.

Investigators may be appointed to investigate and report on the nature, conduct or state of an institution's business, or any aspect of it, where to do so appears desirable in the interests of its depositors or potential depositors; they may also be appointed to investigate the ownership and control of an institution (s.41(1)). Persons connected with an institution under investigation, such as its directors, controllers and employees, may be required to

[1] s.38(1), (2).

[2] Large exposures undertaken by institutions authorised under the Banking Act 1987, BSD/1987/1.

[3] s.39(1), (3). The power to order disclosure is not negated by a court order restraining an institution from disclosing documents to any third party pending trial of an action against it: *A and others* v. *B Bank, Bank of England intervening, Financial Times*, May 15, 1991.

[4] s.39(6), (7), (10).

produce documents, to attend before investigators and otherwise to give them all assistance in connection with the investigation which they are reasonably able to give (s.41(5)). A failure 'without reasonable excuse' to comply with a requirement imposed in the exercise of these powers, is a criminal offence.[1] The Act also makes it an offence, for a person to falsify, conceal, destroy or otherwise dispose of documents relevant to an investigation unless he can prove that he had no intention of concealing the facts disclosed by the documents (s.44). Investigators have been appointed on a total of 21 occasions in the last five years.

POWERS OF INTERVENTION

Revocation

The ultimate sanction at the Bank's disposal is the revocation of an institution's authorisation. The grounds on which the Bank's power of revocation are exercisable are set out in section 11 of the Act. They cover a wide diversity of circumstances ranging from the making of a winding-up order against an institution in the United Kingdom – in which case revocation is mandatory – to a failure to comply with any obligation imposed on an institution by or under the Act.[2] Some of the grounds are drawn in extremely wide terms. Thus the Bank may act to revoke an institution's authorisation where any of the criteria specified in Schedule 3 'is not or has not been fulfilled *or may not be or may not have been fulfilled*' (s.11(1)(a)); in other words it may act where the position is unclear. It may also revoke an institution's authorisation where the interests of its depositors or potential depositors 'are in any other way threatened, whether by the manner in which the institution is conducting *or proposes to conduct its affairs or for any other reason*' (s.11(1)(e)). In the final analysis, therefore, an institution's authorisation may be revoked wherever the Bank considers it warranted in the interests of depositors.

The exercise of the power of revocation is subject to elaborate safeguards. Except where revocation is mandatory, an institution whose authorisation the Bank is minded to revoke must be given notice and an opportunity to make representations which the Bank must take into account before reaching a final decision.[3] If the Bank decides to revoke, the institution has a right of appeal to the tribunal and the revocation of its authorisation does not have effect until either the time-limit for lodging an appeal has expired or its appeal is determined or withdrawn (s.27(4)). The protection of depositors during this period is secured by empowering the Bank, when it initiates revocation proceedings, to give an institution directions *with immediate effect* as to the

---

[1] s.41(9). As to the concept of reasonable excuse, see *Governor of the Bank of England* v. *Riley*, above, p. 118.
[2] s.11(6)(a), 1(b).   [3] s.13(1), (3), (5)–(7).

conduct of its business (s.19(1)(a)). The directions which may be given are such as appear to the Bank to be desirable in the interests of the institution's depositors or potential depositors, whether for the purpose of safeguarding its assets or otherwise. They may, in particular, require an institution to take certain steps or to refrain from adopting or pursuing a particular course of action or to restrict the scope of its business in a particular way; impose limitations on the acceptance of deposits, the granting of credit or the making of investments; prohibit the institution from accepting deposits either generally or from persons who are not already depositors; prohibit it from entering into any other transaction or class of transaction; and require the removal of any director, controller or manager (s.19(2)). It is an offence for an institution to fail to comply with any requirement or to contravene any prohibition imposed on it by a direction (s.19(6)).

Restriction

Where there are grounds for revoking an institution's authorisation the Bank is empowered, as a less drastic alternative, to restrict its authorisation (s.12(1)). It may do so by imposing a time-limit, which must not exceed three years, by imposing conditions, or by imposing a combination of a time-limit and conditions. The conditions which may be imposed are such as the Bank thinks desirable for the protection of the institution's depositors or potential depositors (s.12(2)(b)). They include the same requirements as to the conduct of an institution's business as may be imposed by means of directions with the addition of 'requirements to be fulfilled otherwise than by action taken by the institution' (s.12(4)(b)). This would cover, for example, action to be taken by the parent of a banking subsidiary. The same procedural requirements as attach to the revocation of an institution's authorisation attach to its restriction, with the difference that the requirement of notice can be dispensed with in cases of urgency.[1] It is an offence for an institution to fail to comply with any requirement or to contravene any prohibition imposed on it by a condition (s.12(6)).

The power to restrict rather than revoke an institution's authorisation is expressed to be exercisable where 'the circumstances are not such as to justify revocation' (s.12(1)(b)). In deciding whether the circumstances justify revocation the Bank has primary regard to the prospects for remedial action, its policy being to 'preserve' banks wherever possible. 'We take the view that it must be right except in an overwhelming case to try to preserve rather than to try to terminate a banking institution.'[2] As a general rule, therefore, it will only revoke an institution's authorisation where there is 'no reasonable prospect of speedy and comprehensive remedial action'; in such circumstances it will do

[1] ss.13(1)–(3), (5)–(7), 14(1).
[2] Treasury and Civil Service Committee, *Banking Supervision and BCCI* 1990–1 HC 636-i, p. 2.

so 'even though the threat to depositors [is] not immediate, for example because the institution currently [has] adequate capital and liquidity'.[1] An institution's authorisation is likely to be restricted, on the other hand, 'where the Bank considers that the imposition of conditions is necessary to underpin the institution's efforts to improve matters, and that there is a reasonable prospect that all the relevant criteria for authorisation will be fulfilled again within a reasonable period'.[2] A time-limited authorisation is normally imposed to facilitate an orderly repayment of deposits by avoiding liquidity pressures which could arise from a sudden loss of authorisation. An institution's authorisation may also be restricted as a holding measure to protect depositors and potential depositors whilst further information is sought.

The Bank has exercised the power to revoke authorisation on a total of six occasions in the last five years and its power to restrict authorisation on thirteen occasions over the same period. These figures are not a full record of the exercise of the Bank's powers, since some institutions prefer to surrender their authorisation rather than face outright revocation. An institution which has surrendered its authorisation remains subject to the Bank's supervision until it has repaid all its deposit liabilities.

The Bank's powers to revoke and restrict authorisation do not preclude remedial action by other means. In its *Statement of principles*, the Bank states that it would be generally reluctant to revoke or restrict an institution's authorisation where adequate and speedy remedial steps are likely to be taken by an authorised institution and such action would protect the interests of depositors and potential depositors. It will therefore explore fully the prospects of remedial action in so far as this is consistent with the interests of depositors. If, however, 'the financial position of the institution is weak or is deteriorating rapidly, the scope for such inquiries will be limited. The Bank has to balance the interests of existing depositors, for whom it may be desirable to continue the authorisation in order to allow more time for the scope of remedial action to be explored, and the interests of potential depositors who could be exposed to a risk of loss.'[3]

The Bank's policy towards remedial action and the exercise of its powers of intervention has come under intense scrutiny in the wake of the closure of the Bank of Credit and Commerce International in July 1991. At the time of writing the Bingham inquiry is not yet complete, but in its report on *Banking Supervision and BCCI* the Treasury and Civil Service Committee concluded that there was little evidence to suggest that the remedial action on which the Bank had initially pinned its faith satisfied the requirements of adequacy and speed laid down in its *Statement of principles*.[4] It also questioned whether the Bank was not too committed to 'preserving' rather than 'terminating'

[1] *Statement of principles*, para. 5.4.   [2] para. 5.5.   [3] paras. 5.3–5.5.
[4] Fourth Report from the Treasury and Civil Service Committee (1992, HC 177), para. 32.

institutions: while the desirability of continuing an authorisation in order to allow more time for the scope for remedial action to be explored was fully understandable, it appeared to have led to a climate of opinion in the Bank which 'favoured reconstruction and reform rather than restrictions and closure.' In the Committee's view a clear distinction fell to be drawn between cases involving a lack of solvency and those involving a lack of probity. Where the latter was involved the criteria for authorisation should be strictly enforced.[1]

APPEALS

An institution which is aggrieved by a decision of the Bank to refuse its application for authorisation, to revoke or restrict its authorisation or to give it directions has a right of appeal to a tribunal (s.27(1)). A person who is adjudged not to be fit and proper or whose removal from office is required also has a right of appeal (s.27(2)).

The scope of appeals is confined to the *legality* of the Bank's decision, the question for the determination of the tribunal being whether for the reasons adduced by the appellant the decision was unlawful or not justified by the evidence on which it was based.[2] The tribunal may confirm or reverse the Bank's decision, or if the Bank's decision was to revoke the institution's authorisation it may direct the Bank to restrict it instead. The tribunal may also direct the Bank to impose different restrictions or directions. In such cases it is for the Bank to decide what restrictions or directions to give.

Both the appellant and the Bank may appeal to the High Court (or the Court of Session in Scotland) on any question of law arising from the tribunal's decision. If the court is of the opinion that the decision was erroneous in law, it must remit the matter to the tribunal. A further appeal lies, with leave, to the Court of Appeal (or the House of Lords in Scottish cases).[3]

Although the knowledge that its decisions may have to be defended before a tribunal undoubtedly serves as a check on the exercise by the Bank of its powers, the right of appeal is one that is seldom exercised. The majority of institutions, it would appear, prefer not to proceed with an application, or to surrender quietly, rather than face outright refusal or revocation. Of the few appeals that are lodged, most are withdrawn and of those that have proceeded to a determination none has been successful.

COMPENSATION

The Banking Act 1979 established a deposit protection scheme which is

---

[1] *Ibid.*, para. 40; the Committee also questioned the Bank's failure to restrict BCCI's authorisation once doubts about the probity with which its operations were being conducted had arisen: para. 36.
[2] s.29(1), (5).   [3] s.31.

continued by its successor. The scheme makes provision for the payment of compensation to depositors with failed institutions from a deposit protection fund. The fund is financed by contributions from authorised institutions and administered by a separate Deposit Protection Board whose members are drawn from the Bank of England and contributing institutions (s.50).

The measure of compensation payable under the scheme is currently fixed at 75 per cent of the first £20,000 of sterling deposits made with the United Kingdom offices of an institution.[1] Secured deposits and deposits with a term of more than five years are excluded for the purpose of determining an institution's liability to a depositor, as are deposits made after an institution ceased to be authorised (s.60(6)). The ceiling of £20,000 effectively confines the scope of protection to relatively small personal depositors; large depositors are expected to look out for their own interests. The limitation of cover to 75 per cent, however, is designed to give even small depositors an incentive to be discerning, though whether it is at all realistic to expect depositors to judge the soundness of an institution must be doubted.[2]

The Banking Act 1979 provided for a fund of between £5 million and £6 million to be raised by initial contributions from institutions. New institutions are required to make an initial contribution to the fund (s.53). Should the amount of the fund fall below £3 million the Board is empowered to levy further contributions to restore it to its original amount (s.54). Special contributions may be levied whenever payments are expected to exhaust the resources of the fund before the end of a financial year (s.55). Contributions are calculated as a percentage of each institution's sterling deposit base. A maximum of £300,000 is specified for initial and further contributions and an institution's contributions under all calls must not exceed 0.3 per cent of its sterling deposit base (s.56). The Board also has power to borrow.[3]

Payments fall to be made either on the insolvency of an authorised (or formerly authorised) institution or on an administration order under the insolvency legislation being made against it.[4] The Board may adjust the amount of compensation to reflect the availability of compensation under other schemes (s.58(3)). It may also decline to make a payment to a depositor who may have had any responsibility for, or may have profited from the circumstances giving rise to the institution's financial difficulties (s.58(5)). Since the scheme's inception payments have been made to depositors with some sixteen failed institutions. For most of this period the amount paid in compensation has been very small, but in the last two years it has risen steeply.

---

[1] ss.58(1), 60(1).   [2] See above, p. 72.
[3] s.64; the Deposit Protection Board (Increase of Borrowing Limit) Order 1991, SI 1991/1604.
[4] s.58(1), (2).

9
Building Societies

Background

Building societies, like banks, are deposit-taking institutions; what distinguishes them from banks is that their purpose and powers are defined by statute. They were first recognised by statute in 1836, when provision was made for the application of the friendly societies legislation to them. But in 1874, following the report of the Royal Commission on Friendly Societies, a separate legal framework was established for them. This defined the purpose for which a building society could be established as that 'of raising by the subscription of the members a stock or fund for making advances to members out of the funds of the society upon security of freehold, copyhold or leasehold estate, by way of mortgage . . .'[1] The effect of this definition of their purpose, in combination with the powers permitted them by the legislation, was to confine societies to a narrow range of relatively low-risk activities – making advances on the security of mortgage, raising funds from which advances could be made and activities ancillary to these purposes.

The trend of subsequent amendments to this legislation, which was consolidated in 1962, was to restrict still further the activities building societies were allowed to undertake. The Building Societies Act 1960, for example, was enacted following the exposure of malpractice at the State Building Society, one of a number of 'rogue' societies which 'presented themselves to potential investors as normal building societies, but used the money invested with them to finance property transactions far removed from the bulk of normal building society lending'.[2] If the practice of raising risk capital 'by trading on the good will and prestige which has grown up around the building societies' were to continue unchecked, Viscount Hailsham argued in moving the second reading of the legislation,

---

[1] Building Societies Act 1874, s.13.
[2] Cleary, *The Building Society Movement* (1965), p. 260.

a number of people who were under the impression that they had put their savings into an institution engaged in lending money to owner-occupiers on mortgage, which should offer them a very large measure of security, would find from time to time that they had lost some, or all, of their investment . . . [and] if there were . . . a series of events of this kind, it might be expected that a general loss of confidence might be engendered in building societies generally.[1]

The Act therefore limited the amounts societies could lend to companies and in large single amounts.

Building societies continued to be governed by the narrow definition of their purpose adopted in 1874 until their powers were redefined, and their legal framework recast, by the Building Societies Act 1986. This legislation was enacted principally in response to the increased competition to which societies found themselves exposed in the markets for housing finance and personal savings from 1980 onwards. Faced with an upsurge in competition from a combination of the banks and National Savings, the Building Societies Association argued that its members were prevented from responding as they would have liked by the restrictions on their powers, which prevented them from offering a full range of financial (and house buying) services to their customers. It therefore sought the freedom for its members to compete on more equal terms with other providers of financial services.[2] Among building societies particular importance was attached to securing an increase in their powers by the small number of very large societies, which had grown to dominate the movement, and which chafed increasingly at the restrictions to which societies were subject.

The Building Societies Act loosened the restraints to which societies had been subject by empowering them to hold new forms of assets and to provide new types of services. But it stopped short of removing them entirely. In its initial response to the Building Societies Association's proposals, which had been revised with a view to increasing the likelihood of their acceptance, the Government agreed that societies should be allowed to diversify their business, but insisted that their primary role should continue to be that of specialists in housing finance and personal savings: 'Our purpose is to ensure that the building societies continue primarily in their traditional roles – holding people's savings securely and lending for house purchase – while loosening the legal restraints under which they have operated for a century or more so that they can develop in other fields.'[3] The Act therefore made it a condition of the establishment of a building society that its primary (if not its only) purpose must continue to be that 'of raising, primarily by the subscriptions of the members, a stock or fund for making to them advances secured on land for their residential use'.[4]

[1] HL Debs, 5th ser. vol. 222, col. 1009, April 12, 1960.
[2] Building Societies Association, *New Legislation for Building Societies* (1984).
[3] *Building Societies: A New Framework*, Cmnd. 9316 (1984), p. 1.   [4] BSA, s.5(1).

No sooner had the Building Societies Act come into force, however, than criticisms of the narrowness of the terms in which the powers to provide new services were expressed forced a comprehensive review of them. This review led to a further increase in the range of services building societies were permitted to provide, so that a building society may now provide, subject to certain limitations, banking, investment, insurance, trusteeship, executorship and land services (and a relaxation of the associated limits on the amount of ancillary business they can carry on).[1] It did not, however, result in any alteration of the basic stipulation that the primary purpose of a building society must remain that of raising funds from individual members for lending to other members on the security of first mortgage on owner-occupied residential property.

Building societies, unlike banks, are therefore subject to two systems of control. One is a system of prudential supervision akin to that applied to banks which, in the anticipation of societies' diversification into more risky kinds of business, is designed to ensure that they remain a safe place for investors' money. 'The free play of competition between financial institutions must always be tempered by the need to ensure the protection of investors. Any move by societies into the provision of new services should not detract from their traditional security for investors.'[2] Although the prudential regime operated by the Registry of Friendly Societies had been strengthened prior to the Act's introduction, the Registry's powers were in some respects deficient. The Act therefore gave the Commission the necessary powers 'to complete the shift of the Registry's prudential system from [a] "reactive approach", with the supervisor only intervening when something had started to go wrong, to the more positive and forward-looking approach implicit in an authorisation system'.[3]

The second system of control, which has no banking counterpart, is a system of 'nature limits' designed to preserve the distinctive character of building societies as member-based institutions, primarily engaged in raising funds from their members and lending them to other members for the purpose of owner-occupation. These limits have been described as the price which a building society must pay to retain its mutual status and the right to call itself a building society.[4] For societies which find this price too high, the legislation offers the alternative, subject to the agreement of its members, of conversion to a company regulated in respect of its deposit-taking business by the Bank of England. Despite criticisms that the price is too high, only one society – the Abbey National Building Society – has converted so far.

---

[1] The Building Societies (Commercial Assets and Services) Order 1988, SI 1988/1141; amended by the Building Societies (Provision of Services) Order 1989, SI 1989/839.

[2] *Building Societies: A New Framework*, para. 1.11.

[3] *Annual Report of the Building Societies Commission 1986–87*, para. 2.8.

[4] *Report of the Chief Registrar 1983–1984*, p. 20.

AUTHORISATION

A building society requires authorisation to raise funds and to borrow money. Section 9(1) of the Act provides that, subject to limited exceptions, a society 'shall not raise money from members or accept deposits of money unless there is in force an authorisation of the Commission'. Breach of this prohibition is a criminal offence punishable in the case of a society by an unlimited fine and in the case of its officers by imprisonment for up to two years or an unlimited fine or both (s.9(11)). Civil liability in respect of acceptances and of money accepted is expressly preserved by the Act and an investor may therefore sue for their recovery (s.9(11)).

The Act makes provision for applications for authorisation to raise funds and borrow money to be made in three sets of circumstances. The first is where a newly formed society seeks authorisation for the first time (s.9(4)). New societies are rare: only one has been registered under the provisions of the 1986 Act. The second is where an authorised society is directed by the Commission to seek renewal of its authorisation (s.41(1)); and the third is where a society's authorisation has either expired, following a refusal by the Commission to renew it, or been revoked on one of the discretionary grounds provided by section 43(1) of the Act (s.44(1)).

In all three cases, authorisation may be granted unconditionally or subject to conditions. The power to grant or renew authorisation subject to conditions relieves the Commission of the necessity of making a difficult choice between refusing to grant or renew authorisation, in the certain knowledge that it would spell the end of a society, or prevent its revival, and granting or renewing authorisation while retaining reservations about the security of investments placed with it. It can therefore address its prudential concerns by attaching suitable conditions to a society's authorisation.

Initial authorisation

Section 9(4) of the Act sets out four requirements which an applicant for initial authorisation must satisfy.

(i) *Minimum qualifying capital.* The first requirement is that the society must have qualifying capital of an amount which is not less than the prescribed minimum, which is currently set at £100,000 (s.9(13)). This amount represents a compromise between the minimum capital requirement of £1 million for deposit-taking institutions under the Banking Act, and the need in the case of a mutual institution, without access to conventional risk capital, not to set a threshold so high that it is impossible for a new society to become authorised in future.[1] In the absence of access to outside capital, provision is made for this

---

[1] Chief Registrar of Friendly Societies, *Building Societies Act 1986: Capital Adequacy* (1986), para. 8.13.

sum to be raised by the issue of deferred shares without prior authorisation up to a maximum of £250,000.[1]

(ii) *'Fit and proper' persons*. The second requirement is that the holders of specific key posts in the direction and management of the society – the chairman of the board of directors and any executive directors, the chief executive, the secretary and the managers (if any) – must each be fit and proper persons to hold their respective offices. In common with other investor protection legislation the concept of a fit and proper person is not defined, but in considering whether this requirement is satisfied, the Commission will take account of both the context, including the nature and scale of the business proposed to be conducted, and the specific duties, responsibilities and powers assigned to a particular post, and factors personal to the individual, ranging from his integrity, reputation and character, through his qualifications, experience and competence to possible conflicts of interest and his commitment to fulfilling the duties involved.[2]

(iii) *'Prudent management'*. The third requirement is that the board of directors, together with the chief executive and secretary, must have the capacity and intention to direct the affairs of the society in accordance with 'the criteria of prudent management', and insofar as those criteria fell to be satisfied before the date of the application, must have secured that they were satisfied. The criteria of prudent management are set out in section 45(3) of the Act. Like the analogous 'prudent manner' requirement applicable to banks, they embrace a series of specific requirements in relation to societies' capital and liquidity, structure of commercial assets, arrangements for assessing the adequacy of securities for advances secured on land, records and systems of control, direction and management and the conduct of their business. These requirements constitute the core of continuing prudential obligations upon authorised building societies. A failure by an authorised society to satisfy any of them entitles the Commission to assume that it has prejudiced the security of the investments of shareholders and depositors, so that it may be expedient for it to intervene in order to protect those investments.[3]

(iv) *Protection of investments*. The final requirement, which reflects the fact that authorisation may be granted subject to conditions, is that the investments of shareholders and depositors (who include potential shareholders and depositors (s.119(1)) will be adequately protected without the imposition of conditions.

Authorisation falls to be granted unconditionally where the Commission is satisfied that all four requirements are met; if it is so satisfied it *must* grant unconditional authorisation (s.9(4)). Authorisation falls to be granted subject

[1] s.9(3)(a); Building Societies (Deferred Shares) Order 1991, SI 1991/207.
[2] Guidance Note: Authorisation Under Section 9. [3] See below, pp. 156–7.

to conditions, on the other hand, if the Commission is satisfied that the first two requirements at least are met and that the imposition of conditions would secure the protection of the investments of shareholders and depositors; if it is so satisfied it is obliged to grant authorisation subject to such conditions as it thinks fit to secure their protection (s.9(5)(b)). If, however, it is not satisfied that the first two requirements are met, or that the imposition of conditions would secure the protection of the investment of shareholders and depositors, it must refuse to grant authorisation (s.9(5)(a)).

Renewal of authorisation

The Act did not require societies that were already authorised to seek fresh authorisation.[1] Most of these societies had been automatically authorised when the requirement of authorisation was first introduced in implementation of the First Banking Co-ordination Directive in 1981.[2] To guard against the possibility that they might include societies that would not satisfy the requirements for authorisation, the Act gave the Commission the power (for five years in the first instance) to direct any society whose business it has reason to believe is, or may be, being conducted in a way that may not adequately protect the investments of shareholders and depositors to apply for renewal of its authorisation.[3] If a society fails to apply for renewal of its authorisation within the period allowed, its authorisation must be revoked (s.43(3)(c)). The same requirements as apply to applications for initial authorisation apply to applications for the renewal of authorisation, save that an applicant must also satisfy the requirement, which forms part of the criteria of prudent management, that it has adequate reserves and other designated capital resources. Authorisation must be renewed unconditionally if the Commission is satisfied that all five requirements are met, and subject to conditions if it is satisfied that their imposition would secure protection of the investments of shareholders and depositors.[4] Otherwise authorisation must be refused (s.41(7)(b)).

Reauthorisation

The normal consequence of the revocation of a society's authorisation is for its business to be transferred to another society. The Act, however, leaves open the possibility of its reauthorisation. Applications for reauthorisation fall to be assessed against the same requirements as applications for the renewal of authorisation. Authorisation must be granted unconditionally if the Commis-

---

[1] Sch. 20, para. 6.   [2] Building Societies (Authorisation) Regs. 1981, SI 1981/1488.
[3] s.41(1). This power was continued for a further five years by the Building Societies Act 1986 (Continuation of section 41) Order 1991, SI 1991/1518.
[4] s.41(6), (7)(a).

sion is satisfied that all five requirements are met, and subject to conditions if the Commission is satisfied that the minimum capital and fit and proper persons requirements at least are met, and that the imposition of conditions would secure the protection of the investments of shareholders and depositors.[1] Otherwise authorisation must be refused (s.44(5)(a)).

The conditions to which a society's authorisation may be made subject in the exercise of these powers may relate to any of its activities, not just those for which authorisation is required – the raising of money from members and the acceptance of loans and deposits. They may require the society to take certain steps or to refrain from adopting a particular course of action or to restrict the scope of its business in a particular way. In particular, they may impose limitations on the issue of shares, acceptance of deposits or the making of advances or other loans; require the society to take steps with regard to the conduct of the business of any subsidiary or associated body; and require the removal of any director or other officer.[2] A failure to comply with conditions to which its authorisation is subject renders a society liable to have its authorisation revoked.[3]

Applications for initial authorisation or reauthorisation must normally be determined within six months of the date of their receipt; where additional information is required this period is extended to a maximum of twelve months.[4] Where the application is for the renewal of a society's authorisation these periods are reduced to three months and six months.[5] A society whose application the Commission proposes to refuse or to grant subject to conditions must be informed of its intention, the reasons for it, and given an opportunity to make representations, which the Commission must take into account before reaching a final decision.[6] If the application is refused or granted or renewed subject to conditions, the society has a right of appeal to a tribunal (s.46(1)). The same safeguards are extended to individuals whom the Commission adjudges not to be fit and proper or whose removal from office is required.[7]

FINANCIAL REGULATION

Building societies, like banks, are required to observe specific capital adequacy and liquidity requirements. The sole reference to capital adequacy in the Building Societies Act is contained in the criteria of prudent management, the first of which requires a society to maintain reserves and other designated capital resources, at a level which is adequate, having regard to the range and scale of the present and proposed business of the society including the business of any subsidiaries or other associates.[8] A building

---

[1] s.44(4), (5)(b). [2] ss.9(6), (7); 41(9); 44(6). [3] ss.9(12); 43(1)(c).
[4] Sch.3, para. 2(7), (8). [5] Sch. 3, para. 2(9). [6] Sch. 3, paras. 2(4),(6), 4(1),(3).
[7] Sch.3, paras. 2(5), 4(2); s.46(2). [8] s.45(3)1, (10).

society's primary capital consists of its reserves, that is, the excess of its assets over its liabilities, built up from accumulated operating surpluses over the years. Traditionally, a building society's sole source of capital was its reserves, but provision has been made for the issue of subordinated long-term debt and permanent interest bearing shares (PIBS) by societies, which may be aggregated with their reserves for the purpose of assessing their capital adequacy.[1]

The Commission's approach to capital adequacy is set out in a series of prudential notes issued after consultation with the industry.[2] Like the Bank of England's approach to capital adequacy for deposit-taking institutions, on which it is modelled, it is designed to ensure that the various financial risks to which building societies are exposed are taken into account in assessing their capital adequacy.[3] Capital adequacy requirements for building societies are set on an individual basis. Two requirements are set for each society: the 'minimum acceptable level', below which a society and the investors in it will be at risk, and 'the desired capital', which is a higher figure designed to reduce the risk of the minimum acceptable level being breached. These requirements are arrived at by applying a calculus to the main elements of the society's balance sheet and some 'off balance sheet' items as a starting point for a dialogue between its board and senior management and the Commission as a result of which definitive versions of these requirements are fixed.

The third criterion of prudent management requires a building society to maintain adequate assets in liquid form (s.45(3)3.) 'Adequate' and 'liquid form' are both defined by reference to section 21(1) of the Act, which provides that 'a building society shall secure that, of its total assets, it keeps such a proportion of them having such composition as will at all times enable the society to meet its liabilities as they arise.' In deciding on the amount and composition of its liquid assets for this purpose, a society must have regard to the range and scale of its business, including business it proposes to carry on, and the composition and character of its assets and liabilities; it must also have regard to the range and scale of the business, and the composition and character of the assets and liabilities, of any associated bodies.[4] Liquidity margins are set by building societies themselves, rather than by the Commission, in the light of guidance from the Commission on the management and composition of liquid assets portfolios.[5]

A building society may keep a greater proportion of its assets in liquid form

---

[1] Building Societies (Supplementary Capital) Order 1988, SI 1988/777; Building Societies (Designated Capital Resources) (Permanent Interest Bearing Shares) Order 1991, SI 1991/702.

[2] 1987/1: Capital Adequacy – A Framework for Assessment; 1988/2: Capital Requirements for Off-Balance Sheet Mortgage Lending; 1990/1: Capital Adequacy and Class 1 Advances; 1991/1: Capital Adequacy for Class 1 Lending.

[3] These risks are discussed in Prudential Note 1987/1, section 3.   [4] s.21(3), (4), (10).

[5] Prudential Note 1987/3: Liquidity.

than is required for the purpose of meeting its liabilities (s.21(2)). The proportion must not, however, exceed 33.33 per cent of its total assets (s.21(3)(a)). This is a 'nature' rather than a prudential limit, designed to ensure that the bulk of a building society's funds are applied to its primary purpose – the provision of housing finance – rather than investment in gilt-edged stocks and other money market instruments.[1] A society which exceeds this limit may be required by the Commission to submit a restructuring plan for its approval, which will bring it back within the limit, or a resolution to its members for the transfer of its business to a company.[2]

A building society is also restricted in the investment of its liquid funds, whether held for the purpose of meeting its liabilities as they arise or otherwise, to assets of a character authorised by the Commission.[3] The liquid assets which a society may hold are prescribed by the Building Societies (Liquid Asset) Regulations 1991.[4] They include Treasury Bills, gilt-edged securities, bank deposits, certificates of deposit and floating rate notes issued by a bank or building society, and local authority securities and loans.

Building societies are subject to less intensive monitoring of their capital and liquidity than banks. No criminal penalties are prescribed for the provision of information which is false or misleading, or for a failure to provide information relevant to a building society's supervision,[5] but each society is required to establish and maintain systems of control and of inspection and report such as to secure that its business is so conducted and its records so kept that 'the information regularly obtained by or furnished to the Commission under or for the purposes of [the] Act is sufficiently accurate for the purpose for which it is obtained or furnished and is regularly furnished'.[6] A failure to comply with this requirement, which constitutes one of the criteria of prudent management, creates a presumption that the society has prejudiced the interests of investors, and so raises the question of whether the Commission should use its prudential powers to make its continued authorisation subject to conditions or to revoke its authorisation altogether.

The directors and chief executive of a building society are required to make and send to the Commission each year a statement of their opinion as to whether this requirement has been met (s.71(11)). A further check is provided by requiring the society's auditors to report annually to the Commission on whether in their opinion its systems comply with it.[7] This involves checking a sample of the returns made. This is only one aspect of the wider relationship between the Commission and building society auditors which may involve, for example, bilateral meetings between the Commission and a society's auditors to discuss the approach to be adopted to its audit. Trilateral meetings between

---

[1] *Building Societies: A New Framework*, para. 2.10. [2] s.21(9); see below, p. 154.
[3] s.21(3)(b). [4] SI 1991/2580.
[5] Contrast the position under the Banking Act: above, p. 136.
[6] s.71(1), (6), (7); Prudential Note 1987/4: Systems. [7] s.82(1)–(3).

the Commission, a society and its auditors may also be held, but in contrast to banking supervision such meetings are not a regular feature of the supervisory process.[1]

Auditors are also entitled, under section 82(8) of the Act, to furnish information obtained during the course of their audit work to the Commission when either they or the Commission are satisfied that it is expedient for them to do so in order to protect the investments of shareholders or depositors. Prudential Note 1986/2 – Relationships between Auditors and the Commission – sets out the circumstances in which the Commission expects auditors to take the initiative and approach it with information in order to protect the investments of shareholders or depositors. It provides that they should do so where there has been an occurrence, including a change in circumstances, or a change in the auditor's perception of an existing situation, which involves an actual or potential risk which is or may be relevant to the security of investments of shareholders and depositors, and which is such that investments might be better safeguarded if the Commission was aware of the position (para.13). It envisages that the auditor should first seek to persuade the society itself to inform the Commission, but that in the most exceptional circumstances – where the auditor is of the opinion that informing the society of his concern might of itself prejudice the security of investors – the Commission should be informed without the society's knowledge.[2]

PORTFOLIO REGULATION

To retain its mutual status and the right to describe itself as a building society, a society must confine its activities to those allowed to building societies by the legislation. It must also observe limits on its pattern of business as expressed in certain balance sheet ratios. These limits are not of themselves prudential. Instead, their purpose is to ensure that the mainstream business of building societies continues to be that of raising funds from the public and lending them for the purpose of owner occupation. However, they also contribute to the prudential strength of building societies in that they limit their exposure to riskier forms of borrowing and lending.

On the assets side of the balance sheet, these ratios are expressed in the form of commercial asset structure requirements, a building society's commercial assets being its assets other than its fixed and liquid assets. For the purpose of setting these requirements, a society's commercial assets are divided into three classes: class 1 assets, which consist of societies' traditional business, namely advances secured by first mortgage of residential property occupied by the borrower; class 2 assets, which consist of other advances fully secured on land;

---

[1] Prudential Note 1986/2: Relationships between Auditors and the Commission.
[2] paras. 16–17; see also Auditing Practices Committee, *Building Societies in the United Kingdom* (1989), paras. 166–77.

and class 3 assets, which consist of unsecured loans, ownership of land for residential purposes and investment in subsidiaries and associates.

Under the limits originally imposed by the 1986 legislation, class 1 assets had to account for at least 90 per cent of a building society's total commercial assets with no more than 5 per cent of the remaining 10 per cent taking the form of the riskier class 3 assets.[1] However, these limits were found almost immediately to be too restrictive, and the decision was therefore taken to relax them in stages, to the maximum extent allowed by the legislation, so that by 1 January 1993 class 1 assets will have to account for a minimum of only 75 per cent of a society's total commercial assets with up to 15 per cent of the remaining 25 per cent being in the form of class 3 assets.[2]

On the liabilities side of the balance sheet, the Act introduced for the first time a limit on the proportion of its funds a building society may raise from the wholesale markets. This limit was intended to maintain societies' traditional role as a home for personal savings, and also to limit their exposure to a more volatile source of funding. It was initially fixed at 20 per cent of a society's total liabilities in respect of shares and deposits in the confident expectation that it would be some considerable time before it would have to be reviewed, but it was raised almost immediately to the maximum of 40 per cent permitted by the legislation to allow societies to remain competitive in the mortgage market, graphically illustrating the continuing tension between the desire to retain the traditional character of building societies on the one hand, and the need to give them sufficient freedom to prosper on the other.[3]

There is no automatic entitlement to raise this amount from wholesale sources. Because of the more volatile character of non-retail funding, a society that wishes to raise more than 5 per cent of its funds from wholesale sources is required to agree with the Commission a limit on the proportion of non-retail funds it may hold, linked to a funding policy, and to satisfy it that it has the necessary management capacity and expertise to operate that policy within the agreed limit.[4] Increased reliance on wholesale funding may also reduce the security of shareholders, since their claims on a building society's reserves rank after those of depositors and other non-traditional providers of funds in the event of its being wound up. A society whose wholesale funding rises significantly may therefore be required to increase its capital backing to offset the dilution of the protection which its reserves afford to shareholders.[5]

The 1986 Act also stipulates that at least 50 per cent of a building society's funds must be subscribed in the form of shares rather than deposits (s.8(1)). The significance of this requirement lies in the fact that shareholders are members of a building society, with a voice in the running of its affairs, unlike

---

[1] s.20(2), (3).   [2] The Building Societies (Limits on Commercial Assets) Order 1988, SI 1988/1142.
[3] s.7(3), (15); Building Societies (Limit on Non-Retail Funds and Deposits) Order 1987, SI 1987/2131.
[4] Prudential Note 1987/2: Funding.
[5] *Annual Report of the Building Societies Commission 1987–88*, para. 5.13.

depositors, who as a general rule are not. It is intended, therefore, to ensure that building societies remain mutual institutions, owned by and accountable to their members.[1] The choice of the figure of 50 per cent as the dividing line between mutuality and non-mutuality is to some extent arbitrary, but in the Government's view a building society which raised less than 50 per cent of its funds in the form of shares could no longer be said to be based on the concept of mutuality.[2]

A building society the pattern of whose business does not conform to these limits (or the limit on the proportion of its assets that may be held in liquid form) may be required by the Commission to submit for its approval a restructuring plan which will bring its business back within the relevant statutory limits, or to submit the requisite resolutions to its members for the transfer of its business to a company, or to adopt either course at its option.[3] If the society fails to comply, or if the restructuring plan or transfer resolutions are not approved or implemented, the Commission may either present a petition to the court for the winding up of the society or apply to it for an order directing the society to carry out the restructuring plan.[4] It may also present a petition for the winding up of a society, or make an application for an order directing a society to modify its business, where it has reason to believe that its purpose or principal purpose has ceased to be that of raising, primarily by the subscription of the members, a stock or fund for making to them advances secured on land for their residential use.[5]

The maintenance of a structure of commercial assets which satisfies the statutory requirements is also one of the criteria of prudent management. A failure to maintain the requisite structure may therefore lead to the imposition of conditions on a society's authorisation, or to the revocation of its authorisation, as an alternative to the invocation of the special machinery for the enforcement of these limits provided by the Act.

INFORMATION AND INVESTIGATIONS

The Building Societies Act gives the Commission extensive powers to obtain information and to appoint investigators modelled on those conferred on the Bank of England by the Banking Act 1979.[6] The Commission's information powers extend to any information, documents or explanations of matters, relating to the business or plans for future development of a building society or its associated bodies, which it considers it needs for the purpose of its supervisory functions.[7] It can also require information or documents to be accompanied by a report from an accountant approved by it (s.52(5)(d)). A failure without reasonable excuse to comply with a requirement imposed in

[1] See above, pp. 56–7.　[2] St. Cttee. A col. 90, January 28, 1986.
[3] BSA, s.36(3), (5), (6).　[4] s.37(1)(a), (2)(a).　[5] s.37(1)(b), 2(b).
[6] ss. 16–17; see now BA, ss.39, 41, above, pp. 137–8.　[7] BSA, s.52(5)(a)–(c).

the exercise of these powers is an offence, as is the provision knowingly or recklessly of information which is false or misleading.[1]

Investigations are normally carried out on a voluntary basis, but section 55 of the Act empowers the Commission to appoint one or more persons to investigate and report on the state and conduct of the business of a building society, or any aspect of it, where to do so appears desirable for the purposes of its supervision. Officers, employees and agents of the society (and of its associated bodies if investigation of their business is thought necessary) may be required to produce documents, to attend before investigators and otherwise to give them all assistance in connection with their investigation which they are reasonably able to give (s.55(3)). A failure without reasonable cause to comply with a requirement, including a requirement to answer questions, is an offence (s.55(4)). The Act also makes it an offence to knowingly or recklessly furnish an investigator with information which is false or misleading (s.55(5)). The power to appoint investigators has been exercised on one occasion since it was first introduced.

In addition to its prudential power to appoint investigators, the Commission also has a more general power under section 56 of the Act to appoint inspectors to investigate and report on the affairs of a building society. Like inspectors appointed to inquire into the affairs of a company under sections 431 or 432 of the Companies Act, inspectors may be appointed upon the application of members of a society as well as on the Commission's own initiative (where it is of the opinion that an investigation should be held into a society's affairs).[2] The principal difference between inspectors' powers and those of investigators appointed under section 55 of the Act is that they have power to examine witnesses on oath, whose answers may be used in evidence against them.[3]

The appointment of inspectors is infrequent. The last inspection into a building society was in 1978 into the Grays Building Society, which was the victim of 'exceptional villainy, ingenuity and misfortune'.[4] The perpetrator of this villainy, and the source of its misfortune, was the Grays' chairman and secretary, Harold Percy Jaggard, who between 1938 and 1978 stole in excess of £7 million from the Society. Jaggard was married three times and supported two households between 1942 and 1960, which prompted the inspectors to comment: 'It is clear that this must have placed a considerable strain upon his finances, or to be more precise, upon the finances of the Grays.'[5] Jaggard was also often seen at race meetings with women, and briefcases stuffed with money; his betting alone cost an estimated £1.6 million.[6]

[1] s.52(10), (12); s.52(11) makes it an offence for a society to provide false or misleading information.

[2] s.56(2).   [3] ss.57(4), (5).

[4] *Halifax Building Society* v. *Registry of Friendly Societies* [1978] 1 W.L.R. 1544 at 1546 *per* Templeman J.

[5] Grays Building Society. Investigation under Section 110 of the Building Societies Act 1962, Cmnd. 7557 (1979), p. 7.

[6] Barnes, *Building Societies: The Myth of Mutuality* (1984), p. 127.

POWERS OF INTERVENTION

Revocation

The ultimate sanction at the Commission's disposal is the revocation of a building society's authorisation. A society's authorisation may be revoked at the discretion of the Commission on four grounds: (i) that it has failed to make use of it; (ii) that it has failed to send a copy of its annual accounts to the Commission within six months of the end of its financial year; (iii) that it has failed to comply with a condition to which its authorisation is subject; and, finally, (iv) that the Commission 'considers it expedient to do so in order to protect the investments of shareholders or depositors'.[1] In certain circumstances revocation is mandatory. These include a failure by a society to apply for renewal of its authorisation within the period allowed when directed to do so by the Commission (s.43(3)(c)).

Section 45 of the Act applies for the purpose of determining whether intervention is 'expedient' to protect investors (s.43(2)). It provides that a failure by a society or its directors to satisfy one or more of the criteria entitles the Commission to assume that it has prejudiced the security of the investments of shareholders or depositors, and so to intervene to protect those investments.[2] The creation of a statutory presumption entitling the Commission to intervene whenever the criteria of prudent management are breached would appear to be a response to the New Cross Building Society case.[3] The New Cross was a small society which grew rapidly under the direction of Mr Reg Rowland, a well-known dealer in plantation shares and fringe properties. On two occasions its reserves fell below the prescribed minimum, but on both occasions it was let off with a warning. When, however, it broke the limit on special advances the Registry intervened to prohibit it from accepting investments or deposits from the public, although its soundness was not in question. Rather than merge quietly with another society, the New Cross chose to fight the Registry through the courts, arguing that a breach of prudential requirements of itself did not justify the extreme step of effectively closing a society down in the absence of a risk of actual loss to investors. It succeeded in the High Court before losing in the Court of Appeal, which interpreted the phrase 'expedient . . . in the interests of investors and depositors' in the 1962 Act as conferring a wide discretion on the Chief Registrar to intervene whenever he apprehended a risk of loss to investors rather than waiting until actual loss was virtually certain (by which time intervention would be too late). The significance of the statutory presumption created by section 45 is thus to prevent the possibility of another society seeking to buck the authority of the Commission in this way.

[1] BSA, s.43(1).   [2] ss.43(2), 45(1), (2).
[3] *R* v. *Chief Registrar of Friendly Societies, ex p. New Cross Building Society* [1984] 2 All E.R. 27 C.A.

Although it is unlikely that the revocation of a society's authorisation would not involve a breach of the criteria of prudent management, expedience cannot be defined exhaustively in terms of them. As the Government explained in the Green Paper which preceded the legislation,

it is not posible to anticipate in advance, and then specify in statute or regulations, all the ways in which the board of a society might put investors' money at risk. It would negate the whole purpose of the prudential supervision if the Chief Registrar were to find himself in a position in which he considered that there was a clear case for revoking authorisation in the interests of investors, but he could not do so because it did not fit one of the pre-ordained categories.[1]

Section 45 therefore provides that the Commission may take account of factors other than the criteria of prudent management in deciding whether to revoke a building society's authorisation.[2]

Safeguards are provided for the management of societies. Save where revocation is mandatory, a building society must be given notice of the Commission's intention to revoke its authorisation, the reasons for it, and an opportunity to make representations, which the Commission must take into account before reaching a final decision.[3] Should the Commission decide to revoke its authorisation, the society has a right of appeal to a tribunal (s.46(1)). Revocation does not have effect until the end of the period within which an appeal can be brought or the appeal has been determined or withdrawn (s.46(3)). The protection of investors during this period may be secured by the imposition of conditions on the society, whose operation is not affected by an appeal unless the tribunal orders their operation to be suspended (s.46(5)). The Commission also has power to prohibit a society from advertising (s.51).

Conditions

The Commission also has an intermediate power to impose conditions on a building society's authorisation, which complements its power to grant or renew authorisation subject to conditions. The sole ground upon which this power is exercisable is that the Commission 'considers it expedient to do so in order to protect the investments of shareholders or depositors' (s.42(1)). Section 45 again applies for the purpose of determining whether the imposition of conditions is expedient, so that their imposition is most likely to (but need not) follow a failure by a society or its directors to satisfy one or more of the criteria of prudent management.[4]

The conditions that may be imposed in the exercise of this power are the

[1] *Building Societies: A New Framework*, Appx.2, para. 29.   [2] s.45(4).   [3] Sch. 3, para. 6.
[4] ss.42(2); 45(1), (2).

same as may be imposed on the initial grant or renewal of authorisation; they need not be confined therefore to the raising of funds or the acceptance of deposits, and they may require the society to take certain steps or to refrain from adopting or pursuing a particular course of action or to restrict the scope of its business in a particular way.[1] The same safeguards apply to their imposition as apply to the revocation of a society's authorisation with the difference that an appeal does not stay their operation.[2] A failure by a society to comply with conditions imposed on its authorisation renders it liable to have its authorisation revoked (s.42(3)).

Unlike the banking legislation, the building societies legislation provides no guidance as to when the imposition of conditions is to be preferred to the revocation of authorisation and vice versa.[3] As is the case under the banking legislation, however, the decisive factor is likely to be the prospects for remedial action, so that if there are no realistic prospects for remedial action the Commission will have no alternative but to revoke a building society's authorisation. If, on the other hand, the prospects for remedial action are good, and the Commission considers that the direction and management of a society have the capacity and willingness to respond, it is likely to make the society's continued authorisation subject to conditions, or to accept informal assurances about its future conduct, rather than to revoke its authorisation.

The Commission does not generally report on the exercise of its powers to impose conditions, or to direct a society to apply for renewal of its authorisation, on the grounds that 'publication could well damage confidence in a society, and so risk a run on it, thereby defeating the object of the use of either power, namely the protection of investors'.[4] Clearly, publication of the details of action it has taken in individual cases may well have the consequences the Commission fears, but it does not follow that – unlike the Bank of England, for example – it should provide no information whatsoever on its exercise (or non-exercise) of its intermediate powers of intervention.

The Commission's powers of intervention do not preclude other action being taken to protect investors. The most common means is by a transfer of engagements, that is by a merger with another society. Since the requirement of authorisation was first introduced in 1981 the number of authorised societies has fallen as a result of mergers by more than half, from 236 at the end of 1981 to 101 at the end of 1990. At first this fall was overwhelmingly concentrated among the smallest societies, who had the greatest difficulties in meeting the requirements of authorisation, including the criteria of prudent management, and who therefore sought to merge with larger societies. The majority of these mergers took place voluntarily, but in a minority of cases the Registry gave a board the choice of either demonstrating its ability to make good shortcomings which had been uncovered so that the society would

---

[1] ss.42(4), (5).   [2] Sch. 3, para. 4; s.46(5).   [3] See above, pp. 139–40.
[4] *Annual Report of the Building Societies Commission 1989–90*, para. 4.20.

continue to justify authorisation, or of recommending a merger proposal to the members.[1] More recently, however, the Commission has embarked on a fresh round of forced mergers involving much larger societies, such as the Leamington Spa and the Town and Country, as the recession in the housing market has deepened, exposing societies to the risk of losses on their core business for the first time for most of this century.

APPEALS

A society which is aggrieved by a decision of the Commission to refuse authorisation, to revoke authorisation or to impose conditions, or as to the conditions imposed has a right of appeal to a tribunal.[2] A person who is adjudged not fit and proper or whose removal from office is required also has a right of appeal (s.47(2)).

The scope of appeals is confined to the legality of the Commission's decision, the question for the determination of the tribunal being whether, for the reasons adduced by the appellant, the decision was unlawful or not justified by the evidence on which it was based (s.47(4)). The tribunal may confirm or reverse the Commission's decision, or vary it where the decision was to refuse or revoke authorisation by directing it should be granted or continued subject to conditions; it may also direct the Commission to grant or continue authorisation subject to different conditions from those imposed (s.47(6)). Where the tribunal's determination is that authorisation should be granted or continued subject to conditions, it is for the Commission to determine the conditions to be imposed (s.47(7)).

Both the appellant and the Commission may appeal on any question of law arising from the tribunal's decision to the High Court (or Court of Session in Scotland). If the court is of the opinion that the tribunal's decision was erroneous in law, it must remit the matter to the tribunal. A further appeal lies, with leave, to the Court of Appeal (or to the House of Lords in Scottish cases).[3]

COMPENSATION

The Building Societies Act established an investor protection scheme, administered by a separate Building Societies Investor Protection Board, under which payments are to be made to investors with failed societies (s.24). This scheme replaced a non-statutory scheme, established by the Building Societies Association in 1982, at the instigation of the Chief Registrar, following the collapse of the Grays in 1978. This non-statutory scheme covered investors in all building societies, but a minority of societies did not subscribe to it, thereby denying their members the higher measure of protection

---

[1] *Report of the Chief Registrar 1983–84*, p. 25.   [2] BSA, s.47(1).   [3] s.49.

available to members of participating societies. The opportunity provided by the legislation was therefore used to replace it with a statutory scheme to which all authorised societies have an obligation to contribute.

The measure of compensation payable under the scheme is 90 per cent (or such lesser percentage as the Board determines to apply) of the first £20,000 of an investor's protected investment.[1] Under the Government's original proposals the percentage covered would have been the same as that for banks – 75 per cent – but under pressure from MPs, who argued that investors had higher expectations of the security of investments placed with building societies than with banks, it agreed to increase the percentage to 90 per cent, with power to the Board to apply a lesser percentage if it considered it 'expedient'. Attempts to increase the percentage to 100 per cent were resisted on the grounds that it would remove all incentive for investors to be discerning, but the Act empowers societies to enter into voluntary arrangements supplementing the protection afforded by the statutory scheme (s.31). No society has done so.

In contrast to the position under the Banking Act there is no standing fund, contributions only being levied in the event – which has not yet happened – of a building society becoming insolvent (s.26(2)). Contributions would be calculated as a fixed percentage of each society's share and deposit base, with an upper limit of 0.3 per cent on each society's contributions (s.26(10)). As is the case under the banking scheme, the Board is empowered to decline to make payments to any person who, in its opinion, has any responsibility for, or may have derived any profit from, the circumstances which gave rise to a society's financial difficulties (s.27(4)).

---

[1] s.27(2), (5); The Building Societies Investor Protection Scheme (Maximum Protected Investment) Order 1987, SI 1987/1349.

10
Insurance Companies

BACKGROUND

The regulation of insurance companies in the United Kingdom began with the Life Assurance Companies Act 1870, which was enacted following the 'spectacular' failure of the Albert Life Assurance Company in 1869.[1] This enactment established the principle of 'freedom with publicity', which principle subsequent enactments extended to forms of insurance other than life insurance. The essence of freedom with publicity, or freedom with disclosure, was that companies were required to make public such information about their affairs as would enable members of the public and their advisers to make an informed assessment of their financial stability, but were otherwise left free to conduct their business as they thought fit. It was thus an attempt to combine the protection of policyholders and shareholders – on the theory that publicity was the best check on unsound underwriting methods – with the maximum freedom of enterprise.[2]

The principle of freedom with disclosure continued to govern the regulation of insurance in the United Kingdom until it was effectively abandoned as a result of a series of scandals in the 1960s and early 1970s, which led to the introduction of a system of substantive regulation which was to provide the model in several respects for those subsequently established in relation to banks and investment businesses by the Banking Act 1979 and the Financial Services Act 1986. The first of these scandals arose as a result of the failure of a number of cut price motor insurers, the most notorious of which was that of Dr Emil Savundra's Fire, Auto and Marine. It led to the introduction of a system of prior authorisation and to the vesting of powers of intervention in the Board of Trade by Part II of the Companies Act 1967. This increase in the Board's powers was not, however, accompanied by any change in its approach to insurance supervision, which continued to be dominated by what the Wilson Committee was later to describe as a 'relatively relaxed' view of its responsibilities.[3] That this relaxed view of its responsibilities was incom-

---

[1] Supple, *The Royal Exchange Assurance. A History of British Insurance 1720–1970*, (1970), p. 142.
[2] See above, pp. 45–9. [3] Wilson Report, para. 1074.

patible with effective policyholder protection was quickly demonstrated by Vehicle and General, which crashed in 1971 leaving about one million policyholders uninsured.[1] Its collapse led in turn to the reorganisation of what was now the Department of Trade and Industry, a further increase in its powers as a result of the Insurance Companies Amendment Act 1973 and, following difficulties among a number of life companies of which the most prominent was Nation Life, to the establishment of a compensation scheme by the Policyholders Protection Act 1975.

Notwithstanding the abandonment of freedom of disclosure in favour of a system of substantive regulation, the existing system of insurance companies regulation, the framework for which is provided by the Insurance Companies Act 1982, is commonly described as being based on the principle of freedom with disclosure.[2] Freedom with disclosure, however, is hardly an apt description of a system of regulation whose principal features include a requirement of authorisation, solvency requirements and a compensation scheme. If the description means anything, it must be that the United Kingdom system of regulation is rather more liberal than the systems applied in many other countries. For example, controls over premium rates and policy conditions, while commonplace elsewhere, have never been a feature of insurance business regulation in the United Kingdom.[3] It is thus this broad contrast between more and less liberal approaches to insurance regulation – rather than the method of regulation adopted – which the continued characterisation of the United Kingdom system as being based on the principle of freedom with disclosure appears to be intended to capture.

THE SCOPE OF THE REGIME

The scope of the insurance business regime is delimited by the basic prohibition in section 2(1) of the Insurance Companies Act 1982, which provides that 'no person shall carry on any insurance business in the United Kingdom unless authorised to do so'. What is struck at by the Act, therefore, is the unauthorised carrying on of insurance business in the United Kingdom. To gain a fuller understanding of the regime's scope we need to examine the various elements that make up this prohibition.

Insurance business

The term 'insurance business' is not fully defined by the Act, but it refers

---

[1] *Report of the Tribunal appointed to inquire into certain issues in relation to the circumstances leading up to the cessation of trading by the Vehicle and General Company Limited* (HL 80, HC 133, 1971–2).

[2] See e.g. DTI, *EC Third Non-Life Insurance (Framework) Directive. A Consultative Document*, Feb. 1991, para. 4.1.1.

[3] Tapp, 'Regulation of the UK Insurance Industry' in Finsinger and Pauly (eds.), *The Economics of Insurance Regulation* (1986), pp. 27–61.

primarily to 'the business of effecting and carrying out contracts of insurance'.[1] The term 'contract of insurance' is not exhaustively defined by the legislation either, but a contract of insurance may be defined as 'one whereby one party (the "insurer") promises in return for a money consideration (the "premium") to pay to the other party (the "assured") a sum of money or provide him with some corresponding benefit, upon the occurrence of one or more specified events'.[2] However, insurance business for the purpose of the legislation does not only consist of the business of effecting and carrying out contracts of insurance in this sense; it also includes the business of effecting and carrying out contracts of guarantee, tontines, capital redemption contracts, contracts to manage the investments of pension funds and contracts to pay annuities, all of which are defined as contracts of insurance for the purpose of the legislation.[3]

The conclusion that insurance business means the business of effecting and carrying out contracts of insurance, in the specialised sense given to that term by the legislation, is partly derived from the division, for the purposes of the legislation, of insurance business into long-term business and general business, long-term business and general business being in turn subdivided into a number of classes, the definition of most (but not all) of which begins with the words 'effecting and carrying out contracts of insurance . . .'[4] Our interest is in the regulation of long-term business since it is long-term business (rather than general business) which provides a vehicle for saving and investment as well as protection (though not all long-term contracts are 'investments' for the purposes of the Financial Services Act).[5] It consists of seven classes of business: life and annuity; marriage and birth; linked long-term; permanent health; tontines; capital redemption; and pension fund management. It is regulated in essentially the same way as general business with the addition of a number of special requirements for the protection of policyholders.

Carrying on business

The Insurance Companies Act does not prohibit the effecting of insurance transactions without authorisation. What it prohibits is the carrying on of insurance business without authorisation. This is a different matter. One can effect insurance transactions without being in the business of insurance. A consumer who buys insurance, for example, is effecting an insurance transaction.

---

[1] *Medical Defence Union* v. *Department of Trade* [1979] 1 W.L.R. 686.

[2] *MacGillivray and Parkington on Insurance Law* (8th edn, 1988), p. 1, a definition based on *Prudential Insurance Company* v. *Inland Revenue Commissioners* [1904] 2 K.B. 658.

[3] ICA, ss.95, 96(1).   [4] s.1(1). Sch. 1, Sch. 2 Part 1.   [5] See below, pp. 232–3.

The concept of 'carrying on business' was discussed in relation to the regulation of deposit-taking business.[1] Its broad purpose, as we saw, is to distinguish that which is done for non-commercial reasons and on isolated occasions from that which is done for gain, and repeatedly.

The territorial dimension

To fall within the scope of the prohibition insurance business must be carried on in the United Kingdom. Section 81A(5) of the Act provides that an insurance company shall not be regarded as carrying on insurance business in the United Kingdom by reason only of the fact that it provides insurance in the United Kingdom. The mere presence of the assured in the United Kingdom will not therefore bring the insurer within the scope of the prohibition if the contract is neither effected (by the acceptance of risks) nor carried out (by the payment of claims) in the United Kingdom. Where, on the other hand, contracts are both effected and carried out in the United Kingdom insurance business is carried on in the United Kingdom. Insurance business would also appear to be carried on in the United Kingdom if contracts are either effected or carried out in the United Kingdom.[2]

Exemptions

The Act provides only a limited number of exemptions from the prohibition against the unauthorised carrying on of insurance business. For our purposes the most important is that in favour of registered friendly societies.[3] Also exempted are members of Lloyd's, societies other than friendly societies registered under the friendly societies legislation, and trades unions and employers' organisations providing benefits exclusively for their own members.[4]

UNLAWFUL INSURANCE BUSINESS

Contravention of section 2(1) of the Insurance Companies Act is a criminal offence punishable with up to two years imprisonment or an unlimited fine or both.[5] The possible civil consequences of a contravention of the prohibition depend on whether or not the insurance business carried on without authorisation or exemption is also investment business for the purposes of the Financial Services Act. If it is not – that is to say, the contract entered into is not an 'investment agreement' to which section 5(1) of the Financial Services

---

[1] See above, p. 128.

[2] *Bedford Insurance Co. Ltd.* v. *Instituto de Resseguros do Brasil* [1984] 2 W.L.R. 26; *Stewart* v. *Oriental Fire & Marine Insurance Co. Ltd.* [1984] 3 W.L.R. 741.

[3] ICA, s.2(2)(b), (3).   [4] s.2(2)(a)–(c).   [5] ICA, s.14(1), (3).

Act applies – it is unenforceable by the insurer and voidable at the instance of the insured, unless the court is persuaded that the insurer reasonably believed that in entering into the contract he was not contravening the prohibition, and that it is just and equitable for the contract to be enforced.[1] If, on the other hand, it is an investment agreement to which section 5(1) applies, comparable consequences follow, subject to the court's discretion, by virtue of that section, unless the insurer is an authorised or exempted person under the Financial Services Act.[2] The carrying on of insurance business which is investment business without authorisation or exemption under the Financial Services Act also exposes the insurer to the risk of injunctions and restitution orders under that Act.[3]

AUTHORISATION

Section 3 of the 1982 Act empowers the Secretary of State to authorise a body corporate to carry on in the United Kingdom such classes or parts of classes of insurance business as may be specified. By virtue of section 4 of the Act, insurance companies that were already authorised were not required to seek fresh authorisation. Separate provision is made with respect to the authorisation of applicants from the United Kingdom, applicants from other Member States and applicants from outside the Community, but once the proposed 'framework' directives are adopted and implemented insurers authorised in other Member States will no longer require additional authorisation to set up branches or agencies in the United Kingdom.

(a) Applicant with head office in the United Kingdom
The Act lays down three conditions which United Kingdom applicants must satisfy: (i) the applicant must be a body corporate, i.e., a company within the meaning of the Companies Act, or a registered society (or a body corporate established by royal charter or Act of Parliament, and already authorised to carry on insurance business of a class or classes other than those for which the application is made); (ii) it must not have issued any share capital on or after January 1, 1982 which is not fully paid up; and (iii) its directors, controllers, managers and main agents (as defined in the Act) must be 'fit and proper' persons to hold their positions.[4]

(b) Applicant with head office in another Member State
An applicant from another Member State must satisfy two conditions: (i) it must have appointed a representative resident in the United Kingdom with power to act on its behalf; and (ii) its 'relevant executives', i.e., those executives responsible for its United Kingdom operation, and main agents must be fit and proper persons to hold their positions.[5]

---

[1] FSA, s.132(1), (3); for the background to this provision, see above, pp.62–3.
[2] See below, pp. 247–53.   [3] See below, pp. 244–6.   [4] ICA, s.7(1)–(3).
[5] s.8(1)–(2); subs.3 makes separate provision in respect of applicants seeking authorisation to do reinsurance business only.

(c) Applicant with head office outside the Community

An applicant from outside the Community must satisfy five conditions: (i) it must be a body corporate entitled to carry on in the country in which it is incorporated the type of business (long-term or general) for which authorisation is sought; (ii) it must have appointed a representative resident in the United Kingdom with power to act on its behalf; (iii) its representative together with its directors, controllers, managers and main agents must be fit and proper persons to hold their positions; (iv) it must have assets of a prescribed value in the United Kingdom; and (v) except where authorisation is sought to do reinsurance business only, it must have made a deposit of a prescribed amount.[1]

Satisfaction of these conditions does not entitle an applicant to authorisation. Before granting an application, the Secretary of State must be satisfied, on the basis of the business plan which the applicant is required to submit and any other information available to him, that the application 'ought to be granted'.[2] Should the Department not be satisfied that the application ought to be granted, it will generally tell the applicant what changes would be required before it would be prepared to issue authorisation. By this means it may induce an applicant to modify its original intentions.[3] Because authorised insurance companies are automatically authorised to carry on investment business, the DTI is also bound to consult SIB before issuing an authorisation.[4]

The Department has power, which it routinely exercises, to impose conditions on newly-authorised companies.[5] Companies subject to such conditions are typically restricted in the investment of their assets to a range of 'safe' investments, such as narrower range trustee investments, shares quoted on recognised stock exchanges, land and loans secured by first mortgage on land, or life assurance policies. They may also be required to obtain ministerial approval before investing in or entering into other transactions with 'connected persons', to restrict the growth of their premium income to the levels assumed by their business plans, and to submit returns for monitoring purposes on a quarterly rather than a normal annual basis. Conditions imposed in the exercise of this power may be maintained in force for a maximum of ten years from the date of authorisation.

Applications must be decided within six months of the receipt of the applicant's business plan.[6] There are no formal pre-decisional requirements to be complied with. Nor is there a right of appeal. An applicant must, however,

---

[1] s.9(1), (3)–(5); Insurance Companies Regs. 1981, SI 1981/1654 regs.14–20 (prescribed deposits), reg.30 (prescribed assets).

[2] ICA, s.5(1); the information which must be submitted as part of the business plan is specified in the Insurance Companies Regs. 1981, SI 1981/1654, reg.29 and Schs. 4 and 5.

[3] Wilson Committee, Second Stage Evidence, Department of Trade, para. 7.

[4] FSA, s.22, Sch. 10, para. 10(1).   [5] ICA, s.37(5).   [6] ICA, s.5(2).

be informed in writing of the reasons for the refusal of an application (s.5(2)). This requirement, which was introduced partly in implementation of the requirement in the Life (and Non-Life) Establishment Directive that applicants should be given 'a right to apply to the courts' in respect of a refusal of authorisation,[1] is apparently intended to facilitate judicial review. But since review, unlike appeal, is not available as of right, it is doubtful whether a requirement to give reasons is of itself sufficient to fulfil the underlying Community obligation. Nevertheless, the comment by one civil servant that 'nothing is sacred. Applicants for authorisation even have to be told why, if they are refused it. What more need I say?',[2] suggests a reluctance to go even this far and a continuing preference for the days when the refusal of an application could be treated as a 'subjective judgment made by an instructed person upon a question of experience'.[3]

The Single Market

The Non-Life and Life Establishment Directives gave practical effect to the right of establishment in the context of insurance services by allowing an insurer with a head office in one Member State to set up a branch or agency in another Member State, which branch or agency is subject to the control of the host state.[4] The Establishment Directives are complemented by the Non-Life and Life Services Directives which give practical effect to the right of an insurer to provide insurance services in one Member State from an establishment in another.[5] But instead of providing that the writing of long-term business is subject to the control of the home state, the Life Services Directive, which has to be implemented by May 1993, establishes a 'dual system' of control, depending on whether or not the contract is entered into at the initiative of the policyholder. If it is entered into at the policyholder's initiative, the insurer will be subject to home state control only, but if it is not, the host state will retain the freedom to require the insurer to obtain prior authorisation and to conform to its rules (an option which the United Kingdom does not intend to exercise.)[6]

The proposed Non-Life and Life Framework Directives mark a shift away from this system of multiple authorisations in favour of the concept of a single licence similar to that adopted for banking, so that an insurer authorised in one Member State would not require fresh authorisation to write insurance business direct or through a branch elsewhere in the Community. Under this system, responsibility for the authorisation and supervision of an insurer,

[1] Dir.79/267/EEC OJ 1979 L63/1, art. 12.
[2] Reid, 'Department of Trade Regulation – A Review of the Current Situation' (1980), p. 10.
[3] See above, p. 101. [4] Dir.73/239/EEC OJ 1973 L228/3; Dir.79/267/EEC OJ 1979 L63/1.
[5] Dir.88/357/EEC OJ 1988 L172/1; Dir.90/619/EEC OJ 1990 L330/50.
[6] DTI, *Implementation in the United Kingdom of the Second Council Directive on Direct Life Assurance* (December 1991).

including branch and services business elsewhere in the Community, would remain with the authorities of the insurer's home state. On the Commission's present proposals, the minimum standards which national regimes would have to match as a condition of their mutual recognition would not include prior approval or systematic notification of policy terms and conditions, premium scales and marketing literature.

Changes of control

Once a company has been authorised, the Department must be informed of any changes of controllers, directors, managers and main agents.[1] It has power to object to a proposed change of controller, managing director or chief executive on the ground that the person is not fit and proper to be a controller of a company or, in the case of managing directors and chief executives, to be appointed to the position in question.[2] Before serving a notice of objection, it must give the person (and the company where the objection is to a change of managing director or chief executive) an opportunity to make representations which it must take into account before reaching a final decision.[3] There is no provision for reasons to be given or for an appeal. A change of control is also grounds for the exercise of the Department's powers of intervention at any time in the next five years.[4]

FINANCIAL REGULATION

The key financial requirement imposed on insurance companies is that they should maintain a minimum solvency margin, a company's solvency margin being the excess of the value of its assets over the amount of its liabilities.[5] The requirement of a solvency margin was first introduced in respect of general business in 1946,[6] but it was only extended to long-term business in 1981, in implementation of the Life Establishment Directive (in place of a requirement that the appointed actuary certify that the fund was able to meet its liabilities).

To calculate its actual and required solvency margins, an insurance company must first value its assets and determine its liabilities. Statutory provision has been made with respect to both the valuation of assets and the determination of liabilities,[7] but the requirement with respect to general business liabilities is merely that they should be determined 'in accordance with generally accepted accounting concepts, bases and policies or other generally accepted methods appropriate for insurance companies'.[8] Having valued its assets and determined its liabilities, the company's solvency margin

---

[1] ICA, ss.62–4.   [2] ss.60–1.

[3] ss.60(5), (4); both subsections provide that representations shall be taken into consideration 'before serving the notice of objection', which is presumably not what is intended.

[4] s.37(5); see below, pp. 174–7.   [5] ICA, s.32.   [6] Assurance Companies Act 1946.

[7] SI 1981/1654, Parts V and VI.   [8] Reg.52(1).

is then calculated according to a statutory formula, which is based in the case of general business on premium income or claims experience, and in the case of long-term business on actuarial liabilities.[1]

Should a company fail to maintain the required margin of solvency it may be required to take remedial action. The action it may be required to take will depend on the severity of the shortfall. Should its solvency margin fall below the required amount but nevertheless exceed a minimum solvency requirement (the 'minimum guarantee fund') it may be required to prepare and implement an approved plan 'for the restoration of a sound financial position'.[2] Should its solvency margin fall below the minimum requirement, however, it will have no choice but to seek to arrange (and secure approval for) a rescue operation in the shape of a 'short-term financial scheme'.[3] Because of the seriousness of the position in either case, it is unlikely that additional requirements for the protection of policyholders would not be imposed in the exercise of the Department's powers of intervention.[4]

Insurance companies are also subject to requirements with respect to the matching and localisation of assets.[5] Matching is a device to render companies less vulnerable to fluctuations in exchange rates by ensuring that assets are held in the currency in which liabilities will be expressed. Where the liabilities of an insurance company in any particular currency exceed 5 per cent of its total liabilities, it must hold matching assets to cover at least 80 per cent of its liabilities in that currency. Localisation requires assets to be held in a specific country, so that, for example, assets held to cover liabilities in sterling must be held in the United Kingdom.

Insurance companies are required to make an annual return to the Department, the form and content of which are prescribed by regulation.[6] A company carrying on long-term business must include an abstract of an actuarial investigation of its financial condition in respect of that business; it must also prepare a statement of its long-term business at least once every five years.[7] Although the annual return is primarily intended to enable the Department to monitor the solvency of insurers, it is also available on request to policyholders and shareholders and open to public inspection at the appropriate Companies House.[8]

The reliability of supervisory returns is sought to be ensured in a number of ways. First, the Act makes it an offence to knowingly or recklessly cause or permit a statement which is false in a material particular to be included in a return.[9] Second, the directors of a company are required to certify that the return has been properly prepared and that the solvency requirements have

---

[1] Part III, Schs. 1 and 2.
[2] ICA, s.32(4).   [3] s.33(4), (5).   [4] See below, pp. 174–7.
[5] ICA, s.35; SI 1981/1654, regs.25–7.
[6] ICA, s.22, Insurance Companies (Accounts and Statements) Regs.1983, SI 1983/1811.
[7] ICA, s.18.   [8] ss.23, 65.   [9] s.71(1)(c).

been complied with; in the case of a company carrying on long-term business the appointed actuary must also certify whether in his opinion proper provision has been made with respect to its liabilities, which certificate may include such qualification, amplification or explanation as may be considered necessary.[1] Finally, returns must be audited, the task of the auditor being to state not whether they provide a 'true and fair' view, but whether they conform to the requirements and whether it was reasonable for the directors to have given their certificate.[2]

Auditors have also been empowered to furnish information obtained during the course of their audit work to the Department.[3] Guidance in respect of general business insurers issued by the accountancy bodies and approved by the Department, which is duplicated in draft guidance in respect of life insurers, provides that an auditor should take the initiative in making an *ad hoc* report to the Department when he considers it expedient to do so in order to protect the interests of policyholders. 'Expedient' is defined as an adverse occurrence, or a change in the auditor's perception of an existing situation, which has given rise to a material loss or the reasonable probability of such a loss, and which is such that the interests of existing and prospective policyholders might be better safeguarded if the DTI were aware of it. The guidance provides that the auditor should normally ask the insurer to report matters about which he is concerned to the Department, but that in exceptional circumstances, where it is in the interests of protecting policy-holders that the management of the insurer should not be informed in advance, he should report direct to the DTI.[4]

PORTFOLIO REGULATION

Apart from prohibiting a company carrying on long-term business from investing more than 5 per cent of its long-term funds in shares in subordinate companies, loans to such companies or their controllers,[5] the insurance companies legislation imposes no direct restrictions on a company's choice of investments. However, the valuation of assets regulations, which were introduced in the aftermath of Vehicle and General and strengthened after the failure of Nation Life, exercise a significant indirect influence over a company's investment policy. They do so by providing, first, that certain more volatile assets are totally inadmissible for the purpose of calculating a company's solvency margin[6] and, second, that others involving excessive concentrations of risk (for example, investments in a single piece of land, or a single company) may only be taken into account up to specified limits for the

---

[1] SI 1983/1811, reg.26.

[2] SI 1983/1811, reg.27.   [3] ICA, s.21A, inserted by FSA, s.135.

[4] Auditing Practices Committee, *General business insurers in the United Kingdom* (March 1991); *Life insurers in the United Kingdom*, Exposure draft (August 1990).

[5] ICA, s.31.   [6] SI 1981/1654, reg.38(3).

same purpose.[1] They thus create an incentive for a company to favour less volatile assets, and to spread its investments, since it is the primary aim of all insurers to hold sufficient admissible assets to cover their solvency margin requirements. A company is therefore only free to invest in inadmissible assets, or in excess of the limits, to the extent that its assets exceed those necessary to meet its solvency requirement. 'Those who are handsomely covered can take a chance with a few way-out investments. Those who live near the margin must operate with rather more circumspection.'[2]

LONG-TERM BUSINESS

The 1982 Act provides a number of additional safeguards for life policy-holders. First, a company carrying on long-term business is required to identify by means of separate funds the assets and liabilities attributable to its long-term business (s.28). A requirement that separate funds be maintained in respect of long-term and general business has long been a feature of insurance companies legislation in the United Kingdom, but until 1973 there was no obligation to allocate specific assets to the separate funds. If no such allocation was made, life policyholders enjoyed no priority over other creditors in the event of insolvency.[3] Since 1973, however, a company carrying on both kinds of business has been required to maintain the assets attributable to its long-term business in a separate fund, which assets are applicable only for the purposes of that business and are transferable so as to be available for other purposes only in limited circumstances.[4] Should a company be wound up, its 'long-term' assets are available only for meeting the liabilities of the company attributable to that business.[5]

The prohibition on the transfer of a company's long-term assets does not apply, *inter alia*, where their value exceeds the amount of its liabilities, the surplus being available for distribution among its policyholders and, in the case of a proprietary company, its shareholders (s.29(2)). Once a surplus has been allocated to eligible policyholders, however, the proportion of any subsequent surplus allocated to policyholders cannot be reduced by more than a prescribed amount (0.5 per cent) unless the company makes public its intention to do so (s.30). This provision is intended to impart a measure of stability to the expectations of policyholders by compelling a company which wishes to increase the percentage of its profits it allocates to shareholders to run the gauntlet of informed opinion, with the consequences for new business that that may entail.

Finally, although SIB's conduct of business rules do not apply to the management of life funds (in contrast to pension funds),[6] a company carrying

---

[1] SI 1981/1654, reg.49, Sch. 8.   [2] Reid, *op. cit.*, p. 4.
[3] *Re London General Insurance Co Ltd.* [1939] Ch. 505.   [4] ICA, ss.28–9.   [5] s.55(3)–(6).
[6] FSA, Sch. 10, para. 4.

on long-term business is expected to observe 'the single most important principle of investment management: that of dealing fairly as between different clients'.[1] To this end it is required to have adequate arrangements in place to avoid unfairness between funds.[2] A company's directors are required to certify that this requirement has been fully complied with.[3]

LINKED LIFE INSURANCE

Special provision has also been made for the protection of holders of linked life policies – i.e., policies under which the benefits payable to the policyholder are calculated by reference to the value of property or to an index of the value of property.[4] The Insurance Companies Regulations specify the types of asset and the indices of the value of assets by reference to which benefits may be determined.[5] The purpose of specifying the types of assets to which they may be linked is to ensure that they are only linked to those assets that are capable of fair and reasonably accurate valuation; those to which policies may be linked include listed securities, shares traded on the Unlisted Securities Market, and land. Similarly, the purpose of specifying the indices of the value of assets to which they may be linked is to ensure that they are only linked to those that are generally recognised and independently calculated; those to which they may be linked include the FT Industrial Ordinary Stock Index and the FT–SE 100 Share Index. The specification of the types of assets to which benefits may be linked does not entail any obligation to hold those particular assets.

These restrictions are markedly less onerous than those that apply in respect of authorised unit trusts, which are subject to a requirement of prior authorisation as well as to detailed portfolio and pricing controls.[6] The possibility that linked life assurance should be regulated under the Prevention of Fraud (Investments) Act as well as under the Insurance Companies Acts was considered by the Scott Committee, but rejected in favour of its regulation under the insurance legislation alone on the basis that linked life assurance was no different from any other form of life assurance in providing 'a medium for saving and investment as well as a means of helping the policyholder to make financial provision for his dependants'.[7]

The Committee proposed tackling the anomalies between the treatment of linked life assurance and unit trusts to which this would give rise, by taking account of the safeguards thought appropriate for other kinds of investment in framing recommendations for safeguards specifically designed

---

[1] HL Vol. 479, col. 663 (July 28, 1986).   [2] ICA, s.31A, inserted by FSA, s.136.
[3] SI 1983/1811, inserted by Insurance Companies (Accounts and Statements) (Amendment) Regs. 1989, SI 1989/1952.
[4] ICA, s.78(1)(a).   [5] SI 1981/1654, reg.72, Sch. 13.   [6] See below, Chapter 12.
[7] *Linked Life Assurance: Report of the Committee on Property Bonds and Equity-Linked Life Assurance*, Cmnd. 5281 (1973), para. 71.

for the particular circumstances of linked life assurance. In contrast to the regulation of unit trusts, however, the safeguards it proposed were firmly based on the principle of freedom of disclosure:

we have concluded that the best means of securing effective protection for policyholders without imposing unreasonable burdens on the life company issuing such policies is to follow the philosophy of the Insurance Companies Acts by retaining the life company's freedom of operation but substantially extending the area where disclosure is mandatory, and requiring disclosure to the policyholder as well as the Department.[1]

The Committee therefore rejected controls over the investment of unit-linked funds:

. . . in our view policyholders should be free to choose between schemes linked to more or less speculative assets, and they should similarly be free to opt for a scheme linked to a narrower or wider spread of assets. We do not consider that it is the function of the supervisory authorities to attempt to regulate the investment risk that the policyholder may accept or conversely the extent to which he may benefit from successful investment.[2]

It also rejected any attempt to regulate the conduct of internal funds, again on the basis that this was an area 'where policyholders can in the main be adequately protected by full disclosure'.[3]

INFORMATION AND INVESTIGATIONS

In common with other regulatory authorities, the Department has widely drawn powers to obtain information from and to investigate insurance companies. Among the grounds upon which its information powers may be exercised are that their exercise is 'desirable' for protecting policyholders or potential policyholders against the risk that a company may be unable to meet its liabilities, or, in the case of long-term business, to fulfil the reasonable expectations of policyholders or potential policyholders.[4] In the exercise of these powers it may require a company to furnish specified information at specified times or intervals; it may also require a company's annual return to be submitted early and a company which carries on long-term business to make an actuarial investigation into its condition in respect of that business.[5] Failure to comply with a requirement imposed in the exercise of these powers is an offence (s.71(3)).

The Department's investigation powers extend to any body (whether incorporated or not) which appears to be an insurance company (s.37(4)). They are exercisable on the same grounds as the Department's information powers so that they may be exercised whenever the Department considers it

[1] para. 75. [2] para. 139. [3] para. 158; see also para. 159. [4] ICA, s.37(2).
[5] ss.44(1), 42–3.

desirable (s.37(2)). In their exercise a company may be required to produce specified documents, and present and past controllers, directors, employees and auditors may be required to provide an explanation of any of the documents produced.[1] A statement made by a person may be used in evidence against him (s.44(5)). A failure to comply with a requirement imposed in the exercise of these powers is an offence (s.71(3)). It is also an offence in purported compliance with a requirement imposed in the exercise of these powers knowingly or recklessly to furnish information which is false in a material particular (s.71(1)(b)).

POWERS OF INTERVENTION

Withdrawal of authorisation

Section 11 of the Act empowers the Secretary of State to withdraw, in whole or in part, a company's authorisation to take on new business. A company's authorisation may be withdrawn (other than at its own request) on a number of grounds of which the most important are: (i) that it no longer satisfies the conditions of authorisation, for example because its controllers, directors, managers or main agents are not fit and proper persons; and (ii) that it has failed to comply with any obligation under the Act (or the Financial Services Act, or an obligation of a self-regulating organisation of which it is a member).[2] A company's authorisation may also be withdrawn on the grounds (iii) that it has failed to comply with an obligation imposed by another Member State in implementation of the general insurance directives; and (iv) that authorisation has been withdrawn from the company elsewhere in the Community.[3]

Before a company's authorisation can be withdrawn, it must be informed of the ground for the proposed action and given an opportunity to make representations (both orally and in writing) which must be taken into account before a final decision is made.[4] The same safeguards apply to a person whose fitness is in question.[5] If the company's authorisation is withdrawn reasons must be given (s.11(3)). There is no appeal.

The withdrawal of a company's authorisation to take on new business does not prevent it from carrying out its existing business. It can thus continue to pay claims until its business has been run off. If necessary, the interests of policyholders during this period can be safeguarded by requiring the company to maintain assets in the United Kingdom in the custody of an approved trustee.[6] Once its outstanding liabilities have been run off its authorisation may be finally withdrawn under section 13, which makes provision for the final

---

[1] ss.44(2)–(4).   [2] s.11(2)(a), (b).   [3] s.11(2)(aa), (c).   [4] s.12(1), (6).
[5] s.12(2), (6).   [6] ss.39–40, see below, p. 175.

withdrawal of authorisation from a company which has ceased to carry on insurance business.

The Department's annual report provides information on the use made of these powers, but it does not distinguish between those cases in which authorisation to take on new business is withdrawn at the request of a company, and those in which it is withdrawn on the initiative of the Department. It is impossible, therefore, to form a picture of the frequency with which authorisation is withdrawn contrary to a company's wishes. Even if a breakdown were provided the picture would still be incomplete since no doubt some companies prefer to request the Department to withdraw their authorisation rather than have it withdrawn.

Other powers

In addition to the power to withdraw a company's authorisation to write new business, the legislation confers various other powers of intervention on the Department. These include powers: (i) to require specified investments not to be made, or the realisation of specified investments (s.38); (ii) to require the maintenance in the United Kingdom of assets proportionate to home liabilities, and further to require that they be held in trust for the company by an approved person (s.40); (iii) to limit premium income (s.41); and (iv) to obtain further or earlier information.[1] They also include a residual power (v) 'to take such action as appears . . . to be appropriate for the purpose of protecting policy holders or potential policy holders of the company against the risk that the company may be unable to meet its liabilities or, in the case of long-term business, to fulfil the reasonable expectations of policy holders or potential policy holders' (s.45). This power can only be exercised when the purpose for which it is conferred cannot appropriately be achieved by the exercise of the Department's other powers (s.37(6)). A failure to comply with a requirement imposed in the exercise of these powers is an offence as well as grounds for withdrawal of authorisation.[2]

Section 37 of the Act sets out the grounds on which these powers may be exercised. The powers to impose requirements about investments, to limit premium income, to require further and earlier information and to require a company to take such action as appears appropriate, may be exercised where there has been a failure to comply with an obligation imposed by the legislation (or the Financial Services Act); where misleading or inaccurate information has been furnished to the Department; where a company's reinsurance arrangements are not satisfactory; where the conditions of authorisation are no longer satisfied; where there has been a substantial departure from a business plan; and where authorisation has been withdrawn from a company elsewhere in the Community.[3] They may also be exercised

---

[1] ss.42–4, see above, p. 173.   [2] ss.71(3), 11(2)(a).   [3] s.37(2)(b)–(g).

where their exercise is considered 'desirable for protecting policy holders or potential policy holders of the company against the risk that the company may be unable to meet its liabilities or, in the case of long-term business, to fulfil the reasonable expectations of policy holders or potential policy holders' (s.37(2)(a)). In the final analysis, therefore, the Department, like other financial regulators, has the power to intervene whenever it considers it desirable (rather than necessary) for the protection of policyholders and not just when specific infringements or shortcomings have been identified.

The powers to require assets to be maintained in the United Kingdom and to require them to be vested in an approved trustee (as well as the power to require a company to take appropriate action where it is used to restrict a company's freedom to dispose of its assets), are exercisable on an overlapping but more restricted set of grounds. Like the Department's other powers they too may be exercised where a company's authorisation has been withdrawn, but otherwise they may only be exercised where a company is in breach of its financial obligations or where its liabilities, as reported to the Department, have been improperly determined (ss.37(3), 45(2)). A company's freedom to dispose of its assets can only be limited, therefore, where to do so is the only appropriate form of intervention (because of the risk that the assets available may be insufficient to meet its liabilities).

Some, but not all, of these powers may also be exercised on the grounds that a company is newly authorised (i.e., within the last five years) or that there has been a change of control (again, within the last five years) (s.37(5)). The powers that may be exercised on these grounds are the powers to impose requirements about investments, to limit premium income, to require further and earlier information and to require a company to take such action as appears appropriate, but not the powers to require assets to be maintained in the United Kingdom or in the custody of an approved trustee. Requirements imposed in the exercise of these powers remain in force for ten years from the date of authorisation or change of control unless they are relaxed or cancelled beforehand (s.37(5)).

The Act provides few safeguards against the misuse of these powers. Only where a power is exercised on the ground that a person is unfit to be a director, manager or main agent of a company, but not a controller, is there a requirement that an opportunity to make representations be provided before a decision is taken (s.46). Otherwise the company is merely required to be informed of the ground on which a power is exercised (s.37(7)). The provision of more elaborate safeguards was robustly rejected by the Scott Committee:

> It may be said that it is in principle wrong that a Government Department should have . . . a power to take action, which will sometimes be tantamount to requiring the company to close down permanently, without the company having the right to make prior representations. On the other hand it could well be that where a company is insolvent or in danger of insolvency . . . if, as at pesent, there must be a delay before

action by the Department can come into effect, then intervention may be too late to be effective, or as effective as it could have been with wider powers, to the detriment of the interests of policyholders. It seems to us that in the case of insurance companies . . . the substantial amounts of money involved and social importance of doing everything possible to prevent a serious financial collapse justifies wider powers of investigation and intervention than might be appropriate in some other types of business . . . Once a case for intervention has been established in that the Department are not satisfied that the company is solvent or in that they consider that the business of the company is being so conducted that there is a risk of its becoming insolvent, then in our opinion the interests of policyholders require that the Department be empowered to take immediate and effective action.[1]

The experience of other regimes, however, suggests that it is possible to reconcile the conflicting demands of regulatory effectiveness and fairness to regulated companies by combining a power to impose requirements with immediate effect with a right of appeal.[2]

Intervention most commonly proceeds on the grounds that the company is newly authorised or that there has been a change of control. In only a handful of cases each year are the Department's powers exercised on other grounds. In some cases remedial action is undertaken on an informal (non-statutory) basis.

COMPENSATION

The Policyholders Protection Act 1975 imposed a compulsory compensation scheme on the industry following its failure to agree a voluntary scheme acceptable to the Government in the wake of the collapse of Nation Life. The scheme is administered by a separate Policyholders Protection Board, which is responsible for the protection of policyholders affected by the inability of insurance companies carrying on insurance business in the United Kingdom to meet their liabilities.[3] The Board consists of five members appointed by the Secretary of State, at least three of whom must be drawn from the insurance industry and at least one of whom must be qualified to represent the interests of policyholders.[4]

Under the Act protection is confined to policyholders of authorised insurance companies who hold 'United Kingdom policies', i.e., policies the performance by the insurer of his obligations under which constitutes the carrying on of insurance business in the United Kingdom.[5] Where insurance is compulsory, liabilities to all policyholders must be met in full.[6] In the case of non-compulsory general insurance, liabilities to private policyholders (but not corporate policyholders, who are expected to take professional advice) must be met to the tune of 90 per cent, a limit fixed so as 'to leave an incentive for

---

[1] *Linked Life Assurance*, paras. 126–7. [2] See e.g. above, p. 141.
[3] Policyholders Protection Act 1975, s.1(2)(a). [4] Sch. 1, para. 1. [5] ss.3–4. [6] s.6.

prospective policyholders to choose carefully, insofar as information permits, a company of maximum reliability'.[1] In the case of long-term business, 90 per cent of any payment due must be paid and 90 per cent of future benefits must be secured (or the policyholder must be paid 90 per cent of the value of his policy).[2] But in a further concession to the disclosure philosophy, designed to encourage a potential policyholder 'to view with caution the more seductive over generous policies',[3] the Board has power to reduce or disregard any benefits payable under a long-term policy which in the opinion of an independent actuary are excessive.[4]

The Board's expenditure is financed by levies on companies – one for general business expenditure and one for long-term business expenditure.[5] There is no fund, levies being imposed only to meet expenditure as and when it is incurred. The amount of any levy must not exceed 1 per cent of a company's net premium income in the relevant year. Since its inception the scheme has been invoked on seven occasions, four of which have involved long-term insurers.

---

[1] s.8; Hansard 5th Ser. HL Debs. Vol.360, col. 205, May 6, 1975.   [2] ss.10–11.
[3] HL Debs. Vol. 360, col. 206.   [4] s.12.   [5] ss.18–21.

11
Friendly Societies

Friendly societies are unincorporated voluntary associations, registered under the Friendly Societies Act 1974, whose main purposes are the relief or maintenance of members and their families during sickness, unemployment or retirement and the provision of life insurance. They were first recognised by statute in 1793 (when provision was made for their registration in exchange for the removal of some of the disabilities to which they were subject as unincorporated associations and the extension of various financial privileges to them), but the definitive legislation relating to them was laid down in 1875 following the report of the Royal Commission on Friendly Societies. This defined the object of a friendly society as being that of providing by voluntary subscriptions of the members for a limited number of purposes, including the relief or maintenance of members and their families.[1] Friendly societies, like building societies, were thus confined to a narrow range of purposes (now set out in Schedule 1 to the 1974 Act) from which, in contrast to building societies, they have yet to escape.

The heyday of friendly societies was during the nineteenth century when they were effectively 'the only means by which the majority of the working population were able to protect themselves against loss of income through sickness or unemployment, or to make provision for retirement, for their widows and orphans, and for a decent burial'.[2] Even after the first National Insurance Act of 1911, which set up a state scheme for unemployment and health insurance, societies continued to prosper. Those which registered as 'approved societies', which administered sickness benefit under the state scheme, 'gained new opportunities for recruitment; a valuable contribution to their administrative costs; and the "cachet" attached to official recognition and the title "approved" '.[3] But since 1948, when approved society status was

---

[1] Friendly Societies Act 1875, s.8(1).
[2] *Friendly Societies: A New Framework*, Cm. 919 (1990), para. 2.2.
[3] Morgan, *The Friendly Societies in the Welfare State* (1986), p. 12.

ended and responsibility for the administration of benefits transferred to central government, the history of societies has been one of almost universal decline, broken only by the success of a minority in turning themselves into what are in substance, but not in form, small-scale mutual insurance companies.

Faced with the prospect of their continuing decline and eventual disappearance, friendly societies have responded by seeking powers to undertake a wider range of business than that currently open to them. 'If they were freed from the major legal constraints that hamper their activities, and given more favourable tax treatment, they could reverse the decline of the past forty years and continue to perform an important social role in stimulating the virtues of thrift, responsibility and self-reliance that the government claims to value so highly.'[1] In a Green Paper, *Friendly Societies: A New Framework*,[2] published in 1990, the Government declared itself sympathetic to the movement's request for wider powers. Under its proposals societies would be enabled to incorporate, by registering under the Industrial and Provident Societies Acts, in which form they would be empowered to undertake, through subsidiaries, a wider range of activities, while retaining their mutual constitution and continuing their 'unique combination of business and caring mutual support'.[3]

Pending the implementation of these proposals, the regulation of the larger, more successful societies has been assimilated to that for insurance companies in implementation of the Life Establishment Directive. This has entailed the subjection of the 38 'directive' societies, which are now formally authorised to carry on long-term insurance business, to solvency requirements similar to those applied to insurance companies.[4] It also means that those societies have been freed from the limitations on their powers of investment formerly imposed by the 1974 Act (section 46 of which confines non-directive societies to those investments allowed by the Trustee Investments Act), and are now restricted only by valuation provisions which, like those applicable to insurance companies, provide that certain assets are to be left out of account altogether, and others are to be taken into account only within specified limits, in calculating their solvency.[5] They can therefore invest more widely, or in excess of the limits, to the extent that their assets exceed those necessary to meet the required solvency margin.

A non-statutory Friendly Societies Investor Protection Scheme has also been established, with the encouragement and approval of the Chief Registrar,[6] to provide cover broadly equivalent to that given to policyholders in insurance companies under the Policyholders Protection Act. By the end of September 1990, 244 societies, accounting for 97.75 per cent of the funds of the movement, had joined or applied for membership. But a further 149 societies

[1] *Ibid.*, p. 4.   [2] *supra.*   [3] *Annual Report of the Chief Registrar for 1989–90*, para. 2.11.
[4] Friendly Societies' (Long Term Insurance Business) Regs. 1987, SI 1987/2132, Part III.
[5] SI 1987/2132, Part VI.   [6] FSA, s.141.

had yet to subscribe despite having been exhorted to do so at least twice by the Registry.

If the proposals set out in the Green Paper are implemented, friendly societies – like building societies under the 1986 Act – will be subject to two systems of control. The first of these will consist of an enhanced system of prudential supervision designed to ensure that the extension of their activities does not lead to increased risk for investors: '. . . it is a necessary concomitant of this extension of powers that the framework of prudential supervision to protect investors be brought up to the standards now applied to other organisations holding other peoples' money – building societies and insurance companies are the closest analogues.'[1] (The system of supervision for the larger societies has already begun to move in this direction.) The second will be a system of 'nature' limits designed to ensure that the primary purpose of a society continues to be that of providing its members with some or all of services permitted to societies by the legislation. Should a society transgress these limits, the Chief Registrar will be empowered to require it to bring its activities back within the prescribed purpose or to convert into a company.[2]

[1] *Friendly Societies: A New Framework*, para. 3.6.   [2] paras. 5.13–5.14.

12
Collective Investment Schemes

BACKGROUND

A collective investment scheme is simply one kind of device whereby investors pool their funds so as to create a common fund for investment. In the United Kingdom the main type of collective investment scheme is the unit trust. Occupational pension schemes and life assurance also offer pooling but, as we shall see, they are not defined as collective investment schemes in UK law. Unit trusts were first introduced in 1931. The rapidity of their growth (within five years there were 67 schemes with £50 million invested in them), together with their use of 'extensive display advertising' and 'enterprising salesmanship',[1] drew attention to the lack of promotional restraints to which they were subject compared with other investment media such as companies or, as regards investment management, members of the Stock Exchange, who were debarred from advertising. The question of their regulation was first considered by a Stock Exchange sub-committee in 1935 which concluded that since the Exchange was powerless to control 'the activities of trusts which were content to find their own market elsewhere', i.e., those trusts (the majority) whose promoters chose to make a market in their units outside the Exchange, they should be regulated by the state. 'The ultimate conclusion . . . is that full protection can only be achieved by legislation universally enforced, which lies outside the scope of the Stock Exchange.'[2]

The Anderson Committee, which was appointed in 1936 to inquire into what action, if any, was desirable in the public interest, accepted that properly conducted unit trusts offered 'small investors' a unique combination of access to investment in securities and risk-spreading, but expressed concern, *inter alia*, that investors did not always appreciate that, to use the modern idiom, the value of units might go down as well as up.

We are far from satisfied that this point is fully appreciated by the great mass of small

---

[1] *Fixed Trusts: Report of the Departmental Committee Appointed by the Board of Trade*, Cmd. 5259 (1936), para. 32.

[2] *Report of the Stock Exchange Sub-Committee on Fixed Trusts* (1935), reprinted *The Economist*, 7 March 1936, pp. 49–52.

investors when they buy units. On the contrary, we have had evidence that some unit holders are under a misapprehension as to the security that their units really possess. The possibility of misunderstanding upon this vital point is increased by much of the advertisement by which the sale of units has been fostered.[1]

The Committee rejected the possibility that unit trusts should be licensed as both inadvisable and impracticable, and recommended instead that their regulation should be assimilated to that of companies.

No immediate action was taken to implement the recommendations of the Anderson Committee, but the Bodkin Committee which was appointed a year later to examine the problem of sharepushing was sufficiently concerned about the use of 'pools' such as finance or commodity pools, or pools in stocks and shares, as a vehicle for fraud, to urge some control over and regulation of them 'in the interests of those imprudent persons who, influenced by the persuasive literature distributed in connection with these operations and the promise of guaranteed profits, are induced to participate'.[2] It recommended that the distribution of invitations to the public to contribute to or participate in schemes for financing any undertaking or to contribute to or participate in share or commodity pools of any kind should be deemed to be dealing in stocks and shares, and hence should be prohibited unless undertaken by registered persons.[3]

The Bodkin Committee's recommendations were implemented by the Prevention of Fraud (Investments) Act 1939. The original draft of the legislation made provision for the approval (rather than registration) of trustees, whose responsibility it would be to ensure that managers were fit and proper and that trusts were properly conducted, but in response to criticisms from corporate trustees about the power proposed to be conferred on the Board of Trade to vary their responsibilities as defined in trust deeds, the legislation was amended to provide for the approval of unit trust schemes by the Board of Trade. From enjoying greater promotional freedom than any other channel of investment, unit trusts thus found themselves, largely as a consequence of their supposed association with mushroom farms, apple orchards and other dubious investments, subjected to a regime under which alone among investments they were subject to a requirement of prior authorisation before they could be promoted to the investing public.

The framework for the regulation of unit trusts established by the Prevention of Fraud (Investments) Act survived essentially unchanged until it was recast by the Financial Services Act. The groundwork for the new regime was laid by Professor Gower, who was commissioned by the Secretary of State for Trade in 1981, following the collapse of a number of licensed dealers in securities, to undertake a review of the protection required by investors in, *inter*

---

[1] *Fixed Trusts*, para. 30.
[2] *Report of a Departmental Committee on Sharepushing*, Cmd. 5539 (1937), para. 18.
[3] para. 85, recommendation r.

alia, unit trusts and open-ended investment companies (which are the dominant form of collective investment scheme outside the United Kingdom). In his initial discussion document he acknowledged that the record of the unit trust movement was one of 'on the whole, scandal-free operation'.[1] But he was critical of what he saw as the excessive paternalism of the existing regime, and in particular of the restriction of the kinds of schemes that could be promoted to the general public under it to those whose underlying investments took the form of securities as defined in the legislation. He saw no reason why unit trusts should not serve as a vehicle for investment by members of the public in real property, commodities, financial futures and the like 'so long, at any rate, as the body operating the trust is adequately regulated, the nature and risk of the investment is adequately described and the investor is advised by a professional who is adequately controlled'.[2]

In its subsequent White Paper the Government accepted that unit trusts were in some respects over-regulated.[3] There was, it conceded, 'no reason to maintain restrictions on the promotion to the public of unit trusts investing in assets such as money market instruments, commodities and property, as long as there are adequate safeguards where the underlying assets are illiquid or prone to large price fluctuations'.[4] It therefore proposed extending the range of authorised unit trust schemes capable of being promoted to the general public, and introducing a new category of 'restricted unit trusts' in which form arrangements of 'a more speculative character' might be offered to investors with 'appropriate financial resources and experience',[5] a proposal criticised by Gower, who questioned whether, in view of the risks of abuse and the proposed range of investments for authorised schemes, it was desirable to open further opportunities to this extent.[6] But the opportunity presented by reform to replace the existing system of regulation with one based on the principle of registration with publicity along the lines originally advocated by the Anderson Committee was passed up without apparently being considered – although it would have brought the regulation of unit trusts more into line with, for example, that of linked life assurance.[7]

One obstacle to radical revision of the existing system was the UCITS (undertakings for collective investment in transferable securities) Directive[8] which requires a UCITS to be approved by the authorities of its home state if units in it are to be freely marketed throughout the Community. But the UCITS Directive applies only to unit trusts whose assets are invested in transferable securities. It was not, therefore, a barrier to reform of the rules governing unit trusts investing in other types of assets.

[1] *Disc. Doc.*, para. 8.18.

[2] para. 5.08. He was also critical of the Department's apparent preoccupation with matters of detail to the general neglect of practices which were actually or potentially undesirable: para. 8.18.

[3] FSA White Paper, para. 9.1.   [4] para. 9.10.   [5] paras. 9.1, 9.15–17.

[6] *Report*, Part 11 para. 5.12.   [7] See above, pp. 172–3.

[8] Dir.85/611 EEC OJ 1985 L375/19.

The Financial Services Act did not therefore drastically alter the course of unit trust regulation. One respect in which the new regime does differ from its predecessor, however, is that it is much more extensively rule-based. Under the Prevention of Fraud (Investments) Act the Department lacked any regulation-making power, a lack for which it compensated to some extent by using its discretion in the authorisation of schemes to compel those promoted to the general public to meet additional, unpublished requirements. Under the Financial Services Act, by contrast, SIB possesses powers, transferred to it by the DTI, to make regulations governing virtually every aspect of the constitution and management of authorised schemes. Its possession of these powers has made possible a redistribution of regulatory requirements between the trust deeds, by which schemes have been traditionally governed, and regulations made by SIB, with the bulk of the obligations imposed on scheme managers and trustees now being set out in regulations rather than trust deeds.

THE CONCEPT

A collective investment scheme, as defined by the Financial Services Act, has three essential characteristics. The first is *participation in profits or income*. Section 75(1) of the Act defines a collective investment scheme as 'any arrangements with respect to property . . . the purpose or effect of which is to enable persons taking part in the arrangements . . . to participate in or receive profits or income arising from the acquisition, holding, management, or disposal of the property or sums paid out of such profits or income'. The second is that the *participants must not have day-to-day control* over the management of the scheme property, although they may have the right to be consulted or to give directions (s.75(2)). The scheme property must therefore be managed by someone else, on whose investment management skills the participants by implication rely. And the third is that either the participants' contributions and the profits or income out of which payments are to be made to them must be *pooled*, or else the scheme property must be *managed as a whole* by or on behalf of the operator of the scheme (s.75(2)–(3)).

The 'scheme property', i.e. the underlying assets of the scheme, need not be confined to 'investments' as defined in the Financial Services Act, but may take any form, including money (s.75(1)). There is therefore no limit to the possible diversity of collective investment schemes. A scheme may exist to invest in securities, futures and options, old cars, plantations, bloodstock, theatrical productions or anything else.

A number of arrangements which might otherwise fall to be treated as collective investment schemes are excluded from the definition. Section 75(5) of the Act excludes certain *common management schemes* such as mass-produced (as opposed to individualised) personal equity plans which are managed together, on the basis of a series of discretionary investment management contracts on standards terms, as if they were a single plan. The effect of excluding such schemes from the definition is to allow them to be promoted to the general public without being authorised as unit trusts. To gain the benefit of the exclusion a scheme must satisfy a number of conditions. It must be limited to certain types of investments (paragraph (a)). Among the investments which are permitted are corporate and government securities but not futures or options. The participants must retain ownership of their share of the scheme property and they must be entitled to withdraw it at any time (paragraph (b)). Finally, there must be no pooling and the property must be dealt with as a whole only because more than one participant's holding is dealt with at a time and not, for example, because it is not owned by the participants (paragraph (c)).

Section 75(6) of the Act excludes miscellaneous other arrangements. They include:

(a)   arrangements operated *'otherwise than by way of business'* (paragraph (a)). Investment clubs that do not carry on a business are therefore excluded.

(b)   *employee share schemes* (paragraph (d)). Current public policy favours the establishment of such schemes as a way of rewarding employees and of encouraging them to identify more closely with the firms for which they work. Their exclusion is designed to ensure that employers are not discouraged from establishing or continuing to operate schemes by the need to comply with the requirements in respect of collective investment schemes.[1]

(c)   *timeshares* (paragraph (g)), but only those whose 'predominant purpose' is enjoyment rather than profit. Timeshares marketed as investment opportunities are not excluded.

(d)   *contracts of insurance* (paragraph (j)), investors in which are of course protected by a separate regime. The same rationale underlies the exclusion of *occupational pension schemes* (paragraph (k)), although the protection their members are afforded is much less extensive, and *deposit-based arrangements* (Schedule 1, paragraph 35(a)).

(e)   *business expansion scheme funds* (Schedule 1, para. 34). As with the exclusion of mass produced personal equity plans (and employee share schemes) the exclusion of business expansion scheme funds reflects the tension between investor protection and other public policy goals, which in this case has been resolved in favour of encouraging investment in new ventures.[2]

[1] See also, Sch. 1, para. 20.

[2] Also excluded are commercial joint ventures, intra-group arrangements, franchises, arrangements involving the issue of certificates representing securities, and clearing services.

Section 75(7) of the Act, finally, excludes *bodies corporate*, other than open-ended investment companies, from the definition. Investment trust companies are therefore not collective investment schemes. The rationale for the exclusion of bodies corporate is, of course, that they are subject to the disciplines of company law. Their exclusion, however, leaves open the possibility that the restrictions that the financial services legislation seeks to impose on the promotion of collective investment schemes may be negotiated – at the cost of complying with the prospectus requirements of the companies legislation – by constituting a scheme as a closed-ended registered company.[1] *Building societies* and *industrial and provident societies*, which are also bodies corporate but which are regulated under legislation specific to them, are also excluded, as are *friendly societies*.

As well as defining the concept of a collective investment scheme, the Act defines the concepts of a unit trust and an open-ended investment company. A unit trust is a collective investment scheme the property in which is 'held on trust' for the participants (s.75(8)); the scheme property must therefore be vested in a trustee, separate from the manager of the scheme, who must hold it for the benefit of participants ('unitholders') in the scheme. An open-ended investment company, on the other hand, is a collective investment scheme the property in which is beneficially owned by a company (rather than by the participants in the scheme) whose purpose is 'the investment of its funds with the aim of spreading investment risk and giving its members the benefit of the results of the management of those funds' (s.75(8)(a)). The rights of participants are represented by shares or securities in the company, which the company must either stand ready to buy back or which it must ensure can be sold on an investment exchange at a price related to the value of the scheme assets (s.75(8)(b)).

In the Financial Services Act White Paper, the Government announced its intention to amend the law to make the formation of open-ended investment companies a practicable proposition.[2] This was not done, but the Unit Trust Association has urged the Government to act, believing that its members would find it easier to export open-ended companies – the form of collective investment scheme which is familiar elsewhere in the European Community – than the unfamiliar concept of the unit trust.

PROMOTION

Section 76 of the Financial Services Act severely restricts the promotion of collective investment schemes to the general public. Subject to limited exceptions, it prohibits an *authorised person*[3] from promoting a scheme, i.e.

---

[1] See below, p. 188.

[2] para. 9.8. One of the obstacles to their formation has been the rule against the purchase by a company of its own shares.

[3] Unauthorised persons are prohibited from promoting schemes by the combined effects of section 3 (which prohibits the unauthorised carrying on of investment business), and section 57 (which prohibits the issue of an investment advertisement by an unauthorised person unless its contents have been approved by an authorised person – and approval is prevented by SIB CBRs (1990) 7.04(3)(b) and core rule 5.3).

advertising a scheme or advising or procuring persons to become participants, in the United Kingdom, unless it is either an *authorised unit trust scheme* or a *recognised scheme*. The distinction between authorised and recognised schemes corresponds to the distinction between United Kingdom schemes which may be authorised in the form of a unit trust, and overseas or offshore schemes which may be recognised. Breach of this prohibition is not a criminal offence, but it exposes an authorised person to the risk of civil and administrative penalties.[1]

This ban is the direct successor of the ban on the promotion of unauthorised schemes first introduced by the Prevention of Fraud (Investments) Act 1939. A possible justification for its retention is that 'unregulated' schemes, i.e. schemes that are neither authorised nor recognised, are not suitable for promotion to the public at large because they are not subject to the same regulatory disciplines – as to the composition of their underlying assets, the pricing of their units and so on – as regulated schemes.[2] This would be an altogether more compelling argument, however, were it not possible to side-step the ban on the promotion of unregulated schemes altogether by simply constituting a scheme as a closed-ended registered company, in which the public can then be invited to subscribe for shares in accordance with the prospectus requirements of the Companies Acts.

An alternative justification for banning the promotion of unregulated schemes is that it creates an incentive for promoters to submit to the discipline of regulation. As SIB puts it, a ban is needed so that 'operators intending to promote to the general public schemes eligible for authorisation or recognition should thereby have a sufficient incentive to seek authorisation or recognition with their attendant safeguards for investors.'[3] As we have seen, the introduction of the original ban had nothing to do with making authorised unit trust status more attractive, but this undoubtedly constitutes an important element of the contemporary justification for its retention. It must therefore be counted an anomaly of unit trust regulation that the incentive of authorised unit trust status is not one to which all promoters of collective investment can respond. A promoter of collective investment in, say, money market instruments, can seek authorisation because money market funds are one of the categories of funds permitted by the regulations. But a promoter of collective investment in, say, classic cars, must seek public participation by another route because classic car funds are not eligible for authorisation.

There are a number of exceptions to the general ban on the promotion of schemes, which are discussed below.[4] Also exempted are single property schemes, i.e. schemes unitising real property such as office blocks.[5] No such schemes exist.

---

[1] See below, pp. 000–000.
[2] SIB, *Promotion of Unregulated Collective Investment Schemes*, CP32 (1990), paras. 2–4.
[3] CP32, para. 7.   [4] See Ch. 18.   [5] FSA, s.76(4)–(7).

AUTHORISATION

Authorised unit trust schemes are the only form (apart from exempt single property schemes) in which United Kingdom collective investment schemes can be lawfully promoted to the general public. To obtain an order declaring a scheme to be authorised a number of conditions must be satisfied. One set of conditions applies to the unit trust scheme itself. It must comply with the requirements of the regulations, made under section 81 of the Act, relating to the constitution and management of schemes.[1] In addition, the name of the scheme must not be 'undesirable or misleading', and its purposes must be 'reasonably capable of being successfully carried into effect' (s.78(5)). SIB is therefore required to vet the scheme. Once a scheme has been authorised it cannot be altered without SIB's approval (s.82).

A second set of conditions applies to the manager and trustee of the scheme who, the Act stipulates, must not only be 'different persons' but also 'independent of each other'.[2] This stipulation forms the basis of a system of 'devolved self-regulation'[3] under which it is in the first instance the responsibility of the trustee, rather than an external regulator such as SIB or IMRO, to ensure that the manager acts in accordance with the regulations as well as the trust deed. As well as being independent of each other, the manager and trustee must each be incorporated, either in the United Kingdom or another Member State of the European Community. If the management company is incorporated in another Member State, the scheme must not qualify for recognition under section 86 of the Act.[4] The affairs of each must be administered in the country in which it is incorporated and each must have a place of business in the United Kingdom. Finally, each must be authorised to carry on investment business under the Financial Services Act and neither must be prohibited from acting in their chosen capacity (s.78(4)). A subsequent change of manager or trustee requires the approval of SIB (s.82).

A final condition relates to the redemption of units in the scheme. Section 78(6) of the Act provides that unitholders must be entitled to have their units redeemed in accordance with the scheme 'at a price related to the net value of the property to which the units relate . . .'. The purpose of this condition is to ensure that an investor can 'liquidate his holding at a fair price, without incurring penalties for so doing and with the minimum of fuss and delay'.[5] Redemption by the manager is the traditional method of redemption, but as an alternative units can be listed on an investment exchange, in which case the

---

[1] FSA, s.78(1).

[2] ss.77(1), 78(2); SIB, *Independence of Trustees/Managers of Unit Trusts*, Guidance Release 1/90.

[3] DTI, *The Regulation of Authorised Unit Trust Schemes: A consultative document on the proposed regulations for unit trust schemes authorised under the Financial Services Bill*, August 1986, para. 6.5.

[4] FSA, s.78(3); see below, pp. 190–1.

[5] DTI, *The Regulation of Authorised Unit Trust Schemes*, para. 9.8.

manager must ensure, for example by intervening in the market, that their price does not vary significantly from the net asset value of the fund.

Authorisation is at the discretion of SIB, which 'may' authorise a unit trust scheme which 'appears' to satisfy these conditions (s.78(1)). In *Allied Investors' Trust Ltd* v. *Board of Trade*[1] it was held that the Board of Trade was not obliged, under the similarly worded provision of the previous legislation, to authorise a unit trust scheme, even though it satisfied the conditions prescribed for authorisation by that legislation. Despite the elevation of the 'discretionary requirements' which the Board of Trade imposed in the exercise of this power to the status of statutory requirements, which has arguably diminished the need for discretion in the authorisation of schemes, and the change in judicial attitudes towards the control of administrative decision-making which has taken place over the last 30 years, the use of the permissive 'may' rather than the mandatory 'shall' makes it unlikely that a court would not hold that SIB, too, possesses a residual discretion to refuse authorisation even though the statutory requirements are satisfied.

Applications must be decided within six months of the date of their receipt.[2] If SIB is minded to refuse an application, it must give the applicants written notice of its intention to do so, stating the reasons for which it proposes to refuse the application, and informing them of their right to make representations, both orally and in writing, which must be taken into account in the determination of the application (s.80). There is no right of appeal against the refusal of authorisation, which leaves judicial review as the sole means of legal redress. But given that (in England and Wales) judicial review is not available as of right, it is questionable whether the lack of a right of appeal is compatible with the United Kingdom's obligation under the UCITS Directive to 'provide that decisions taken in respect of a UCITS are subject to a right to apply to the courts'.[3]

RECOGNITION

Recognised schemes, like authorised schemes, can be freely promoted to the general public. There are three routes by which an overseas scheme can seek recognition. First, a scheme which is constituted in another Member State and which invests in transferable securities can seek recognition by way of notification under section 86 of the Act. This section implements the UCITS Directive which allows a transferable securities scheme authorised in a Member State to be marketed throughout the Community without the need for further authorisation but subject to a notification requirement and compliance with local marketing rules. At least two months' notice must be given of the intention to market a scheme in the United Kingdom and

---

[1] [1956] Ch. 232.   [2] FSA, s.78(7).   [3] Dir. 85/611/EEC, art.51.2.

recognition can be refused if the proposed marketing arrangements do not comply with UK law.

Secondly, schemes from countries or territories designated by the Secretary of State (not SIB) can seek recognition under section 87 of the Act. A country or territory cannot be designated unless its regime affords to United Kingdom investors protection at least equivalent to that provided by the United Kingdom authorised unit trust regime. The Isle of Man, Jersey, Guernsey and Bermuda have been designated. Finally, offshore schemes that do not qualify for recognition under section 86 or 87 can seek recognition under section 88 of the Act. Recognition may be granted if a number of requirements are satisfied including the provision of adequate protection to participants.

As is the case with the refusal of authorisation, there is no right of appeal against the denial of recognition under any of these provisions. Notice must be given, however, and an opportunity to make representations[1] which must be taken into account before a final decision is taken in the case of schemes which qualify for recognition under section 87 or 88 but not section 86.[2]

PORTFOLIO REGULATION

Under the Prevention of Fraud (Investments) Act the property of an authorised unit trust scheme could only be invested in securities, which were defined narrowly by the legislation. Under the Financial Services Act, by contrast, the range of permitted assets has been widened to include money market instruments, futures and options, real property and warrants, as well as conventional securities. This does not mean that scheme managers have a free hand in the investment of scheme property. Schemes must belong to one (and only one) of a limited number of categories of schemes or funds allowed by regulations made under the Act,[3] for each of which categories the regulations prescribe, in the form of portfolio or asset structure requirements, minimum standards of risk-spreading and liquidity. The categories of funds allowed by the regulations include securities funds, money market funds, futures and options funds, geared futures and options funds (which are potentially riskier than futures and options funds), property funds and warrant funds. They also include feeder funds, funds of funds and umbrella funds.

Securities funds must invest mainly in approved securities, that is, transferable securities traded on an approved market (reg.5.09). The approved markets are the Official Lists of the EC Member States plus the other principal markets of Europe, North America and the Far East (they include the Unlisted Securities Market). Up to 10 per cent of a fund's assets can be invested in transferable securities that are not approved. The use of futures,

[1] FSA, ss.86(4)–(6). 89(5)–(7).   [2] ss.89(7), 86(5).
[3] Financial Services (Regulated Schemes) Regs. 1991, reg. 2.07.

options and contracts for differences (derivatives transactions) is permitted for the purpose of efficient portfolio management, that is, for the purpose of reducing relevant risks or costs or for achieving almost certain gains, but not for the purpose of speculation; such transactions must be covered by cash or other property sufficient to meet any obligations to which they may give rise. As to spread, the basic principle (which does not apply to government and other public securities) is that no more than 5 per cent of a fund can be invested in transferable securities issued by the same issuer, but this proportion may be increased to 10 per cent providing that the total of such investments is less than 40 per cent of the value of the fund (reg.5.10). Where more than 35 per cent of a fund is invested in government and other public securities issued by the same issuer, at least six different issues must be held, and a single issue cannot account for more than 30 per cent of the value of the fund (reg.5.11). There is also a limit of 10 per cent on the proportion of the voting shares of a company that can be held by a fund (reg.5.14), which limit is designed partly to ensure that the interests of unitholders remain paramount and partly to prevent holdings being so dominant that they unduly influence the market in the shares, making it difficult to sell the holdings and leading to the market price ceasing to be a reliable indicator of their value.[1]

Money market funds must confine investment (subject to the use of derivatives in the context of efficient portfolio management) to a variety of money market instruments: permitted investments include certificates of deposit, short-term corporate bonds, treasury bills and short-term bank deposits (reg.5.16). To avoid difficulties of valuation and realisation, at least 50 per cent of the fund must consist of instruments or deposits which are either redeemable or repayable within two weeks or capable of being transferred without the consent of a third party (reg.5.17). There are various requirements as to spread so that, for example, no more than 5 per cent of the fund can consist of instruments (other than government and other public securities) issued by the same issuer and no more than 10 per cent can be kept on deposit with one person; a limit of 30 per cent applies to government and other public securities of the same issue (reg.5.18).

Futures and options funds (FOFs) and *geared futures and options funds (GFOFs)* provide a vehicle for collective investment in futures, options and contracts for differences by way of speculation as well as by way of efficient portfolio management. Both futures and options enable investors to achieve a high degree of market exposure for a relatively small outlay. But whereas the most an investor in options stands to lose is the premium he paid for a contract, the losses an investor in futures faces are potentially unlimited. In the case of FOFs a ceiling is set on the level of risk to which unitholders are exposed, by requiring most if not all derivatives transactions to be fully covered by cash,

---

[1] *The Regulation of Authorised Unit Trust Schemes*, para. 7.11.

securities or other derivatives from within the fund (reg.5.20). This requirement does not apply to GFOFs, which are permitted to devote 20 per cent of
assets to initial outlay on derivatives transactions (reg.5.28). They therefore
involve greater potential exposure to risk than FOFs. There are no detailed
requirements as to spread, but the manager of a GFOF is under an obligation
to ensure that investment in derivatives is prudently diversified (reg.5.29).
Both FOFs and GFOFs may invest up to 10 per cent of assets in gold.

A *property fund* must invest between 20 per cent and 80 per cent of its assets
directly in land and buildings ('approved immovables') (reg.5.32). There are
detailed requirements governing the spread of land and buildings so that, for
example, a single property cannot account for more than 15 per cent of a fund
(reg.5.38). The balance must be invested either in property related assets,
such as shares in property companies, or, to help alleviate problems of
liquidity, in government and other public securities. Not more than 35 per cent
of assets may be held in the form of government and other public securities. A
property fund must secure a minimum subscription of £5 million during the
initial offer period: if it does not, an application for revocation of the scheme's
authorisation must be made.

Warrant funds were established as a separate category of authorised unit trust
in response to the marketing in the United Kingdom under the UCITS
arrangements of warrant funds based in other Member States. A warrant fund
is similar in all respects to a securities fund, except that it may invest up to 100
per cent in warrants (which give their holders the right to buy securities at a
particular price) (reg.5.42). Warrants are highly geared instruments in the
sense that their prices rise and fall far more sharply than those of the securities
on which they are based. Like GFOFs, warrant funds are therefore a risky
form of investment.

Feeder funds are funds which invest exclusively in other funds (or in 'eligible'
investment trust companies) for personal pension purposes; only relevant
pension schemes can be feeder funds (reg.5.43). The purpose of requiring a
unit trust or investment trust-based personal pension to be constituted as a
feeder fund is to ensure that an investor 'who contributes to a personal pension
arrangement and who obtains tax concessions on those contributions is not
able to redeem his units in the normal way before retirement and thus walk
away with his investment enhanced by the tax concessions'.[1] A feeder fund can
be invested only in units of one authorised unit trust or recognised scheme or in
shares of one eligible investment trust company. There are restrictions on the
categories of authorised unit trust scheme and their recognised scheme
equivalents in which feeder funds can be invested so that they cannot, for
example, be invested in GFOFs or warrant funds.

---

[1] SIB, *Regulations for Collective Investment Schemes: Investment and Borrowing Powers and New Products*, CP 49
(1990), para. 70.

Funds of funds, as their description implies, invest exclusively in other funds. A fund of funds may invest (subject to the efficient portfolio management facility) either in funds within one only of the permitted categories of authorised unit trust scheme, apart from feeder funds or other funds of funds, or else it may combine investment in money market funds with investment in any one other permitted category of scheme, apart again from feeder funds or other funds of funds (reg.5.45). No more than 20 per cent of assets can be invested in a single fund, so that there must be investment in at least five funds.

An *umbrella fund* consists of a number of constituent parts, each of which must have the characteristics of one of the other permitted categories of scheme, participants in the fund being entitled to switch all or part of their investment from one part to another (reg.5.47). Proposals for *mixed funds*, which in contrast to funds of funds would be able to invest in any combination of funds, have been shelved until experience has been gained of the operation of futures and options funds and property funds.

The extension of the range of unit trust schemes capable of being promoted to the general public was not effected without controversy. The proposal that unit trust schemes should be permitted to invest in futures and options attracted criticism from the Unit Trust Association in particular, which feared that failures among funds investing in riskier types of assets would quickly destroy the reputation of unit trusts as a relatively low-risk investment vehicle. The distinction between FOFs and GFOFs was one response to this concern; the tougher marketing regime for GFOFs and warrant funds another. It is possible, however, that a more satisfactory balance might have been struck between the competing demands of product innovation and investor protection by the development of a new vehicle for collective investment in these assets rather than by reliance on the unit trust concept.[1]

PRICING REGULATION

Pricing regulation is unique to authorised unit trust schemes. The need for it arises because the market in the units of most trusts is made by their managers rather than by competing market-makers. To prevent the abuse by managers of their monopoly position, the prices at which they sell and buy back units are regulated. The principle on which pricing regulation is based is that of fairness between incoming, outgoing and continuing participants.

Prices are fixed at the discretion of the manager within the overall limits set by the regulations. Two prices are fixed: an *issue* or offer price at which units are bought by investors, and a *redemption* or bid price at which units are sold by investors. The limits within which issue and redemption prices are fixed are set by creation and cancellation prices calculated in accordance with the

[1] CP 49, para. 9.

regulations, plus, in the case of the issue price, an initial charge paid to the manager. The creation price is calculated on the basis of the offer net asset value of the fund (the cost of buying the whole of the existing fund), while the cancellation price is calculated on the basis of the bid net asset value of the fund (the amount that would be realised on the sale of the fund).[1] In this way the price at which unitholders are entitled to have their units redeemed is related to the net asset value of a fund. The actual prices quoted will depend on whether the fund is expanding or contracting. If it is expanding (on an offer basis) the issue and redemption prices quoted will be higher than if it is contracting (on a bid basis).

The United Kingdom system of 'dual pricing' under which prices are determined by the offer and bid net asset values of a fund contrasts with the system of 'single pricing' employed in other countries, under which prices are calculated on the same basis regardless of whether units are being bought or sold and irrespective of whether a fund is expanding or contracting. The possibility of bringing the United Kingdom into line with practice elsewhere has been mooted. As well as being simpler, single pricing has the attraction of eliminating managerial discretion in the pricing of units. It is also probably essential if United Kingdom funds are to be marketed successfully abroad. However, a shift to single pricing bases, for example, on the mid-market value of the underlying assets would not be without difficulty. One difficulty would be that it would penalise existing investors to the benefit of new and departing ones, since incoming investors would have to pay less than the cost of acquiring the underlying assets represented by the units purchased and outgoing unitholders would receive more than the proceeds of realising the assets represented by their holdings.

Prices may be fixed on an historic or forward basis. Historic prices are fixed by reference to the valuation preceding a transaction, while forward prices are fixed by reference to the valuation which next follows a transaction. Historic and forward prices have different properties. Historic prices combine certainty with the possibility of unfairness as a result of changes in the value of the underlying assets: 'The fact that unit prices are based on an out of date valuation of the fund opens up opportunities for professional market operators and managers to profit at the expense of other unit holders. They are in a position to effect transactions on the basis of current information not yet reflected in unit prices.'[2] Forward prices, on the other hand, avoid the possibility of unfairness at the expense of uncertainty as to the price at which a bargain will be concluded.

Authorised unit trusts have traditionally been priced on an historic basis. Because of the opportunities which historic pricing provides for the exploitation of inequalities of information, SIB tried unsuccessfully to make forward

---

[1] Financial Services (Regulated Schemes) Regs. 1991, regs. 4.09, 4.11.
[2] SIB, *Collective Investment Schemes* (October 1987), para. 21.

pricing compulsory. However, although managers normally retain the freedom to deal on the basis of historic prices, there are numerous occasions on which dealing must take place on the basis of forward prices. For example, if a manager knows or has reason to believe that there is a 2 per cent or greater difference between the current value of a fund and its last calculated value he must move forward (or carry out a special valuation).[1] GFOFs, property funds and warrant funds must always be priced on a forward basis.

SUPERVISION

The primary role in the supervision of authorised unit trust schemes is played by SIB and IMRO, which is the normal regulator both of managers and trustees. But a role is also played by trustees who are responsible in addition for the custody of scheme assets. Apart from their duties under the general law of the land,[2] the trustees' specific responsibilities include ensuring that the relevant portfolio requirements are observed and that unit prices are within the prescribed limits.[3] In the exercise of its responsibilities the trustee company has power to obtain information from the manager concerning the operation of the scheme (reg.7.08), and the power ultimately to replace the manager if it is of the opinion 'for good and sufficient reason' that a change of manager is desirable in the interests of participants (reg.7.17). A manager may also, in a concession to the notion of 'unitholder democracy', be removed by an extraordinary resolution of unitholders.

Behind the trustees (and unitholders) stand IMRO and SIB, which has the conventional array of powers of investigation, intervention and revocation at its disposal. In the exercise of its powers of investigation, which are exercisable concurrently with the DTI, SIB may appoint inspectors to investigate and report on the affairs of an authorised unit trust scheme, or of its manager or trustee, if it appears that it is in the interests of unitholders to do so or that the matter is of public concern.[4] It may also appoint inspectors to investigate and report on the affairs of a recognised scheme, or of its operator or trustee (but only in relation to activities carried on in the United Kingdom), or of an unregulated scheme, or of its operator or trustee. Like inspectors appointed under the Companies Act, inspectors appointed to investigate the administration of collective investment schemes have power to require persons in possession of relevant information to produce documents, to attend before them and to otherwise assist them with an investigation; they also have power to examine witnesses on oath, and witnesses' answers to inspectors' questions may be used in evidence against them.[5] A failure to comply with a requirement

---

[1] Financial Services (Regulated Schemes) Regs. 1991, reg. 4.26.

[2] Section 84 of the Act renders void any provision in the deed of an authorised scheme which would enable a trustee to avoid liability for failure to exercise due care and diligence in the discharge of his functions.

[3] Financial Services (Regulated Schemes) Regs. 1991, reg. 7.09.   [4] FSA, s.94(1).

[5] s.94(3), applying with appropriate modifications ss.434–6 of the Companies Act.

imposed in the exercise of these powers, including a requirement to answer questions, may be punished as a contempt of court.

SIB's powers of intervention are confined to regulated collective investment schemes: unregulated schemes by definition are not amenable to intervention. Its powers of intervention are more extensive and varied in relation to authorised schemes than in relation to recognised schemes, the primary responsibility for intervention in relation to the latter resting with the authorities of their home state. In the case of recognised schemes SIB's powers are confined to the suspension of recognition and then only recognition obtained under section 87 or 88 but not section 86 of the Act (s.91(5)). In the case of authorised schemes, by contrast, it has power to require dealings in units to be suspended and schemes to be wound up as well as power to apply to the court for an order removing a manager or trustee (or both a manager and trustee) and either replacing them or appointing an authorised person to wind up a scheme.[1] These powers may be exercised where any of the conditions for authorisation or recognition (where recognition is obtained under section 88) are no longer satisfied, where a manager, trustee or operator are in breach of their obligations, or where intervention appears otherwise 'desirable in the interests of participants or potential participants in the scheme'.[2] Failure to comply with a direction requiring dealings in units to be suspended or a scheme to be wound up renders the manager and trustee of an authorised unit trust scheme liable to a range of sanctions, including public censure and actions for damages as well as loss of their authorisation to carry on investment business (s.91(4)).

There is no right of appeal against the exercise of these powers. Nor, in the interests of the protection of investors, is there any right to make representations which must be taken into account before deciding whether or not to intervene. Decisions must be reasoned, however, and SIB has power to withdraw or vary a direction on the application of the manager, trustee or operator of a scheme as well as of its own motion.[3]

Finally, SIB has power, exercisable on the same grounds as its powers of intervention, to revoke authorisation and to withdraw recognition, again where recognition was obtained by virtue of section 87 or 88 but not 86.[4] Revocation of authorisation and withdrawal of recognition both have the consequence that a scheme can no longer be lawfully promoted to the public at large. There is no right of appeal against the revocation of authorisation or the withdrawal of recognition, but SIB must give notice of its intention and an opportunity to make representations, which must be taken into account before a final decision is made.[5] During this period the interests of investors and

---

[1] ss.91(2), 93.   [2] ss.91(1), (4), 93(1).   [3] ss.92, 91(8).   [4] ss.79(1), 89(1).
[5] ss.80, 89(5)–(7).

potential investors can be safeguarded by the exercise of SIB's powers of intervention.

13
Occupational Pension Schemes

BACKGROUND

An occupational pension scheme is an arrangement made by an employer under which benefits are paid to scheme members on their retirement and to their dependants on death. Employers' motives for establishing the first schemes varied. In some cases they were a formalisation of *ad hoc* arrangements whereby *ex gratia* payments were made to long serving, valued employees. In others they were aimed at encouraging the savings habit among the workforce. But the most common motive for establishing schemes was to improve the length and quality of key employees' working commitment to firms; they also made easier the compulsory retirement of employees whose useful working lives were drawing to a close.[1]

After a slow start the coverage of schemes grew rapidly, particularly in the years after the Second World War when the fiscal treatment of schemes became especially favourable. In 1936 about 2.5 million employees, or about 15 per cent of the workforce, were members of occupational pension schemes. By 1967 scheme membership had climbed to a peak of 12.2 million, or 49 per cent of the workforce. Since then the proportion of the workforce covered by schemes has remained roughly constant at around 50 per cent, although the number of members has fallen – to 10.6 million in 1987. Meanwhile, the number of pensioners receiving pensions has risen from less than a million in 1953 to some 6 million in 1987.[2]

The growth of occupational provision for old age has been paralleled by the growth of state provision. Nineteenth-century orthodoxy insisted that provision for old age was the responsibility of the individual – there was no other way of providing for old age, the Chief Registrar of Friendly Societies wrote in 1891, than by 'thrift, self-denial and forethought in youth'.[3] But acceptance of old age as the single greatest cause of poverty led to the introduction of a non-contributory state pension scheme in 1908, followed by a contributory scheme in 1925. After the Second World War the state's aim came increasingly to be defined in terms of income maintenance rather than the simple relief of

[1] Hannah, *Inventing Retirement* (1986), pp. 21–30.
[2] *Occupational Pension Schemes 1987: Eighth Survey by the Government Actuary* (1991).
[3] Quoted in Gosden, *Self-Help* (1973), p. 266.

poverty. A graduated pension scheme was introduced in 1961 and replaced by a more ambitious state earnings-related pension scheme (SERPS) in 1978. But within a decade of its introduction hostility to state provision coupled with concern about the cost to future generations of funding SERPS led to its being drastically cut back. At the same time, measures were taken to encourage, on an individual as well as a collective basis, private provision for old age. Personal pensions – one of the fruits of this 'pensions revolution' – are discussed in the next chapter.

The regulatory regime for occupational pension schemes differs markedly from that for the other savings and investment media with which we are concerned. The key difference is that there is no system of prudential supervision akin to that applied to banks, building societies and insurance companies. (Nor is there any system of devolved self-regulation, involving the imposition of specific responsibilities upon trustees, akin to that applied to authorised unit trusts.)[1] There is thus no requirement of authorisation, although investment managers require authorisation under the Financial Services Act,[2] no solvency or investment requirements, although limited requirements apply to contracted out schemes,[3] no supervisory authority equipped with powers of intervention, although the Occupational Pensions Board exercises some powers but again only for the purpose of supervising contracted out schemes,[4] and no compensation arrangements, although other compensation arrangements may be brought into play by the kinds of assets, for example, insurance policies, in which scheme resources are invested, and the Department of Social Security has power, which it has not exercised, to prescribe compensation arrangements in respect of schemes contracted out of the state scheme on a money purchase basis.

This difference in regulatory treatment is not attributable to any features of occupational pension schemes that set them apart from other investment media. Pension schemes are 'no less custodians of their members' savings than are banks of their depositors', or life assurance companies of their policy-holders' '.[5] Nor do they present less scope for fraud and mismanagement than do other financial institutions, as has been graphically illustrated by the revelations of 'stealing on a massive scale' from the pension schemes controlled by Robert Maxwell, which 'may force into near destitution many of the people covered by these schemes who otherwise had every prospect of retirement free from major financial worries.'[6] Instead, it is partly attributable to the apparent lack of any need for a full-scale system of prudential supervision – before the Maxwell scandal there had been only a handful of scheme failures –

---

[1] See above, pp. 189, 196.   [2] See below, pp. 237, 240.   [3] See below, pp. 205–10.
[4] See below, pp. 205–10.
[5] Richardson, 'The provision of pensions' (1983) 23 *Bank of England Quarterly Bulletin* 502 at p. 508.
[6] Second Report from the Social Security Committee, *The Operation of Pension Funds* (1992; HC 61-II), para. 6.

and to the much greater scale of the task that would be involved (whereas there are only some hundreds of banks, building societies and insurance companies, there are nearly 140,000 pension schemes).[1] Accordingly, the argument went, 'it would represent a very heavy commitment in skilled manpower to supervise the funding of all schemes other than those under which the benefits were fully secured by means of insurance policies and the investment of all self-administered schemes and one that would be unnecessary in the great majority of schemes.'[2]

Also relevant has been the perception that so long as occupational pension schemes are provided purely at the discretion of employers, any increase in their costs as a result of the imposition of new regulatory requirements may have the undesired – though arguably desirable in view of the risks to which their members may be exposed and the difficulty of their effective regulation – consequence of diminishing the extent of occupational provision for old age. The Occupational Pensions Board, for example, prefaced its report, *Protecting Pensions*, in 1989 with the comment that: 'we have sought to tailor our recommendations to ensure that whilst in certain areas they provide greater security to the member, the additional cost to the employer is kept to a minimum. This to our mind is important, because nothing should be done to deter employers from providing a company scheme and to burden them with heavy additional cost could well prove counter-productive.'[3] But if, as the Government insisted in the Financial Services Act White Paper, occupational pension rights are to be 'at least as well protected as other forms of investment', the nettle of additional costs may have to be grasped.[4]

LEGAL BASIS

Most occupational pension schemes are set up in the form of a trust. The reasons for this are first and foremost fiscal: to gain the full range of tax reliefs and exemptions pension schemes must be set up as irrevocable trusts, the idea being to deny employers access to assets set aside for pension purposes and thus to prevent schemes being used for tax avoidance or evasion.[5]

Apart from its fiscal advantages the trust device has other advantages. From the standpoint of employers perhaps the most important of these advantages is its flexibility, which allows schemes to be tailored to the circumstances of an individual firm. The pioneers of trust-based schemes discovered that the trust was 'agreeably flexible: creative lawyers could draw up a trust deed with

---

[1] DHSS, *Greater Security for the Rights and Expectations of Members of Occupational Pension Schemes*, February 1984, para. 46. According to the National Audit Office there are some 725,000 pension schemes attracting tax relief, 5 per cent of which are self-administered and the rest of which are insured: *Inland Revenue: Control of Tax Reliefs on Occupational Pension Schemes* HC 666 (1991).

[2] *Occupational Pension Schemes – The Role of Members in the Running of Schemes*, Cmnd. 6514 (1976), para. 45.

[3] OPB, *Protecting Pensions: Safeguarding Benefits in a Changing Environment*, Cm. 573 (1989) p. iii.

[4] FSA White Paper, para. 11.2.   [5] See below, pp. 204–5.

virtually any characteristic the employer chose'.[1] From the standpoint of pension scheme members, the trust device, as well as putting scheme assets beyond the reach of employers, also has the advantage of putting them beyond the reach of creditors in the event of an employer's insolvency. They are thus, in theory at least, insulated from any misfortune that may befall an employer. Moreover, the trustees are under a fiduciary obligation to act in accordance with the best interests of the present and future beneficiaries of the trust.[2]

Notwithstanding these advantages, the suitability of the law of trusts as a legal basis for occupational pension schemes has been questioned. Although pension schemes are now financially the most important form of trusts, the law of trusts was not devised with the needs of pension schemes in mind but principally 'to prevent the dispersal of large family estates and to protect the needs of children who were considered unable to administer their own assets'.[3] As a result, critics argue, many of the concepts used in trust law become somewhat strained when applied to modern pension schemes. 'In the days when pension schemes were looked upon as a form of employer benevolence it may have been easier to equate the employer with a *paterfamilias* endowing his infant successors with an inheritance held in trust, but the notion now seems increasingly incongruous.'[4]

Of greater moment is the criticism that the roles of the various parties are insufficiently clearly defined. Most obviously lacking in definition is the role of the employer upon whose continuing goodwill the payment of the promised benefits may depend, but about whose obligations the law is largely silent.[5] The economic dependence of funds on employers also has implications for trustees whose task in law is to serve the best interests for the beneficiaries, but who may feel that the beneficiaries' interests are best served by complying with the wishes of the employer. In some cases the underlying economic reality may be reflected in the appointment of an employer as the sole trustee. The protection afforded beneficiaries by the appointment of trustees is thus open to question: '. . . the idea that the trustees represented the beneficiaries' interests was no more than a legal fiction. *De facto*, the great bulk of trustee boards and management committees worked in the interests of employers.'[6] Moreover, securing legal redress for beneficiaries in the event of an alleged breach of trust is costly and difficult.

Considerations such as these led the Wilson Committee in 1980 to recommend the adoption of a Pension Scheme Act, analogous to the Companies Acts, under which schemes would be formally constituted. As conceived by the Wilson Committee, the main purpose of statutory interven-

[1] Hannah, *op. cit.*, p. 19.   [2] See above, p. 18.

[3] OPB, *Greater Security for the Rights and Expectations of Members of Occupational Pension Schemes*, Cmnd. 8649 (1982), para. 4.9.

[4] *Ibid.*, para. 8.2.

[5] See, however, *Imperial Tobacco Pension Trust Ltd.* v. *Imperial Tobacco Ltd.*, *FTLR* Dec. 5, 1990.

[6] Hannah, *op. cit.*, p. 140.

tion would be 'to produce a clear and systematic statement of the legal duties and obligations of employing companies, scheme trustees and their professional advisers and to make it easier for members of a scheme and their representatives to monitor its management and solvency'.[1] Two years later the Occupational Pensions Board concluded that 'the present structure of trust law does not provide satisfactory safeguards for members' rights and expectations in occupational pension schemes', and called on the Government 'to initiate a wide-ranging review of the relevant law, with particular regard to the desirability and feasibility of taking pension schemes out of trust law completely and putting them on a new statutory basis'.[2]

The Government responded to this pressure by setting up a working party to examine the law and conventions governing the conduct of pension funds. It claimed to detect a 'substantial' movement in opinion 'in favour or retaining trust law as an appropriate legal basis, provided that it is clarified so as to remove ambiguities and unsatisfactory aspects, and to fill identified gaps'.[3] No evidence of this substantial movement in opinion was offered but the Government announced itself satisfied that, contrary to the criticisms that had been made, trust law did provide a suitable framework for regulating the conduct of pension schemes.[4]

The Government's conclusion was later endorsed, in a surprising volte-face, by the OPB, which saw 'no immediate advantage of clarity or simplicity in a consolidation of the numerous strands of separate legislation that are involved'.[5] But the question of the appropriate legal basis for pension schemes has now been reopened in the light of the shortcomings in the practical operation of trust law revealed by the Maxwell affair. In its report on the *Operation of Pension Funds*, the Social Security Committee recommended the implementation as a matter of priority of the Wilson Committee's recommendation that the law of trusts be replaced by a Pensions Act; the lack of other scandals equivalent in scale to that perpetrated on the Maxwell-controlled pension funds, the Committee concluded, owed more to the decency of employers and the integrity of trustees than to the law of trusts.[6]

REGULATION

The regulatory controls to which occupational pension schemes are subject fall into three distinct groups. One group applies to schemes approved for tax

---

[1] para. 1224.
[2] *Greater Security for the Rights etc.*, para. 8.7; see also Gower, *Report*, Part 1, para. 11.03.
[3] DHSS, *Greater Security for the Rights etc.*, para. 59.   [4] *Ibid.*, para. 60.
[5] *Protecting Pensions*, para. 8.14. The Government's rejection of the case for reform prompted Gower to remark: 'The Government obviously have greater confidence than I have in reliance on pristine trust law in relation to modern commercial developments . . . which its founding fathers never contemplated': *Report*, Part II, para. 5.23.
[6] *The Operation of Pension Funds*, paras. 74–75.

purposes: their purpose is to ensure that tax reliefs are confined to genuine pension schemes and that schemes are not used for tax avoidance or evasion. A second group applies to schemes used for contracting out of SERPS. Their purpose is to ensure that benefits standing in place of state benefits meet certain criteria and are paid when they fall due. The third group is made up of a miscellany of controls which apply to occupational pension schemes generally, regardless of whether or not they are approved for tax purposes or used for contracting out of SERPS. One of these controls is a product of the Financial Services Act, the others address some of the hazards occupational pension scheme members face.

'Exempt approved' schemes

Occupational pension schemes enjoy significant tax advantages. To qualify for full tax relief on contributions and investment income, schemes must not only be approved by the Inland Revenue under sections 590 or 591 of the Income and Corporation Taxes Act 1988, but must also secure 'exempt approved' status, i.e. they must be shown to the satisfaction of the Inland Revenue to be established under 'irrevocable trusts'.[1] The original purpose of limiting tax reliefs to schemes established under irrevocable trusts seems not to have been to encourage the use of the trust device 'as a safeguard for members' rights but rather to ensure that the money invested in them was genuinely alienated from the employer, who could not then use the scheme as a vehicle for tax avoidance'.[2] This does not prevent the trust device from providing a safeguard for members' rights as well as means of preventing tax avoidance and evasion, but Inland Revenue supervision of occupational pension schemes is directed to safeguarding public revenues rather than members' rights.

To qualify for exempt approved status the Inland Revenue does not require a scheme to be operated by means of a formal trust deed, but it does require the scheme assets to be set aside to provide relevant benefits for employees, and that they be held by a trustee or trustees (who may be, or include, the employer) on trusts that ensure that they are not normally available to the employer.[3] The Occupational Pensions Board has claimed to detect in various other of the conditions of approval operated by the Inland Revenue a contribution to the protection of members,[4] but their contribution seems slight. Thus, although it is a requirement of Inland Revenue approval of a scheme that an employer must contribute to it, and a scheme will not be approved if 'the employer's contributions appear to be mere token contributions of insignificant amounts i.e. less than 10 per cent of the total contributions',[5] there is no requirement on the employer to see that his scheme

[1] ICTA, s.592.   [2] OPB, *Greater Security for the Rights etc.*, para. 3.6.
[3] Inland Revenue Practice Notes, *Occupational Pension Schemes*, IR12 (1991), paras. 2.3 and 2.5.
[4] *Greater Security for the Rights etc.*, paras. 4.17–4.21.   [5] IR12, para. 5.1.

is adequately funded.

Provision is made, on the other hand, to prevent overfunding and for the elimination of actuarial surpluses.[1] Should an actuarial valuation, which must be carried out at not less than three-and-a-half yearly intervals, reveal a scheme's assets to exceed its liabilities by more than 5 per cent, proposals must be made to the Inland Revenue for eliminating the surplus. This may be done by improving existing benefits or by providing new benefits, by suspending or reducing contributions for up to five years, by returning the surplus to the employer (which attracts a tax liability), or by any combination of these measures. A surplus cannot be returned to an employer, however, unless the scheme rules make provision for pensions payable under the scheme to be increased in accordance with the statutory requirements.[2] Should a scheme's rules prohibit refunds to the employer or contribution holidays the Occupational Pensions Board has power to authorise their modification to allow this.[3]

'Contracted out' schemes

Just as employers have an incentive, in the shape of tax concessions, to secure exempt approved status for schemes, so too they have an incentive, in the shape of reduced national insurance contributions, to secure approval for schemes as a vehicle for contracting employees out of SERPS. In return for a rebate in national insurance contributions, employers are required to provide the earnings-related part of the pension that would otherwise have been payable under the state scheme, and regulation is applied to ensure that those benefits which are standing in place of the state scheme benefits are paid when they fall due.

Schemes may contract out on a final salary or (since April 6, 1988) a money purchase basis. A final salary or 'defined benefit' scheme is one in which the benefits are calculated on the basis of the levels of pensionable pay during the last year or years of pensionable service. A money purchase or 'defined contributions' scheme, on the other hand, is one in which the contributions are invested, effectively as a personal savings account, for each individual scheme member, and the benefits are simply those that can be purchased with the sum of the contributions and the investment return on them at retirement.

The introduction of contracting out on a money purchase basis marks a return to a form of pension provision which earlier had been largely abandoned, because in inflationary conditions it 'simply did not produce pensions sufficient to permit people to retire on a decent proportion of their final income'.[4] Final salary schemes, by contrast, effectively compensate for inflation during working life (but not after retirement) by providing a pension linked to pay levels near the time that the pension becomes payable. Their

[1] ICTA, ss.601–2, Sch. 22.   [2] SSA 1990, s.11(3), see below, pp. 213–14.   [3] SSA, s.64(3).
[4] Hannah, *op. cit.*, p. 72.

disadvantage, from the standpoint of employers, is that they involve – morally if not legally – an open-ended financial commitment, the precise scale of which depends on the future rate of growth of earnings and the rate of return on investments, which is one reason why employers may be unwilling to set up or continue schemes in this form. Provision was thus made for contracting out on a money purchase basis by the Social Security Act 1986 in the expectation (which so far at least appears not to have been realised) that 'more employers would be prepared to start up schemes if they could contract out of the state earnings-related scheme but keep their commitments to a known level.'[1]

Contracting out is governed by sections 30–32 of the Social Security Pensions Act 1975 which lay down alternative tests for contracting out depending on whether a scheme is contracted out on a salary related or money purchase basis. In the case of a *final salary scheme* the basis requirement, which has been rendered less onerous as a result of the cutting back of SERPS, is that the scheme must provide a 'guaranteed minimum pension' (GMP), broadly equivalent to the earnings-related part of the state pension which the member would have earned had his employment not been contracted out of the state scheme.[2]

This guaranteed minimum pensions test cannot be applied to money purchase schemes since they do not provide defined benefits. The GMP test is therefore replaced in *money purchase schemes* by a guaranteed minimum level of contributions test, whereby the employer must make a contribution to the scheme at least equal to the 'contracted out rebate', i.e. the difference between full rate national insurance contributions and the lower rate which members of contracted out schemes and their employers pay, to which may be added (until 1993) an incentive payment in respect of schemes contracted out for the first time. These minimum contributions and incentive payments must be applied, except insofar as they are used to defray administrative expenses and to pay commissions, so as to provide money purchase benefits.[3] These money purchase benefits, which are known as 'protected rights', are in concept the money purchase equivalent of the pension an employee would have earned as a member of SERPS. Whether they in fact match the pension which would have been earned under SERPS depends on the performance of the fund and annuity rates at retirement, but for the purpose of calculating an individual's entitlement under SERPS it is assumed that they match the GMP which would have been provided by a salary related scheme. Certainty for employers as to the level of their commitment is therefore secured in a money purchase scheme at the expense of uncertainty for employees as to the size of their pension on retirement.

---

[1] *Reform of Social Security: Programme for Action*, Cmnd. 9691 (1985), para. 2.27.   [2] SSPA, s.30(1).

[3] SSPA, s.30(1); power is conferred by SSA 1986, Sch. 1, para. 4 to control charges, but this power has not been exercised.

As well as requirements in relation to guaranteed minimum pensions or protected rights, schemes must satisfy other requirements, designed for the protection of members, if they are to be used for contracting out. In the case of final salary schemes, the Occupational Pensions Board must be satisfied generally as to the arrangements in force for securing guaranteed minimum pensions; in particular it must be satisfied that guaranteed minimum pensions are 'secured' by an irrevocable trust, insurance policy or annuity contract.[1] There must also be a scheme rule which gives priority to any liabilities of the scheme in respect of, *inter alia*, guaranteed minimum pensions in the event of its being wound up.[2]

In the case of *money purchase schemes* there are restrictions on the investment of scheme resources.[3] These restrictions have no final salary scheme equivalents. The basic justification for their imposition is that it is the employee – rather than the employer – who bears the risk that the performance of the fund will be insufficient to match his expectations on retirement. 'Because the distinctive characteristic of money purchase occupational schemes, as opposed to salary-related occupational schemes, is that there will normally be no guaranteed benefits for members, the Government consider it particularly important to seek to guard against an unwise investment policy being adopted by trustees.'[4]

The restrictions are of three kinds. First, there are limits on the classes of assets in which scheme resources may be invested; these limits are not tightly drawn so that scheme resources may be invested in ostensibly riskier investments such as futures and units of unauthorised unit trust schemes, as well as safer investments such as deposit accounts and gild-edged securities. Second, there are limits ('class limits') on the proportion of scheme resources that may be invested in certain classes of assets, so that, for example, no more than 10 per cent of a fund may be invested in the 'riskier' forms of permitted investments. Finally there are limits ('concentration limits') on the proportion of scheme resources that may be invested in the securities of a single issuer, the basic principle, which is derived from the regulation of unit trusts, being that no more than 5 per cent of the resources of a scheme can be invested in securities issued by the same issuer, but this proportion may be increased to 10 per cent so long as the total of such investments does not exceed 40 per cent of the value of the fund.

Section 41 of the Social Security Pensions Act requires the Occupational

---

[1] SSPA, s.40(2), Occupational Pension Schemes (Contracting-Out) Regs. 1984, SI 1984/380, reg.30; 'secured' in this context is interpreted as meaning only that money is set aside for pension benefits in such a way that it is kept apart from the employer's business: OPB Memorandum No.77, *Scheme Rule Requirements for Contracting-Out Salary Related Schemes*, (1988), para. 60.

[2] SSPA, s.40(3). [3] Money Purchase Contracted-out Schemes, Regs. 1987 SI 1987/1101, reg.2.

[4] DHSS, *Reforming Social Security: Investor Protection Requirements for Personal and Occupational Pension Schemes* (April 1987), para. 8.

Pensions Board to be satisfied that the resources of a pension scheme contracted out on a *salary related basis* are sufficient for meeting, *inter alia*, all claims in respect of guaranteed minimum pensions.[1] The adequacy of scheme resources is checked by means of a system of periodic actuarial certificates and annual returns. Under this system a valid actuarial certificate (certificate A) is required for each scheme, confirming that in the event of the scheme being wound up in the period covered by the certificate its financial resources are likely 'in the normal course of events' to be sufficient to meet GMPs in full or to make payments to the state scheme to secure equivalent benefits, having first met other liabilities given equal or higher priority in the scheme rules. Details of any self-investment, i.e. investment in a scheme's sponsoring employer or investment closely connected with that employer, and concentrations of investment must be reported, and the actuary must state whether self-investment needs to be taken into account before he can be satisfied that the GMPs and other priority liabilities are covered.

An annual return is also required in respect of each scheme. This return is made either by an insurance company or by the scheme's trustees depending on whether the scheme is insured, i.e. one for which a life office certifies that it is administering an insurance contract designed to provide the benefits required for contracting out, or self-administered. In the case of an insured scheme, the life office is required to confirm either that all premium payments are up-to-date or that any arrears are not substantial. The life office also undertakes to inform the Occupational Pensions Board if it becomes aware of circumstances which give rise to concern in relation to the ability or intention of the scheme authorities to pay the premiums demanded. In the case of self-administered schemes the trustees are required to confirm, *inter alia*, that contributions at the 'appropriate rate', i.e. the rate considered by the actuary satisfactory for meeting the liabilities of the scheme *as a whole*, rather than just those listed in the actuarial certificate, have been paid for the last scheme year, and that the actuary has been given an opportunity to consider any changes which might affect the scheme's current actuarial certificate.

The supervision of *money purchase schemes* is based on a system of annual returns only, there being no possibility of a deficiency or surplus in such schemes (since the total fund is made up of the sum of the individual balances) and hence no need for a system of actuarial certificates. Returns are again made by life offices or scheme trustees depending on whether a scheme is insured or self-administered. In the case of insured schemes, confirmation is sought about the procedures relating to the payment of premiums and the requirements relating to the receipt and investment of minimum payments. In the case of self-administered schemes confirmation is sought that minimum payments have been made, that payments which give rise to protected rights

---

[1] SSPA, s.41(1): see also SI 1984/380, reg.27.

have been invested promptly and can be identified and attributed to each member, and that the restrictions on the investment of scheme resources have been observed.

The Occupational Pensions Board's supervision of schemes is backed by powers of intervention. In the case of salary-related schemes, the Board has power to impose such conditions as it thinks fit for securing that it is kept informed as to any matter affecting the security of the minimum pensions guaranteed under a scheme, and that the resources of a scheme are brought to and maintained at a satisfactory level; in the exercise of this power it may require a scheme's resources to be increased.[1] Non-compliance with conditions imposed by the Board in the exercise of this power is grounds for cancellation of a contracting-out certificate.[2] In the absence of any obligation to make an annual report, no information is publicly available on the exercise of these powers.

The Occupational Pensions Board also has power to make it a condition of contracting out that no part, or no more than a specified proportion, of a salary-related scheme's resources should be invested in investments of a specified class or description, and that the whole or a specified proportion of investments of a specified class or description should be realised within a specified period.[3] In the case of contracted out money purchase schemes, the Board has power to give directions to the same effect, limiting the proportion of a scheme's resources that may be invested in assets of a specified class or description or requiring the realisation of specified investments.[4]

Finally, the Board has power to cancel (or vary) a contracting out certificate where a condition of contracting out ceases to be satisfied.[5] Cancellation of a certificate renders an employer liable to pay national insurance contributions at the higher rate. The Board may also cancel a certificate where it considers that there are 'circumstances which render it inexpedient' that a scheme should continue to be contracted out.[6] The Board has stated that it would consider the continued contracting out of a scheme inexpedient 'when it becomes manifest that the employer is failing to pay the contributions which the scheme's actuary has assumed would be paid'.[7] A scheme whose contracting out certificate has been cancelled (or surrendered) continues to be subject to the supervision of the Board so long as it retains any liability for GMPs or protected rights.[8] No information is publicly available on the exercise of these powers; according to the Social Security Committee,

---

[1] SSPA, s.41(2)–(3). [2] *Ibid.*

[3] SSPA, s.41(5). In the absence of specific powers over self-investment, the Board used this power to impose a ceiling on the level of self-investment by schemes.

[4] SSA 1986, Sch. 1, para. 3 as modified in its application to money purchase schemes by s.32(2B) of the SSPA.

[5] SSPA, s.32(3). [6] s.32(4). [7] *Greater Security for the Rights etc.*, para. 5.27.

[8] SSPA, s.49.

however, the OPB has carried out its role 'in the most passive manner possible.'[1]

These controls, it must be stressed, apply only to contracted out schemes: they have no application to schemes that are not used for contracting out. The proposition that there should be funding and investment controls on all schemes and not just on those used for contracting out was considered by the Occupational Pensions Board in 1975, and again in 1982, but rejected on both occasions on the grounds that 'an apparatus of controls was not justified unless members' pension rights seemed to be in danger on a significant scale and voluntary action seemed unlikely to correct the problem.'[2] The Board's conclusion was subsequently endorsed by the Government: 'Experience of corresponding problems overseas does not necessarily lead to the conclusion that funding controls would prove sufficiently valuable in this country, in the absence of evidence of significant abuse or malpractice.'[3] In the light of the systematic 'looting' of the Maxwell pension funds, that conclusion plainly needs to be re-assessed.[4]

Miscellaneous controls

(a) *Occupational pension schemes and the Financial Services Act.* Rights under occupational pension schemes are not investments for the purposes of the Financial Services Act.[5] But the trustees and managers of an occupational pension scheme, including in-house managers, require authorisation for managing scheme assets unless they have delegated all day-to-day investment decisions to authorised persons or the scheme is in a class which, in view of its small size and the control exercised over its affairs by its members, has been exempted from this requirement.[6] The management of a scheme's underlying assets is thus intended to be subject to broadly the same safeguards as those which apply to the management of investments generally.[7]

(b) *Preservation.* Employees who left pension schemes before retirement – early leavers – traditionally got back their own contributions (if any) but not those of their employer. The loss by early leavers of their pension rights was

---

[1] *The Operation of Pension Funds*, para. 242.

[2] *Greater Security for the Rights etc.*, para. 6.20; see earlier *Solvency, Disclosure of Information and Member Participation in Occupational Pension Schemes* Cmnd. 5904 (1975), para. 65.

[3] DHSS, *Greater Security for the Rights etc.*, para. 34.   [4] *The Operation of Pension Funds*, para. 285.

[5] Sch. 1, para. 11, note 1.

[6] FSA, s.191; Financial Services Act 1986 (Occupational Pension Schemes) (No.2) Order 1988, SI 1988/724. Guidance on what constitutes day-to-day management is given in SIB Guidance Release 2/88.

[7] But note that SIB's compensation scheme does not apply to managers of occupational pension schemes acting as such. In the case of the Maxwell pension schemes, the Social Security Committee impugned the effectiveness of these safeguards: the way in which IMRO (the SRO for pension fund managers) had gone about carrying out its duties, it averred, 'suggests that this aspect of the system of self-regulation is – when the chips are down – little short of a tragic comedy.' IMRO's role, it recommended, should be taken over by a reconstituted Occupational Pensions Board: *The Operation of Pension Funds*, para. 243.

treated as central to the purpose of schemes, which was to attract and retain employees, and which therefore sought to induce employees to stay by penalising those who left early. As well as being part and parcel of the attainment of the purpose of pension schemes, the loss by early leavers of their pension rights was also vital to the financial viability of schemes which relied on the forfeit of employer's contributions by leavers to meet their commitment to those who stay until retirement.[1] Widespread criticism of the treatment accorded early leavers, however, coupled with concern that non-transferability of pensions was a barrier to labour mobility, led to the introduction by the Social Security Act 1973 of a requirement for the preservation of pension benefits for scheme members with a five (later reduced to two) year contribution record who left before pension age.[2]

The weakness of the preservation requirements of the 1973 Act was that they made no allowance for the effects of inflation on the value of preserved pensions in the period up to retirement. The introduction of SERPS brought about some improvement in the position of early leavers from contracted out schemes, since the GMP element of the preserved pension had to be revalued in line with earnings up to the attainment of state pension age, but it was only in 1985, following the report of the Occupational Pensions Board on *Improved Protection for Early Leavers*, that provision was made for the compulsory revaluation of the non-GMP element in preserved pensions in line with prices up to a ceiling of 5 per cent a year.[3] (As an alternative to leaving preserved rights in a scheme, early leavers were given the right to have the actuarially determined cash equivalent of their preserved rights transferred to a new occupational pension scheme or to an approved individual arrangement.)[4] This revaluation requirement applied only to benefits earned by service after January 1, 1985, a limitation which was subsequently removed by the Social Security Act 1990, so that all non-GMP pension benefits now have to be revalued.[5] However, the ceiling on the revaluation of benefits was retained. Whether a preserved pension is protected against inflation thus depends on the rate of inflation between leaving and the pension coming into payment.

(c) *Self-investment*. As we have seen, controls over the investment of scheme assets going beyond those imposed by the law of trusts[6] have been avoided, other than in the context of contracting out, in the absence of any evidence of a threat to the financial viability of schemes. An exception has been made, however, in the case of self-investment, i.e. investment in a scheme's sponsoring employer or investment closely connected with that employer in the form, for example, of a loan or investment in property occupied by him,[7]

[1] Hannah, *op. cit.*, p. 100. [2] SSA 1973, s.63. [3] SSPA, s.52A.
[4] SSPA, s.52B, Sch. 1A, Pt. 11. [5] SSA 1990, s.14, Sch. 4, para. 4.
[6] As to which, see *Cowan* v. *Scargill* [1984] 2 All E.R. 750; *Martin* v. *City of Edinburgh District Council* 1988 S.L.T. 329.
[7] See e.g. *Evans* v. *The London Co-operative Society*, *TLR*, July 6, 1976.

because of the potential double risk to jobs and pensions such investment entails. A National Association of Pension Funds report on *Self-Investment by Pension Funds* in 1988 described the practice as 'undesirable and unhelpful'; and a year later the Occupational Pensions Board, in its report on *Protecting Pensions*, while stopping short of blanket condemnation of the practice, acknowledged that 'if carried to extremes it can represent a grave weakening of that security which a separate trust fund is created to provide', and recommended that power be taken to set a maximum level of self-investment for schemes.[1]

Now under section 57A of the Social Security Pensions Act 1975, which was inserted by paragraph 3 of Schedule 4 to the Social Security Act 1990, the Department has power to prescribe by regulation the proportion of a scheme's resources that may be invested in 'employer-related assets', which concept covers shares or other securities issued by an employer or connected person, land and other property which is occupied by or used for the purposes of any business carried on by an employer or connected person and loans to an employer or connected person.[2] The Occupational Pension Schemes (Investment of Scheme's Resources) Regulations 1992, which were made in the immediate aftermath of the Maxwell pension fund scandal, impose a limit of 5 per cent on the proportion of a scheme's resources that may be invested in such assets.[3] Schemes which exceed this limit[4] will be allowed two or five years, depending on the types of assets involved, to bring their levels of self-investment within the permitted maximum of 5 per cent.

(d) *Inflation-proofing.* Inflation is no less corrosive of the value of pensions in payment than of the value of deferred pensions. Its effects on pensioners' standards of living were highlighted by the Occupational Pensions Board in its 1982 Report: 'Whereas most schemes were set up to provide their members with a reasonably secure standard of living in retirement, fixed in relation to the standard achieved in the last years of working life, today many schemes find themselves paying pensions which diminish in real terms at a continuous but uncertain rate as the pensioner grows older.'[5] Some schemes had tried to maintain the original relationship between pensions and payments by increasing the money value of pensions in payment, but others had adjusted to inflation at the expense of pensioners and early leavers by allowing the 'saving' on pensions to offset increases in the contribution rate which might otherwise have arisen from higher than expected pay rises or scheme improvements.[6] But although the Board was of the view that 'the present widespread practice of relying on discretionary, *ad hoc*, unfunded increases diminishes the security

---

[1] *Protecting Pensions*, para. 15.15.   [2] s.57A(2).   [3] SI 1992/246.

[4] A report commissioned by the Department estimated that there were between 300 and 500 large (12 or more members) self-administered schemes with self-investment in excess of 5 per cent of which between 150 and 200 had self-investment in excess of 10 per cent: Study on Self-Investment by Pension Funds (1991).

[5] *Greater Security for the Rights etc.*, para. 9.1.   [6] *Ibid.*

given by the system of externally funded pension schemes built up over the last 60 years',[1] it nevertheless declined to recommend the mandatory revaluation of pensions in payment (partly on grounds of cost and partly because it was optimistic about the prospects for progress by voluntary action). It confined itself instead to recommending that schemes should aim as far as possible to maintain the full real value of the retired members' pension income (insofar as this was not fully price-indexed through the state scheme by way of the GMP arrangement).[2]

Seven years later the Board felt moved to put on record its view that:

> time is running out for a structure of fully discretionary payments. Although this has worked satisfactorily in many cases, we believe in future years it will seem extraordinary that generations of pensioners should have been so exposed to uncertainty as to their standard of living from one year to another, and so dependent on the decisions of company managers whose main preoccupations and responsibilities were, necessarily, elsewhere.[3]

Nevertheless, it again refrained from proposing statutory intervention, recommending instead that employers and trustees should be urged 'as a matter of good practice' to guarantee, on pensions in payment other than GMPs, 'limited price-indexing', i.e. increases in line with prices up to a maximum of 5 per cent a year.[4]

A more robust line was taken by the Government, which proposed initially that limited price-indexing should be mandatory in relation to schemes which were wound up (the idea being to deter predators from winding up schemes and appropriating the surplus). Under pressure, the restriction of limited price-indexing to schemes being wound up was dropped, so that under section 58A of the Social Security Pensions Act, which was inserted by section 11 of the Social Security Act 1990, all *final salary* (not money purchase) occupational pension schemes will be obliged to increase pensions earned after an appointed day once they come into payment in line with prices up to a maximum of 5 per cent. As regards pension rights earned before the appointed day, schemes will be required to use surpluses identified following actuarial valuations to index them by as close to the target rate of 5 per cent as possible. To preserve surpluses for distribution among pensioners, schemes were prohibited with immediate effect (from August 17, 1990) from making payments to employers (but not from reducing contributions), unless they made provision for present and future pensions payable under a scheme to be increased in accordance with the statutory requirements.[5]

The prohibition against the return of any surplus to an employer apart, these requirements are not yet in force. It was originally intended to bring them into effect from January 1, 1992, but their implementation has been

---

[1] para. 9.23. [2] para. 9.21. [3] *Protecting Pensions*, para. 11.10. [4] para. 11.28.
[5] SSA 1990, s. 11(3).

postponed pending clarification of the financial implications of the *Barber* case (which requires equality of treatment in pension matters for men and women).[1]

(e) *Independent trustees*. Section 57C of the Social Security Pensions Act, which was inserted by paragraph 1 of Schedule 4 to the Social Security Act 1990, requires the powers of the trustees of a scheme (other than a money purchase scheme or small self-administered scheme) to be administered by an independent trustee when an employer becomes insolvent. This requirement is intended to avoid any conflict of interest between the interests of the scheme members on the one hand and the interests of the employer or the employer's creditors on the other. It should therefore prevent a recurrence of the situation in *Icarus (Hertford) Ltd.* v. *Discroll*,[2] where a liquidator was allowed to exercise an employer's powers as sole trustee of a scheme in favour of the employer's creditors. An independent trustee must have no interest in the assets of the employer or of the scheme and must not be connected or associated with the employer or the insolvency practitioner or official receiver who is acting; nor must he have provided services to the trustees, managers or employer in the three years preceding the application of the requirement.[3]

(f) *Deficiencies in assets*. Section 58B of the Social Security Pensions Act, finally, which was inserted by paragraph 2 of Schedule 4 to the Social Security Act 1990, makes any deficiency in the assets of a scheme on its winding up a debt due from the employer to the trustees of the scheme. Like limited price-indexing, this requirement was also conceived as a deterrent to a new owner winding up a scheme.[4]

DISCLOSURE

Disclosure to scheme members

In the absence of a full system of prudential supervision, disclosure assumes greater importance as a means of protecting members of occupational pension schemes.

Such a measure, stimulating employees' interest in their schemes and enabling them or their representatives to obtain information and explanations in order to satisfy themselves about the running and the finances of the scheme, would of itself tend to discourage malpractices and contribute to the greater security of pension rights. It would enable members to draw attention, either generally or in individual cases, to

---

[1] *Barber* v. *Guardian Royal Exchange Assurance Group* [1990] 2 All E.R. 660; HC Debs, 6th Ser. 1991.

[2] December 4, 1989.

[3] SSPA, s.57C(3); see also Occupational Pension Schemes (Independent Trustees) Regs. 1990, SI 1990/2075.

[4] *Protecting Pensions*, paras. 10.6 and 10.17.

circumstances where trustees were in breach of their obligations under the scheme, and to press for remedial action; and it would reveal any weaknesses in the scheme rules or organisation, which could be taken up in negotiation with the employer.[1]

Despite the evident importance of disclosure to the effective monitoring of the solvency and management of schemes, there was for a long time no provision for the mandatory disclosure of information to scheme members. In its 1975 report the Occupational Pensions Board dismissed suggestions that members would be unable to comprehend detailed information, and that statutory intervention was unnecessary because members were already entitled to the requisite information under the law of trusts, before recommending greater disclosure and greater member participation in the running of schemes.[2] Its proposals were accepted by the Government but never implemented.[3]

In its 1982 report the Board returned to the issue, describing adequate disclosure as 'a prerequisite for the maintenance of confidence in any voluntary system for the provision of occupational pensions'.[4] The freedom enjoyed by schemes, it continued, entailed risks, 'but as far as possible they should be known risks, knowingly accepted: not unknown risks imposed unilaterally'.[5] It renewed its recommendations for compulsory disclosure, which were accepted and implemented by the Social Security Act 1985.[6]

The Occupational Pensions Schemes (Disclosure of Information) Regulations 1986,[7] made under the Social Security Act 1985, confer on members of occupational pension schemes extensive rights to information about their schemes. Provision is made for the disclosure, on request, of the documents constituting a scheme; an annual report including audited accounts[8] and an actuarial statement; and an actuarial valuation report. Provision is also made for the disclosure, automatically or on request, of scheme information, which may be provided in the form of a scheme booklet or leaflet, and individual statements which must be provided in various specified circumstances.

These requirements, in the Occupational Pensions Board's experience, 'have yet to make a significant impact on employees' and managers general level of knowledge of pension schemes, or interest in them'.[9] The Board attributed this not to a continuing lack of information – the amount of disclosure it described as ample – but to a lack of 'effective communication',

[1] DHSS, *Greater Security for the Rights etc.*, para. 15.

[2] *Solvency, Disclosure of Information etc.*, paras. 25–6.

[3] *The Role of Members in the Running of Schemes.* As to progress towards increased member participation, see Schuller and Hyman, 'Pensions: The Voluntary Growth of Participation', (1983) 14 *Industrial Relations Journal*, and *Occupational Pension Schemes 1987, op. cit.*, 63.

[4] *Greater Security for the Rights etc.*, para. 2.22.   [5] paras. 2.37–2.38.

[6] s.3, inserting a new s.56A in the SSPA.   [7] SI 1986/1046.

[8] Provision is made for the appointment of auditors by the Occupational Pension Schemes (Auditors) Regs. 1987, SI 1987/1102.

[9] *Protecting Pension*, para. 12.1.

which 'cannot be brought about by statutory requirements, but without [which] disclosure loses much of its force'.[1] It therefore urged trustees and employers to approach disclosure as much more than simply a statutory requirement that had to be met, i.e. in accordance with its spirit rather than its letter.[2]

Registration

The Social Security Act 1990 makes provision for the compulsory registration of occupational (and personal) pension schemes with a registry which is compiled and maintained by the Occupational Pensions Board.[3] This is a reduced version of a proposal originally put forward by the Board in 1975 for the establishment of a system of registration of occupational pension schemes, whose functions would have included the policing of disclosure requirements and the provision of assistance in tracing schemes with which members had lost contact, but which was rejected by the Government on the grounds that the manpower requirements of such a system would be out of proportion to the benefits obtained.[4]

In 1981 the Board put forward a less ambitious proposal, identical in all essential respects to that which has now been implemented, for a register of the names and addresses of employers and their schemes to which members could turn in case of difficulty in tracing the person responsible for payment of their pension,[5] but this too was rejected: in favour of a fuller system of registration along the lines originally proposed by the Board in 1975 and rejected by the Government in 1976! Statutory provision for a full registration system was made by the Social Security Act 1985[6] but the system was never implemented because of the apparent scale of the task involved. The present system by contrast is confined to the provision of a tracing facility only and has no wider role in relation to schemes.

REDRESS

The Social Security Act 1990 makes provision for the appointment by the Secretary of State of a Pensions Ombudsman with powers to investigate and make binding determinations in respect of disputes of fact or law as well as complaints of injustice sustained in consequence of maladministration by the trustees or managers of an occupational or personal pension scheme.[7]

---

[1] para. 12.7.   [2] *Ibid.*

[3] s.13, inserting a new s.59K in the SSPA; Register of Occupational and Personal Pension Scheme Regs. 1990, SI 1990/2278.

[4] *The Role of Members in the Running of Schemes*, para. 46.

[5] *Improved Protection for the Occupational Pension Rights and Expectations of Early Leavers*, Cmnd. 8271 (1981), ch. 10.

[6] s.3.   [7] s.12 and Sch. 3, inserting new ss.59B–59K in the SSPA.

The Pensions Ombudsman has no power to investigate complaints or disputes in respect of which legal proceedings have been commenced; if legal proceedings are started after a complaint or reference has been made, the court may stay the proceedings if it is satisfied that there is no sufficient reason why the matter should not be investigated by the Pensions Ombudsman and the applicant is ready and willing to co-operate with the investigation.[1] Complaints and disputes which can be investigated by, or under arrangements by, SIB or an SRO under the Financial Services Act – other than a complaint or dispute relating to the management of a personal pension scheme – are also excluded from his jurisdiction.[2]

The Pensions Ombudsman may refer any question of law arising for determination in connection with a complaint or dispute to the High Court or, in Scotland, Court of Session.[3] His determination is 'final and binding', save that an appeal on a point of law lies to the High Court (or Court of Session in Scotland).[4]

---

[1] SSPA, ss.59C(5), 59E.
[2] The Personal and Occupational Pension Schemes (Pensions Ombudsman) Regs. 1991, SI 1991/588.
[3] SSPA, s.59G(7). [4] ss.59H(3), (4).

14
Personal Pensions

The Social Security Act 1986 introduced personal pensions as part of the Government's policy of giving people more choice in the way they save for old age. The practice of making occupational pension scheme membership a condition of employment was ended,[1] and employees were given the right to take out a personal pension which could be used to contract out of the state earnings-related pension scheme (SERPS). Employees were also given the right to make additional voluntary contributions (AVCs) to their employer's pension scheme, and to make contributions to a free-standing AVC scheme (FSAVC) independent of their employer's pension scheme.

REGULATION

Personal pension schemes are subject to two main groups of controls. One group applies to schemes approved for tax purposes; like the equivalent controls in respect of occupational pension schemes, their purpose is to ensure that tax reliefs are confined to genuine schemes and that schemes are not used for the purposes of tax avoidance or evasion. The second group applies to schemes used for contracting out of the state earnings-related scheme; like the equivalent controls in respect of occupational pension schemes, their broad purpose is to ensure that benefits standing in place of state benefits are paid when they fall due. Personal pension schemes are also subject to disclosure requirements analogous to those applicable to occupational pension schemes.[2]

Approval for tax purposes

A personal pension scheme needs Inland Revenue approval in order to be able to offer tax advantages to its members; it also needs Inland Revenue approval

---

[1] s.15.
[2] Personal Pension Schemes (Disclosure of Information) Regs. 1987, SI 1987/1110.

if it is to be used to contract out of SERPS.[1] From the standpoint of investor protection, the most important feature of Inland Revenue approval is that it is restricted to schemes established by persons who are already subject to investor protection regulation in one form or another, namely banks, building societies, insurance companies, friendly societies and authorised unit trust scheme managers.[2] The protection of personal pension scheme members therefore takes as its starting point the various controls to which these providers are subject.

Personal pension schemes must satisfy various other conditions in order to secure and retain approval for tax purposes. One such condition is that its 'sole purpose' must be the provision of approved benefits,[3] and that schemes established by providers other than insurance companies and friendly societies must be set up under irrevocable trusts.[4]

Approval is at the discretion of the Inland Revenue which has power to withdraw approval if the facts concerning a scheme, its administration, or its arrangements, cease to warrant approval.[5] An appeal to the Special Commissioners lies against the refusal or withdrawal of authorisation.[6]

Contracting out

A personal pension scheme used to contract out of SERPS is known as an 'appropriate' personal pension scheme. The provider of an appropriate personal pension scheme undertakes, in exchange for 'minimum contributions' from the Department of Social Security, to provide scheme members with pension benefits, known as protected rights, in place of those which would have been payable to them had they remained members of the state scheme. The minimum contributions which schemes are qualified to receive consist of two elements: a contracted out rebate, which represents the difference between the full rate national insurance contributions and the lower rate which members of contracted out occupational pension schemes and their employers pay, and an incentive payment (payable until April 1993) in respect of those members of a scheme who qualify for its receipt.[7] However, since personal pension schemes are money purchase schemes, providing benefits related to contributions rather than earnings, there is no guarantee that the benefits

---

[1] Personal Pension Schemes (Appropriate Schemes) Regs. 1988, SI 1988/137, reg.2.

[2] ICTA, s.632.

[3] ICTA, s.633; the sole purpose test entails restrictions on the investment of scheme assets, as to which see IR 76, *Personal Pension Schemes*, paras. 8.10–8.13.

[4] IR 76, *op. cit.*, para. 2.5.   [5] ICTA, ss.631, 650.   [6] ICTA, s.651.

[7] The cost of rebates and incentive payments over the period 1988–93 has been estimated at some £9.3bn against a saving of only £3.4bn: Eighth Report from the Committee of Public Accounts, *The elderly: information requirements for supporting the elderly and the implications of personal pensions for the National Insurance Fund* (HC 124; 1990–1).

payable will match those which would have been payable under the state scheme. The personal pension scheme member therefore bears the risk that the return on contributions will not match the amount of the pension which would have been payable under the state scheme.

A personal pension scheme must satisfy a number of requirements over and above approval for tax purposes in order to become and remain 'appropriate'. These requirements include a requirement that a scheme take one of the following forms:[1]

(a) an arrangement for the issue of insurance policies or annuity contracts;

(b) an authorised unit trust scheme of a kind listed (however, neither the list of authorised unit trust schemes nor their definitions appears to have been revised to take account of the Financial Services (Regulated Schemes) Regulations 1991);[2] and

(c) an arrangement for the investment of contributions in an interest-bearing account, or shares in or deposits with a building society.

The rules of schemes in the last category (deposit-based schemes) must include provision for cooling-off periods as a condition of appropriateness.

The Occupational Pensions Board must also be satisfied that adequate compensation arrangements exist to cover a scheme's liability in respect of protected rights in the event of the commission of a criminal offence or insolvency.[3] Normally this requirement will be satisfied by access to the relevant statutory compensation arrangements (for example, the Financial Services Act scheme in the case of a scheme based on authorised unit trusts, or the Policyholders Protection Act arrangements in the case of a scheme based on insurance policies), but where a scheme does not have access to the relevant statutory arrangements (as may be the case with deposit-based arrangements since the contributions are not 'repayable' and hence may not fall to be treated as deposits for the compensation purposes)[4] the OPB must be satisfied that compensation will be payable to scheme members at a level as least as generous as that which would be available if access to the relevant statutory arrangements existed.[5]

The Social Security Act confers various other powers of control on the Department of Social Security. These include a power to control the investment of scheme resources,[6] which the Department has not exercised, save to impose restrictions on the types of authorised unit trusts in which contributions may be invested, on the grounds that, given the controls to

---

[1] Personal Pension Schemes (Appropriate Schemes) Regs. 1988, SI 1988/137, reg.2.
[2] See above, pp. 191–4.   [3] SSA 1986, Sch. 1, para. 10.
[4] DHSS, *Investor Protection Requirements for Personal and Occupational Pension Schemes*, April 1987, para. 15.
[5] Personal Pension Schemes (Compensation) Regs. 1988, SI 1988/2238, reg.3.
[6] SSA 1986, Sch. 1, para. 3.

which scheme providers are subject, further restrictions on the investment freedom of personal pension schemes are not warranted.[1] Also included is a power to control administrative charges, which the Department has not exercised 'in the expectation that charges will stabilise at acceptable levels as a result of competition and disclosure'.[2] There is also a residual, open-ended power to impose other requirements, which in accordance with standard administrative law principles must be read subject to the limitation that any requirements imposed must be for the protection of members.[3]

Supervision of appropriate schemes is based on a system of annual returns analogous to the system employed in respect of contracted out money purchase schemes. It is backed by limited powers of intervention, which include power to give directions limiting the proportion of a scheme's resources that may be invested in assets of a specified class or description, or requiring the realisation of specified investments.[4] The OPB also has power to cancel an appropriate scheme certificate where a condition of contracting out ceases to be satisfied or where it considers that there are 'circumstances which make it inexpedient' that a scheme should continue to be appropriate.[5] Where a scheme ceases to be appropriate, protected rights must either be made subject to approved arrangements or a state scheme premium in respect of those rights (referred to as a personal pension protected rights premium) must be paid.

---

[1] DHSS, *Investor Protection Requirements etc.*, para. 7. [2] *Ibid.*, para. 4. [3] *Ibid.*, para. 6.
[4] *Ibid.*, para. 3. [5] *Ibid.*, s.2(3)(4).

Part III

INTERMEDIARIES AND PROMOTION

15
The Financial Services Act: Background and Scope

BACKGROUND TO THE ACT

The Financial Services Act 1986 superseded an earlier piece of legislation, the Prevention of Fraud (Investments) Act 1958 (the 'PFI Act'), which was concerned primarily with the licensing of dealers in securities and with the authorisation of unit trust schemes. The 1958 Act, like its 1939 predecessor, was largely designed to regulate the activities of 'fringe' stock and share dealers, while leaving alone the more respectable firms, such as the stockbrokers who were members of the Stock Exchange and subject to its own self-regulatory system. By the mid-1970s changes in the character of the investment industry led the government of the day to acknowledge that the 1958 legislation was deficient with respect to both its coverage of investment practitioners and the powers of enforcement it conferred on the licensing authority, the Department of Trade and Industry.[1] But nothing was done to amend the Act, a policy decision having been taken to give priority to the preparation of fresh companies legislation.[2]

In February 1981, however, Norton Warburg, an investment management firm with licensed dealer status, collapsed taking some millions of investors' money with it. This failure embarrassed the authorities sufficiently to prompt the Secretary of State for Trade to commission Professor L. C. B. Gower to conduct a one-man review with the following terms of reference:

(a) to consider the statutory protection now required by (i) private and (ii) business investors in securities and other property, including investors through unit trusts and open-ended investment companies operating in the United Kingdom;

(b) to consider the need for statutory control of dealers in securities, investment consultants and investment managers; and

---

[1] Cmnd. 6893.
[2] Parliamentary Commissioner for Administration, *First Report: Selected Cases 1983*, Vol. 3, p. 110, para. 9.

(c) to advise on the need for new legislation.[1]

While the Gower Review proceeded, the DTI set about strengthening its Licensed Dealers Rules ('LDRs') as a holding measure. The opportunity was taken to affirm that, although only licensed dealers were bound by the rules,

> The Department has always 'expected' those investment managers who by virtue of Exemption Orders are not subject in law to the LDRs to comply with them . . . Those 'expected' but unable to comply may 'show cause', on the basis that their own arrangements afford at least equivalent protection to the investor.[2]

Here we see the precursor of the 'principle of equivalence' subsequently enshrined in the Financial Services Act. Professor Gower produced his initial discussion document in January 1982. It was a cogent critique of the existing patchwork of regulatory arrangements and stated the case for the establishment of a single, comprehensive investor protection framework within which would operate self-regulatory agencies subject to residual government supervision. Of equal significance for subsequent developments was Gower's forceful argument that life insurance policies used as vehicles for savings or investment fell within the scope of his review and should not be left outside the new investor protection framework.

In his discussion document Gower observed that, if the experience of most enquiries was anything to go by, the most likely outcome of his own would be that nothing would be done.[3] Over the next three years, however, a number of factors combined to persuade the government that root-and-branch reform, broadly along the lines suggested by Gower, was the best approach. A general desire to enhance the UK's international reputation as a clean place to do business, and to look after the moderately affluent private investors (created, for example, by the impact of parental home ownership on patterns of inheritance) who might be regarded as a natural object of Conservative government concern, combined with more specific factors. On the Stock Exchange the Big Bang made it necessary to devise a new set of rules to cope with the shift from a floor-based dealing system, and with the conflicts of interest engendered by the abandonment of the single capacity system. The question was how the Exchange could keep its regulatory grip as the possibility grew that dealings in internationally traded equities might drift outside the confines of the Exchange altogether. A comprehensive regulatory framework with statutory backing to which all firms would be subject offered the prospect of preserving a centralised market in securities, since bypassing the Exchange would be less attractive if it did not afford a means of side-

---

[1] L. C. B. Gower, *Review of Investor Protection: A Discussion Document* (January 1982), para. 1.01.

[2] *Revision of the Licensed Dealers Rules: Memorandum by the Department of Trade* (January 1982), para. 4; DTI, *Licensed Dealers in Securities: Draft Rules and Regulations Proposed to be Made under the Prevention of Fraud (Investments) Act 1958* (September 1982), para. 7.

[3] *Disc. Doc.*, para. 7.02, n. 59.

stepping regulatory controls. At the same time a system of self-regulation with statutory teeth came to be seen as the key to sorting out the problems of the life assurance sector – in particular, the threat of a commissions war which would undermine the independence of intermediaries and increase the cost of insurance products.[1]

The blueprint for the new legislation was set out in the White Paper of January 1985.[2] The Act that followed in 1986 departed from the model of the PFI Act in various ways. First, its coverage was much wider, extending beyond 'securities' to other 'investments'. Secondly, while the PFI Act dispensed exemptions liberally, the Financial Services Act did so only sparingly. Thirdly, section 62 of the 1986 Act gave a civil right of action where loss was suffered through breach of its provisions. And the Securities and Investments Board was charged with responsibility for supervising the new system, although the Secretary of State retained the power to define the boundaries of the new regime and, in the final analysis, to divest the Board of its responsibilities.

Initially, the plans for the new investment business regime were well received in the investment industry. But as the new regime was implemented, a strong current of hostility developed. This was expressed in complaints about the complexity of the Act, the 'legalism' and 'inflexibility' of SIB and its rulebook, and the costs of implementation. Within a couple of years of its establishment in the summer of 1985, and even before the regime was brought fully into force in 1988, SIB was being heavily criticised by almost every section of the investment industry: stockbrokers and investment managers complained of the costs of drawing up customer agreements and of the difficulty of getting their clients to go through the formalities of bringing them into force; unit trust companies resented the lost latitude to profit from implicit charges; life offices bemoaned the costs of revising promotional literature and issuing product particulars to each purchaser; the clearing banks disliked the loss of commercial freedom occasioned by the policy of 'polarisation'; and insurance intermediaries subject to regulation for the first time denounced what they saw as bureaucracy and 'red tape'.

Two factors in particular tended to be singled out for blame. It was averred, firstly, that SIB's approach to the 'principle of equivalence' (i.e. the principle that the rules of self-regulating organisations and professional bodies must achieve at least the same standard of investor protection as the rules of SIB) was unnecessarily rigid, and that by insisting on equivalence to its own detailed rulebook SIB had deprived the SROs and RPBs of the latitude to devise rules tailored to the situation of their own member firms. In fact, SIB's approach to the equivalence of SRO rulebooks was less rigid than this

---

[1] See further Chapter 17.

[2] DTI, *Financial Services in the United Kingdom: A New Framework for Investor Protection*, Cmnd. 9432 (January 1985).

implied: the test was equivalence of effect rather than of wording. And indeed the rulebooks which emerged from the equivalence process were actually quite diverse.

Secondly, section 62 of the Act, which made breaches of investment business rules civilly litigable, was blamed for creating a fear of litigation which prompted some investment firms to draft their documentation in a precautionary, legalistic way, and some SROs to adopt the same approach to the contents of their rulebooks. Again, it is arguable that the fear of litigiousness was exaggerated: there has been little litigation founded on section 62. But the perception was what counted, and the damage was done.

SIB sought to defend its approach by reference to the significance of its rules both for the equivalence test and for section 62:

> It is because of these legal consequences that the FS Act provides for an approach to regulation based on rules rather than codes on the Highway Code model. These rules have to be drafted in 'legal language' precise enough to enable both the regulators and the courts to establish whether they have been broken. Rules of this sort cannot be as 'user-friendly' as the Highway Code . . .[1]

It was at this crucial juncture in the development of the new regulatory system that Sir David Walker succeeded Sir Kenneth Berrill as Chairman of SIB.

The new Chairman took office in June 1988 and immediately set in motion a redrafting process designed to bring about the simplification of the SIB rulebook. The initial idea was to introduce statements of principle that would summarise and explain the more detailed rules which would be couched in less obscure language. A draft of the proposed new conduct of business rules was published in November 1988.[2] It was heavily criticised for failing to simplify and shorten the existing rules significantly, while adding an extra layer of requirements which might actually conflict with the more detailed rules. The November 1988 draft was dropped. Instead there emerged, over the next few months, a proposal reflecting the combined wisdom of SIB, the DTI, and the SROs for a 'new settlement' which would aim to reconcile the need for a degree of uniformity or harmony in the requirements of the various regulatory bodies with the desire for enough latitude and flexibility to allow each body to respond to the circumstances of its own members.[3] Under the new settlement, SIB would act as the guardian of the overall coherence of the system by declaring overarching principles and by laying down a *common core* of rules, while leaving to each SRO the job of 'elaboration, adaptation and individual tailoring' of detailed requirements for its own members within the overall framework.[4] Thus it was hoped, 'greater uniformity and cohesiveness at the

---

[1] *The Securities and Investments Board's Application for Designated Agency Status under the Terms of the Financial Services Act and the Revised Rule Book Dated February 1987: Explanatory Statement*, para. 5.

[2] SIB, *Conduct of Business Rules: A New Approach* (November 1988).

[3] *Possible Changes to the Financial Services Act 1986* (March 1989), esp. paras. 3,8.

[4] SIB, *Regulation of the Conduct of Investment Business: A Proposal* (August 1989), para. 13.

level of principles and core rules [would] make it possible for SIB to be less intrusive in relation to the detail of the SRO's own rules and other arrangements where these are supportive of the principles and core rules'.[1] To the same end, SIB would judge SRO and RPB arrangements by reference to a criterion of 'adequacy' rather than equivalence. The adequacy test differs from its predecessor in three ways:[2] (i) it substitutes SIB's 'subjective' judgement of adequacy for the theoretically 'objective' yardstick of equivalence; (ii) it allows account to be taken not only of a body's hard rules but also of softer material such as guidance, ethical statements and codes of practice; and (iii) it focuses not only on the formal content of the rulebooks, but also on 'the nature of the investment business carried on by members of the organisation, the kinds of investors involved *and the effectiveness of the organisation's arrangements for enforcing compliance*'.[3] So the test is how the rules work in practice, not what they look like in the rulebook.

The Companies Act 1989 amended the Financial Services Act in the ways necessary to enable the new structure to be introduced: SIB was given the power to make authoritative statements of principle,[4] to create a common core of 'designated' rules,[5] and to judge SRO and RPB rulebooks by reference to the concept of adequacy.[6] At the same time, the Secretary of State was given the power to restrict the right of civil action under section 62,[7] and SIB was put under an explicit obligation to take compliance costs into account when framing its rules.[8] The structure developed within the framework of these amendments is described in greater detail at the start of Chapter 17.

THE SCOPE OF THE REGIME

The scope of the investment business regime established by the Financial Services Act is determined by the basic prohibition laid down in section 3: 'No person shall carry on, or purport to carry on, investment business in the United Kingdom unless he is an authorised person ... or an exempted person. ...' The crucial concept, therefore, is the carrying on of investment business in the UK – crucial not only because it defines the circumstances under which the need to be authorised under the Act arises, but also because, generally speaking, it defines the scope of the various rules and regulations made by the Securities and Investments Board.

To elaborate the concept of carrying on investment business in the UK it is necessary to consider its various elements in turn. We can then pause briefly to note the main exemptions for which the Act provides.

---

[1] *Ibid.*, para. 23.   [2] *Ibid.*, para. 22.   [3] FSA Sch. 2, para. 3(2), italics supplied.

[4] Companies Act 1989, s.192, FSA s.47A.   [5] Companies Act 1989, s.194, FSA s.63A.

[6] Companies Act 1989, s.203(1), (2); FSA Sch. 2, para. 3, Sch. 3, para.3.

[7] Companies Act 1989, s.193(1), FSA s.62A.

[8] Companies Act 1989, s.206(1), FSA Sch. 9, para. 12(1).

Investments

The Financial Services Act does not attempt to give any general definition of an investment. Rather Part I of Schedule 1 enumerates certain specific instruments which are to be regarded as investments for the purposes of the Act. A rough and ready summary of the Act's long and complicated list appears in the first column of Table 2 below. The second column in the table highlights certain assets which in everyday discourse are often referred to as investments but which are not investments within the meaning of the Act.

As one would expect, *company shares* (para. 1) are classed as investments. Subject to one exception, a share in a building society (created by opening a share account) is not caught: this reflects the separate regulation of building societies under the Building Societies Act and the absence of a market in building society shares. The exception is provided by PIBS (permanent interest bearing shares). As their name suggests, PIBS are perpetual – i.e. irredeemable – building society shares, designed to be bought and sold on the secondary market (in practice, the Stock Exchange), and hence akin to securities in character. The first issues of PIBS took place in 1991, the attraction for the building societies concerned being that PIBS count as core capital for the purpose of capital adequacy requirements.[1]

Debentures – that is, instruments creating or acknowledging indebtedness – are also defined as investments (para. 2). Fixed interest stocks issued by companies as a form of borrowing are an example of debentures. So are certificates of deposit (CDs) (marketable documents acknowledging the deposit of a large sum of money at a bank). The concept of a debenture is so wide that the Act specifically excludes a number of instruments from its ambit: one set of exclusions is of cheques and other bills of exchange, banker's drafts, letters of credit, banknotes, and instruments acknowledging or creating indebtedness in connection with the consideration payable under a contract for the supply of goods or services. The purpose of these exclusions is to draw a line between debentures which serve investment purposes and those used for ordinary trade and commerce. Also excluded are statements showing a balance in a current, deposit or savings account. The institutions with which such accounts are held are, of course, regulated under the banking or building societies legislation.

Government and public securities – that is, instruments creating or acknowledging indebtedness issued by or on behalf of a government, local authority or public authority – are excluded from paragraph 2 but are investments by virtue of paragraph 3. This category includes, for example, gilts (British government stocks) and local authority negotiable bonds. National Savings products are excluded.

---

[1] PIBS were classified as FSA investments by the Financial Services Act 1986 (Extension of Scope of Act) Order 1991, SI 1991/1104.

Table 2

	INVESTMENTS	NOT INVESTMENTS
Schedule 1 paragraph		
1	Company shares	Building society shares (except deferred shares, e.g. PIBS)
2	Debentures (e.g. Eurobonds, certificates of deposit)	Current/deposit/savings accounts in building societies and banks (e.g. TESSAs), deposit-based personal pensions, National Savings investments
3	Government/local authority/ public authority securities (e.g. gilts)	
4	Investments entitling to shares/securities (e.g. share warrants)	
5	Certificates representing securities (e.g. American depositary receipts)	
6	Units in collective investment schemes (e.g. units in authorised unit trusts, shares in open-ended investment companies)	
7	Options (including currency options)	Currency
8	Futures	Contracts made for commercial and not investment purposes
9	Contracts for differences (e.g. stockmarket index bets)	
10	Long-term insurance contracts (e.g. with-profits/unit-linked endowment policies, whole of life policies, personal pension policies, annuities)	Policies with no saving or investment element (e.g. term assurance)
11	Rights and interests in investments within 1–10 above	Interests under trusts of an occupational pension scheme Property (e.g. land, collectibles)

Certain 'derivative' instruments are also defined as investments. A derivative instrument is one which gives the holder some kind of a claim to an underlying asset.[1] Under paragraph 4 of Schedule 1 *warrants or other instruments* entitling the holder to subscribe for shares or securities are classified as investments, while paragraph 5 catches certificates representing securities. One example of the latter is an American depositary receipt, a marketable document representing securities registered in the name of a US bank. *Options* are defined as investments by virtue of paragraph 7 which, it should be noted, extends not only to options to acquire or dispose of 'investments' as defined in the other paragraphs of Schedule 1, but also to currency options and to gold, silver, palladium and platinum options. *Futures* too are investments (paragraph 8). Futures are defined as 'Rights under a contract for the sale of a commodity or property of any other description under which delivery is to be made at a future date and at a price agreed upon when the contract is made.' The trouble with this definition, of course, is that it covers contracts entered into for genuine trading purposes, where actual physical delivery of the underlying property is expected, as well as contracts entered into for investment, hedging or speculative reasons. Paragraph 8 accordingly disapplies itself 'if the contract is made for commercial and not investment purposes', and lays down a number of tests for determining the purpose of a contract. However, all contracts made or traded on a recognised investment exchange[2] – such as LIFFE, the London International Financial Futures Exchange – are regarded as being made for investment purposes. Similar in function to futures and options are *contracts for differences*, caught by paragraph 9.[3] One example is a bet on the movement of a stock market index.[4]

The most important kinds of pooled investment also fall within Part I of Schedule 1. *Units in collective investment schemes*, such as unit trusts and open-ended investment companies, are classed as investments by paragraph 6. So, therefore, are personal pension schemes based on authorised unit trusts. The concept of a collective investment scheme was discussed in Chapter 12.

Life assurance policies (paragraph 10), when used as a vehicle for saving or investment, are also investments within the meaning of the Financial Services Act. The main types of policy caught are with-profits endowment policies (very commonly used as a means of saving to repay a mortgage loan), unit-linked policies, and personal pension policies. Pure term assurance policies, which pay out *only* on the death of the life insured and whose function is

---

[1] Note, however, that in practice the label 'derivative' is usually reserved for instruments falling within paras. 7 to 9 of Sch. 1.

[2] See p. 97.

[3] Along with other contracts 'the purpose or pretended purpose of which is to secure a profit or avoid a loss by reference to fluctuations in the value or price of property of any description or in an index or other factor designated for that purpose in the contract'.

[4] If such a bet is not a contract for differences it is some 'other contract' caught by para. 9: *City Index Ltd* v. *Leslie* [1991] 3 All E.R. 180.

protection (of dependants) rather than saving or investment, are treated as investments only in exceptional circumstances (for example, if the policy can be converted into an investment-type policy).

Finally, there is a sweeping-up clause (paragraph 11) which defines as investments 'rights to and interests in anything which is an investment falling within any other paragraph' of Part I of Schedule 1. However, the interests which members of an occupational pension scheme have by virtue of being beneficiaries of the scheme's trust are not to be treated as investments because of paragraph 11.

Overall, the Financial Services Act's approach to the concept of an investment reflects the 'touch-and-see principle'. During the Parliamentary stages of the Act, the government was urged by the National Association of Pension Funds to extend the scope of the legislation to cover real property (other than residential property). The argument in favour of taking this step was that property is an alternative store of value to gilts, equities and the like, and that it is commonly promoted and purchased as an investment, in the broad sense, with a view to subsequent resale at a profit.

The government responded with a statement of the philosophy underlying Part I of Schedule 1:

The general principle underlying the definition of 'investments' . . . is that it excludes physical property which a potential purchaser can inspect and which passes under his direct control on purchase. A person wishing to buy a building can have it surveyed and can establish its physical condition, the cost of any essential repairs and the likely maintenance costs. Once he has purchased it, he will be able directly to influence at least that part of its value which relates to its structural condition. This distinguishes real property from investments as defined in the [Act], where the purchaser acquires rights, directly or indirectly, in underlying assets which he generally cannot inspect or control.

Besides, why draw the line at real property?

A wide range of things, such as stamps and limited edition porcelain plates, are promoted on the basis that they will rise in value and they are certainly bought in that expectation or at least that hope. It would be wholly impracticable to extend the scope of the [legislation] so as to cover all these areas.[1]

The reader may suspect that it was this pragmatic argument that was decisive from the government's point of view rather than the philosophical distinction between tangible and intangible property. The touch-and-see principle can be viewed in two ways. On the one hand, it can be seen as asserting that *laisser-faire* is the best approach to land and collectibles. The difficulty with this approach is that an investor who buys land or gold or works of art on the strength of professional advice may be just as dependent on the

[1] HL Debs., vol. 479, cols. 64–5, 21 July 1986 (Lord Lucas of Chilworth); HC Debs., vol. 99, cols. 552–53, 12 June 1986 (Mr Howard).

integrity and expertise of his professional advisers as a purchaser of stocks and shares who puts his faith in the advice of his stockbrokers. Alternatively, the touch-and-see principle can be seen as an argument against including property and collectibles within the same protective regime as that established by the Financial Services Act. On this view, tangible investments, the markets in which they are bought and sold and the investors who buy them are so different in character that, to the extent that regulation is required (if at all), a different system of regulation would have to be created.

Investment activities

Part II of Schedule 1 to the Financial Services Act identifies five activities which the heading to Part II somewhat misleading describes as 'activities constituting investment business'. These activities are: (i) dealing in investments; (ii) arranging deals in investments; (iii) managing investments; (iv) giving investment advice; (v) establishing, operating or winding up collective investment schemes.

It is slightly misleading to describe these as activities constituting investment business because, according to section 1(2) of the Act, 'investment business' is actually *the business* of engaging in one or more of the listed activities. One can give investment advice without being in the business of giving investment advice. But the activities listed are authorisable in the sense that authorisation will normally be necessary if one carries on the business of engaging in any of them.

While Part II of Schedule 1 identifies the activities which are authorisable in this sense, Part III creates a number of specific exceptions ('excluded activities') to the definitions laid down in Part II. If all of one's business activities are excluded activities (or, of course, beyond the scope of the legislation in the first place), the need for authorisation is eliminated. Before we examine the authorisable activities, it is convenient to deal with certain exclusions of general application.

General exclusions

Part III of Schedule 1 contains certain exclusions which relate to all the activities identified as authorisable in Part II, except establishing, operating or winding up a collective investment scheme. One exclusion covers *trustees and personal representatives* in their relationships with each other and with the beneficiaries of the will or trust in question. This exclusion was designed to enable solicitors, for example, who act as trustees to perform their responsibilities as such without having to be authorised. It was not intended to exempt firms which hold themselves out as investment firms, and so it is not, broadly speaking, available to persons who hold themselves out as providing investment services or are separately remunerated for such services.[1]

[1] Sch. 1, para. 22.

The other general exclusions reflect the attempt to draw the boundaries of the Financial Services Act in a way that would exclude the normal activities of industrial and commercial companies on the footing that

These are not the sort of companies to whom the [Act] was intended to apply. Their investment activities are only peripheral to their main commercial activities, and they generally confine themselves to a professional market place and do nothing which would affect the ordinary investor.[1]

The first of these exclusions covers the situation where one company in a corporate *group* deals with or acts on behalf of other companies in the same group. Plainly, normal investor protection considerations do not arise in this context. The same exclusion also operates as between participators in a *joint enterprise*, i.e. an enterprise embarked upon by the various participants for commercial reasons related to a non-investment business carried on by them.[2] The second of these exclusions has effect where a *supplier of goods or services* engages in what would otherwise be an investment activity with or on behalf of his customer, and that activity is bound up with the commercial transaction which is the supplier's main purpose.[3] This exclusion thus recognises that major commercial transactions (e.g. in the export markets) often have an investment side to them which is part and parcel of the overall commercial package.

Dealing and arranging deals in investments (paragraphs 12 and 13)
(i) Dealing in investments. This is defined as: 'Buying, selling, subscribing for or underwriting investments or offering or agreeing to do so, either as principal or as an agent.'[4] Since dealings in an agency capacity are included, this covers, for example, the execution by a stockbroker or unit trust intermediary of his clients' instructions to buy or sell.

The inclusion of dealing as principal would mean that anyone whose dealings on his own account amounted to carrying on a business would need authorisation. But this outcome is prevented by the complex 'own account' exemption in paragraph 17 of Schedule 1, the general effect of which is that the only dealings as principal which are authorisable are those of a committed market maker (i.e. a person who 'holds himself out as willing to enter into transactions . . . at prices determined by him generally and continuously rather than in respect of each particular transaction'), or an occasional market maker (i.e. a person who 'holds himself out as engaging in the business of buying investments with a view to selling them'), or a person who regularly solicits members of the public to buy or sell investments.

The extent to which dealings as principal give rise to a need for

[1] HL Debs., vol. 480, col. 690, 14 October 1986 (Lord Lucas of Chilworth).   [2] Sch. 1, para. 18.
[3] Sch. 1, para. 19.   [4] Sch. 1, para. 12.

authorisation is further limited by the 'permitted persons' exclusion (paragraph 23). This exclusion is unique in Schedule 1 in that its operation depends on the grant of a permission by the Securities and Investments Board. The permitted persons procedure was introduced into the Financial Services Bill at the last minute[1] because of fears that, notwithstanding the 'group' and 'sale of goods/supply of services' exclusions already described, some commercial and industrial companies pursuing their usual business might technically be carrying on investment business, with all the criminal and civil law consequences which that entails if one is not authorised.[2] SIB may, at its discretion, give a 'permission' to an applicant whose main business is not investment business, but whose activities are likely to involve dealing as principal within the meaning of paragraph 12 if it would be 'inappropriate' to require the applicant to be subject to regulation as an authorised person.[3] In keeping with the philosophy of the investment business regime, permission is held to be appropriate only in cases where the investment dealings of the company concerned do not involve the public.[4] At March 1991 there were 146 permitted persons.[5]

(ii) Arranging deals in investments. Two kinds of arrangement are covered in paragraph 13: (*a*) arrangements with a view to another person buying, selling, subscribing for or underwriting a particular investment; (*b*) arrangements with a view to a person who participates in the arrangements buying, selling, subscribing for or underwriting investments.

Subparagraph (*a*) catches a person who *brings about* a *particular* investment deal without actually being a contracting party.[6] However, there is a difference between bringing a transaction about and merely making it possible. For example, a lawyer who merely prepared the documentation for a transaction, acting on instructions, would not be regarded as bringing it about.

Subparagraph (*b*) was put into the Act to make operating an investment exchange an authorisable activity.[7] Only later was it appreciated that subparagraph (*b*) catches the activities of 'introducers' to 'product companies' (i.e. of those who, by organising meetings or making referrals, introduce prospective customers to life insurance or unit trust companies). The benign effect (benign in the sense that it fits in with the Securities and Investments Board's policy of 'polarisation' – explained in Chapter 17) is to require the introducer to reveal his hand by becoming the appointed representative of the company concerned or to seek authorisation under the Act as an independent adviser.

---

[1] HL Debs., vol. 480, cols. 755–7, 14 October 1986.   [2] See pp. 244–6.   [3] Sch. 1, para. 23(3).
[4] SIB, *Permitted Persons* (December 1987), para. 11.
[5] *Report of the Securities and Investments Board for 1990/91*, p. 58.   [6] Sch. 1, para. 13, Notes (1), (2).
[7] *Recognised* investment exchanges are exempted persons under s.36 of the Act. Unrecognised exchanges need authorisation.

(iii) Special exclusions applicable to dealing and arranging deals. Paragraph 20 allows a company operating an employees' share scheme to establish facilities (for example, a 'share shop') for transactions in the company's shares for the benefit of its employees and their close relatives without having to worry about authorisation. The encouragement of employees' share schemes has been a feature of public policy since the late 1970s, and paragraph 20 reflects the concern that employers would think twice about laying on low-cost dealing facilities for their employees if doing so entailed authorisation under the Financial Services Act. Such facilities must, however, operate on an 'execution-only' basis; a company which offered an advice service to its employee shareholders (and 'carried on the business' of doing so) would have to be authorised.

Paragraph 21 excludes the transfer of control of a whole company from one set of hands to another, the measure of control being a holding of at least 75 per cent of the voting shares. In this situation the acquisition of the shares is in effect the acquisition of a business to be managed by the acquirer, and the exclusion can thus be regarded as an application of the touch-and-see principle. Paragraph 21 extends to advice given in connection with the transfer of control.

Managing investments (paragraph 14)
The Act's conception of investment management is a wide one. It covers not only the management of investments (other than one's own), but also the management of assets other than investments (as defined in the Act) where these form part of a managed portfolio which includes investments. So an investment manager who looks after his client's properties, cash, collectibles etc., as well as his 'investments' in the sense of the Financial Services Act, must comply with the requirements of the investment business regime in his management of these non-investment assets. Indeed the concept of 'managing investments' extends to portfolios which do not include investments (e.g. a fund of cash) if the portfolio has included investments (since the passage of the Act) or the portfolio manager has created the impression that it will eventually do so.

The concept of 'managing' investments is not wholly unproblematic. It clearly covers discretionary management, where the investor delegates to the manager the power to take on his own initiative and act upon decisions to acquire or dispose of assets. How far (if at all) it extends into arrangements where the manager in some sense 'looks after' the investor's portfolio, but cannot act without his instructions, is not so clear.

Giving investment advice (paragraph 15)
(i) The concept of investment advice. The core of paragraph 15 is as follows: 'Giving . . . to persons in their capacity as investors or potential investors advice on the

merits of their purchasing, selling, subscribing for or underwriting an investment. . . .'

Paragraph 15 is not as wide-ranging as it might appear at first glance. Both the DTI[1] and SIB draw a distinction between general advice on investments and specific advice on 'an investment':

General or generic advice on investments is not 'investment advice'. For example, advice on the merits of investing in the USA as opposed to Japan. Or on the merits of investing in engineering rather than leisure stocks. Or on the merits of investment trusts as opposed to unit trusts.

On the other hand:

Advice on the merits of specific investments is 'investment advice' if it is given to people in their capacity as investors or potential investors. For example, recommending a specific company share. Or the endowment policy of a particular life office. Or 'highlighting' some particular share or product in such a way as to indicate approval or disapproval of it.[2]

Moreover, what is caught is advice on the *merits* of an investment. In other words there must be some suggestion that the investment in question is a good (or a bad) buy, that the recipient of the advice should take steps to acquire (or dispose of) that investment. Giving advice on the merits of an investment is to be contrasted with neutral accounts of an investment's past performance or forecasts of its future prospects which leave the investor to draw his own conclusions. At the margin, of course, this distinction between advice on the merits and mere analysis is by no means easy to draw.

The final element in the paragraph 15 concept of investment advice is the audience. To be caught, the advice must be given to persons 'in their capacity as investors or potential investors'. This means, for example, that the recommendation of one's products to investment advisers in the hope that they in turn will recommend them to their clients, is not in itself investment advice.

(ii) The 'freedom of the press' exclusions. If absolutely everyone in the business of giving investment advice had to be authorised, a large number of newspapers (Sunday newspapers in particuar) and general financial magazines would be subject to the investment business regime because they contain columns in which shares or other investments are tipped. If investor protection were the sole objective of public policy this would be a justifiable state of affairs: after all, newspapers and magazines are a major source of investment advice for many comparatively unsophisticated private investors. In this context, however, the value of investor protection competes with that of the freedom of the press. In deference to press freedom, paragraph 25 of Schedule 1 to the Act excludes, from the concept of investment advice, advice given in a publication

---

[1] Statement by Francis Maude, 20 January 1988.
[2] SIB, *The Financial Services Act and the Press* (March 1988), paras. 9, 11 (emphasis and punctuation modified).

whose 'principal purpose' is not to lead persons to invest in any particular investment. The effect is to exempt from the need for authorisation publishers whose publications are read out of a general interest in current affairs or financial matters.[1] Paragraph 25 does not, however, exempt 'tipsheets' – i.e. publications whose main *raison d'être* is to give investment recommendations. Publications other than tipsheets automatically get the benefit of the freedom of the press exemption, but their exempt status can be conclusively confirmed if need be (e.g. in cases of doubt) by a certificate granted by the SIB.[2] The freedom of the press exemption also applies to television, radio and cable programmes – and neither the programme in question nor the channel as a whole need pass the 'principal purpose' test.[3]

The government's decision to exempt publications other than tipsheets from the rigours of the Financial Services Act was made easier by the *Declaration of Principle on Financial Journalism* made by the Press Council in June 1985. This voluntary code enjoins financial journalists to disclose to their editors personal interests in shares about which they write. Journalists should not buy or sell shares to exploit the price movements their articles can be expected to produce, and indeed are urged to abjure short-term speculation in general. Some publishers reinforce these ethical guidelines by requiring their observance as a matter of contract.

(iii) Necessary advice. There is also a narrow exclusion from the definition of investment advice in favour of advice given in the course of carrying on a profession or a non-investment business when it is 'necessary' to give that advice as part of other advice or services being given (paragraph 24). In effect, 'necessary' advice is advice which it would be negligent not to give. An example would be an accountant reviewing his client's tax position and observing that a special tax advantage could be gained by the realisation of one particular holding of shares. In this situation it would be 'necessary' for the accountant to advise his client which shares to sell.[4]

Establishing etc. collective investment schemes (paragraph 16)
The final investment activity with which the Act is concerned is the establishment, operation and winding up of collective investment schemes. As we saw in Chapter 12, these include unit trusts and open-ended investment companies, and may include, depending on the legal structure adopted, various other arrangements such as timeshares marketed as investment opportunities and some arrangements under which 'angels' back theatrical productions.

---

[1] The exemption covers only the published word: publishers who reply individually to readers' letters still need to be authorised if their doing so amounts to the carrying on of investment business: *The Financial Services Act and the Press*, para. 14.
[2] para. 25(2).   [3] para. 25A; Broadcasting Act 1990, Sch. 20, para. 45(2).
[4] HC Debs., Standing Committee E, 4 February 1986, col. 104.

Carrying on investment business

The Financial Services Act does not prohibit, for example, the giving of investment advice without authorisation. What it prohibits is *carrying on the business* of giving investment advice without authorisation. This is a different matter: passing a share tip to a chum in the pub does not require one to be an authorised person.

'Carrying on business' is an elusive concept, but it has two main elements. The first is *commercial motivation*: 'Advice given out of friendship or for philanthropic reasons is not caught by the Act. On the other hand, giving advice for a fee or a commission is caught.'[1] The second element, with which the first must normally be coupled, is *repetition or continuity*: 'A person will be regarded as carrying on the business of engaging in an activity only if his engaging in that activity were taken . . . as amounting to a substantial number of transactions amounting to carrying on a business.'[2]

The result of combining these tests is that the Act catches two kinds of businesses – those who specialise in investment activities and those who engage in them as a sideline to their mainstream business activities. A businessman is not caught merely by virtue of being in business and giving an isolated piece of investment advice. So, for example, an electronics company does not need to be authorised to give advice on a one-off basis to an employee who seeks advice on a personal pension. But a company which for industrial relations reasons operates a regular investment advice service for its employees may well be in a different position.

In one case – that of occupational pension schemes – the concept of carrying on investment business has an extended meaning. Under section 191 of the Act someone who engages in the activity of managing the assets of an occupational pension scheme is *deemed* to be carrying on investment business, even if he would not on the application of the normal test be regarded as doing so.[3]

The territorial dimension

As we have seen, the need to become an authorised person under the Financial Services Act arises only if one is carrying on investment business *in the United Kingdom*. Under section 1 of the Act there are two situations in which a person is regarded as doing this. The first is if he carries on investment business 'from a permanent place of business maintained by him in the United Kingdom' (s.1(3)(a)). The second is if he engages in the United Kingdom in one or more investment activities without being able to get the benefit of any exclusion, and his doing so constitutes the carrying on by him of a business in the United

---

[1] *The Financial Services Act and the Press*, para. 13.

[2] HL Debs., vol. 480, col. 694, 14 October 1986 (Lord Lucas of Chilworth).

[3] Thus it does not matter whether the fund manager is carrying on business, or whether he could otherwise claim the benefit of the 'trustees' exclusion in para. 22 of Sch. 1 (described above, p. 234). See further p. 210 above.

Kingdom (s.1(3)(*b*)). It is, of course, possible to fall within paragraphs (*a*) and (*b*) simultaneously. But a person who falls within paragraph (*b*) and not paragraph (*a*) – i.e. one who does not have a permannt UK base – is known as an 'overseas person', and special provisions apply.

Persons with a UK base

Section 1(3)(*a*) is designed to catch firms with a *permanent* presence in the UK. This emphasis on permanence means, for example, that business conducted from a stand at a money show by a foreign firm without a branch in the UK would not be caught by paragraph (*a*).[1] On the other hand, investment business done abroad by a firm with a UK base ('export business') sometimes is caught. This is because the purpose of the Financial Services Act is not just to protect investors in the UK but also to inspire confidence overseas in British firms and thereby to encourage overseas investors to do business with them. So the Act covers a UK firm's overseas investment business if it is carried on 'from' a UK base. This coverage extends, for example, to investment advice given from the UK base by telephone or letter. And if a UK-based salesman flies to Germany and spends a week or two working from a hotel bedroom to sell investments to British servicemen (or indeed Germans), he is carrying on investment business 'from' the UK. On the other hand, if a UK firm establishes a branch or a subsidiary in Germany, investment business conducted from there is not investment business 'in the United Kingdom'.

Overseas persons

The Financial Services Act sets up a system of investor protection, but it is not intended to be 'protectionist' in the economic sense. It is not designed to shelter UK investment businesses from foreign competition or to deprive British investors of the freedom to invest overseas. The Act's provisions on overseas persons are therefore an attempt to strike a balance between this open-door policy and the need to protect British investors from dubious overseas businesses. The balance is struck by tempering the general principle that the conduct of investment business in the UK requires authorisation with special provisions in Part IV of Schedule 1, the effect of which is that certain business done in the UK is deemed to have been done outside the UK, with the result that the doer does not require authorisation after all.

Part IV of Schedule 1 creates two main 'exclusions' for overseas persons. The first excludes *dealing* with or through an authorised (or exempted) person.[2] The rationale for this is that authorised and exempted persons can look after themselves and any of their own customers who happen to be involved.[3]

The second exclusion relates to unsolicited or *legitimately solicited transactions*.[4]

---

[1] SIB, *Carrying on Investment Business in the United Kingdom*, CP19 (March 1989), para. 9.   [2] para. 26(1).

[3] SIB, CP19, para. 6. There is an analogous exclusion for the arranging of deals: Sch. 1, para. 26(2).

[4] Sch. 1, para. 27.

This makes it possible for an unauthorised overseas person to seek business in the UK provided it is done in a way that does not break the Act's provisions on either advertising or the making of unsolicited calls. In relation to advertising, this usually means that the advertisement cannot be issued without the approval of an authorised person. The safeguard for investors lies in the fact that the giving of approval is conditional on compliance with the advertising rules to which the authorised person is subject by virtue of having authorisation. These are described in Chapter 18. In relation to unsolicited calls, an overseas person wishing to take advantage of the legitimate solicitation exclusion must not cold-call anyone save in the exceptional categories and circumstances (e.g. customers signed up when they were expatriates) enumerated in SIB's Unsolicited Calls Regulations. Again these are described in Chapter 18.

If an unauthorised overseas business operates within the framework of the 'legitimate solicitation' exclusion it cannot only *promote* dealing, advisory and investment management services in the UK, it can also enter into actual deals with those whose business has been legitimately solicited and give investment advice. However, the exclusion does not enable an unauthorised overseas person actually to manage investments in the UK.

Exemptions

The Financial Services Act creates a number of exemptions from its authorisation requirement. In keeping with the general policy of applying a light regulatory touch to inter-professional dealings, section 43 creates an exemption for 'listed money market institutions' – i.e. players on the markets in sterling, foreign exchange and bullion, which are subject to the Bank of England's non-statutory 'Grey Book' regime – in respect of their mutual and wholesale transactions.[1] The other two main exemptions relate to appointed representatives and Lloyd's underwriting agents.

Appointed representatives (s.44)

An appointed representative is a self-employed individual or a company for whose investment activities an authorised person (the appointed representative's principal) has accepted responsibility. The effect of this is that the principal will be responsible at civil law for the relevant acts and omissions of the appointed representative as if they were his own (s.44(6)). In other words, the position of the appointed representative is equated with that of an employee (employees do not need to be authorised because it is their employer who is 'carrying on business'). The exemption of the appointed representative is confined to his 'selling' activities ('procuring' persons to enter into

---

[1] For a detailed account, see B. Rider, C. Abrams and E. Ferran, *Guide to the Financial Services Act 1986* (2nd edn, 1989), pp. 84–6.

investment agreements with his principal), and giving advice to them[1] and does not extend to investment management. The appointed representative concept was introduced with the life assurance and unit trust sector in mind because of the large numbers of self-employed, commission-remunerated salespersons working in that sector. But there is nothing in section 44 to prevent a corporate entity – of whatever size – from becoming the appointed representative of a life company, and many have in fact done so. In particular, most large building societies have 'tied' to life insurers. Many estate agencies and mortgage brokerages are also tied. The theory behind section 44 was that the principal's liability for any misdemeanours committed by its appointed representatives while acting within the scope of their appointment would provide a sufficient incentive for the principal to supervise their activities adequately. In practice, however, LAUTRO has found it necessary to specify with increasing rigour and precision both the scope of its members' responsibility for their appointed representatives and the steps they must take to control and monitor their conduct.[2]

Lloyd's (s.42)

Lloyd's is a *general* insurance market – no life policies falling within the definition of 'investment' are underwritten – with virtually unique features. The normal pattern in insurance markets is for policies to be underwritten by entities incorporated with limited liability. But at Lloyd's the risks are assumed by *individual* underwriting members with unlimited personal liability. These individuals are combined in syndicates whose affairs are handled by underwriting (or 'managing') agencies. Underwriting members are divided into working members (professionals in the Lloyd's market) and external members, known as 'names', passive underwriters who put their assets at risk in the hope that their managing agents will make a profit for them. In a sense, therefore, Lloyd's names are investors; and indeed a Lloyd's syndicate falls within the Financial Services Act's definition of a collective investment scheme.[3] Hence managing agencies operate collective investment schemes and give advice on units in them to names and potential names. In addition, they look after members' insurance funds – a form of investment management.[4] Hence Lloyd's managing agencies would need authorisation under the Act, were it not for the fact that section 42 makes them exempted persons 'as respects investment business carried on in connection with or for the purpose of insurance business at Lloyd's'.

[1] s.44(3).
[2] See generally LAUTRO, *Appointed Representatives*, Consultative Bulletin No. 3 (1990); core rule 13; LAUTRO (Representatives) Rules 1991.
[3] FSA s.75; see pp. 185–7.   [4] HC Debs., Standing Committee E, 4 February, 1986, cols. 121–2.

The rationale for this exemption lies partly in the distinctive character of business at Lloyd's, which would have required investment business regulators to acquire a specialised expertise, partly in the need for the regulation of Lloyd's to strike a balance between the interests of names and those of Lloyd's policyholders, and partly in the fact that self-regulation at Lloyd's had only just been overhauled following the enactment of the Lloyd's Act 1982.[1] The exemption of Lloyd's managing agents was hotly contested by the Labour opposition during the passage of the Financial Services Bill, and the government sought to strengthen its defences by appointing the Neill Committee to consider whether the Lloyd's regulatory system provided protection for names 'comparable' to that afforded to investors in general under the Financial Services Act.[2] If the Committee's report had recommended the removal of the exemption for Lloyd's managing agents, this could have been done by means of an order under section 46 of the Financial Services Act. But the report published in January 1987, although concluding that the regulatory arrangements then in place at Lloyd's did not provide comparable protection, did not make such a recommendation. Instead it argued for a 'solution specially devised to fit the particular requirements of Lloyd's' which could be implemented within the framework of the 1982 Act.[3] In particular, the Neill Committee felt that the degree of external supervision to which SROs and RPBs are subject by virtue of the role of SIB within the investment business regime was lacking in relation to Lloyd's. Accordingly the Committee recommended that more independent outsiders should be appointed to the Council of Lloyd's, and that the working members should lose their built-in majority. These and other recommendations were implemented, and on that basis the Lloyd's exemption remains undisturbed, although the scale of the losses suffered by some syndicates in recent years has made the principle of unlimited personal liability seem increasingly problematic, and allegations of serious malpractice have been made.

UNLAWFUL INVESTMENT BUSINESS

The Financial Services Act attaches a number of possible legal consequences to the contravention of section 3 – that is, to the carrying on of investment business in the United Kingdom without authorisation or exemption. Carrying on investment business unlawfully (i) is a criminal offence, (ii) may taint with unenforceability contracts made while doing so, and (iii) may enable SIB to obtain injunctions or restitution orders. However, the right to pursue an action for damages conferred upon private investors by section 62 of the Act does not arise in connection with breaches of section 3.

[1] See Ferguson, 'Self-Regulation at Lloyd's: The Lloyd's Act 1982', (1983) 46 *Modern Law Rev.* 56.
[2] *Regulatory Arrangement at Lloyd's: Report of the Committee of Inquiry*, Cm. 59 (January 1987).
[3] *Ibid.*, para. 1.9.

(i) *Criminal offence.* Section 4 of the Act makes the contravention of section 3 a criminal offence for which the maximum penalty is two years imprisonment. Under section 3 it is even an offence to 'purport' to carry on investment business. This means that it might be possible to secure a conviction against somebody who *held himself* out as carrying on investment business, even without proof that specific transactions caught by Schedule 1 to the Act were entered into.

The definition of investment business is, as we have seen, so complex that it is quite possible for people to carry on investment business without appreciating that they are doing so. If a person can prove that he 'took all reasonable precautions and exercised all due diligence' to avoid carrying on investment business without authorisation he is not guilty of the offence. SIB has issued several pieces of formal guidance[1] on the concept of carrying on investment business.[2] It is probable that someone who could show that he was led by the SIB's guidance not to seek authorisation (and that he had interpreted it in a reasonable way) would have this defence. Reliance on the advice of one's own solicitors might also have this effect.

(ii) *Unenforceability.* One of the most striking features of the Financial Services Act, from a legal point of view, is the way in which it seeks at various points to reinforce criminal or administrative law sanctions by the provision of civil law remedies. One example is the way in which agreements tainted by a contravention of section 3 may turn out to be legally unenforceable.

Prima facie unenforceability arises in two situations. The first is where someone, in the course of carrying on investment business in contravention of section 3, enters into an agreement the making or performance of which constitutes an investment activity.[3] In this situation the other party will be able to enforce the agreement if he wants to, but the law-breaker may find himself unable to do so. However, the court may allow the agreement to be enforced against the other party if the plaintiff reasonably believed himself not to be breaking section 3 by entering into the agreement.[4] The other situation is where the investment firm is duly authorised or exempted, but the agreement is entered into as a result of something said or done by a third party (e.g. an introducer) who is carrying on investment business without authorisation or exemption.[5] In this situation again the agreement will be enforceable against, but not necessarily by, the firm. However, the court may allow the agreement to be enforced against the other party if the firm did not know that the third party was in contravention of section 3.[6] Moreover, in both situations, the court may allow the agreement to be enforced if that would be 'just and equitable'.[7]

[1] As defined in FSA, s.114(12).

[2] e.g. *Pensions Advice and Management*, Guidance Release; *The Financial Services Act and the Press* (March 1988, Part 1).

[3] s.5(1)(a).   [4] s.5(3)(a).   [5] s.5(1)(b).   [6] s.5(3)(b).   [7] s.5(3)(c).

(iii) Restitution orders. Section 6 of the Financial Services Act enables the Securities and Investments Board to assume the role of investor's champion by taking a person who has been unlawfully carrying on investment business to court for the benefit of investors who have done business with that person. The order sought from the court is called a restitution order, but this is a misnomer because SIB can not only seek compensation for investors who have suffered loss but also ask the court to require the person concerned to disgorge his profits for distribution among the investors – even if they have not suffered loss or been adversely affected by their dealings with that person.[1]

While it is for SIB to seek a restitution order (and SIB cannot be compelled to go to court by any investor or group of investors), it is for the court to decide whether the order should be made. There must, of course, have been a contravention of section 3 (but not necessarily an offence under section 4, where there is a due diligence defence). But where the ground for seeking the restitution order is that investors have lost out, it is also necessary to show that this resulted from either a contravention of section 47 (which bans misleading statements and market manipulation) or section 56 (the ban on unsolicited calls),[2] *or else* a failure to act substantially in accordance with some rule or regulation made under Chapter V of the Act. (Non-conformity to SIB's Conduct of Business Rules could thus form part of the grounds for a restitution order against an unauthorised person, even though those rules do not 'apply' to unauthorised persons.) Where, on the other hand, the ground for seeking the order is that profits have accrued to the person concerned as a result of his unlawful investment business, no further non-compliance need be shown.[3]

If the court decides in favour of a restitution order, the amount to be disgorged will be 'such sum as appears to the court to be just' having regard to the profits accrued or the loss suffered. The court will also determine the allocation of the proceeds among the investors whose transactions with the unauthorised person gave rise to the profits or losses in question.[4]

---

[1] Between 1988 and 1991 SIB raised restitution actions (under s.6 or 61) in six cases: *Report of the Securities and Investments Board for 1990/91*, p. 32.

[2] Oddly enough, a contravention of s.47 or 56 *by itself* enables SIB to seek a restitution order under s.61. It is not clear what occasion SIB would ever have to tackle such a contravention under s.6, where a contravention of s.3 would also have to be proved.

[3] s.6(3).   [4] s.6(4)–(6).

16
The Financial Services Act: Regulation of Investment Firms

ROUTES TO AUTHORISATION

The Financial Services Act provides for no less than seven different ways of obtaining authorisation.

Direct authorisation

It is open to any person to seek authorisation directly from SIB itself. It was always envisaged that virtually all investment businesses would get authorisation through membership of a self-regulating organisation or professional body recognised by SIB rather than directly from SIB itself and so it has turned out. Of the 28,000 or so authorised persons only about 80 are directly authorised by SIB.[1] In view of these figures it would be tempting to argue that there was no need to provide for the possibility of direct authorisation in the Financial Services Act at all. However, it was felt necessary to make provision for direct authorisation in case there were investment businesses for which no SRO or RPB provided a suitable 'home', and to lend credibility to the possibility that SIB might 'de-recognise' recognised body.

Seeing itself mainly as a standard-setting body with a strategic role to play in the regulation of the investment industry, SIB has never encouraged applications for direct authorisation. But when all is said and done applicants have a statutory *right* to direct authorisation provided they pass the fit and proper test.[2] In practice direct authorisation has attracted in particular building societies and bank and building society subsidiaries who were reluctant to join FIMBRA, perceiving it as an SRO for small businesses rather than large-scale organisations. Firms directly authorised by SIB have no right to participate in the governance of SIB – they have no voting rights

[1] *Report of the Securities and Investments Board for 1990/91*, pp. 19–20.
[2] FSA, s.27(2).

nor any right to be represented on the Board – but this seems not to have troubled the building societies, who have a tradition of being subject to external regulation in the form of the Building Societies Commission.

Persons seeking direct authorisation must submit to SIB a business plan detailing the kinds of investment business they propose to carry on, and their subsequent conduct of investment business must be confined to the areas indicated in the plan, although changes may be notified.[1] The point is to enable SIB to assess the firm's competence and the adequacy of its compliance systems *in relation to* the activities it proposes to pursue. If a directly authorised firm engages in investment business outside the scope of its business plan it is not guilty of a criminal offence against section 4 of the Act – for it remains an authorised person – but it exposes itself to the possibility of civil and disciplinary sanctions.

If SIB proposes to refuse an application for authorisation it must first give the applicant written notice of its intention to do so, setting out its reasons for proposing to refuse the application and informing the applicant of his right to have the case referred to the Financial Services Tribunal. If the reasons involve a named third party, and are 'prejudicial to that person in any office or employment',[2] a copy of the notice must be served on that party, unless it is impracticable to do so. The applicant and any third party on whom a copy of the notice has been served have the right to require the case to be referred to the Financial Services Tribunal. If after 28 days the applicant has not exercised his right to have the matter referred, SIB must give him written notice of its final decision. Since SIB is not bound by its initial statement of intention this procedure provides an opportunity to correct any errors upon which its notice of intention may have been based. There have been two references to the Tribunal following notice of an intended refusal of an application, neither of which has been successful.

Membership of an SRO

SIB recognises four self-regulating organisations under the Financial Services Act and membership of any one of them confers authorisation to carry on investment business. Each SRO is required to have a 'scope' rule which delimits the kinds of investment activity in which a member firm may engage by virtue of its membership.[3] The function of the scope rules is to establish a division of labour between the different SROs and to ensure that each SRO assumes regulatory responsibility only for areas of business which it has the competence and resources to regulate. Chapter 6 contains a brief outline of each SRO's scope.

Within an SRO, an individual firm may be further constrained by the scope

[1] FSA, s.26(2)(b); SIB CBRs (1990) 2.01(1)(b).   [2] FSA, s.29(3)(b).   [3] FSA, s.10(3).

of its business plan or (in the case of FIMBRA members) by its membership categorisation. However, as with firms directly authorised by SIB, it is not a criminal offence for a firm to go beyond its individual scope or that of its SRO.

The inevitable consequence of the functional differentiation of SROs is that financial conglomerates involved in a wide range of investment activities become involved with more than one SRO, either because a single entity finds it necessary to have multiple membership or because different entities within a group must join different SROs. In addition, there may be non-Financial Services Act regulators to be contended with, such as the Bank of England. In relation to financial regulation (i.e. the enforcement of capital adequacy requirements) the problem of co-ordination has been mitigated by the establishment of 'lead regulator' arrangements under which one regulator (e.g. the Bank or the Building Societies Commission) assumes paramount responsibility for monitoring compliance on behalf of all the interested regulators.

Corporate groups which have two or more SRO rulebooks to reckon with tend to display an understandable preference for uniformity of approach to matters which recur in more than one set of rules. The old 'principle of equivalence' by and large operated to ensure that each rulebook attained a certain standard of investor protection, but it did not prevent the emergence of technical differences in the means by which legal effect was given to the common standards. Under the 'new settlement' the core rules are designed to secure a minimum level of uniformity among SROs on fundamental issues, but the scope for disparity at the level of detail (i.e. the 'third tier') between different SRO rulebooks remains. This is an unavoidable byproduct of a system that is both self-regulatory and decentralised.

Certification by an RPB

In itself, membership of one of the professional bodies recognised by SIB – i.e. the three Law Societies, the three Institutes of Chartered Accountants, the Chartered Association of Certified Accountants, the Institute of Actuaries, and the Insurance Brokers Registration Council – does not give authorisation under the Financial Services Act. Authorisation depends on the issue of an investment business certificate, and such certificates can only be issued where two conditions are satisfied: (i) the firm must be managed and controlled by individuals each of whom is a member of an RPB and at least one of whom is a member of the certifying RPB, and (ii) the firm's main business must be the practice of the profession in question, excluding the practice of investment business.[1] This means, for example, that a firm of solicitors could not be certified by the Law Society of Scotland if its investment business outweighed

---

[1] FSA, s. 16 and Sch. 3, para. 2.

its other professional business. The purpose of this provision is to ensure that firms whose main line of business is investment business must join the appropriate SRO, even though they happen to be members of a recognised professional body.

It is striking that the Act does not require the process of certification by an RPB to involve a fit and proper test. The theory of the Act is that the fitness and properness of professional firms for certification can be taken as read because each *individual* member of the profession has to demonstrate his fitness and properness on entry to it. But this overlooks the relativity of fitness and properness: someone who has shown he is fit and proper to engage in mainstream legal or accounting work may not, as a matter of fact, be competent to engage in investment business. Of course, judgments of fitness and properness made by RPBs *since* the passage of the Financial Services Act should take into account the possibility that the individual concerned may join a certified firm and be called upon to engage in investment business.

Authorised insurers and registered friendly societies

Under the Insurance Companies Act 1982 the Department of Trade and Industry has the function of authorising insurance companies to carry on *insurance* business in the UK. Some insurance business – in particular, the writing of life policies with a savings or investment element, and pension fund management – is also investment business.[1] A separate process of authorisation under the Financial Services Act would therefore have been necessary, but section 22 of the Act gives automatic FSA authorisation to insurance companies with ICA authorisation from the DTI. This automatic authorisation covers not only the activities specified above but also connected activities – in particular, the marketing of life assurance. Authorisation is given only 'as respects' these kinds of investment business. Thus an insurance company which exceeds the latitude given by section 22 becomes liable to criminal sanctions for carrying on investment business without authorisation.

The fact that the prudential regulation of insurance companies is already undertaken by the DTI makes it inappropriate for the investment business regime in its entirety to apply to them. So the only investment business rules which apply are those which relate to marketing of life assurance and pension fund management.[2] The applicable rules are those of SIB itself unless the company joins Lautro. In fact, only six insurance companies are directly regulated by SIB;[3] the rest have chosen to subject themselves to Lautro's rules. But this does not mean that their authorisation derives from membership of Lautro; it still flows from section 22. So if Lautro expelled an insurance company, the normal consequence of being expelled from an SRO – loss of

---

[1] Insurance Companies Act 1982, Sch. 1, long-term business classes I and VII.
[2] FSA, Sch. 10, para. 4(2).   [3] SIB, *Report*, note 1 above, p. 57.

authorisation – would not follow. Neither Lautro nor SIB has the power to deprive an insurance company of its authorisation. If an investment business regulator felt that an insurance company should be deauthorised, it would have to ask the Secretary of State for Trade and Industry to withdraw the company's authorisation under the Insurance Companies Act. That Act specifies contravention of SIB or Lautro rules as a ground for withdrawal of authorisation.[1] In short, the fitness and properness of a DTI-authorised insurance company to carry on investment business is, in the final analysis, for the Secretary of State to determine. However, he is under an obligation to consult with SIB before he exercises his power to authorise an insurance company.[2]

Under the Friendly Societies Act 1974 the supervision of friendly societies is the responsibility of the Chief Registrar of Friendly Societies. Accordingly, the Financial Services Act makes special provision for friendly societies broadly parallel to the special regime for insurance companies.[3]

UCITS operators

Pursuant to the UK's obligations under the UCITS Directive, section 24 of the Financial Services Act confers automatic authorisation upon the operator of a recognised UCITS as respects the operation of the scheme and for connected purposes (e.g. promoting the scheme). A UCITS operator whose authorisation derives from section 24 alone (and not, for example, from membership of an SRO) is subject to SIB's conduct of business rules only to the extent that they make provision for marketing matters (and so, for instance, the rules on contract notes do not apply).[4]

SIB has published guidance to the effect that automatic authorisation under section 24 comes about only if the operator carries on investment business *in the UK*.[5] The basis of this view is that otherwise authorisation, with all that it entails in the way of obligations, would be thrust upon operators who confine their investment business to jurisdictions outside the UK. Nevertheless it is remarkable what an operator can accomplish in the way of promotional activity without technically carrying on investment business in the UK. An unauthorised operator can advertise his scheme in the UK,[6] take advantage of the exemption in favour of legitimately solicited transactions,[7] canvass independent intermediaries to recommend his scheme[8] and, if the

---

[1] Insurance Companies Act 1982, s.11(2)(a) as amended by FSA Sch. 10, para. 7(1).

[2] FSA, Sch. 10, para. 10(1).   [3] FSA, Sch. 11.   [4] FSA, s.86(7).

[5] SIB, *Marketing in the United Kingdom: Guidance for Operators of Recognised Collective Investment Schemes*, Guidance Release 3/89 (July 1989), paras. 21,23.

[6] FSA, s.58(1)(c).   [7] Above, pp. 241–2.

[8] Advice given to independent intermediaries does not constitute investment advice as defined in paragraph 15 of Schedule 1 because it is not given to them in their capacity as 'investors or potential investors'.

operator is in a corporate group which includes a UK marketing company with authorisation, rely on that company to sell to UK investors. In consequence, no authorisations under section 24 have hitherto been notified to SIB.

Europersons

Section 31 of the Financial Services Act confers UK authorisation upon persons authorised under the law of another EC Member State to carry on investment business (or some particular kind of investment business), but only if certain conditions are satisfied. In the first place, the person claiming authorisation must be carrying on investment business in the UK, but not from a permanent place of business maintained by him in the UK. His head office must be situated in a Member State other than the UK. And the law of that State must recognise him as a national of one of the Member States (not excluding the UK).[1]

Secondly, the law of the Member State concerned must pass one of two tests. The first test is an application of the principle of equivalence: does the law in question afford investors in the UK protection at least equivalent to that provided by Chapter III of the Financial Services Act in relation to SRO member firms, or directly authorised persons?[2] In effect, this means that the Member State must have an adequate system for ensuring that only fit and proper persons become and remain authorised for the conduct of investment business. Alternatively, the EC Member State in question must have implemented an EC harmonisation directive and the implementing legislation must give him authorisation to carry on the investment business in question. This authorisation must be evidenced by a certificate issued by the authorising authority.[3] Only two firms have claimed authorisation on the basis of section 31.[4]

The Single Market

When the Second Banking Co-ordination Directive[5] comes into force, banks authorised in other Member States will be able, depending on the scope of their authorisation, to do investment as well as banking business in the United Kingdom without the need for further authorisation. This is because the list of activities which a bank may be permitted to undertake by means of the single banking licence includes investment banking business, such as dealing in securities, money broking and portfolio management, as well as conventional retail banking business. In the provision of these services, banks authorised in other Member States will be subject to the supervision of their home state

---

[1] FSA, s.31(1),(2).   [2] FSA, s.31(3)(a).   [3] FSA, s.31(3)(b), (5).
[4] SIB, *Report*, note 1 above, p. 20.   [5] Dir.89/646/EEC.

regulator, but they will be required to comply with United Kingdom conduct of business rules and to participate in the Investors Compensation Scheme (unless services are provided on a cross-border rather than branch basis in which case their domestic compensation arrangements, if any, will apply). UK banks by contrast will not possess the same freedom to provide investment services in other Member States unless the scope of their authorisation under the Banking Act is widened, which is likely to happen, contrary to the functional principle upon which the UK system of regulation is based, in order to avoid this potential competitive disadvantage.

The provision of investment services by non-bank institutions, on the other hand, is the subject of a separate proposal for an Investment Services Directive,[1] conceived along lines similar to the Second Banking Co-ordination Directive, which has not yet been adopted. If it is adopted in its proposed form, investment firms authorised in other Member States will also be free to provide investment services in the United Kingdom without the need for separate authorisation. In the provision of such services they will be subject to supervision by their home state authorities, but they will again be required to adhere to United Kingdom conduct of business requirements and to join the compensation scheme (in respect of branch business).

Neither of these directives apply to life insurance. The availability of a 'single licence' for life insurance will depend on the progress of the Third Life Directive (the Life Framework Directive), as we saw in Chapter 10.

FINANCIAL RESOURCES

The Financial Services Act makes provision for the imposition of financial resources or capital adequacy requirements on investment firms in respect of their business.[2] The requirements prescribed by SIB follow the three-tier structure adopted as part of the 'new settlement'.[3] They consist of a top tier of principles, which apply across the board, a middle tier of core rules[4] which apply to SRO members as well as to directly authorised firms, i.e. firms authorised under section 25 or 31 of the Financial Services Act, and a bottom tier of detailed rules which apply, with exceptions, to directly authorised firms only.[5] One of the rationales for the adoption of this three-tier structure was to allow SROs greater freedom to tailor requirements to the circumstances of their members. SIB, however, has taken the view that, because of the need to ensure consistency of treatment of individual risks and firms with similar risk profiles, there is less scope for flexibility in the application of financial resources requirements to SRO members than there is in the application of conduct of business rules. SRO members are therefore subject to essentially the same requirements as directly authorised firms.

---

[1] OJ C42 (22 February 1990), p. 7.   [2] FSA, s.49.   [3] As to which, see below pp. 266–8.
[4] Financial Supervision Rules 1990, rule 1.04.   [5] Rule 1.05.

The basic financial resources requirement applicable to investment firms, encapsulated in principle 8, is that a firm 'should ensure that it maintains adequate financial resources to meet its investment business commitments and to withstand the risks to which its business is subject'. Core rule A does not add to this requirement save to enjoin a firm to have available 'at all times' the amount and type of financial resources required by its regulator. The amount and type of resources required by regulators are expressed in the form of general rules, rather than individual decisions as is the case, for example, in relation to banks or building societies. Complete uniformity is avoided, however, by the division, for the purpose of setting these requirements, of firms into different categories according to the type of risks to which they are exposed.

The Financial Supervision Rules distinguish four categories of firms – low risk firms, medium risk firms, higher risk firms and special firms. *Low risk firms* comprise investment advisers and intermediaries which limit themselves to certain low risk activities, such as advising on and arranging transactions in life policies, and which do not handle clients' money or assets (rule 2.01): they are merely required to satisfy a basic solvency test whereby they must be able to meet their liabilities as they fall due (rule 3.02). *Medium risk firms* comprise firms involved in similar types of activity which handle clients' money or assets and carry out limited types of investment management (rule 2.02): they are required to meet a 'current liquidity' test, whereby they must be able to meet their short-term liabilities out of their current assets (rule 4.02), and a modified 'net liquid assets' test whereby their liquid assets must exceed their total liabilities by a margin which is sufficient to allow them to wind down their business, if necessary, and repay all claims by customers and counterparties (the base requirement) and to cover any position risk, counterparty risk or foreign currency risk to which they may be exposed (rule 4.03). *Higher risk firms* include firms broking or dealing in securities and general investment managers: (rule 2.03) they are required to meet a more demanding 'net liquid assets' test (rule 5.02). *Special firms*, finally, which category currently includes only trustees of authorised unit trusts (rule 2.04), are required to have gross capital of at least £4 million (rule 6.02).

The financial resources requirements applicable to investment firms are complemented by record keeping and reporting requirements whose content is summarised by principle 9, which provides that a firm should, *inter alia*, keep proper records, and principle 10 which provides that a firm should 'deal with its regulator in an open and co-operative manner and keep its regulator promptly informed of anything concerning the firm which might reasonably be expected to be disclosed to it'. These principles are amplified by core rules which require a firm to ensure that it maintains adequate accounting records, and to prepare and submit such reports as are required by its regulator in a timely manner,[1] to ensure, for the purpose of compliance with rules on

---

[1] Core rule B; the reports required are specified in the third-tier rules which distinguish between the various categories of firm so that, whereas higher risk firms are required to submit monthly reports, low risk firms are required to complete half-yearly questionnaires and an annual declaration of solvency.

financial supervision, that its internal controls and systems are adequate for the size, nature and complexity of its activities,[1] and to notify its regulator immediately it becomes aware that it is in breach of, or that it expects shortly to be in breach of, the core rules on financial resources, records and reporting or internal controls and systems.[2]

All firms, whether incorporated or not, with the exception of those conducting only low risk investment business, are required to appoint a suitably qualified auditor who is required to make certain reports to the appropriate regulator.[3] The precise reporting requirements vary, but as a general rule auditors are required to report on annual financial statements and accounting records, statements of financial resources and the adequacy of systems of control over clients' money and other assets.

As well as being required to report to the appropriate regulator on prescribed matters, an auditor also has power to draw to the regulator's attention matters of concern of which he becomes aware in his capacity as the auditor of an authorised business.[4] Guidance issued by the professional bodies on the circumstances in which matters should be brought to the attention of a regulator provides that an auditor should take the initiative and ensure that an *ad hoc* report is made, either by the authorised business or by himself, 'if he considers investors have incurred, or are at significant risk of incurring, a material loss as a result of persons regulated under the Act carrying on business in a manner that is not fit and proper or that is in breach of the regulations'.[5] The guidance provides that normally an auditor should ask the authorised business to draw matters about which he is concerned to the attention of the regulator, but that in exceptional circumstances, where the auditor doubts whether management are fit and proper persons to carry on investment business and it would be in the interest of protecting investors that the management of the authorised business should not be informed in advance, the auditor should report direct to the regulator.[6] Examples of such circumstances include where an auditor believes that a fraud or other irregularity has been committed by the directors or senior management, or where he has discovered that the directors or senior management are acting in an irresponsible or reckless manner with respect to the affairs of the business or its clients.

---

[1] Core rule C.   [2] Core rule D.

[3] See e.g. rule 10.02; core rule E requires a firm to make available to its auditor the information and explanations he needs to discharge his responsibilities as required by the firm's regulator. SIB has power to require a second audit of directly authorised firms: FSA, s. 108.

[4] FSA, s. 109.

[5] Auditing Practices Committee, *Communications between Auditors and Regulators under sections 109 and 180(1)(g) of the Financial Services Act 1986* (1990), para. 29.

[6] paras. 33 and 35.

CLIENT MONEY AND INVESTMENTS

Client money regulation is specific to investment firms. Like compensation schemes, it is designed to mitigate the impact of insolvency on investors, in this case by seeking to ensure that client money is not available to meet the claims of creditors in the event of a firm's insolvency but is preserved for distribution among clients.[1] This aim is sought to be achieved by requiring client money to be held separately from a firm's own money, in a separate bank account, and by making provision for it to be held on trust (or, in Scotland, as agent) for clients.

The Financial Services (Client Money) Regulations 1991 (CMRs) set out the requirements which apply to firms handling client money. They have been designated so as to apply directly to members of SROs as well as to directly authorised firms.[2] One reason for their designation is that only SIB has power to create binding trusts.[3] But their designation so as to apply to firms regulated by SROs is not solely attributable to the limitations of contractual (as opposed to statutory) law-making. Another reason why 'commonality' has been preferred is that it is administratively more convenient for firms as well as regulators.[4] For this reason too a more specific approach to rule making has been adopted: 'in the field of client money, where the regulatory requirements have considerable systems and administrative consequences, and where investors' interests are affected in a particularly tangible way, a more specific approach to rule making is appropriate than may be felt necessary in the general field of conduct of business.'[5]

The Financial Services (Client Money) (Supplementary) Regulations 1991 (SCMRs) prescribe requirements in respect of the handling of money for margined transactions and the payment for securities. As well as applying to firms regulated by SIB, they apply to FIMBRA and Lautro members but not to IMRO or SFA members. The reason why they do not apply to members of IMRO and SFA is to allow IMRO and SFA the flexibility – within the limits set by the test of adequacy – to respond quickly to new developments (which might not be possible were the regulations applicable to their members in these areas to be alterable only by SIB). In the interests of uniformity, however, they have initially adopted the same rules as SIB.

The basic requirement imposed on firms with regard to client money is summarised by principle 7, which governs the treatment of client assets generally, not just client money. It requires a firm which has control of, or is otherwise responsible for, assets belonging to a customer which it is required to safeguard to 'arrange proper protection for them, by way of segregation and

---

[1] SIB, *Proposals for amended Client Money Regulations*, CP53 (1991), para. 17; a second purpose is to prevent firms using client money to finance their business.

[2] Regs. 1.02, 1.05.   [3] CP53, para. 6.   [4] para. 9.   [5] para. 8.

identification of those assets or otherwise, in accordance with the responsibility it has accepted'.

The CMRs impose two basic requirements on a firm in respect of client money.[1] The first requirement is to keep client money separate from its own money in a client bank account with an 'approved bank'.[2] An approved bank in relation to client bank accounts opened at branches in the United Kingdom is defined by the CMRs as an institution authorised under the Banking Act or a building society which offers, unrestrictedly, money transmission services.[3] The second requirement is to hold client money on trust (or, in Scotland, as agent) for clients so that in the event of default it is available to be repaid.[4] Should there be insufficient money in the client accounts to meet the claims of clients, the available money is distributed among clients in proportion to their claims on it.[5] Clients therefore share equally in the risk of a shortfall. These requirements are complemented by record keeping and audit requirements whereby a firm's compliance with the client money requirements may be policed.[6]

Turning to client *investments*, the basic requirements are laid down in core rule 32, which applies when a firm has custody of a customer's investments 'in connection with or with a view to regulated business' (and thus not when a firm provides safe custody services – which are not in themselves an investment business activity – independently of and apart from its investment services).[7] The primary requirement is to keep safe the customer's documents of title, or to arrange for their safekeeping. As we have seen, principle 7 itself suggests one means of accomplishing this – namely by segregation and identification. In the case of *registrable* investments (such as most UK company shares) bought or held for a customer, the core rule adds that they must be properly registered in the customer's name or, if he has given his consent, in the name of an 'eligible nominee'. There are three types of eligible nominee – UK-authorised banks, nominee companies with no other business, and individuals chosen by the customer and not associated with the firm. Finally, core rule 32 also addresses the case where title to investments is recorded *electronically*: here the firm's obligation is to ensure that customer entitlements are separately identifiable from its own in the relevant system.

---

[1] As to the definition of client money, see reg. 2.01.   [2] Regs. 2.05 and 2.12.

[3] Reg. 5.04. Although approved status is therefore at the discretion of the Bank of England or Building Societies Commission, this need not prevent action by SIB where it entertains doubts about the suitability of an institution as a custodian of client money, as was illustrated by the case of British and Commonwealth Merchant Bank where SIB adopted the simple expedient of amending the CMRs (by the Financial Services (Clients' Money) (Amendment) Regs. 1990) to provide that BCMB should cease to be an approved bank and designating the amendment so as to apply to members of SROs.

[4] Regs. 3.02–3.05.   [5] Reg. 3.05.   [6] Regs. 4.03–4.06 and 4.11–4.12.

[7] Blair, *Financial Services: The New Core Rules* (1991), p. 132.

INFORMATION AND INVESTIGATIONS

SIB possesses extensive information and investigation powers. In the exercise of its information powers it may require such information from authorised insurers, operators and trustees of recognised collective investment schemes and directly authorised firms as it may reasonably require for the exercise of its functions under the Act.[1] It has no power to require information from members of SROs or RPBs but it may require information from their regulators.[2] Failure to comply with a requirement imposed in the exercise of these powers exposes a firm to the risk of public censure, injunctions and restitution orders and actions for damages.[3]

SIB's powers of investigation are exercisable concurrently with the DTI. They may be used, where it appears there is good reason to do so, to investigate the affairs, or any aspect of the affairs, of any person so far as relevant to any investment business which he is or was or appears to be or to have been carrying on.[4] They may not be used to investigate the affairs of an exempted person, other than an appointed representative, or a member of an SRO or an RPB unless the SRO or RPB has requested an investigation, or it appears to SIB that the SRO or RPB is not prepared to investigate the affairs of the firm properly.[5] In the exercise of its powers, SIB (or investigators authorised by it under section 106 of the Financial Services Act) may require anyone to produce documents, and persons under investigation and connected persons to answer questions, which may be used in evidence against the person giving them.[6] Failure without reasonable excuse to comply with a requirement imposed in the exercise of these powers is a criminal offence.[7] In the last three years SIB's powers of investigation have been used on 34 occasions in respect of authorised firms.[8]

POWERS OF INTERVENTION

SIB's investigation powers are backed by powers of intervention modelled on those possessed by the DTI under the Insurance Companies Act. In the exercise of its powers SIB may restrict the business, including non-investment business, directly authorised firms may undertake, freeze the assets of such firms and their appointed representatives, have them vested in an approved trustee, or require them to be maintained in the United Kingdom.[9] These

---

[1] FSA, s.104(1).   [2] s.104(2).   [3] s.104(4).

[4] s.105(1). In *R* v. *Secretary of State for Trade and Industry, ex p. R* [1989] 1 All E.R. 647, it was held that the power conferred by s.105 could not be used to investigate activities which took place before 18 December 1986, the date on which the material provisions of the Act came into effect.

[5] s.105(2).   [6] s.105(3)–(5).   [7] s.105(10).

[8] *Report of the Securities and Investments Board for 1990/91*, p. 27. Action taken following an investigation has ranged from business being stopped to the institution of restitution proceedings by SIB. See also Third Report from the Trade and Industry Committee, *Company Investigations*, HC 36, 1989–90, pp. 128–34.

[9] FSA, ss.65–8.

powers are exercisable on three grounds: (i) that their exercise is 'desirable for the protection of investors', (ii) that a firm is not fit to carry on investment business of a particular kind, or to the extent to which it is carrying it on or proposing to carry it on, or (iii) that a firm is in breach of its obligations or has furnished SIB with false, inaccurate or misleading information.[1] Breach of a prohibition or requirement imposed in the exercise of these powers exposes a firm to the risk of public censure, injunctions and restitution orders and actions for damages as well as suspension or loss of authorisation.[2]

These powers are exercisable in relation to directly regulated firms (or appointed representatives of such firms) but not in relation to members of SROs or RPBs (or appointed representatives whose principals are members of SROs or RPBs), with the exception of the power to require assets to be vested in an approved trustee which may be exercised in relation to an SRO or RPB member (or an appointed representative of an SRO or RPB member) at the request of the SRO or RPB of which the firm (or, in the case of an appointed representative, its principal) is a member.[3] It is a condition of their recognition that SROs have, so far as practicable, powers corresponding to those of SIB.[4] Most intervention is undertaken by SROs or RPBs: in the last three years there have been a total of 697 'actions', only 18 of which have been taken directly by SIB.[5]

When SIB imposes (or on its own initiative rescinds or varies) a prohibition or requirement, written notice must be given.[6] A notice (other than a notice rescinding a prohibition or requirement) must state the reasons for intervention and give the firm particulars of its right to have the case referred to the Financial Services Tribunal.[7] If the reasons involve a named third party and are 'prejudicial to that person in any office or employment', a copy of the notice must be served on that person unless it is impracticable to do so.[8] The same requirements apply to the refusal of an application for the rescission or variation of a prohibition or requirement.[9]

A notice takes effect on the date specified in it.[10] SIB may therefore intervene with immediate effect. The reference of the imposition or variation of a prohibition or requirement to the Financial Services Tribunal does not affect the date on which a notice comes into effect.[11]

The exercise of the corresponding powers of Lautro to prohibit an insurance company from accepting or soliciting investment business from one of its appointed representatives was unsuccessfully challenged in judicial review proceedings (in the absence of a right of appeal) in *R* v. *Lautro ex parte Ross*.[12] The Court held that Lautro was under no duty to consider representations from affected third parties before intervening to protect investors.

---

[1] s.64(1).   [2] s.71.   [3] s.64(4).   [4] Sch. 2, para. 3(3).
[5] *Report of the Securities and Investments Board for 1990/91*, p. 26.   [6] s.75(1).   [7] s.70(3), (5).
[8] s.70(4).   [9] s.70(2), (3)–(5).   [10] s.70(1).   [11] s.97(6).
[12] [1992] 1 All E.R. 422.

Withdrawal and suspension of authorisation

SIB also has power to withdraw or suspend the authorisation of directly authorised firms. Section 28 of the Financial Services Act provides that it may do so on two grounds: (i) that the firm is not fit and proper to carry on investment business, or (ii) that the firm is in breach of its obligations or has furnished false, inaccurate or misleading information.[1] SIB has no power to withdraw or suspend the authorisation of members of SROs or RPBs, but RPBs are required as a condition of their recognition to have arrangements for the suspension or withdrawal of certification in the event that either the conditions governing certification are no longer satisfied or the rules governing the conduct of investment business have not been complied with.[2]

Whether a firm's authorisation is withdrawn or merely suspended, the result is the same: its authorisation ceases to have effect and it becomes subject to the basic prohibition in section 3 of the Act. Suspension may be for a specified period or until the occurrence of a specified event or until specified conditions have been complied with. Like the subjection of authorisation to conditions in other regulatory contexts it thus provides an opportunity to remedy shortcomings that have been uncovered, with the difference that the firm cannot carry on investment business for so long as its authorisation is suspended. A firm whose authorisation is suspended remains subject to SIB's powers of intervention.[3]

Where SIB proposes to withdraw or suspend a firm's authorisation, it must give the firm notice of its intention to do so. A notice must set out the reasons for the proposed action, the date on which the withdrawal or suspension is to take effect (and, in the case of the latter, its proposed duration) and particulars of the firm's right to have the case referred to the Financial Services Tribunal.[4] If the reasons involve a named third party, and are 'prejudicial to that person in any office or employment', a copy of the notice must be served on that party unless it is impracticable to do so.[5] If after 28 days the firm has not required the case to be referred to the Tribunal, SIB must give the firm a further notice of its final decision.[6] As in the case of the proposed refusal of an application for authorisation SIB is not bound by its initial notice of intention.

Censure

Finally, SIB has power to publicise misconduct on the part of directly authorised firms, regulated insurance companies (i.e. companies authorised under section 22 of the Act) and operators or trustees of recognised collective investment schemes.[7] It has no power to publicise misconduct on the part of

---

[1] Section 33 confers an equivalent power in respect of firms authorised under s.31.
[2] Sch. 3, para. 4.   [3] s.64(3).   [4] s.29(1)–(2), (4).   [5] s.29(4).   [6] s.29(5).
[7] s.60(1).

SRO or RPB member firms, but SROs or RPBs may have power to do so. By itself censure has no consequence other than the damage to a firm's reputation potentially involved, which may of course be considerable. The same safeguards apply to the proposed censure of a firm as apply to the proposed withdrawal or suspension of authorisation.[1]

APPEALS

Persons affected by the exercise of SIB's powers to refuse authorisation, to suspend or withdraw authorisation, to impose prohibitions or requirements in the exercise of its powers of intervention, to make public statements of misconduct and to issue disqualification directions, may require SIB to refer the matter to the Financial Services Tribunal, normally in advance of action being taken but if necessary after action has been taken in the case of the exercise of its powers of intervention.[2] Third parties on whom copies of notices are served in the exercise or proposed exercise of these powers may also require the matter to be referred to the Tribunal.[3]

The task of the Tribunal is to investigate the case and to report to SIB what would in its opinion be the appropriate decision in the matter, and the reasons for that opinion.[4] Where the matter referred is the refusal of an application, the Tribunal may report that the appropriate decision would be to grant or refuse the application; alternatively, it may report that the appropriate decision would be to vary a suspension, direction, consent, prohibition or requirement in a specified manner, in the case of an application for their variation, or to vary a prohibition or requirement in a specified manner in the case of an application for their rescission.[5]

Where the matter referred is action other than the refusal of an application, the Tribunal may report that the appropriate decision would be to take or not to take the action proposed to be taken or to take any other action that could be taken in the exercise of any of SIB's powers to suspend or withdraw authorisation, to issue public statements of misconduct or to impose prohibitions or requirements in the exercise of its powers of intervention.[6] It is therefore open to the Tribunal to take a harsher view of a firm's conduct than SIB, which is a considerable disincentive to referring a matter to the Tribunal in any case in which SIB is not proposing to withdraw a firm's authorisation. Once the Tribunal has made its report SIB is under a duty to decide the matter forthwith in accordance with the Tribunal's report.[7] Since no appeal lies from the report of the Tribunal to the courts, action taken by SIB in implementation of a report can only be challenged by way of judicial review.

Where the case is referred by a third party named in a notice, the task of the

[1] s.60(2)–(5). [2] s.97(1)(a). [3] s.97(1)(b). [4] s.98(1). [5] s.98(2).
[6] s.98(3). [7] s.98(1).

Tribunal is to report whether the reasons for the action which involve the person are substantiated.[1] A finding that the reasons are not substantiated clears the person's name but has no effect on the action taken or proposed to be taken.

COMPENSATION

The Investors Compensation Scheme operates within the framework of rules made by SIB under s.54 of the Financial Services Act,[2] but it is administered by a separate management company, the Investors Compensation Scheme Ltd. The investment firms participating in the scheme are SRO members and those directly regulated by SIB. The Act does not compel RPBs to bring their members into the scheme, and none has chosen to seek admission.[3] The RPBs have compensation schemes of their own (which must, however, satisfy the adequacy test in Schedule 3 of the Act). The SROs are represented on the board of the management company, which also includes directors appointed by SIB to represent the interests of investors.

Receiving compensation

Scope for the payment of compensation arises when the management company determines a SIB or SRO regulated firm to be 'in default'. That determination cannot be made unless it appears to the management company that the firm 'is unable, or likely to be unable, to satisfy claims in respect of any description of civil liability incurred in connection with its investment business' (rule 2.01.1). Eligibility for compensation is confined to investors who are not business or professional investors,[4] and to trustees of trusts which are principally for the benefit of individuals who are eligible investors or which are charitable trusts. An eligible investor needs to be able to show that his claim passes two main tests:

(i) Is it a *scheme business claim?* The most important type of scheme business claim covers liabilities owed by the firm in connection with investment business done by it after its 'participation date' – i.e. after it became an SRO member or SIB regulated firm, or from 28 August 1988 (when the scheme came into force), if it was already fully authorised by then. The business must have been done 'with the investor or as agent on his behalf' (rule 2.03.1). The rules also admit 'property claims' – i.e. claims relating to property which was held by the firm before its participation date and which, on that date, it was 'reasonably believed to continue to hold' (rule 2.03.2). The concept of the

---

[1] s.99.   [2] Financial Services (Compensation of Investors) Rules 1990.   [3] s.54(3).

[4] 'Business investor' and 'professional investor' are defined in Financial Services (Glossary and Interpretation) Rules and Regulations 1990. Compare the concept of a non-private customer in the core rules.

property claim was introduced so that investors would not need to withdraw and reinvest property held by a firm before its accession to the scheme in order to get the benefit of the scheme. The drawback is that the recognition of property claims means that money has to be found, out of current contributions, to pay for delinquencies perpetrated before the scheme came into force. However in *SIB* v. *FIMBRA*[1] it was held that no claim would be based on events prior to 18 December 1986, that being when the provisions of the Act introducing the concept of 'investment business' were brought into force.

(ii) Is it a *compensatable claim*? There are two types of 'basic' compensatable claim – claims for property held (e.g. claims based on theft or embezzlement), and claims arising from uncompleted transactions (e.g. failure to deliver stock, or the proceeds of a sale of stock). Other claims (e.g. a claim based on negligence, or on breach of a conduct of business rule such as the suitability rule) are also compensatable – but 'only where the Management Company considers that this is essential in order to provide fair compensation to the investor' (rule 2.04.1). All claims, basic or not, have to satisfy a credibility test (rule 2.04.2): have they been established in court, or would they be established if proceedings were brought?

There is also an important exclusion from the definition of compensatable claim. To the extent that a claim 'relates to or depends upon . . . failure of investment performance to match a guarantee given or representation made', it is not compensatable.[2] So investors told by the firm now in default that they would get 15 per cent per annum, or that they were bound to get their original investment back, do not have a claim by reason only of this not coming to pass. The exclusion of guarantees of investment performance and similar representations reflects concern that firms should not be seen to be able to write blank cheques on the compensation scheme. Firms bold enough to guarantee investment performance or to represent that a certain performance will be achieved are obliged by virtue of core rules 5.4 and 10[3] to disclose the position under the compensation scheme to their customers; and third-tier rules contain further restrictions on the offering of purported 'guarantees'.[4]

When a claim is made out, there are limitations on how much of it can be met. The maximum amount payable to one investor on a default is £30,000 plus 90 per cent of his loss between £30,000 and £50,000, i.e. £48,000 in total (rule 2.07.1). Individual compensation payments may be scaled down if the management company is of the view that 'payment of the full amount would provide a benefit to the investor which is greater than the benefit which he

[1] [1991] 4 All E.R. 398.
[2] Rule 2.04.3a; contractual obligations and promises to pay are also excluded if the management company considers them to have been undertaken without 'full consideration' passing to the firm: rule 2.04.3b.
[3] See pp. 304, 273.
[4] SFA rule 5–9(8), Table; IMRO, Advertising Code, para. 22; FIMBRA Rules, Vol. 1, rule 3.3.2.

might reasonably have expected or than the actual benefit available on similar investments made with other firms' (rule 2.06.2). There is also an overall ceiling of £100 million on the amount of compensation payable in any financial year (rule 2.07.2), and this could also occasion the scaling down of payments (rule 2.08.1); but hitherto this has not happened.

Funding the compensation scheme

The cost of operating the compensation scheme is met by levies on participant firms. The membership of each SRO constitutes a contribution group (as do the firms directly regulated by SIB) and, in the event of a default by a firm in a particular contribution group, the rule is that the cost of that default should be met by the other firms in that group. The underlying theory is that:

> If a particular activity has a high claims record, the costs of compensation should be reflected in the pricing structure of the activity. This means that an important goal will be to tie the costs, caused by the failure of a firm involved in a particular activity, to other firms in that activity. It is not possible to do this exactly but it can be done approximately if the costs caused by the failure of a firm in one SRO are borne by the other members of that SRO.[1]

The trouble is that a single SRO may embrace widely diverse activities, and that one activity may be regulated by several SROs. So, for example, the default of a FIMBRA-authorised portfolio manager specialising in gilts becomes a charge upon the FIMBRA membership, even though most of them are insurance intermediaries.

The principle that each SRO membership must pay for its own defaulters is, however, carried only to a certain point. For each SRO there is a threshold figure, the reaching of which would trigger 'cross contributions' from the other contribution groups. Provision for cross contribution 'reflects the fact that . . . without cross contribution, failures in some of the SROs, involving very substantial claims, would impose a burden on the members of those SROs which might be disproportionate to their financial resources'.[2]

The cross contribution threshold for FIMBRA firms in 1990 was set at £19 million. It became clear, however, without the threshold being reached, that anxiety about the scale of compensation scheme liabilities after a series of defaults on the part of FIMBRA members was damaging the morale of FIMBRA firms. As SIB put it, 'The potential impact of a levy of up to £19m . . . gives rise to a substantial risk that firms will decide to leave FIMBRA and of a diminution in the size and scope of the independent sector. As FIMBRA membership declines, so the financial pressures on the remaining members intensify.'[3] A short-run solution was found when Lautro and its members

---

[1] SIB, *Review of the Investors Compensation Scheme*, CP28 (1989), para. 13.3.   [2] *ibid.*, para. 13.4.
[3] SIB, *Financing the Compensation Liabilities of FIMBRA Members*, Retail Regulation Review Discussion Paper 1 (June 1991), para. 3.

(mainly life insurance and unit trust companies) undertook to cover the liabilities of the FIMBRA membership beyond £5 million up to £19 million. The need to find a longer-run solution was one of the main factors prompting the announcement of the Retail Regulation Review in April 1991, a review which would examine not only the question of future arrangements for the funding of the compensation scheme, but also the relationship and boundaries between the retail SROs.[1] The financial pressures of the compensation scheme thus helped to trigger a fundamental reappraisal of the viability of a separate SRO for independent intermediaries.[2]

[1] SIB, *Retail Regulation: Issues for Review* (April 1991).
[2] See now SIB, *Retail Regulation Review: Report of a study by Sir Kenneth Clucas on a new SRO for the Retail Sector* (March 1992).

17
Conduct of Investment Business

STRUCTURE OF THE RULEBOOKS

The three tiers

We saw in Chapter 16 how SIB's original rulebook and the 'equivalent' rulebooks of the SROs and RPBs were criticised for legalism, complexity and impenetrability. The 1989 amendments to the Financial Services Act paved the way for a new three-tier structure whose implementation is not yet complete:[1]

(i) The first tier consists of the ten *principles* for investment business promulgated by SIB in March 1990. (They are reproduced below in the Appendix.) The principles are in effect a code of ethics for investment business ('a universal statement of the standards expected', as the introduction to the principles puts it), and as such couched at a high level of generality and abstraction. They apply to the conduct of investment business and the financial standing of all authorised persons (s.47A(1)). Breach of a principle is a ground for disciplinary action or the exercise of powers of intervention, but cannot 'of itself' provide the basis of an action for damages (s.47A(2)).

(ii) The second tier consists of *core rules and regulations* – those made by SIB and 'designated' by it under s.63A so as to apply to SRO members. The power to designate extends to four sets of provisions – conduct of business, financial resources, clients' money and unsolicited calls – but the Core Conduct of Business Rules made in January 1991 are often just referred to as the 'core rules'. The power of designation does not extend to firms certified by RPBs,

---

[1] The Core Conduct of Business Rules were brought into force in respect of members of IMRO on 30 November, 1991 at the same time as IMRO's third tier. In respect of members of SFA they were due to come into force on 1 April, 1992 along with SFA's third tier. At the end of 1991 the commencement date for the core rules as respects members of FIMBRA and LAUTRO, and for firms directly regulated by SIB, had not been settled.

perhaps because it would have been regarded as too gross a violation of the traditional autonomy of the professions. Breaches of the Core Conduct of Business Rules can found actions for damages.

(iii) Then there are the *third-tier* provisions of the various FSA regulatory bodies – i.e. the provisions laid down by each SRO for application to its own members, and SIB's requirements for directly regulated firms. To the extent that third-tier provisions are expressed as rules, breach of them may give rise to actions for damages under s.62. But third-tier provisions which take the form of 'guidance' or 'codes of practice' do not of themselves afford a basis for such an action.[1]

A structure of this kind poses the question of the balance to be struck between SIB and the SROs, and between uniformity via the core rules and diversity via the third tiers. It was always envisaged that third-tier require- ments might elaborate or add to the obligations imposed by the core, and no problem arises where the third tier complements the core rules in this way.[2] It was also foreseeable that SROs might, in certain circumstances, seek to modify the impact of the core rules on their members – for example, in order to accommodate the distinctive circumstances of a particular kind of investment business. Section 63A(2) anticipates this possibility by empowering SIB to provide for core provisions to have effect, 'generally or to such extent as may be specified', subject to the rules of an SRO. SIB's policy is not to make derogations available on demand, but to require a case to be made out. That case is most likely to succeed where there is a valid argument for an exception, but it relates to members of one SRO only, or amendment of the core rule itself would be too complex or cumbersome.[3]

In practice, there are two ways in which the SROs have been given limited latitude to make rules which diverge from the requirements of the core rules:

(i) Some of the provisions of the core rules apply 'subject to any exceptions contained in the rules of an SRO'. This formula is designed to provide flexibility where the SROs may need to make adjustments to fit the core rule to a particular type of business, or indeed where a listing of all the appropriate exceptions in the core rule itself would have made it too long-winded. But an SRO is not free to devise exceptions which would eat up the core provision: the specification of exceptions must be explicit and selective.[4]

---

[1] On the status of guidance and codes of practice, see Ferguson, 'The Legal Status of Non-Statutory Codes of Practice', [1988] *J. Business Law* 12.

[2] Indeed core rule 38.1 endows third-tier guidance on core rules with a special status: where a firm relies on such guidance, and believes on reasonable grounds that it was acting in accordance with the core rules, it is *deemed* to have followed the rules, even if in fact it broke them.

[3] SIB, *The Proposed Core Rules: Derogations and certain other points*, CP47 (1990), para. 6.

[4] See the definition of 'exception' in the Financial Services Glossary 1991 (2nd Edition). The Financial Services Glossary contains definitions of a large number of terms used in the core rules: core rule 40.4.a.

(ii) Special 'derogation instruments' have been made by SIB in conjunction with the introduction of the IMRO and SFA third tiers. The main reason is to enable the SROs to devise special regimes for special situations. For example, IMRO has special regimes for operating collective investment schemes, managing the assets of occupational pension schemes and trusteeship, and these involve derogations from the core rules.[1]

Notwithstanding these safety valves the risk remains of an SRO third-tier requirement turning out to be drafted in terms which inadvertently conflict with a core rule. In this event the core rule (which is statutory) would override the third-tier requirement (whose status is merely contractual).

Actions for damages

Section 62 of the Financial Services Act confers a right of action for loss suffered as a result of breaches of SIB, SRO and RPB conduct of business rules (or of various other provisions).[2] Originally, as we saw in Chapter 15, that right of action could be exercised by *any person* (ranging from private clients to investment business competitors) who suffered loss because of a breach. But the Restriction of Right of Action Regulations now generally confine the right of action to private investors.[3] The definition of private investor in these regulations is significant not only in the context of s.62 but also more generally because it provides a building block for the categorisation of customers in the core rules. 'Private investor' is defined as 'an investor whose cause of action arises as a result of anything he has done or suffered – (a) in the case of an individual, otherwise than in the course of carrying on investment business; and (b) in the case of any other person, otherwise than in the course of carrying on business of any kind . . .' (reg.2(1)).

Thus, the effect is that a flesh and blood individual counts as a private investor, except where the basis of his claim would be something that was done to him while he was carrying on *investment* business himself (e.g. as an authorised or exempted person). Corporate entities, on the other hand, fall outside the private investor concept if they were wronged in the course of carrying on *business of any kind.*[4]

---

[1] Core Conduct of Business Rules Commencement (IMRO) Order 1991.

[2] A s.62 action can be based on SIB's Conduct of Business Rules (s.48), Cancellation Rules (s.51) and Clients' Money Regulations (s.55), but not on the Financial Resources Rules (s.49): s.62(1)(a). It can also be based on the corresponding rules of an SRO or RPB: s.62(2). Note that the relevant SRO or RPB rules 'are not only those which correspond to the SIB's actual rules and regulations, but also those which correspond to the rules and regulations which the SIB might hypothetically make': Sweet & Maxwell's Annotated Financial Services Act 1986 (1987), 76. In addition, in certain other cases s.62 is imported by cross-reference: see Rider et al., *Guide to the Financial Services Act* (2nd edn, 1989), p. 244.

[3] Financial Services Act 1986 (Restriction of Right of Action) Regulations 1991, SI 1991/489. There is a different definition of 'private investor' for the purpose of actions against friendly societies: Financial Services Act (Restriction of Right of Action) (Friendly Societies) Regulations 1991, SI 1991/538, reg. 2.

[4] A government, local authority or public authority can never be a private investor.

Although in general the Restriction of Right of Action Regulations confine the right of action to private investors, they also specify a number of cases where a non-private investor could still sue. One example is where there has been abuse of unpublished price-sensitive information, contrary to core rule 28. Another is where a trustee company sues for the benefit of trust beneficiaries.[1]

Categories of customer

The basic concept employed to delineate the object of protection in the core rules and in the third tiers is not 'investor' but 'customer'. The Financial Services Glossary does not give an exhaustive definition, but indicates exclusions, inclusions and subdivisions of the concept.

Private and non-private customers

The key distinction in the core rules is between private and non-private customers. There are two types of *private customer*. The first is 'a customer who is an individual and who is not acting in the course of carrying on investment business'.[2] The other is a 'small business investor', which is a company, partnership or trust below a stipulated size. In the case of a company, the line is drawn at called-up share capital or net assets of £5 million (a figure which falls to £500,000 if the company has more than 20 shareholders); in the case of a partnership, at net assets of £5 million; and in the case of a trust, at aggregate cash and investments valued at £10 million (before deduction of liabilities). The precise dividing line is inevitably arbitrary to some extent, but the underlying objective is to extend to the small business investor, whose sophistication in investment matters may well be no greater than that of most private individuals, the same degree of protection as private individuals enjoy. 'Ordinary business investors' – i.e. companies, partnerships and trusts falling on the other side of the line, and also governments, local authorities and public authorities of any size – are deemed to be more capable of looking after themselves, and accordingly fall outside the protective ambit of a substantial number of the core rules.[3]

The classification of small business investors as private customers under the core rules does not alter their status under s.62A: they are business investors and their right to bring a s.62 action is restricted accordingly.

---

[1] Reg. 3(c), (d).　[2] Cf. the definition of 'private investor', above, p. 268.

[3] An SFA derogation allows small business investors to be treated as ordinary business investors if they can be classified as 'trade customers'; to be a trade customer one must be entering into the transaction as an integral part of one's main business, have sufficient experience and understanding, and have been warned of the protections forgone: SFA rule 5–5(4).

Experienced customers

The general stance of the core rules is that firms cannot enter into agreements with private customers under which the customers purport to contract out of the rights the rules confer on them.[1] But there is one exception. Core rule 39.1 allows the rules of an *SRO* to make exceptions from the core rules to enable member firms to treat a private customer as if he were a non-private customer if three conditions are met:

a. it [the member firm] can show that it believes on reasonable grounds that the customer has sufficient experience and understanding to waive the protections provided for private customers;
b. it has given a clear written warning to the customer of the protections . . . which he will lose; and
c. the customer has given his written consent after a proper opportunity to consider that warning.

Thus the core rule itself does not allow private customers to waive private customer protections, but it permits SRO third tiers to make provision for that event. The rules of IMRO and SFA in fact do so.

Opting out of private customer status does not, however, change one's classification under s.62A: a private investor retains the private investor's right of action. But such an action cannot be founded on any of the rules whose protection has been relinquished by virtue of contracting out.[2]

Indirect and potential customers

The Glossary stipulates that 'customer' includes a *potential customer* and an *indirect customer*. The effect of the former is to make it clear that there need be no contractual nexus between the firm and the persons to whom the duties imposed by the rules are owed. For example, the obligation in core rule 5 to give adequate and fair information in direct offer advertisements is effectively owed to any private investor who reads the advertisement, not merely to those with whom it has a contractual relationship.

The *indirect customer* concept comes into play in agency situations. Where a firm's immediate customer is known to be acting as an agent, the indirect customer is 'an identified principal who would be a customer if he were dealt with direct'. So, for example, a stockbroker who receives an order from a solicitor acting on behalf of an identified private client owes to the solicitor's client the obligation to provide best execution.[3]

---

[1] Core rule 15.1; see further p.274.

[2] It could, of course, be founded on a breach of the conditions for contracting out reproduced in the SRO rules.

[3] However, by way of derogation, SFA rules provide that an identified principal is not an indirect customer if his agent (e.g. a solicitor or accountant, or a portfolio manager authorised by an SRO) agrees so with the SFA firm. If this is agreed, the agent will be the only customer: SFA rule 5–6. Since the agent will normally be a non-private customer, the effect will be to disapply – as far as the SFA firm is concerned – the obligations which are owed only to private customers, e.g. core rule 10 (customer's understanding). Obligations normally owed by SFA firms to all customers, e.g. best execution, continue to apply. Where the agent is himself an authorised person, he will of course owe a variety of obligations to his customer.

Customers and non-customers
Market counterparties are not customers for the purposes of the rules. 'Market counterparty' is defined as a person dealing with the firm

a. as principal or as agent for an unidentified principal; *and*
b. in the course of investment business of the same description as that in the course of which the firm acts.

The object, of course, is to exclude from the protection of most of the rules fellow market professionals who can be expected to fend for themselves by bargaining the terms of the relationship at arm's length. The problem is how to identify with a sufficient degree of precision what is investment business 'of the same description' as the firm's own. The SFA rules (by way of derogation) attempt to solve this problem by specifically listing kinds of persons who may be treated as market counterparties. The categories on the list include other members of SFA, trading members of an investment exchange, and listed money market institutions. The person whom it is proposed to treat as a market counterparty must be sent a written notice to this effect, and has the right to reject categorisation as a market counterparty under this procedure.[1] But this does not preclude the possibility that the person concerned falls to be treated as a market counterparty *anyway* by virtue of the test laid down in the core rules glossary.

Trust beneficiaries are also excluded from the concept of customer for the purposes of the rules. 'Trust beneficiary' is defined as 'a beneficiary under a trust (not being the settlor) who benefits from the performance by a firm as trustee of investment services relating to the management of the trust assets'.

GENERAL CONDUCT OF BUSINESS REQUIREMENTS

The most general conduct of business requirements are those declared in the principles, which lay down obligations, *inter alia*, to observe 'high standards of integrity and fair dealing' (principle 1), to act with 'due skill, care and diligence' (principle 2), and to observe 'high standards of market conduct' (principle 3). To attribute meaning to these broad precepts, we must look primarily to the core and third-tier rules, many of which can be regarded as elaborations of the principles. But it must not be forgotten that no set of more detailed provisions can exhaust the implications of principles cast at a high level of generality, and that it is therefore possible for a breach of a principle to occur even when all the relevant core and third-tier requirements have been complied with.[2]

[1] SFA rule 5-4.
[2] For a discussion of the content of each principle, see M. Blair, *Financial Services: The New Core Rules* (1991), ch. 2.

Suitability

Core rule 16.1 says:

A firm must take reasonable steps to ensure that it does not . . .
a. make any personal recommendation to a private customer of an investment or investment agreement; or
b. effect or arrange a discretionary transaction with or for a private customer or, subject to any exceptions contained in the rules of an SRO of which the firm is a member, any other customer;
unless the recommendation or transaction is suitable for him having regard to the facts disclosed by that customer and other relevant facts about the customer of which the firm is, or reasonably should be, aware.

This is the suitability rule. In essence, its effect is that a firm providing personal services must tailor them to the circumstances and needs of each individual client. The rule is thus 'a direct statement of one of the basic aims of investor protection – that if an investor puts his trust in the judgment of an investment firm – explicitly or implicitly asking "what do I need?" – that firm should vindicate his trust by tailoring its advice to his needs. . . .'[1]

The first limb of the suitability rule applies in the case of *personal recommendations*. It does not apply where the customer is proceeding on an 'execution-only' basis (i.e. where the firm takes the customer's order without giving him any advice), nor where a firm gives impersonal recommendations, e.g. in a tipsheet. But as long as it is personal, the recommendation need not be of an 'investment'; recommendations of *investment agreements* are also covered. This means that the rule's protection extends to 'sell' recommendations, and to recommendations to enter into a discretionary management agreement, e.g. a discretionary managed PEP. The second limb of the rule applies in the case of *individualised discretionary management*. Where, in contrast, the customer's funds are combined with others into some kind of common management scheme,[2] the firm's obligation in managing the scheme is to be faithful to the investment objectives which have been stated for it.[3] Of course, the customer should not be advised to enter the scheme in the first place unless its stated investment objectives are suitable for him.

In the case of a personal recommendation, no suitability obligation is owed to a non-private customer: such customers are assumed to be capable of making their own judgment of the merits of any recommendations made to them. In the case of discretionary management, on the other hand, non-private customers are also protected, on the argument that, even for a non-private customer, the point of conferring discretion on an investment manager

---

[1] SIB, *Regulation of the Marketing of Investment Products and Services* (1990), para. 3.3.
[2] That is, a collective investment scheme, or a pooled discretionary management service under FSA s.75(5).
[3] Core rule 16.2.

is to avoid having to scrutinise his every decision. But the rule allows SROs to derogate in respect of non-private customers, and IMRO has done so.[1]

Judgments of suitability have to be made by reference to 'relevant facts about the customer of which the firm is, or reasonably should be, aware'. Accordingly, the suitability rule is complemented by the requirement in principle 4 (the 'know your customer' principle) to seek from advisory and discretionary customers 'any information about their circumstances and investment objectives which might reasonably be expected to be relevant' in enabling the firm to fulfil its responsibilities to them. If a customer declines to answer some or all of the questions asked, the firm may still act for him, but not in a way that disregards the facts it does happen to know about him. The collection of information pursuant to the know your customer principle raises issues of data protection, and the Data Protection Registrar has issued guidance on the use of questionnaires or 'factfinds' in this connection.[2]

Understanding of risk

Core rule 10 requires a firm recommending a transaction to a *private* customer, or acting as a discretionary manager for such a customer, to take reasonable steps to enable him to understand the nature of the risks involved. What this requires will depend on the characteristics of the individual concerned; so, as Blair puts it,[3] 'different explanation may be needed for a new or apparently slow-witted customer compared with that for a seasoned or alert one'. In the case of a regular or discretionary customer, it is plainly unnecessary to repeat the same explanation before each and every transaction. Indeed, in the final analysis, there is no need to show that the customer *does* understand, merely that reasonable steps have been taken to enable him to understand.

The role of the customer agreement

SIB's original conduct of business rules introduced the concept of the 'two-way' customer agreement as a necessary preliminary, in general, to the provision of discretionary or advisory services to a private customer. (There was no need to put a customer agreement in place in order to give advice on life assurance and authorised unit trusts.) The customer agreement was a contractual document whose contents had to cover a variety of stipulated matters,[4] the aim being to ensure that the firm's terms of business were clearly defined and disclosed to the customer from the outset. It was a 'two-way' agreement in the sense that no services could be provided under it until (i) it

---

[1] IMRO rule II 3.1(3).
[2] Data Protection Registrar, *Guidance on the Requirement in the First Data Protection Principle to 'Obtain Fairly' for Firms Advising on and Selling Financial Investment Products*, Guidance Note 24 (April 1991).
[3] *Op. cit.*, p.76.   [4] CBRs (1987) 4.03, 4.05.

was signed on behalf of the firm, (ii) it was sent by post to the customer and (iii) it was signed and returned by the customer.[1] The purpose of these notification formalities was to establish a quasi cooling-off period – in other words, to give the customer an opportunity to consider his position at leisure and in privacy, without exposure to sales pressure. Two-way formalities were not required for dealings with non-private customers, but even here a terms of business letter had to be sent.[2]

In practice, however, these concepts did not work well. Many firms devised documentation of inordinate length and complexity and wrote in far-reaching exclusion clauses. The new documentation met with resistance from customers, who were irritated by its complexity and, in the case of long-standing relationships, could see no justification for the sign and return requirements. At the same time, the production of terms of business letters led to a 'battle of forms' between market professionals, who might otherwise have let sleeping dogs lie. SIB's initial response was to prohibit clauses purporting to exclude liability to private customers for breaches of the conduct of business rules,[3] and to introduce a simple model Private Customer Letter for basic stockbroking services, whose use allowed the two-way formalities to be dispensed with.[4]

The core rules, however, make a more far-reaching departure from the original approach. As between professionals, a terms of business letter is no longer required. And, in relation to private customers, the concept of a two-way agreement has been redefined – as 'an agreement in written form to which the customer has signified his assent in writing in circumstances where the firm is satisfied that the customer has had a proper opportunity to consider its terms' – so that it need no longer be signed on behalf of the firm and sent by post to the customer. And such an agreement has to be put in place only in two situations – where discretionary management is to be undertaken, or where there are to be 'contingent liability transactions' (i.e. derivatives transactions in which the customer may lose more than his initial stake).[5] In other situations the provision of services to private customers does not require a written agreement at all (though in practice there will normally be one).

While the original approach to customer agreements has thus been considerably modified, the original objectives are to some extent secured by other means: (i) if there is a written agreement, it must set out in adequate detail the basis on which services are provided;[6] (ii) firms must not seek to exclude or restrict any duty or liability owed to a customer (whether or not a private customer) under the Act or the 'regulatory system';[7] nor – unless it is reasonable to do so in the circumstances – must they seek (in the case of a

---

[1] CBRs (1987) 4.10(1).   [2] CBRs (1987) 4.02(3)(b), 4.10(3).   [3] CBRs (1987) 2.03A.
[4] CBRs (1987) 4.10(2A); SIB, *Customer Agreements*, CP8 (1988), Appendix A.   [5] Core rule 14.2.
[6] Core rule 14.1.
[7] Core rule 15.1; 'regulatory system' is defined to include principles, core rules and third-tier rules.

private customer) to exclude or restrict the common law duty to act with skill, care and diligence, or liability for breaking it;[1] (iii) customer agreements must be presented fairly and clearly.[2]

SECURITIES AND DERIVATIVES BUSINESS

Background

The conduct of business requirements applicable to dealings in securities need to be viewed against the background of the market structures which emerged from the transformation of the London Stock Exchange, the paramount market for dealings in UK equities, in the 1980s. Before the upheaval there was a 'single capacity' dealing system under which stockbrokers dealt in an *agency* capacity on behalf of clients, buying from and selling to stockjobbers who dealt as *principal* and who could not deal directly with non-members of the Exchange. Orders were executed on the floor of the Exchange. The Wilson Committee noted four advantages which the single capacity system was said to possess:

> First . . . it has the effect of concentrating transactions in any given security in one place. This increases the likelihood that prices will be set fairly in relation to supply and demand. . . . Secondly, in contrast to systems where buyers and sellers are brought together directly by brokers, the jobbing system in principle provides continuous dealing. An investor deals through the broker with the jobber acting as principal and does not have to rely upon the existence of a matching order by another broker. . . . Thirdly, a potential conflict between their own interests and those of their clients which could arise if members dealt both as principals and as agents is avoided without the need for special arrangements as in other countries. . . . Finally, the single capacity system is said to be more effectively self-policing than other systems since there are always two parties to every transaction and because, with more than one jobber dealing in each security and competing for brokers' business, market rigging and collusion are more easily detected.[3]

Single capacity dealing was underpinned by fixed minimum commissions for brokers, whose function was to discourage the brokers from developing an appetite for the activities (dealing as principal and taking positions) which were the preserve of the jobbers. American and Japanese securities houses were excluded from the Exchange by rules requiring member firms to be controlled by individual members of the Exchange; the general effect of these rules was 'to ensure that non-members can have only very limited and circumscribed interests in Stock Exchange businesses'.[4]

By the mid-1980s it had become clear – partly because of the dismantling of

---

[1] Core rule 15.2. [2] Core rule 9.2. [3] Wilson Report, paras. 351–5.
[4] *The Stock Exchange: A Discussion Paper* (April 1984), para. 107.

exchange controls in 1979 – that the UK domestic market could no longer be insulated from the pressures of international competition and that these market structures were no longer tenable. The explosive growth of the Eurobond market, with London as one of its main centres, had shown the viability of bypassing official exchanges, and there was growing apprehension that the Exchange's traditional business might also start to go off-exchange. To prevent the fragmentation of the market, membership would have to be opened up to overseas firms. If existing member firms were to compete effectively, they would need more capital; this in turn would require the removal of the restrictions on outside ownership and control.[1] The single capacity system would also have to go, to make the Exchange attractive to 'integrated' American and Japanese firms, and to enable the existing members to compete with them:

> if foreign brokerage houses and other financial institutions are to be encouraged to become Members of The Stock Exchange in order to centralise dealings in securities in the UK, the dealing system must be attractive to them. The unique features of the jobbing system and the constraints it places on dealing practices would be unlikely to prove attractive to brokerage firms which had not grown up with such a system and which had developed the integrated principal trading and retail capabilities necessary in other major securities markets. Competition from such firms, operating outside The Stock Exchange, has led Member Firms, particularly those dealing in internationally traded UK equities, to feel that in order to compete effectively, they must be permitted to act in dual capacity. . . .[2]

The immediate catalyst of change was the deal struck between the Exchange and the Secretary of State for Trade (Cecil Parkinson) in July 1983: in return for legislation removing the Exchange from the jurisdiction of the Restrictive Practices Court, before which it had been brought by the Director General of Fair Trading, the Exchange agreed to end fixed commissions.[3] This decision released and intensified the pressures which had been building up on the single capacity system and on the barriers facing overseas firms.

In the new system, it was decided, all member firms would be free to act as 'broker dealers' – i.e. both as agent and as principal. Some broker dealers would, in addition, register as market makers in specified stocks, thus helping to constitute a 'competing market maker system' in which they would, by continuously quoting prices on the Exchange's electronic price display system, compete for the business of firms acting in an agency capacity as well as for principal trades with those wishing to deal directly with them. Thus the new system would be, like its predecessor, 'quote driven',[4] and its choice reflected a desire to preserve a degree of continuity with the old jobbing system, as well as

---

[1] *Ibid.*, paras. 15,4.
[2] Stock Exchange, *The Choice of a New Dealing System for Equities*, Council Notice 64/84 (July 1984), Report, 3–4.
[3] Restrictive Trade Practices (Stock Exchange) Act 1984.   [4] Stock Exchange, Notice 64/84, 6.

to maximise the liquidity or depth of the market. Even so, the changes in market structure were radical: the 'Big Bang' in 1986 left the Exchange with a screen-based dealing system dominated by global securities houses with 'integrated' (i.e. multi-functional) capacity.

From the outset it was appreciated that the new dealing system would require fresh investor protection arrangements to compensate for the loss of those inherent in the single capacity dealing system. A market in which the players are multifunctional firms requires the elaboration of rules on best execution, visibility of prices and the handling of conflicts of interest. The rules developed by the FSA regulators are a response to this need.

Best execution and soft commission

Best execution

The obligation to provide best execution – to obtain the best price for one's customer or to match it oneself – is the central duty imposed by the core rules in connection with securities and futures business. To provide best execution a firm must (a) take reasonable care to ascertain the price which is the best available for the customer in the relevant market at the time for transactions of the kind and size concerned – this recognises that the prices quoted will depend on the size of the customer's order and whether it is to buy or sell; and (b) unless the circumstances require it to do otherwise in the interests of the customer, deal at a price which is no less advantageous to him.[1] The firm is thus required to shop around to a reasonable extent to ascertain the best price; but having done so, it can deal as principal with its customer – provided it offers him a price at least as good as that available on the market. Whether it deals as principal or as agent, the firm's *own* charges to the customer (whether in the form of a mark-up, mark-down or commission) are left out of the reckoning.[2]

It is open to a firm to entrust the execution of the transaction to another person, and to rely on that other person to provide best execution – 'but only if it believes on reasonable grounds that he will do so'.[3] This provision is designed, for example, to enable a FIMBRA member to pass his customer's orders to a Stock Exchange member for execution, or to enable a Stock Exchange member to arrange for the execution of transactions on other well regulated markets.[4]

The duty to provide best execution is owed whenever a firm deals for or with a *private* customer – i.e. whether as agent or principal.[5] In the case of non-

---

[1] Core rule 22.4.

[2] Core rule 22.4. The amount or basis of charges to a private customer have to be disclosed by virtue of core rule 18.2.

[3] Core rule 22.3.   [4] e.g. one of the investment exchanges 'designated' by SIB.

[5] Core rule 22.1.

private customers it is owed only in certain circumstances – where the firm is acting as discretionary manager, where the firm is instructed to deal as agent, or where the order is given in circumstances 'giving rise to similar duties as those arising on an order to effect a transaction as agent'.[1] In any event, the rules of both SFA and IMRO derogate from the core rule to allow their members to agree waivers of the best execution obligation with non-private customers.[2]

Best execution on the Stock Exchange

While the core rule obligation to provide best execution applies (or will apply) to all authorised persons regulated by SIB and the SROs, membership of the Stock Exchange, where the great bulk of business in UK domestic securities is executed, brings with it a separate (and, from the point of view of an authorised person, an additional) set of requirements. These requirements are bound up with the Exchange's electronic price display mechanism, SEAQ (the Stock Exchange Automated Quotations System), and with the obligations of market makers on the Exchange. The following brief account is based on the regime for dealings in UK domestic equities.[3]

Under the Stock Exchange system the obligations of the market maker depend on whether the security concerned is a 'SEAQ security' or not. SEAQ securities are simply those designated by the Exchange as eligible for inclusion in SEAQ;[4] those left outside SEAQ are generally the most lightly traded, i.e. the least liquid. In the case of non-SEAQ securities the market maker's obligation is to be prepared to give firm two-way price quotations on enquiry.[5] In the case of SEAQ securities, however, the market maker's obligation is to 'display on SEAQ firm two-way prices in not less than the MQS in all SEAQ securities in which it is registered [as a market maker]'.[6] A *firm* price is price at which the market maker must deal, if called upon to do so; and a *two-way* price comprises both a buying price and a selling price. The MQS is the 'minimum quote size' – in other words, the minimum number of shares, as prescribed by the Exchange for each stock, for which the market maker must display a firm price. (The MQS reflects the scale and frequency of dealings in the stock concerned.) The market maker is not obliged to display firm prices for sums in excess of the MQS for each stock; but if it chooses to do so, it 'must be prepared to deal at that price and in up to that size with all enquiring Member Firms'.[7]

Since the display on SEAQ sets the quotes of the competing market makers for each stock side by side, it can be seen how a mechanism for obtaining best execution is created when firm quotes are available. This is the basis of the

---

[1] Core rule 22.2, in conjunction with the definition of 'order' in the Glossary.

[2] SFA rule 5–39(2); IMRO rule II 3.8(2).

[3] For a detailed description of the Exchange's requirements (as at December 1989), see S. R. Sanders, *Fair Exchange: ISE Regulation of the Market-place in UK Equities* (1990).

[4] Stock Exchange rule 350.0g.   [5] Rule 357.1a(ii).   [6] Rule 357.1a(i).

[7] Rule 357.1e. There is an exception where the approach comes from a rival market maker: rule 357.3.

Stock Exchange's best execution requirement in respect of securities *for which there is a firm quotation on SEAQ,* which is to take 'all reasonable steps to ensure that the price obtained by the client is as good as or better than the best price displayed in that security in comparable size on SEAQ'.[1] Moreover, if a firm which is not a market maker (in the stock concerned) decides to execute its client's order by dealing as principal with him, instead of dealing as agent on his behalf with a market maker, its obligation is to ensure that its own price is *better* than the best price available for transactions of that size from a market maker.[2] The point of this 'better than best' obligation is to encourage a flow of business to the market makers in recognition of their role in keeping the market liquid and preventing its fragmentation; it also encourages market makers to display prices in larger sizes.

The SEAQ system also affords a basis for the operation of SAEF – the SEAQ Automatic Execution Facility. SAEF is a facility for the automatic execution – at the best available price – of small orders from retail clients relayed by broker dealers acting on an agency basis.[3] To confine its operations to small bargains, the Exchange sets a 'maximum SAEF size' for each stock to which the facility applies, and broker dealers are not allowed to split client orders larger than the SAEF maximum in order to squeeze them into SAEF.[4] The system works by automatically channelling SAEF orders to the market maker displaying the best price in the relevant size; the market maker, by virtue of his status as such, is committed to accepting SAEF business.[5] If more than one market maker is displaying the best price for the stock in question, SAEF orders are rotated among them. Market makers not displaying the best price can also participate in the rotation, provided they have indicated willingness (by means of a symbol on the SEAQ screen) to deal at the best price.[6]

SEAQ and SAEF thus afford a technological basis for securing best execution in a large number of routine transactions. But if there is no firm quotation on SEAQ – for example, because the size of the desired transaction exceeds the size for which the market makers are quoting, or because the stock is a non-SEAQ security – a less precise requirement applies. This is to take all reasonable care to deal to the client's 'best advantage'.[7] Satisfaction of this requirement will normally involve some shopping around, but it all depends on the circumstances, such as current market conditions.[8]

The Exchange reviewed and adjusted the overall regime for the operation of the UK equity market in 1989–90.[9] It is generally accepted that the competing

---

[1] Rule 354.7a. However, the member firm may settle for less than the best price displayed in comparable size if it judges that it is to the best advantage of the client to deal immediately and it is satisfied that it has taken all reasonable steps to ensure that the price obtained is the best *immediately* available: rule 354.7b. This exception is designed to cater for the problem of congested telephone lines in a fast-moving market.

[2] Rule 354.8. [3] Rule 361.1. [4] Rule 361.3b. [5] Rules 357.1f, 361.3a.

[6] Rule 361.4a. For a detailed account of the operation of SAEF, see Sanders, *op. cit.*, pp. 36–41.

[7] Rule 354.1. [8] Rule 354.5.

[9] *Review of the Central Market in UK Equities: A Consultative Document* (May 1989); *Review of the Central Market in UK Equities: Implementation Plans and Conclusions* (July 1990).

market maker system has worked reasonably well as far as dealings in stocks at the upper end of the market are concern. But among the more thinly traded stocks there are signs that a vicious circle of deteriorating liquidity and widening spreads has set in.[1] At the end of 1991 the Exchange was reportedly flirting with the introduction of a system of sole market makers, with exclusive market making rights, for each of the less liquid stocks.[2] The aim of such a system would be to maximise available liquidity by concentrating such business as there is on a single focus.

Soft commission

The 'full' service provided by stockbrokers to their clients has customarily included not only the execution of bargains but also 'free' investment advice and analysis and sometimes custodianship, and this is reflected in the level of commission charged. Alongside these 'traditional' arrangements, there have emerged in recent years arrangements of a new type, under which fund managers (e.g. pension fund managers, unit trust managers) *commit* themselves to providing a broker with a *specific* amount of business (and hence of commission) in return for services (e.g. portfolio valuation systems and market information services, and the associated computer hardware and software) which the manager will have to pay for if the stipulated amount of commission is not delivered. The distinctive feature of such *soft commission arrangements* is thus that 'there is a commitment from the fund manager to channel a certain amount of commission to the broker, whereas under traditional arrangements there is not'.[3]

Commission paid to stockbrokers by a fund manager is generally a cost that is borne by the fund manager's customers over and above the management fees. Soft commission arrangements therefore present a number of dangers. First, there is the risk that the fund manager may resort to churning to generate the requisite level of business. Secondly, there is the risk that the services obtained will be used to benefit the fund manager in its own-account activities, in other words that the fund under management will be used to subsidise other activities of the manager. The third danger is that a soft commission arrangement might jeopardise the obtaining of best execution, by binding the fund manager to an agency broker who provides poor quality execution or to a market maker with wider spreads.[4]

Core rule 3 is designed to obviate these dangers. On the footing that in the final analysis the integrity of the securities market is at stake, it applies

[1] Waters, 'Stock market goes back to the future', *Financial Times*, 2 July 1991.

[2] 'Monopoly on the exchange', *Financial Times*, 3 November 1991.

[3] SIB, *Soft Commission Arrangements in the Securities Markets*, CP29 (1989), para. 7.

[4] See generally SIB, *Soft Commission Arrangements in the Securities Markets: Discussion Paper* (February 1989), and CP29, cited above.

whether the fund manager's customers are private or non-private. 'Soft commission agreement' is defined as

> any agreement, whether oral or written, under which a firm which deals in securities on an advisory basis or in the exercise of discretion receives goods or services in return for an assurance that not less than a certain amount of such business will be put through or in the way of another person.

The effect of the rule is that soft commission agreements in the securities markets – the rule is confined to securities business because that is where the problems have arisen[1] – must meet five tests:

(i) 'The only benefits to be provided under the agreement are goods or services which can reasonably be expected to assist in the provision of investment services to the firm's customers and which are in fact used for the benefit of those customers.'[2] Examples of services capable of meeting this test include research, computer facilities, safe custody services and performance measurement facilities.[3] If the test is met, it seems the fund manager may also derive benefit.

(ii) There must be adequate disclosure.[4] The detailed disclosure requirements[5] are fairly elaborate, reflecting the fact that most of the customers concerned are 'professionals'.[6]

(iii) The broker must agree to provide best execution,[7] even though in the case of a non-private customer best execution might not otherwise be owed under the best execution rule.

(iv) The fund manager must check that 'the terms of business and methods by which the relevant broking services will be supplied do not involve any potential for comparative price disadvantage to the customer'.[8] So the fund manager must consider, for example, whether he will be faced with a wider spread than would otherwise arise.[9]

(v) If the broker deals as principal, he must not be remunerated by spread alone.[10] This is designed to rule out 'soft for net' arrangements – i.e. arrangements between a fund manager and a market maker (or a broker-dealer acting as principal and not charging commission). The reason is that soft for net arrangements are likely to lead market makers to widen their spreads, thereby jeopardising best execution and market liquidity.[11]

---

[1] SIB *Soft Commission Arrangements in the Securities Markets: Second Policy Statement* (1991), para. 11.
[2] Core rule 3.a.   [3] SFA rule 5–8(2).   [4] Core rule 3.e.   [5] e.g. SFA rule 5–8(3), (4).
[6] SIB, CP29, cited above, para. 36.   [7] Core rule 3.b.   [8] Core rule 3.c.
[9] SIB, Second Policy Statement, cited above, para. 5.   [10] Core rule 3.d.
[11] SIB, CP29, cited above, para. 46; *Soft Commission Arrangements in the Securities Markets: A Policy Statement* (1990), para. 17; Second Policy Statement, cited above, para. 7.

Other dealing obligations

Around the focal obligation to provide best execution are gathered a series of provisions designed to secure the integrity and fairness of the dealing process. These provisions utilise the concept of an 'order' which, it should be noted, includes not only orders given by customers but also, in the case of a discretionary manager, decisions to deal on behalf of a customer.

Core rule 20 requires a firm to deal with customer and own account orders 'fairly and in due turn'. An own account order is one where the firm proposes to deal for itself or an associate.[1] The underlying point, of course, is that in a moving market the order in which transactions are executed may affect the price at which they are executed, and a firm's execution of orders may itself influence the price at which subsequent transactions by the same firm can be effected. The rule is therefore designed to prevent 'front-running' by firms – i.e. giving priority to the firm's own orders or those of favoured customers so as to take advantage of an anticipated price movement, while holding back the orders of less favoured customers.[2] The requirement to proceed 'fairly' does not require the firm to put its own business last, merely to afford itself no higher priority than its customers, and not to practise favouritism among those customers. The requirement to deal with orders 'in due turn' prima facie calls for a 'first come, first served' procedure. But departure from this can be justified – for example, where small orders are aggregated to achieve economies of scale, or where a precondition for the execution of an order is not yet met.

Next, the core rule on timely execution requires orders to be executed 'as soon as reasonably practicable in the circumstances'.[3] This requirement reinforces the prohibition of front-running, but also strikes at dilatoriness in itself. 'Current customer orders' include both orders for immediate execution, and conditional orders once the condition (e.g. the obtainability of a stipulated price) is fulfilled. Delay is permissible, however, if the firm believes on reasonable grounds that it is in the best interests of the customer.[4] Aggregation of small bargains again furnishes a possible example.[5]

Once a transaction has been executed, it must be allocated – in other words, earmarked for a particular customer or customers or for the firm itself, as the case may be – promptly.[6] It is not a legitimate practice to leave bargains in

---

[1] 'Associate' covers undertakings in the same group (which itself has an extended meaning), appointed representatives of group undertakings, and 'any other person whose business or domestic relationship with the first person or its associate might reasonably be expected to give rise to a community of interest between them which may involve a conflict of interest in dealings with third parties'.

[2] Another kind of front-running – dealing to take advantage of the price movements expected to be triggered by the publication of the firm's newsletter or research publication – is addressed by core rule 25.

[3] Core rule 21.1.   [4] Core rule 21.2.

[5] In the case of some investment trust savings schemes, the practice is to accumulate small orders for as much as a month at a time.

[6] Core rule 23.

limbo for a while, so as to be able to decide in the light of market movements subsequent to the transaction itself who should get the benefit (or detriment) of the bargain.

Core rule 24 governs the process of allocation where orders have been aggregated. If each of the individual orders can be met in full, there is unlikely to be a problem. If, however, there is not enough stock to meet each order in full, the apportionment must not give any customer unfair preference over other customers, and the firm must not allocate stock to itself or its associates until other customers' orders have been fully satisfied. But the firm and its associates can participate in the apportionment on equal terms if the firm believes on reasonable grounds that, without its (and their) earlier participation, it would not have been able to execute the orders of the unassociated customers on such favourable terms, or perhaps at all.

A transaction having been executed, the customer must be sent 'with due despatch' a note containing the 'essential details' of the transaction (known as a contract note in the securities markets, and as a confirmation note in the derivatives markets).[1] This requirement is elaborated in SRO third tiers.

Independence

Most of the dealing rules applicable to securities and derivatives firms are concerned with conflicts of interest, in the sense that they lay down substantive requirements requiring the firm to subordinate its own interests to those of its clients – or at any rate to place its own interests no higher than theirs – and to show equal regard for the interests of each client. But there are also, in core rules 1 and 2, broader precepts on the avoidance or handling of conflicts of interest.

Core rule 1 requires firms to abjure the giving or acceptance (or offer or solicitation) 'either in the course of regulated business or otherwise [of] any *inducement* which is likely significantly to conflict with any duties of the recipient (or the recipient's employer) owed to customers in connection with regulated business'. The prohibition does not apply unless the duties whose performance is likely to be undermined by the inducement are owed, broadly speaking, in connection with investment business in the UK. Trivial inducements are not caught; nor (by virtue of the definition of 'inducement') are goods and services provided pursuant to a legitimate soft commission agreement, or disclosable commission from third parties.

Core rule 2 comes into play if a firm has a *material interest* in a transaction involving a customer or a relationship giving rise to a *conflict of interest* in relation to it. Where that is the case, the firm must not 'knowingly' advise the customer on that transaction, or effect it on a discretionary basis, without

---

[1] Core rule 19.1.

taking reasonable steps to ensure 'fair treatment' for the customer. There are several possible ways of complying with core rule 2.[1] First, the firm in question may *refrain* from giving advice or dealing on a discretionary basis when a 'conflict' situation arises. This is plainly not an attractive commercial proposition for an integrated securities house, and putting stocks on a stop list may itself give rise to speculation. Second, it may make *specific disclosure* of the conflict to the customer concerned. But that may be impracticable in the context of a discretionary relationship, and out of the question if a duty of confidentiality is owed to another customer in respect of the relevant information, or if the insider dealing legislation is applicable. Third, under SFA's rules, it may rely on an *independence policy*, under which relevant employees of the firm are required to 'disregard' conflicts of interest when advising customers or exercising discretion on their behalf, and private customers are notified in general terms that the firm may give advice or make discretionary management decisions even where there is a conflict of interest. However, as SFA acknowledges, an independence policy may not always be sufficient for the firm to ensure fair treatment for its customers. In such circumstances, 'the firm should take other steps, such as specific disclosure . . .'.[2]

Fourth, the firm may maintain *Chinese walls* to insulate individuals advising customers or exercising discretion on their behalf from information which might tempt them to act otherwise than in the best interests of those customers. A Chinese wall is an arrangement within a firm (or a group) designed to restrict the flow of confidential or price-sensitive information between departments whose functions are potentially mutually incompatible. It is, in the words of the Act, an arrangement

enabling or requiring information obtained by an authorised person in the course of one part of his business to be withheld by him from persons with whom he deals in the course of carrying on another part and for that purpose enabling or requiring persons employed in one part of that business to withhold information from those employed in another part.[3]

By stopping the right hand from knowing what the left hand is doing, the Chinese wall may serve (i) to secure the confidentiality of information in respect of which a duty of confidentiality is owed to a particular client, (ii) to prevent insider dealing, and (iii) to prevent the exploitation of conflicts of interest. In recognition of this third function, core rule 2 accepts the existence of an effective Chinese wall as an alternative to disclosure and other forms of fair treatment: the firm is not to be regarded as having acted 'knowingly' if none of the individuals involved in giving advice on the relevant transaction (or effecting it on a discretionary basis) acted with knowledge of the

---

[1] Principle 6 enumerates the main ones.   [2] SFA rule 5–29, guidance.
[3] FSA s.48(2)(h); see also core rule 36.1.

information giving rise to the conflict.[1] From the firm's point of view, the attraction of the Chinese wall is that it may enable the firm to continue to provide its full range of services even when disclosure is impossible because it would involve committing a breach of confidence or the offence of insider dealing. The existence of a Chinese wall might, for example, enable the investment advisers in a firm to go on making recommendations about a particular stock, even though the firm's corporate finance division is involved in planning a takeover affecting that stock.

It is scarcely surprising that a good deal of scepticism has been expressed about the effectiveness of Chinese walls. 'I have never', said Gower, 'met a Chinese wall that did not have a grapevine trailing over it.' He concluded:

> They are a legitimate device to protect individual members of a multi-functional business from the risk of criminal liability for insider-dealing. They are not, however, a protection to investors and may, indeed, be a detriment to them as depriving them of the benefit of the knowledge and expertise that they will expect from a financial supermarket.[2]

Certainly the notion that an effective Chinese wall might be maintained in a very small firm strains credulity. In relation to larger firms, however, to the extent that they are characterised by greater impersonality and by the physical separation of departments performing different functions, the Chinese wall concept becomes more credible. The operation of the wall must, of course, be actively policed. The role of the firm's compliance officers in monitoring the effectiveness of the arrangements is therefore crucial.

Even a well designed, properly monitored wall does not solve all conflict of interest problems. Casual or inadvertent leaks may still occur occasionally. Nor is a Chinese wall of any avail once the information it hides is publicly announced, and the conflict of interest becomes patent. That is why Chinese walls need to be buttressed by independence policies and, where appropriate, by specific disclosures.

Derivatives business: additional requirements

Business in options, futures and contracts for differences – known collectively as 'derivatives' – is subject to additional requirements because of the characteristically high volatility of the instruments concerned and because some contracts can expose the investor to losses far greater than his initial deposit.

Accordingly third-tier provisions amplify core rule 10 (customer's understanding) by requiring a Derivatives Risk Warning Notice to be sent to private customers. The notice explains the risks associated with different kinds of derivative instrument. For example, as to futures:

[1] Core rule 36.3.   [2] Gower *Report*, Part II, para. 4.13.

Transactions in futures . . . carry a high degree of risk. The 'gearing' or 'leverage' often obtainable in futures trading means that a small deposit or down payment can lead to large losses as well as gains. It also means that a relatively small market movement can lead to a proportionately much larger movement in the value of your investment, and this can work against you as well as for you. . . . If you trade in futures . . . you may sustain a total loss of the margin you deposit with your broker to establish or maintain a position. If the market moves against you, you may be called upon to pay substantial additional margin at short notice to maintain the position. If you fail to do so within the time required, your position may be liquidated at a loss and you will be liable for any resulting deficit.[1]

The sending of the notice, and the obtaining of the customer's signature on it after he has had a proper opportunity to consider its terms, must occur before *any* derivatives business is transacted (whether discretionary, advisory, or even 'execution-only').[2]

Contingent liability transactions (ones in which the customer risks losing more than his initial investment) are particularly hazardous when effected off-exchange (i.e. otherwise than on a recognised exchange or one designated by SIB). It may prove impossible to liquidate a position and assess its value or the extent of the customer's exposure to risk.[3] For this reason core rule 27 prohibits (subject to one exception) the involvement of private customers in off-exchange contingent liability transactions.

Market manipulation and stabilisation

Section 47(2) of the Financial Services Act makes it a criminal offence to do any act or engage in any course of conduct which creates a false or misleading impression as to the market in or the price or value of any investments, if it is done for the purpose of creating that impression and thereby inducing someone to make an investment decision. This is a provision designed to protect the integrity of the markets. One example of the conduct prohibited would be the mounting of a nefarious share support operation during a takeover; another would be the staging of fictitious trades to foster a specious impression of market liquidity.

Since market participants can quite innocently create an impression that happens to be misleading, the specification of the mental element in the offence is crucial. The prosecution must prove that the accused *intended* to create the impression concerned, and *intended* thereby to induce someone to make an investment decision. It is not enough to show that the accused was reckless as to whether these outcomes would occur. But once the prosecution has shown that the accused intended to create the impression concerned, and that it was as a matter of fact false or misleading, it does *not* have to go on to prove that the

---

[1] SFA Rules, App. 15. Derivatives Risk Warning Notice, paras. 1, 6.   [2] SFA rule 5–30(2).
[3] SFA Rules, App. 15. Derivatives Risk Warning Notice, para. 4.

accused *meant* it to be false or misleading; rather it is for the *accused* to prove that 'he reasonably believed that his act or conduct would not create an impression that was false or misleading' (s.47(3)).

The crime of market manipulation must be distinguished from the legitimate practice of stabilising the price of newly issued or newly offered securities for a limited duration, to give the market time to 'digest' the offering. Stabilisation is primarily a phenomenon of the Eurobond markets. The stabilisation rules made by SIB under s.48(2)(*i*) of the Act allow the 'stabilisation manager' to go into the market to buy the relevant securities for a period of about a month after the sale, provided the possibility of stabilisation has been publicised in announcements and documentation, and provided the stabilising purchases are not at a price in excess of the prescribed ceiling (broadly speaking, the initial offer price).[1]

The SIB stabilisation rules apply only to directly authorised persons and (by virtue of core rule 29) to SRO members. But it is a defence to a charge of market manipulation if the actions in question were done for the purpose of price stabilisation and 'in conformity with' SIB's stabilisation rules.[2] Since it is possible to act in conformity with the stabilisation rules without being subject to them, it is open to an unauthorised overseas person to claim the benefit of this defence.

THE MARKETING OF LIFE INSURANCE

Background

Life insurance companies, as we saw in Chapter 10, have long been accustomed to *prudential* supervision by the DTI. At the same time they have enjoyed (and continue to enjoy) considerable freedom of *product design*, compared to authorised unit trust companies and indeed insurance companies from most other EC jurisdictions. Before the Financial Services Act there was, moreover, comparatively little in the way of the regulation of *marketing*.[3] For companies and intermediaries alike, therefore, the shock occasioned by the Act was considerable, since it led to a restrictive and detailed marketing regime.[4] But this regime must be viewed as a response (not necessarily the only possible response) to the structure and characteristics of the UK life insurance industry.

Leaving aside bank and building society accounts, life insurance occupies a

---

[1] SIB CBRs (1990) Part 10; Blair, *op. cit.*, pp. 125–7.   [2] FSA, s.48(7).

[3] For a review of the marketing position prior to the FSA, see Ferguson, 'Regulation of the Marketing of Life Assurance', [1984] *Scots Law Times* 265.

[4] Note that SIB's power to regulate conduct of business on the part of UK-authorised life offices is in essence confined to marketing matters, and does not extend to product design, ongoing 'administration' of contracts by life offices, or financial resources: FSA, Sch. 10, para. 4(1),(2); Sch. 11, paras. 14(1), (2).

paramount position in the UK as the most widely used vehicle for the personal savings of private investors.[1] Although life insurance can be bought (in the form of term assurance) purely to insure against the contingency of death, most life insurance sold in the UK incorporates a substantial investment component and takes the form of with-profits policies (where the policyholder participates in the profits of the life office by receiving discretionary 'bonuses'), or unit-linked policies (where the value of the investor's policy is directly linked to the performance of a particular investment fund).

One of the factors to account for life insurance's pre-eminence is the way in which it is sold. The life insurance industry is highly proactive in character – geared to making individualised approaches to potential buyers of its product. There exists a vast army of life insurance intermediaries (both 'tied' and 'independent') whose *raison d'être* is to identify and make contact with 'prospects' – for example, by following up referrals from previous contacts and by means of cold calls. Life offices also secure outlets for their products by means of distribution arrangements with businesses involved in the process of buying a home – estate agents, mortgage brokers, and mortgage lenders (building societies and banks).[2] As a result of these arrangements the proportion of house purchasers taking endowment mortgages – i.e. mortgages coupled with an endowment policy – has grown to something like 75 per cent in recent years.[3]

In general, the glue by which life offices maintain their distribution networks is commission. Commission plays a large role in the motivation of direct sales forces (i.e. salesmen tied to a particular life office), in the cementing of relationships with banks and building societies, and in the attraction of business from independent intermediaries. And, as a rule, the commission which can be generated by recommending life products exceeds that to be had from other types of investment such as unit trusts, PEPs and National Savings products.[4] This is reflected in the comparatively heavy 'front-end loading' of most with-profits and unit-linked policies. The expenses of selling and administering the contract are concentrated disproportionately on the initial period of its life. In the case of regular premium contracts the result is poor surrender values in the early years of the contract's life (zero values in the first year are common). The scale of front-end loading means that life policies must be regarded as long-term investment vehicles; yet in fact a

---

[1] At the end of 1989 the value of UK life insurance funds exceeded £200,000 million: Association of British Insurers, *Insurance Statistics 1985–89*, p. 3.

[2] Overall there are at least 200,000 individual insurance intermediaries. Over 190,000 company representatives are on the Lautro register. FIMBRA has over 20,000 registered individuals, most of whom will advise primarily on insurance.

[3] Building Societies Association, Fact Sheet 30 (May 1992).

[4] For example, in March 1990 £1,000 invested in a unit-linked bond yielded an average commission of £50 for an independent intermediary; £1,000 invested in a unit trust yielded an average of £31: *Survey by Lautro of Commission Paid to Independent Intermediaries*, Press Notice (15 June 1990).

large proportion of endowment policies are surrendered before enough time has elapsed to overcome the initial handicap.

In a normal market, competition among producers and distributors puts a break on the extent to which marketing expenses can be run up and loaded into the cost of the product. But the life insurance market is very imperfect in this respect because the complexity of the product makes it exceedingly hard for the investor to judge how much of his money is to be invested, and how much consumed in the form of charges or expenses – and yet this split is of substantial importance when the ultimate return to the investor is not guaranteed but dependent on the investment performance of a fund. The resultant danger is that heightened competition between life offices will tend to confer increased benefits on distributors (i.e. intermediaries of all kinds) rather than on investors. In the words of Sir Mark Weinberg:

> Let's assume that you are running a life company that's anxious to expand its new business, and you can afford to spend £1 million on doing so. Will you attract more additional business by applying that £1 million in the form of lower premium rates and higher bonuses – or by using that £1 million to offer higher commission rates to brokers? Anyone who has any experience in the marketing of life assurance will have little difficulty in answering that question – and I fear that the answer underlies the imperfect competition that is inherent in the market for life assurance. . . .
>
> Where competition is effective is in the area of commissions. Whereas life offices would find it difficult to present information on policy benefits to *consumers* in a form which will sufficiently enable them to compare one product with another, there's no difficulty in presenting information on commission rates in the form which will enable a *broker* to see which life office is offering him more commission for selling the same type of policy. So, yes, the market for a broker's support is a highly competitive one – but it isn't the sort of beneficial competition that most people are thinking of when they press for open markets.[1]

It is against this background that the regulatory developments of the last few years must be viewed. One major objective of regulatory policy has been to increase the transparency of life products by imposing disclosure requirements. Another has been to counter the tendency of commission structures to lead to the sale of long-term products in inappropriate cases. And a third (as we shall see) has been to clarify the nature of the advice given by the insurance salesman.

The original FSA regime

The marketing regime for life insurance devised by the FSA regulators in 1985–7 and introduced in 1988 involved (i) 'polarisation' of advisers, coupled with an obligation on them to give their 'best advice', (ii) controls on

[1] M. Weinberg, Speech to the Insurance Institute of London, 2 February 1989.

commission, (iii) a ban on 'churning', (iv) product disclosure requirements and new cooling-off rules, and (v) controls on illustrations. As we shall see in subsequent sections, some of these elements of the original regime have hitherto remained more or less intact, while others have undergone significant development.

Polarisation and best advice

Polarisation was inspired by the ambiguous and conflicting roles played by many life insurance intermediaries in the pre-FSA market. At one end of the spectrum there were conscientious and reputable firms genuinely independent of any particular insurance company and offering their clients unbiased advice on selection of company and policy. But side by side with these there were firms happy to foster an impression of independence, in order to inspire client confidence, while behind the scenes they had entered into special arrangements with a specific company and were in effect committed to channelling a significant proportion of the business they generated in its direction. Such arrangements could assume a variety of forms. For example, a firm might receive backing from an insurance company in the form of a loan which would be interest-free provided the firm pushed a specified volume of business the life office's way. 'Volume overriders' were becoming widespread – that is, arrangements whereby the crossing of a target threshold for the production of business for a particular company would trigger a higher rate of commission, not only on subsequent business but also on business brought to that company earlier in the year. Volume overriders thus create a powerful incentive to channel more and more business to a single company.

The economic logic of this situation was clear: in the long run, companies that wished to defend their market share could not afford to stand aloof from the need to devise incentives to capture the allegiance of avowedly independent intermediaries. As a result, the 'independence' of independent intermediaries would become increasingly illusory, and their recommendations to clients would be determined by unavowed 'deals' with insurance companies.

At the other end of the spectrum, there were company salesmen whose role was simply to sell the policies of a single company. There were also, however, 'tied agents' – intermediaries acting on behalf of a single company, but not on an exclusive basis, and hence free to place business with other companies in the circumstances specified in their contracts with their main companies. Some intermediaries exploited this freedom by using it to leave their prospects with the impression that they were in some sense 'brokers' giving unbiased advice.

Part of the regulatory response to this stage of affairs was to 'polarise' life insurance intermediaries by requiring them to act (and to declare themselves) *either* as the representatives of a single company *exclusively, or* as fully independent intermediaries with no allegiance to any particular company. In SIB's words:

> . . . the policy of polarisation is essential to secure the necessary clarity of status of the salesman or intermediary in the mind of the consumer and to minimise the scope for conflicts of interest operating to the detriment of the investor. The reasons for this are well known: the great confusion of roles and titles in the market at present; the special difficulties for the customer in making his own judgment given the complexity of the product and the extensive product differentiation; the penalties involved if the customer finds that he has been sold an unsuitable product; and the consequent need for the customer to know whether or not he is being given independent advice.[1]

In close connection with the concept of polarisation there emerged that of 'best advice'. Independent and 'tied' intermediaries would be subject to the same know your customer and suitability obligations, but different standards would govern the *range* of their advice. The obligation of the *tied* intermediary would be not to recommend a product to his customer unless he believed, on reasonable grounds, that there was no other product available *from his company* which would meet his customer's investment objectives more advantageously. In the case of the independent intermediary, on the other hand, the yardstick would be what was available *on the market as a whole*. Thus the independent intermediary's 'know your merchandise' obligation would require a reasonable degree of familiarity with the different types and brands of policy on offer in the UK market, and the application of that expertise with reasonable diligence to find the best practicable answer to the client's investment needs.

The elaboration of these policies in the context of corporate *groups* (such as those of the clearing banks) containing both product providers and independent intermediaries proved to be particularly contentious. The key question was whether it should be open to a group company classified as an independent intermediary to recommend 'in-house' products (e.g. the products of an insurance company within the group). SIB's answer to this question was what came to be known as the 'better than best' requirement: an independent intermediary could recommend an in-house product only if any recommendation of an out-of-house product would be less advantageous for the client. It would not be enough to show that the in-house product was as good as the competitors'. The practical effect of this requirement (as SIB intended) was to make it impossible (save in rare circumstances) for a group company polarised as independent to recommend the products of other companies within the group. SIB's rationale for this policy was as follows:

> . . . the Board's concerns arise because in many circumstances it is inherently very difficult to establish beyond doubt what is the 'best' life assurance . . . product for the customer. . . . Nevertheless, the Board believes that independent intermediaries

[1] Published letter from Sir Kenneth Berrill to the Committee of London and Scottish Clearing Banks, 24 November 1986.

should always be expected to make a genuine and conscientious effort to find the most satisfactory answer to the individual customer's requirements. It does not want to open up the possibility of situations emerging ... in which an allegedly independent intermediary might as a matter of practice sell the group product more often than not unless there were clear reasons why this would be contrary to the customer's interests. This would represent a serious erosion of the standards of independence the Board wishes to see maintained, but might not be so clearly contrary to a 'best advice' rule as to enable corrective action to be taken.[1]

SIB's insistence on the 'better than best' requirement was criticised by the Director General of Fair Trading as likely to 'discourage banks, building societies and other financial conglomerates from seeking to provide independent intermediary services': above all the banks would have little choice but to go tied if they wanted to use their branch networks to sell the products of associated companies.[2] But the Secretary of State rejected the OFT view, arguing that bank branches did not currently provide independent advice on life assurance, and that their broking subsidiaries did not in practice place business with in-house product companies.[3] As it turned out, nearly all the banks did opt for tied status, and nearly all the big building societies did likewise a year or two later. It is doubtful, however, whether the 'better than best' requirement played a major part in these polarisation decisions. Factors of greater significance were the problems of training branch staff to advise on more than one brand of product, and the different commission disclosure requirements applicable to tied and independent intermediaries.

Commission control: the MCA
A fundamental but short-lived feature of the original life assurance marketing regime was the Maximum Commission Agreement (MCA) administered by Lautro. The MCA was designed to help purify independent advice by eliminating 'company bias' – the situation where an independent intermediary directs business to a particular company because it pays higher commission. The MCA put a ceiling on the commission payable on a given contract; and, since in practice all participating companies (virtually all companies did participate) paid the maximum permissible commission, an independent intermediary would receive the same amount of commission whichever company he recommended to his client. The incentive to abide by the MCA was the threat of 'hard disclosure': an intermediary expecting to receive commission *in excess* of the MCA was under an obligation to disclose its quantum, in cash, at the point of recommendation. An intermediary expecting to receive commission *within* the MCA merely had to make 'soft disclosure' to

---

[1] Letter of 24 November 1986, cited above.
[2] OFT Report on the Securities and Investments Board (March 1987), para. 3.20.
[3] DTI memorandum to House of Commons Standing Committee on Statutory Instruments, 30 April 1987.

the effect that he was remunerated by commission and that it accorded with the MCA, whose details were available on request.

At the same time the provision of any but the most trivial non-cash benefits ('benefits in kind') to independent intermediaries was prohibited, since such benefits would have lent themselves to the circumvention of the MCA.

Neither the MCA nor the virtual ban on the provision of benefits in kind applied to the remuneration of tied intermediaries. Company bias is inherent in the concept of a tied intermediary: the important thing was that it should be clearly disclosed.

The MCA did not last long. The Director General of Fair Trading reported that its effects were anti-competitive:

'Soft' disclosure would seriously inhibit any form of price competition between intermediaries. . . . 'soft' disclosure would deprive the intending investor of information vital to a major transaction already marked by a lack of transparency. The investor needs to know what rate of commission the adviser could obtain by selling him different products because this helps him to see how much of his payments would actually be invested for his future benefit. Without this information he is more ill-informed than he needs to be, and competition cannot function effectively in such conditions.[1]

On this occasion the Secretary of State sided with the DGFT – even though the establishment of the MCA had been encouraged by the government in its 1985 White Paper on financial services.[2] Accordingly a new regime for commissions had to be introduced in 1989–90 (see below, pp. 295–7). Leaving aside the OFT criticisms, the fatal flaw in the MCA was that, while it restricted the commission payable to independent intermediaries, it did nothing to inhibit the 'bidding up' of the incentives offered by companies to those willing to go tied. The temptation on independent intermediaries to increase their earnings by voting with their feet was therefore considerable. In the long run the MCA would have contributed to a large erosion of the independent sector.

Churning

A widely recognised problem associated with the retailing of life insurance and other packaged investment products is that of 'churning' (or 'twisting'), which occurs when an intermediary prevails upon the investor to surrender his existing policy, or allow it to lapse, and to take out a new policy instead. Particularly in the case of regular premium policies, the long-term nature of the product and the poor surrender values attaching to early encashment mean that such a course of action is rarely in the interests of the investor. Churning is said to be widespread, especially in the mortgage and remortgage market, but systematic evidence on the scale of the problem is hard to come by. There is no doubt that premature surrender is a widespread phenomenon;

[1] OFT report on Lautro, Part I (March 1988), para. 1.8. [2] FSA White Paper, paras. 10.7–10.11.

what is not so clear is what proportion of premature terminations is attributable to churning by intermediaries.

It is impossible to churn a life assurance customer without breaking the suitability rule. But to affirm the illegitimacy of churning, the rules of SIB and the other FSA regulators have from the outset contained a specific prohibition on churning,[1] and that prohibition has been carried forward into the core rules, where a firm is forbidden to recommend a switch of life policies (or other packaged products) unless it believes, on reasonable grounds, that the switch is 'justified from the customer's viewpoint'.[2] Lautro's rules contain detailed record-keeping requirements designed to encourage observance of the ban.[3]

Product disclosure and cooling-off

Efforts to define the status and obligations of intermediaries were accompanied by measures designed to give the investor a better chance of grasping the main features of the product that he was being invited to buy. A requirement was introduced for companies to supply 'product particulars' to the investor, normally before he was irrevocably committed to the sale. The hope was that the product particulars would summarise the product information that an investor would need to make a well-informed investment decision. Of particular importance was the requirement to disclose *surrender values*, in the form of realistic estimates of how much the policyholder would get back on cashing in his policy at the end of each of the first five years of its life. In principle the disclosure of surrender values should expose the degree of front-end loading and bring home the long-term nature of the commitment. In practice, however, the impact of the disclosure was diluted by the way in which surrender values tended to get buried in the rest of the product information, itself often presented in a form likely to be understood by few consumers.

Along with the introduction of product disclosure requirements came an extension of cooling-off rights. Government legislation in 1978 had already introduced a ten day cooling-off period; SIB increased this to fourteen days and applied it to the investment of lump sums in single premium bonds, which had previously been exempted.[4] The exemption of lump sum investments had reflected concern that shrewd investors would in effect use the cancellation period to place a one-way bet against the life office, cancelling the purchase if the value of the investments underlying the policy fell during the cooling-off period. The solution adopted was to allocate to the investor the risk of a 'shortfall' – i.e. a fall in the value of the underlying investments during the relevant period.[5]

[1] e.g. SIB CBRs (1987) 2.08(4).   [2] Core rule 26.2.   [3] Lautro rule 3.11(2)(a).

[4] Insurance Companies Regulations 1981, SI 1981/1654, reg. 71; Financial Services (Cancellation) Rules 1987 and subsequent re-enactments.

[5] Gower, *Report*, Part I, para. 8.48.

Illustrations

The giving of an illustration of future benefits (also known as a projection) as part of the quotation supplied to the prospective buyer of life insurance is a standard part of the intermediary's repertoire of persuasion as well as a common feature of promotional literature. In effect the 'prospect' is invited to consider what a large sum of money might come his way in 10, 15 or 25 years time, if he is willing to save only £n a month. Except where there is a contractually guaranteed rate of return, illustrations are, of course, highly conjectural, and the assumptions (as to rates of return, costs, tax rates etc.) on which they are based may be vitiated by subsequent events.[1] But the salesman may be tempted to gloss over these limitations.

In the years preceding the Financial Services Act a trend had developed of companies vying with each other in terms of the optimism of their illustrations. As SIB put it, 'projections have been widely used for competitive purposes, resulting in bidding up of projected maturity amounts and an unwillingness on the part of any one company to opt out of this competition'.[2] The regulatory response was, firstly, to *standardise* illustrations on the basis of assumptions prescribed by Lautro – assumptions covering not only the future rate of investment return but also the impact of company charges or expenses on that return. And secondly, a company choosing to give an illustration was obliged to show the effect of two different rates of return – an 'optimistic' rate (normally 10.5 per cent) and a 'pessimistic' rate (normally 7 per cent).[3] This requirement was designed to bring home to the investor the speculative nature of illustrations, while a further requirement for the illustration to be accompanied by a table showing the effect on real values of different rates of inflation was designed to remind the investor that the purchasing powers of sums of money to be collected 25 years hence might be much attenuated.[4]

As a result of these measures all companies give the same illustrations. This has certainly eliminated the specious competition described above; but the price which has been paid is that illustrations fail to discriminate between companies with high and low charges or expenses.

The post-MCA regime

The fundamental shift prompted by the rejection of the Maximum Commission Agreement was from a system which controlled the commission payable to independent intermediaries to one which merely required their *disclosure*. It seems likely that the OFT had assumed that SIB would require independent intermediaries to make automatic disclosure of commission receivable, expressed in cash terms, at the 'point of sale' – i.e. at the time when the

---

[1] SIB, *Regulation of the Marketing of Investment Products and Services* (1990), para. 8.1.

[2] SIB, *Product Disclosure: Illustrations, Surrender Values and Past Performance* (July 1986), para. 8.

[3] Lautro Rules, Sch. 4, Part III.   [4] Lautro Rules, Sch. 6.

intermediary recommended the policy to his customer. In fact, however, the new regime provided for automatic commission disclosure (expressed as a percentage of premium) to be made by the insurance company, and allowed that disclosure to be made as late as the sending of the cooling-off notice – i.e. in practice, after the making of the contract. The independent intermediary himself had to disclose that he was remunerated by commission and that he would give the details on request; but he was not required to disclose the prospective amount automatically.[1]

One of the factors which influenced the formulation of the commission disclosure requirement was concern that regulation should not make tied status a much more attractive posture than independence for large numbers of independent intermediaries. Behind this concern is SIB's belief that it is 'highly desirable' for the investment market to include 'a strong independent financial adviser sector',[2] and the recognition of that sector as a spur to competition between life offices.

The new commission disclosure regime was accompanied by certain other changes. First, an attempt was made to strengthen *polarisation* by means of further status disclosure requirements. In particular, both tied and independent intermediaries were required to hand over a 'Buyer's Guide' right at the start of the sales process, the main function of the guide being not only to identify the individual adviser as tied or independent but also to explain the significance of these labels.[3]

Second, a new dimension was added to *product disclosure* by means of an obligation on the life office to disclose the long run *effect of its charges or expenses* on the investor's prospective return in the product particulars sent to the investor along with the cooling-off notice.[4] The rationale for requiring the effect of such costs to be disclosed derives from two characteristics of with-profits and unit-linked life policies. The first is the open-endedness of the ultimate return to the investor. In the case of a with-profits policy, although a minimum guaranteed sum may be payable on maturity, the bulk of the return to the investor depends on the size of the annual ('reversionary') bonuses and the final ('terminal') bonus declared by the company; and the size of these bonuses is at the discretion of the life company, taking the performance of its fund and other relevant factors into account. In the case of a unit-linked policy, the return to the investor depends on the performance of the fund to which the value of his policy is linked. Since the investor is not, in either case, promised a fixed return, a relevant question is how much of his money is 'working' for him, or in other words, to what extent his premiums or the fund into which they are paid will be reduced by the impact of the life office's charges or expenses.

---

[1] SIB CBRs (1990) 5.13, 5.13A(a).
[2] *Life Assurance and Unit Trust Disclosure: The Regime for 1990* (1988), para. 8.
[3] SIB CBRs (1990) 5.11B.   [4] SIB CBRs (1990) 5.14, App.D.

This is not, however, an easy question to answer because of the second relevant characteristic of products of this kind – the relative opacity and complexity of their cost structures. In the case of a with-profits policy there are generally no *explicit* charges; rather the life office recovers its expenses (e.g. the costs of marketing, administration and investment management) from the fund under management. While the life office's appointed actuary has a role in overseeing the equity of this process, it remains highly opaque from the policyholder's point of view. In the case of a unit-linked policy, on the other hand, the charges are explicit, but highly complex charging structures have emerged, involving not only initial and recurrent charges, but also 'capital units' and 'nil allocation' periods, as well as administration fees. Ordinary policyholders are unlikely to be able to assess the net impact of these various charging devices.

It was against this background that a requirement to disclose the *effect* of the charges or expenses was introduced. The formula chosen to encapsulate this information was that of the 'reduction in yield' (RIY). The RIY indicates the extent to which a postulated rate of return (normally 7 per cent per annum) over the full life of the contract will be reduced by virtue of the life office's expected charges or expenses. Thus an RIY of 1 per cent means that an annual return of 7 per cent would be reduced to 6 per cent. While in principle RIY is a satisfactory device for expressing the net effect of costs, there emerged soon after its introduction widespread doubt as to what ordinary investors could make of it. It is easy, for example, to misread the RIY as representing a deduction from the proceeds of the policy, on which misunderstanding the impact of costs appears much less significant.

One other change attended the introduction of the new commission disclosure regime. Companies offering with-profits policies were required to prepare a 'With Profits Guide', explaining in technical detail such matters as the company's investment policies, bonus philosophy, reserves and expenses.[1] The guide is designed to facilitate assessment by experts – e.g. journalists and professional intermediaries – and there is no requirement to give or offer it to investors.

The emergence of a third disclosure regime

The post-MCA regime phased in during 1989–90 failed to satisfy the Director General of Fair Trading, who reported adversely on it in April 1990. The Director General's primary concern was that 'disclosure [of commission] after the point of sale diminishes the effect of disclosure in encouraging competition between IFAs [independent financial advisers] in the cost and quality of their advice, and will do little to counter the malign effect on competition of the commission system itself'.[2] He also criticised the timing – i.e. at the start of the

---

[1] SIB CBRs (1990) 5.11C.
[2] OFT, *The Disclosure of Information about Life Insurance Products and Commissions Paid to Independent Financial Advisers* (April 1990), para. 4.5.

cooling-off period – of the disclosure of the effect of charges and expenses, and the lack of consistency between the commission disclosure format (percentage of premium) and the format for the effect of charges and expenses (reduction in yield).[1]

In December 1990 the Secretary of State for Trade and Industry accepted that the disclosure rules remained likely to restrict or distort competition to a significant extent. SIB was asked to propose changes to lessen the anti-competitive effect of the rules in a way which would take into account the desirability of:

giving the consumer the comparable and timely information he needs in a form which is readily comprehensible; avoiding unnecessarily burdensome costs on product providers; and ensuring that any changes to the rules on disclosure of commissions do not result in a distortion of competition between IFAs and tied agents.[2]

In response, SIB and Lautro published new disclosure proposals in October 1991.[3] The main changes proposed were (i) the introduction of a 'key features' summary, which would be given to the investor *before* he decides to buy the product, and which would highlight in simple language the *essential* characteristics of the product in question; (ii) the introduction of a 'reduction in proceeds' formula to express the effect of charges or expenses as a sum of money deductible from the proceeds of a policy held to maturity; and (iii) a shift to an 'own charges' basis for illustrations or projections, so that the sum projected by each company would reflect its actual current charges or expenses, rather than a standard figure prescribed by Lautro.

At the same time, SIB explained why it was against changes to the timing and format of commission disclosure by independent intermediaries:

. . . a commission disclosure requirement which applies to independent inter-mediaries, but not the tied, engenders the danger of *distribution bias* – i.e. the risk that independent intermediaries will be put at competitive disadvantage *vis-à-vis* tied intermediaries. Independence is, for insurance intermediaries, to a large extent a voluntary posture: if the commission disclosure regime is perceived as unduly intrusive, intermediaries may arrange to sidestep it by relinquishing their independent status and plying their trade as tied agents. Having regard to the benefits which the existence of a solid independent sector confers upon investors, SIB does not regard this as a prospect to be viewed with indifference. It is sometimes asserted that the problem of distribution bias could be solved at a stroke by the imposition of identical disclosure obligations on tied intermediaries. This is not so. Even leaving aside the argument of legal principle (that the independent intermediary is the agent of his client, the tied intermediary that of the product company), there are insuperable practical difficulties. For example, where a tied entity is in the same group of companies as its principal there may be no flow of commission to disclose. . . .

[1] *Ibid.*, para. 4.21.   [2] DTI Press Notice, P/90/723 (7 December, 1990).

[3] SIB, *Disclosure*: Retail Regulation Review: Discussion Paper 3 (October 1991); Lautro, *Disclosure*, Consultative Bulletin No. 11 (October 1991).

If independent intermediaries were required to make automatic disclosure at the point of sale of the amount of their commission, it would no doubt be open to them to 'put their commission into context' by reference to overall life office costs. It would be naive, however, to regard this as a reliable means of maintaining a competitive equilibrium between tied and independent intermediaries, and the risk of a significant erosion of the independent sector could not be discounted.[1]

At the end of 1991, therefore, the issue of commission disclosure remained to be resolved.

UNIT TRUSTS AND INVESTMENT TRUSTS

By and large authorised unit trusts (and recognised overseas collective investment schemes) are subject to the same conduct of business regime as life products. Thus (i) advice on them is polarised and within the scope of the best advice requirement; (ii) unit trust commission was subject to the MCA and is subject to the disclosure requirements which replaced it;[2] (iii) the ban on churning applies; (iv) with one significant exception,[3] they are subject to similar product disclosure and cooling-off requirements; and (v) any illustrations of possible future returns are controlled in the same way as those on life policies. The virtual completeness of the regulatory assimilation of life assurance and authorised unit trusts for conduct of business purposes is expressed in the use of the term 'packaged product' to cover both in the core rules.

The rationale for this regulatory equation of life insurance and unit trust products is that they are often readily substitutable for each other (this is particularly true of unit-linked life policies and unit trusts), and that they tend to be sold side by side by intermediaries and product providers. Even so, it may be argued that some features of the retail regulatory regime – e.g. polarisation – were designed primarily as a response to problems characteristic of the life industry, and that the unit trust industry has been put in the position of having to swallow the life industry's medicine. But as long as there is such a high level of interchangeability between many of the products of the two sectors, the impulse to assimilate them in regulatory terms will remain a strong one.[4]

Personal equity plans (PEPs) and investment trust savings schemes

---

[1] SIB, *ibid.*, para. 37, 40.

[2] In any event market practice has always been to disclose the commission in the contract note.

[3] Because the product regulations allow authorised unit trusts to utilise only two types of charging device – the initial charge and the periodic charge – they are not yet required to make an effect of charges disclosure: Financial Services (Regulated Schemes) Regulations 1991, regs. 4.17, 8.02. The eventual extension of effect of charges disclosure to authorised unit trusts is, however, contemplated in the discussion papers published in late 1991: see above, p. 298, n. 3.

[4] Note, however, that the idea of 'depolarising' unit trusts was floated in SIB's discussion paper on *Polarisation*: Retail Regulation Review: Discussion Paper 2 (September 1991), paras. 52–4.

(ITSSs) emerged too late to be accommodated satisfactorily in the original regulatory scheme of things, and accordingly became the object of subsequent adjustments. The difficulty posed by PEPs is the variety of forms they can assume – ranging from discretionary portfolio management arrangements to 'pepped' unit trust purchases – which makes it difficult to devise any regime appropriate for them all. The reasonably successful solution found in 1989 was to adopt a 'look through' approach to PEPs, whereby the applicable regulatory requirements depend on the character of the underlying plan investments.[1] So, for example, advice on a PEP with a built-in unit trust component is polarised; advice on a PEP whose plan investments consist wholly of equities is not.

Investment trusts are closed-ended companies, and the initial inclination of the FSA regulators was to treat investment trust shares like shares in any other company. Business involving them thus fell to be regulated along the lines of other securities business. But the growing popularity of investment trust savings schemes[2] from the mid-1980s onwards engendered demands for them to be afforded the same degree of freedom in marketing terms as life insurance and unit trusts. By 1990 SIB had espoused the principle that ITSSs should attract both the freedoms and the constraints of the conduct of business regime applicable to those products. Accordingly ITSSs were defined as 'packaged products' for the purposes of the core rules. At the same time, dealings in investment trust shares remain, for obvious reasons, subject to relevant requirements applicable to share dealings in general – e.g. the best execution requirement.

---

[1] SIB, *Unit Trust Only Personal Equity Plans*, CP22 (1989); Financial Services (Miscellaneous Amendments) (PEPs) Rules and Regulations 1989; see also core rule 17.6.

[2] Investment trust saving schemes do not involve the sale of investment trust shares by the investment trust itself: this is precluded by the closed-ended character of investment trusts as registered companies. Rather an ITSS involves the establishment of a subsidiary with authorised person status, which functions in effect as an agency stockbroker, buying and selling shares in the investment trust on the Stock Exchange on behalf of investors. Thus the core rules glossary defines an ITSS as 'a dealing service dedicated to the securities of a particular investment trust . . .'. From the investor's point of view the advantage of the ITSS is as a cheap dealing facility. The necessary economies of scale are usually achieved by the aggregation of orders.

18
Promotion

This chapter is concerned with ways of promoting investment and savings products. The first part of the chapter briefly outlines the *statutory offences* created specifically to tackle the employment of deception to induce investors to hand over their money. The next part describes regulatory controls on *advertisements*, taking investment advertising (and, in certain cases, other kinds of statement) under the Financial Services Act first, then deposit advertising. The final part deals with restrictions on the making of *unsolicited calls*; again the pattern is to take the FSA regime first, then the regime applicable to deposit-takers.

MISLEADING STATEMENTS

Section 47(1) of the Financial Services Act creates the criminal offence (punishable with up to seven years imprisonment) of making misleading statements. To be more specific, there are three ways of committing the offence: (i) by making a statement, promise or forecast which the maker *knows* to be misleading, false or deceptive; or (ii) by *recklessly* making (*dishonestly or otherwise*) a statement, promise or forecast which is misleading, false or deceptive; or (iii) by *dishonestly concealing* any material facts. In each case the offence is committed only if this is done for the purpose of inducing (or recklessly as to whether it may induce) someone to enter into an investment agreement.[1] Under the Banking Act 1987 (s.35) there is the broadly comparable offence of inducing or attempting to induce someone to make a deposit by any one of the three means outlined above.

The statutory language makes it clear that an offence can be committed if the truth is presented in a misleading way and that there is no need to prove

---

[1] Or to exercise any rights conferred by an investment, or to refrain from entering into an investment agreement, or to refrain from exercising rights conferred by an investment. For the definition of 'investment agreement', see FSA, s.44(9), and p. 303 below.

dishonesty in connection with statements recklessly made.[1] The meaning of 'recklessness' in criminal statutes is a much controverted matter, but at least in the present context it is reasonably clear that guilt does not depend on proof that the accused consciously ran the risk that his statement was misleading, false or deceptive; it is enough to show that there has been a 'high degree of negligence' on the part of the accused.[2]

ADVERTISING

Background

While advertisements by deposit-taking institutions and investment businesses compete with equal vigour for the attention of savers on television, in newspapers and in other media, there is a marked contrast in the character of the regulatory controls which apply. Leaving aside the criminal offence of making misleading statements, the main component of the regime for deposit advertisements is a non-statutory code of practice whose function is to ensure that claims about rates of interest are fair and comparable. This reflects the primary focus of competition between deposit-takers and the relative simplicity of deposit-based products. The regulation of investment advertising under the Financial Services Act, on the other hand, reflects the complexity and diversity of FSA investment vehicles, the focus of competition on past performance and future potential, and the involvement of larger numbers of firms with different backgrounds.

FSA section 57 and the concept of an investment advertisement

The concept of an investment advertisement is introduced by section 57 of the Financial Services Act. That section makes it a criminal offence for anyone except an authorised person to issue in the UK (or cause to be issued there) an investment advertisement unless its contents have been approved by an authorised person. This provision is designed to ensure that for each investment advertisement there will be an authorised person with responsibility for its contents, and thus that investment advertisements, whether or not actually issued by authorised persons, will conform to FSA advertising standards.

Under section 57 there are two types of investment advertisement. The first is any advertisement *inviting* persons to enter or offer to enter into an 'investment agreement' (or to exercise any rights conferred by an investment

---

[1] The interpretation of recklessness in *R.* v. *Mackinnon* [1959] 1 Q.B. 150 is thus rejected.
[2] *R.* v. *Bates* [1952] 2 All E.R. 842; the ruling in this case and in *R.* v. *Grunwald* [1963] 1 Q.B. 935 is broadly consonant with the approach to recklessness taken by the House of Lords in *R.* v. *Caldwell* [1982]

to acquire, dispose of, underwrite or convert an investment). The second is any advertisement *containing information calculated to lead directly or indirectly* to persons doing so. 'Calculated' can be taken to mean intended or likely.

This definition does not just catch advertisements in which investment firms promote their products or services, or the image of the firm itself. It also extends to advertisements by others if they invite entry into an investment agreement or contain information likely to lead to such an agreement. The definition of 'investment agreement'[1] is extremely broad. It is 'any agreement the making or performance of which by either party constitutes an activity which falls within any paragraph of Part II of Schedule I to this Act' (i.e. dealing, managing, advising, etc.) 'or would do so apart from Parts III and IV of that Schedule' (i.e. the exclusions). The effect of these final words is that in *this* context the definitions of the activities constituting investment business apply without the exclusions (e.g. the 'own account' exclusion) which are relevant when the question is whether someone needs to become an authorised or exempted person. In addition, the definition of investment agreement applies irrespective of whether either party to the agreement is 'carrying on the business' of engaging in the Part II activity in question. The upshot is that 'investment advertisement' extends, for example, to advertisements offering company securities for sale, and to corporate image advertising by a company whose privatisation is imminent. But, as we shall see, advertisements offering securities are often exempted from the advertising requirements of the FSA regulators.

Investment advertising standards in the core rules

SIB's core rules (made under section 48) lay down two general requirements for investment advertisements. The first is that the firm issuing or approving the advertisement must be able to show (note that the burden of proof falls upon the firm: this reflects the terms of the Misleading Advertisements Directive)[2] that it believes on reasonable grounds that the advertisement is fair and not misleading.[3] An advertisement may be unfair, for example, if, having indicated the potential benefits of buying the investment advertised, it passes over in silence the risks which accompany the pursuit of those benefits. The generality of the core rule lends itself to amplification by guidance or codes of practice in the 'third tiers' of the SROs, but it also makes it unlikely that any third tier could spell out its implications exhaustively.

The second requirement is that a firm issuing or approving an investment advertisement must 'apply appropriate expertise'.[4] This stipulation is designed to ensure that a firm approving an advertisement brings to bear a

---

A.C. 341, though there are divergences in the language used to characterise recklessness which might turn out to be material in some cases.

[1] s.44(9).   [2] Council Directive 84/450.   [3] Core rule 5.1.b.   [4] Core rule 5.1.a.

sufficient grasp of the business being advertised to make possible a judicious assessment of the advertisement's contents. This does not mean, however, that the approving firm must be in the same line of business. Nor does it mean that it must find all the appropriate expertise in house: it is open to an approving firm to draw on third-party expertise – for example, for the vetting of financial figures. If information supplied by a third party turns out to be flawed, the approving firm will not be held responsible if it reasonably believed the supplier to be independent and competent, and if it was reasonable to rely on the information.[1]

Further provisions apply if the advertisement is of the 'direct offer' type. A direct offer advertisement is one to which an investor can respond by making an immediate contractual commitment by following the procedure laid down in the advertisement itself – for example, by sending off an application form and a cheque.[2] The nub of the matter is that the customer's investment decision may be based on nothing more than the information furnished in the advertisement itself. At one time SIB took the view that advertising to private customers on a direct offer basis was a privilege which should be confined (on the footing that they could be assumed to be suitable for most people) to life assurance, unit trusts and PEPs.[3] However, this restrictive policy was never fully implemented in practice,[4] and core rule 5.4.a reflects SIB's Retail Review conclusion that, in general, freedom with disclosure is the appropriate regulatory philosophy for direct offer advertising.[5] Accordingly direct offer advertisements to private customers must give 'information about the investments or investment services, the terms of the offer, and the risks involved, which is adequate and fair having regard to the (UK or overseas) regulatory protections which apply and the market to which the advertisement is directed.'[6] 'Adequate' means sufficient to enable a private customer reading the advertisement to reach an informed investment decision.[7]

There is a more paternalistic approach, however, in the case of direct offer advertisements offering derivatives (i.e. futures, options or contracts for differences) or warrants. Such an advertisement may be directed at a private customer only if the firm issuing it has satisfied itself that the offer is suitable for the actual recipient.[8] This reflects the comparative volatility of these instruments and the high degree of financial sophistication needed to use them successfully.

Whereas core rule 5 applies only to investment *advertisements*, core rule 9 goes wider. Core rule 9.1 applies whenever a firm makes a 'communication' with another person which is designed to promote the provision of investment services, and requires the firm to be able to show that on reasonable grounds it

---

[1] Core rule 38.2.

[2] SIB, *Regulation of the Marketing of Investment Products and Services* (1990), para. 5.1; Financial Services Glossary 1991.

[3] SIB CBRs (1987), 7.22(2).   [4] SIB CBRs (1990) 17.04.

[5] *Regulation of the Marketing of Investment Products and Services: A Policy Statement* (1991), para. 6.

[6] Core rule 5.4.a.   [7] Cf. the more explicit test in core rule 12.1.   [8] Core rule 5.4.b.

believes the communication to be fair and not misleading. This requirement thus applies to one-off statements (written or oral) made to a single person, which in UK law would not normally be regarded as amounting to 'advertisements'. And it applies even if the communication is made to a non-private customer. In these respects core rule 9.1 reflects the scope of the Misleading Advertisements Directive, which it is designed to implement.[1]

Core rule 9.2, on the other hand, is concerned with the *presentation* of material to private customers, and requires firms to take care that any 'agreement, written communication, notification or information' given to a private customer is presented fairly and clearly. Clarity of presentation is thus the distinctive requirement in this provision.

In certain cases the core rules on *advertising* – but not core rule 9 – are disapplied.[2] The main instances are: (i) an authorised person's issue of an 'exempt' advertisement – i.e. an advertisement which, if issued by an *un*authorised person, would not need to be approved by an authorised person;[3] and (ii) a 'takeover advertisement' – i.e. an advertisement subject to the Takeover Code and hence within the jurisdiction of the Panel on Takeovers and Mergers. In addition, *all* of the core rules are disapplied when a firm *re*issues an investment advertisement which has already been issued or approved by an authorised person.[4] This avoids unnecessary duplication of vetting effort. But if the reissue is directed at a different market from that originally intended – for example, if an advertisement issued to non-private customers is reissued to private customers – the core rules will apply after all.

Investment advertisements by unauthorised persons

Section 57, as we have seen, prohibits an unauthorised person from issuing or causing to be issued an investment advertisement in the UK unless its contents have been *approved* by an authorised person. Contravention of section 57 is a criminal offence, and there is also a presumption that the contravention renders legally unenforceable by the advertiser any relevant investment agreement entered into after the issue of the offending advertisement.[5] In principle, all agreements *subsequent* to the issue of the advertisement are tainted, whether or not they are *consequent* agreements. But the court may allow the tainted agreement to be enforced after all, if it is satisfied that the advertisement was not misleading and fairly stated the risks, or that the decision to contract by the person against whom enforcement is sought was not materially influenced by the advertisement.[6]

---

[1] The Directive defines advertising as 'the making of a representation in any form in connection with a trade, business, craft or profession in order to promote the supply of goods or services, including immovable property, rights and obligations' (Council Directive 84/450, Art.2(1)), and does not discriminate between private and non-private recipients of advertisements.

[2] Core rule 40.2.b.   [3] See below, pp. 306–8.   [4] Core rule 40.2.c.(ii).   [5] s.57(5)(a).
[6] s.57(8).

There are exceptions to the s.57 approval requirement in s.58, the most important of which cover:

(i) advertisements by governments and local authorities for investments issued by themselves (s.58(1)(a)(i),(ii));

(ii) advertisements required or expressly contemplated by the Stock Exchange's Yellow Book, e.g. prospectuses and mini-prospectuses for listed securities and certain advertisements relating to the results of listed companies (s.58(1)(d));

(iii) registered prospectuses inviting members of the public to subscribe in cash for unlisted securities (e.g. shares in a Business Expansion Scheme company), and box advertisements indicating how such a prospectus can be obtained (s.58(2)).[1]

The effect of these exceptions is to remove much of the advertising material associated with the issue of securities from the s.57 approval requirement, and hence from SIB/SRO/RPB advertising rules, but in some situations the s.57 regime is still applicable – for example, where there is a 'private' offering of unlisted securities.

In addition to the exceptions created by s.58 itself, the Secretary of State has exercised his power (s.58(3)) to make further exemptions. Two in particular stand out. The first is the exemption for advertisements issued only to 'persons sufficiently expert' to understand the risks involved, introduced in 1988. The list of 'persons sufficiently expert' includes authorised and exempted persons, governments, local authorities and public authorities, and companies above a certain size.[2] But opportunities for taking advantage of the exemption are circumscribed by the need to ensure (in the case of an advertisement taking the form of a document) that *the only persons* to whom the advertisement is issued are those reasonably believed to fall in the listed categories, and (in the case of other advertisements, e.g. screen displays) that the advertisement 'will not generally be made available' except to those in the listed categories.[3] Thus it is hard to rely on the exemption except in connection with publications access which is carefully restricted to those in the 'expert' categories.

The limitations of the 1988 exemption, and especially the impossibility of relying on it in connection with advertisements appearing in publications (e.g. the *Financial Times*) which are not just read by investment 'professionals', prompted the government to add in 1992 a less restrictive exemption for advertising oriented to professionals.[4] Under this further exemption the test is

[1] At the time of writing the transitional provisions in Sch. 15, para. 8 remained applicable.

[2] Financial Services Act 1986 (Investment Advertisements) (Exemptions) Order 1988, SI 1988/316, art. 9(3). The size criterion parallels that used by SIB to identify 'ordinary' (as opposed to 'small') business investors: above, p. 269.

[3] Art. 9(2).

[4] Financial Services Act 1986 (Investment Advertisements) (Exemption) (No.2) Order 1992, SI 1992/813, art. 2.

not by whom the advertisement is likely to be *seen*, but at whom it is *targeted*. An advertisement is exempt from the approval requirement if it may reasonably be regarded as 'directed at informing or influencing' only persons within certain categories, which include investment advisers, local and public authorities, and also 'persons whose ordinary business involves the acquisition, holding, management or disposal of investments or whom it is reasonable to expect will acquire, hold, manage or dispose of investments for the purposes of a business carried on by them'.[1] This last category covers not only investment managers but also commercial and industrial businesses with a corporate treasury function.

To help advertisers and publishers decide whether a particular advertisement gets the benefit of the exemption or not, the exemption order instances 'indications' that an advertisement is professional-oriented. So, for example, it helps if the advertisement states expressly that it is 'directed at persons with professional experience in matters relating to investment and that it would be imprudent for persons of any other kind to respond to it', or if its matter is 'unlikely to appeal' to persons without professional experience in investment matters.[2]

Where an unauthorised person takes advantage of s.58 by issuing an investment advertisement without the approval of an authorised person, the advertisement concerned is subject to the Control of Misleading Advertising Regulations[3] which were introduced to implement the Misleading Advertisements Directive. The odd thing is that those regulations apply to unauthorised persons' investment advertisements even if they *have* been approved by an authorised person. Such advertisements are thus doubly regulated – by the OFT regime as well as that of the FSA regulators.

Overseas advertisers

Section 57 applies if the issue of the advertisement is 'in the United Kingdom'. But the effect of section 207(3) is that an advertisement issued *outside* the UK is to be treated as issued *in* the UK if it is 'directed' to persons in the UK or is 'made available' to them (though, as we shall see, in the case of 'availability' this does not apply to advertisements carried by media whose principal audience is outside the UK).

Where, by virtue of section 57, an overseas advertiser needs to seek the approval of an authorised person for the contents of his advertisement, that approval cannot be given unless the advertisement complies with the advertising standards outlined above. Moreover, the approving firm must, in certain circumstances, ensure that the advertisement contains a 'prescribed

---

[1] Art. 2(1)(b).

[2] Art. 3(a), (c). For indications that an advertisement is directed at *non*-professionals, see art. 4. In either case, the absence of an indication is not an indication to the contrary.

[3] SI 1988/915.

disclosure' – a statement to the effect that all or most of the protections provided by the UK investor protection system will not apply, and that compensation under the Investors Compensation Scheme will not be available. This is the disclosure that is required in the case of a 'specific' investment advertisement (i.e. one which identifies and promotes a *particular* investment or investment service) which is likely to lead to an overseas person (i.e. an overseas *investment business* with no permanent base in the UK) doing business outside the umbrella of the UK regulatory system with *private* customers in the UK. When these circumstances apply the approving firm is also under an obligation to withhold its approval altogether if it has any reason to doubt that the overseas person will deal with UK investors in an honest and reliable way.[1]

Certain of the exemptions from the section 57 approval requirement are of particular significance for overseas investment businesses. In particular, where the advertiser is the national of an EC state (other than the UK itself), section 58(1)(c) disapplies the approval requirement to an advertisement issued by him in the course of investment business lawfully carried on by him in such a state. The crucial proviso is that the advertisement must comply with SIB's advertising rules. A breach of SIB's advertising rules is not normally a criminal matter, but section 58(1)(c) is an exemption from the criminal prohibition in section 57; accordingly a breach of the advertising rules by an EC national seeking to rely on this exemption will give rise to criminal liability.

There are also narrowly circumscribed 'existing client' exemptions for overseas investment businesses. One enables the overseas firm to send unapproved advertisements to investors in the UK who became clients when they were expatriates.[2] Another allows the operator of an overseas collective investment scheme recognised under section 87 (designated territories) or section 88 (individual recognition) to send unapproved advertisements about the scheme to existing participants in that scheme.[3]

Publishers

The criminal prohibition in section 57 is of direct relevance to the publishers of newspapers and magazines that circulate in the UK in that carrying an investment advertisement in one's publication amounts to 'issuing' it. Publication of an unapproved investment advertisement may therefore expose the publisher as well as the advertiser to a criminal charge. In effect the Act puts the onus on publishers to screen investment advertisements.

The burden on UK-based publishers is, however, greater than on their overseas counterparts. If a newspaper or magazine is published outside the UK and circulates principally outside the UK, the fact that it also has some

---

[1] Core rule 6.   [2] SI 1988/316, art. 8.   [3] SI 1988/316, art. 12; see also art. 3(2).

UK circulation does not bring any investment advertisement it carries within the ambit of section 57 unless the advertisement in question is 'directed' to persons in the UK. 'Direction' implies some particular targeting of the UK audience; it is not enough in the case of an international publication that the advertisement is in the English language.

In consequence, UK-based publishers in particular have felt the need to establish screening systems designed to identify investment advertisements, to determine whether they get the benefit of an exemption or not, and to explain the need for approval to advertisers. Even so, unapproved advertisements may occasionally slip through the net. In this connection, section 57(4) affords the publisher a 'due diligence' defence. The burden of proof is on the publisher to show that he believed on reasonable grounds that the advertisement was issued or approved by an authorised person, or that it was exempt. There is *no* due diligence defence, however, if an investment advertisement is erroneously classified as a non-investment advertisement, or if an overseas publication circulating principally outside the UK erroneously decides that an investment advertisement is not 'directed' at investors in the UK: in these cases the offence is one of strict liability.

Life policies

Section 130 of the Financial Services Act imposes special restrictions on the promotion in the UK (whether by authorised or unauthorised persons) of life policies with an investment element. The restrictions apply both to advertising and to advice given by an intermediary or salesperson. Their inclusion in the Act appears to have been prompted by the failure of Signal Life in the early 1980s (Signal Life was a Gibraltar life office whose policies had been extensively promoted in the UK by certain intermediaries).

Under s.130 the promotion of investment-type life policies is banned unless the policy is that of an insurer which gets through one of the gateways listed in that section. These are: (i) authorised UK insurance companies and registered friendly societies;[1] (ii) insurance companies with an EC connection – a head office or branch or agency in a Member State and entitlement to carry on the relevant class of *insurance* business there;[2] (iii) insurance companies with appropriate authorisation from a country or territory with a s.130 designation from the Secretary of State for Trade and Industry.[3] So far designation orders have covered the Isle of Man, Guernsey and Pennsylvania.[4] It is a precondition of designation that the Secretary of State be satisfied that the supervisory regime of the jurisdiction in question affords 'adequate protection' to policyholders against the risk that the companies subject to it may be unable

[1] s.130(2)(a), (b). [2] s.130(2)(c), (d). [3] s.130(3).
[4] Financial Services (Designated Countries and Territories) (Overseas Insurance Companies) Orders 1988 and 1989, SI 1988/439, SI 1989/2380.

to meet their liabilities.[1] The scrutiny which precedes designation is thus primarily concerned with the arrangements for prudential supervision in the relevant country or territory.

The net effect is that life policies from countries such as Switzerland cannot be promoted in the UK, even to non-private investors. The irony is that Gibraltar, notwithstanding its place in the events which prompted the introduction of the s.130 restrictions, is to be treated as an EC Member State for the purposes of s.130.[2]

The ban in s.130 is backed by civil and criminal sanctions[3] broadly comparable to those associated with s.57.

Unregulated collective investment schemes

As we saw in Chapter 12, promotion of 'unregulated' collective investment schemes – i.e. schemes which are neither UK authorised unit trusts nor recognised overseas schemes – is severely circumscribed by s.76 of the Financial Services Act. Section 76 starts by prohibiting *authorised* persons from promoting unregulated schemes; and promotion covers both advertising schemes and advising or procuring anyone to become a scheme participant (someone is 'procured' to become a participant if, for example, a discretionary manager acquires units on his behalf). There are, however, exceptions which create a number of gateways through which promotional activity can flow. Some of these exceptions are established by s.76 itself; the rest are in regulations made by the SIB under s.76(3). It is important to notice that the SIB's power to make exemptions is not unlimited: it can only be exercised for the purpose of exempting from the general prohibition promotion of schemes 'otherwise than to the general public'.

A number of the gateways are designed to make possible the promotion of unregulated schemes to persons who can be assumed to be capable of fending for themseves. For example, the s.76 prohibition is lifted to permit promotion to: (i) another authorised person;[4] (ii) a person whose ordinary business involves the acquisition and disposal of property of the same kind as the property to which the scheme relates:[5] this would allow, for example, the promotion of a scheme investing in stamps to a stamp dealer; (iii) non-private customers[6] as defined in the core rules;[7] and (iv) 'experienced' private customers who have opted to be treated as non-private customers.[8]

Other gateways allow for promotion to investors who are classified as ordinary private customers. The main gateways are:

(i) the *established customer* exemption.[9] This enables an authorised person to

---

[1] s.130(4).   [2] s.208(1).   [3] ss.130(6)–(8), 131.   [4] s.76(2)(a).   [5] s.76(2)(b).
[6] Financial Services (Promotion of Unregulated Schemes) Regulations 1991 [hereafter cited as PUS regs.], item 6.
[7] See p. 269.   [8] PUS regs., item 7.   [9] PUS regs., item 3.

promote an unregulated scheme to a known client (known in the sense that the know your customer procedure has been followed). The safeguard is that promotion is not permitted under this exemption unless the scheme in question is reasonably judged to be suitable for the client, and this test must be satisfied *before* any promotion occurs.

(ii) the *newly accepted customer* exemption.[1] This permits promotion, subject to the know your customer and suitability safeguards, to a newly acquired client – provided that client was obtained without breaking s.76 in the first place. So, for example, if a discretionary portfolio management firm gains a new client by advertising its general management services, there is an immediate possibility of including unregulated schemes among other investments within the client's portfolio; it is unnecessary to wait until the client is 'established'. But the newly accepted customer exemption does not permit promotion of un-regulated schemes to *potential* customers; indeed a regulation which purported to permit promotion to potential customers as a class would be *ultra vires* of s.76(3), since that would be tantamount to permitting promotion to the general public.

(iii) the *prior participant* exemption.[2] If an investor is already a participant in an unregulated scheme (or has been within the last 30 months), this exemption enables other unregulated schemes to be promoted to him as long as the underlying property and risk profile of the new schemes are 'substantially similar' to those of the scheme in which he has already invested. For example, an 'angel' who has backed a theatrical production structured as a collective investment scheme could be sent details of other theatrical or film production schemes.[3] From the promoter's point of view, the advantage of the prior participant exemption is that it enables promotional literature to be sent without the need for a prior judgment that the investment will be suitable for the recipient. From an investor protection point of view, the justification for this relaxation is that the investor must, by definition, have previous experience of investment in a substantially similar scheme.

A strange feature of s.76 is that the ban it lays down applies to the *issue*, but not to the *approval*, of advertisements by *authorised* persons. It therefore leaves *unauthorised* overseas persons who operate unregulated collective schemes free to advertise their schemes to the general public in the UK, provided a UK authorised person can be persuaded to approve the advertisement under s.57.

The original version of s.57 in the Financial Services Bill[4] would have required all investment advertisements to be issued by authorised persons. When provision was made for approval by authorised persons as an alternative to issue, it seems that some of the consequential amendments needed were overlooked. Hence the mismatch between s.57 and s.76.[5] If

---

[1] PUS regs., item 3.   [2] PUS regs., items 1, 2.   [3] PUS regs., Note 1.   [4] Clause 52.
[5] For other missed consequentials, see s.130(7) and Sch. 10, para. 5(1).

matters had been left there, unauthorised overseas operators would enjoy greater promotional freedom in the UK than their authorised UK counter-parts.

SIB core rule 5.3 is an attempt to put matters right. It provides that a firm must not *approve* a 'specific' investment advertisement relating to an un-regulated collective investment scheme.[1] The effect is to close off the 'approval' route while still permitting UK authorised persons to *issue* advertisements for unregulated schemes operated by unauthorised overseas persons. But of course such issue will be subject to s.76 and therefore confined to the limited number of gateways available under s.76.[2]

Deposit-taking

Under section 32 of the Banking Act 1987 the Treasury has power to make regulations (backed by criminal sanctions)[3] governing the issue, form and content of deposit advertisements. 'Deposit advertisement' is defined in terms parallel to the definition of 'investment advertisement' in the Financial Services Act.[4] The power covers the deposit advertisements of building societies as well as banks, and can therefore only be exercised after consultation both with the Bank of England and the Building Societies Commission. In fact, however, no statutory requirements have been laid down by the Treasury except in connection with advertisements seeking deposits with offices of deposit-takers outside the UK and the other Member States of the European Community.[5] The regulations are designed to ensure that the deposit-taker concerned is properly identified,[6] that its assets and liabilities are disclosed,[7] that the interest on offer is described in a way that is not misleading,[8] and that the position on compensation scheme coverage is made clear by the inclusion of a statement that 'deposits made with . . . are not covered by the Deposit Protection Scheme under the Banking Act 1987'.[9]

The specification of standards for advertisements by domestic deposit-takers is left to the Code of Conduct for the Advertising of Interest Bearing Accounts, which is issued jointly by the British Bankers' Association, the Building Societies Association and the Finance Houses Association.[10] The code standardises the usage of the terms 'gross', 'net', 'tax free' and 'compounded annual rate (CAR)', and stipulates conditions for their use. In

---

[1] As to the definition of 'specific' investment advertisement, see p. 308. Note that generic advertisements for unregulated schemes can still be approved under s.57: this makes it possible for an unauthorised person such as a trade association to mount a campaign to arouse public interest in a certain *type* of unregulated scheme – provided no particular scheme of that type is identified.

[2] Since the core rules do not apply to persons whose authorisation derives from RPB membership, complete closure of the loophole depends on the adoption by RPBs of rules whose effect corresponds to that of core rule 5.3.

[3] Banking Act 1987, s.32(3).   [4] Above, pp. 302–3.

[5] Banking Act 1987 (Advertisements) Regulations 1988, SI 1988/645, reg. 2(1).   [6] reg. 4.

[7] reg. 5.   [8] reg. 7.   [9] reg. 6,   [10] Revised edn, December 1990.

particular, if an advertisement quotes an interest rate at all, it must include the gross rate (i.e. the contractual rate of interest payable not taking account of the deduction of income tax at the basic rate), or the tax free rate (in the case of an account yielding tax free interest, e.g. a TESSA). Quotations of the net rate and the CAR cannot be given greater prominence than the gross rate. The advertisement must either specify a term for which the rate is fixed or indicate that the rate is subject to variation, and it must also contain 'a clear statement of the conditions for withdrawal, including the amount of any charges levied, the period of any notice required and the extent of any interest forfeited' (paragraph 12(a)). There are no special requirements for advertisements inviting deposits 'by immediate coupon response' (i.e. the equivalent of 'direct offer' advertisements in the FSA regime), except that they must state that the full terms and conditions are available on request (if they are not included in the advertisement), and be designed so that the consumer does not relinquish details of the product by returning the response coupon (paragraph 13).

Although the system is thus largely one of self-regulation in the traditional sense, both the Bank of England and the Building Societies Commission have power to issue a binding direction in respect of advertisements by a specific deposit-taker under their jurisdiction. In the case of the Bank, the power is exercisable only if it considers an authorised institution's advertisements to be misleading. If this condition is satisfied, the Bank may prohibit the institution in question from issuing advertisements of a specified kind (or substantially similar advertisements), and require the modification or withdrawal of offending advertisements.[1] In the case of the Building Societies Commission, the power is exercisable if the Commission considers it expedient to do so in the interests of potential depositors or shareholders, and the direction given may extend to prohibiting the society from issuing advertisements of *all* descriptions, though a less compendious direction is also possible.[2]

Finally, there is a special regime for advertisements for *deposit-based* personal pension schemes, i.e. schemes based on investment of contributions in an interest-bearing account. Under regulations made by the Secretary of State for Social Security[3] it is, for example, a criminal offence to issue an advertisement for a deposit-based scheme which conveys any information which is false or misleading, or makes an unfair or misleading comparison with an occupational pension scheme, or the state earnings related pension scheme, or another personal pension scheme (reg.5(a),(c)). In addition, there is a requirement for 'off the page' advertisements (again, the equivalent of 'direct offer' advertisements in the FSA regime) to give various particulars of the scheme (reg.4).

---

[1] Banking Act 1987 s.33(1), (2).   [2] Building Societies Act 1986, s.50(1), (2).
[3] Personal Pension Schemes (Advertisements) Regulations 1990, SI 1990/1140.

UNSOLICITED CALLS

Background

'Cold-calling' – where a business takes the initiative in making contact with potential customers on the telephone, or on the doorstep, or even in the street – has long been regarded as a suspect activity, partly because people associate it with high-pressure salesmanship and misleading sales patter, and partly because it can be a nuisance. But the response of UK law to cold-calling has varied according to the subject-matter of the call.

The cold-calling of company shares first attracted official attention in the 1920s, when the Greene Committee noted the growth of 'share-hawking' – the practice of going from door to door to sell worthless shares, often in overseas companies. The Greene Committee's sympathy for the victims of share-hawking was by no means unalloyed: 'At best their action amounts to the rashest kind of speculation; at the worst it shows a complete absence of first elements of prudence and good sense', but they still recommended that it should be made illegal.[1] And when the Companies Act 1929 was passed, s.356 made it a criminal offence to go from house to house offering shares to any member of the public.

The abject failure of this provision to repress the share-hawkers is evidenced by the establishment of a Board of Trade committee in 1936 (the Bodkin Committee) to consider alternative measures. The Bodkin Committee described in detail the *modus operandi* of the sharepushers – noting for example that they were often 'English-speaking aliens of good appearance' – and recommended the creation of a licensing system for dealing in shares.[2] The ensuing legislation was the Prevention of Fraud (Investments) Act 1939. The Act introduced the licensing requirement, while exempting members of the Stock Exchange. The Licensed Dealers Rules made by the Board of Trade prohibited licensed dealers from dealing in shares during or in consequence of an unsolicited call, and extended that concept to cover unsolicited telephone calls.[3] The rules remained in force for nearly 50 years.

The legal treatment of the cold-calling of life assurance took a different course. The sale of life assurance in working class neighbourhoods was traditionally on a door-to-door basis, with collectors calling weekly or fortnightly to collect the premiums. The cold-calling of life assurance was seen as necessary stimulus to working class thrift and providence.[4] So the legislative response to evidence of abuse in the marketing of life assurance was not to ban cold-calling but to introduce various safeguards.[5] The modern life insurance

---

[1] Cmd. 2657 (1926), para. 92.   [2] Cmd. 5539 (1937), para. 10.

[3] The final version was rule 11 of the Licensed Dealers (Conduct of Business) Rules 1983, SI 1983/585; the previous version was rule 6 of SI 1960/1216.

[4] Gower's reluctant conclusion in 1984 was that cold-calling 'still appears to perform a useful social purpose in relation to life cover in general and industrial assurance in particular': *Report*, Part I, para. 8.47.

[5] In the Industrial Assurance Act 1923.

industry remains geared up to sell proactively, on the footing that life insurance is 'sold, not bought'.

The proactive orientation of the life industry, with its salesmen and independent intermediaries accustomed to 'prospecting' for business and to visiting the homes or business premises of their prospects, is in marked contrast to the traditionally reactive style of banks and building societies, with their staff based in branches waiting for the customer to come in. This contrast is reflected in the absence of regulatory controls over the cold-calling of deposit-based investments: there has been little sign of the kind of activity which might have prompted the development of such controls.

Unsolicited calls under the Financial Services Act

Section 56(1) of the Financial Services Act provides that, subject to exceptions:

> no person shall in the course of or in consequence of an unsolicited call . . . by way of business enter into an investment agreement with the person on whom the call is made or procure or endeavour to procure that person to enter into such an agreement.

The scope of this prohibition is wide:

> It applies to the making of investment agreements both *during* and *as a result* of an unsolicited call (e.g. at a subsequent meeting). It also applies to *attempts* (whether successful or not) to persuade someone to enter into an investment agreement. The concept of an unsolicited call is a broad one – broader than the type of behaviour evoked by colloquial references to 'cold-calling'; an unsolicited call is defined as 'a personal visit or oral communication made without express invitation'.[1] Uninvited *telephone calls* are thus equated with uninvited *doorstep visits* and *street canvassing*. Calls preceded by an introductory letter have the same status as calls 'out the blue'. A call even remains unsolicited if it is a response to an *implicit* invitation to call . . .[2]

Breach of s.56 (which applies both to authorised and to unauthorised persons) is not in itself a criminal offence.[3] Rather, it gives rise to the presumption that the investment agreement tainted by the unsolicited call cannot be enforced against the person on whom the call was made. That presumption may be overturned, however, in certain circumstances – for example if the investor understood the nature of the agreement and the risks it involved, and entered into it following discussions which effectively superseded the initial call.[4] For authorised persons, legal unenforceability is not the only sanction: breach of s.56 may also be dealt with as a disciplinary offence by the regulator concerned.

---

[1] s.56(8). [2] SIB, *Regulation of the Marketing of Investment Products and Services* (1990), para. 4.6.

[3] But it deprives an overseas investment firm of the benefit of para. 27 of Schedule 1 and may thus throw it into breach of s.4: see above, pp. 241–2.

[4] s.56(4)(b); see also paras.(a) and (c).

As we have seen, s.56 is subject to 'exceptions' which permit unsolicited calls in specified cases. By and large the exceptions made when the Financial Services Act was brought into force in 1988[1] were designed to reproduce the pre-FSA pattern. Thus they gave *carte blanche* for unsolicited calls in connection with life assurance products, while withholding this privilege from securities and futures business. The main innovation was to put authorised unit trusts on a par with life assurance, it being hard to see any rational basis for treating unit trusts more restrictively than unit-linked life policies.[2] Alongside these product-based permissions there were also provisions permitting unsolicited calls on established clients and on 'professional' investors. But in 1991, following a review, SIB introduced a more liberal regime. This liberalisation reflected the feeling that the tightness of the old restrictions could no longer be justified now that so many other safeguards (the fit and proper test, the suitability requirement, the best execution obligation etc.) were operative in relation to authorised persons; that the existing controls conferred an unfair competitive advantage on life assurance and unit trust products; and that by truncating the range of products and services on which advice might be given after an unsolicited call, the restrictions inhibited advisers from giving investors the advice best suited to their needs. The main substantive innovation was therefore to allow stockbroking services and portfolio management services to be sold pursuant to unsolicited calls. This liberalisation was matched by an extension of cooling-off arrangements, and did not extend to services involving unquoted shares or futures – the two areas where past abuse of cold-calling has been concentrated.

The 1991 Unsolicited Calls Regulations ('UCRs') are 'designated' regulations under s.63A of the Act. They apply therefore not only to unauthorised persons and to firms directly regulated by SIB (as did the original UCRs) but also to SRO member firms. They do not, however, apply to firms whose authorisation derives from RPB membership. So the position of RPB firms continues to depend on the net effect of s.56 coupled with the exceptions made by the RPB in question.[3] The permissions given by the RPBs reflect their traditional distaste for touting for business and, in general, give freedom to make unsolicited calls only on existing clients.

In content, the 1991 regulations reflect the historical development outlined above. Their main features are:

(i) *Sale of non-geared packaged products.* UCR 2.1 is the descendant of the old permission for life assurance. As well as life assurance it covers sales of authorised unit trusts (including the case where the units are to be housed within a PEP), recognised collective investment schemes, and investment

---

[1] Financial Services (Unsolicited Calls) Regulations 1987, and the corresponding rules of the SROs.
[2] Gower, *Report*, para. 8.47.   [3] FSA, s.56(7A).

trust savings schemes. But it does not extend to geared packaged products such as geared futures and options funds (GFOFs).

(ii) *Supply of callable investment services.* UCR 3 is the liberalising measure described above. Investment services are not callable unless they are confined to non-geared packaged products and readily realisable securities (excluding warrants).[1] As long as they are confined in that way, the service concerned may consist of discretionary management, or advice, or dealing, or some combination of these. In any event there has to be a cooling-off period, generally in the form of a seven-day pause during which no services can be provided under the relevant customer agreement and it can be cancelled without cost.

(iii) *Existing customers.* The s.56 prohibition is also lifted where there is a legitimately established[2] customer relationship such that the investor *envisages* calls of the kind concerned.[3]

(iv) *Non-private investors.* The s.56 prohibition is again lifted where the person called is a non-private *investor* and the aim is to do business with him in his capacity as such (UCR 1.1). The UCRs thus draw the line in a different place from the core rules which, as we have seen, treat 'small' business investors as private customers. The reason for drawing the line differently in connection with unsolicited calls is the feeling that anyone who is in business as a corporate entity must expect to receive unsolicited calls from other kinds of business. If it emerges that the person called is a small business investor, the authorised person who called him must afford him private *customer* treatment under the applicable conduct of business rules.[4]

(v) *Overseas person calls.* Where the unsolicited call is made by an unauthorised 'overseas person' – i.e. an overseas investment business without a UK base and without UK authorisation – a stricter regime applies since the safeguards associated with authorisation under the Financial Services Act – vetting for fitness and properness, subjection to conduct of business requirements, etc. – do not apply. Thus an unauthorised overseas person (e.g. the operator of a collective investment scheme recognised under s.87) does not have the privilege of being able to make unsolicited calls upon UK private customers with a view to selling *packaged products* (though the overseas person may enter into a deal pursuant to an unsolicited call made by a UK authorised or exempted person).[5] Nor is an unauthorised overseas person in a position to

---

[1] 'Readily realisable' securities are those listed or regularly traded on an EC exchange or a recognised investment exchange: Financial Services Glossary 1991 (Second Edition).

[2] e.g. without breach of s.56 or 57.

[3] UCR 4.1. Of course, if the investor does not merely envisage but expressly invites the call it falls outside the scope of s.56 in the first place.

[4] For the distinction between a private investor and a private customer, see above, pp. 268–9.

[5] UCR 2.2.

supply private customers with *investment services* pursuant to an unsolicited call.[1] Calls upon *existing customers* must not only satisfy the conditions outlined in paragraph (iii) above, there is also a requirement that the customer relationship existed while the investor was resident outside the UK, that the investor indicated *in writing* that he envisaged calls, and that the investor has been warned that the normal UK investor protections will not apply.[2] The privileges of the unauthorised overseas person are less highly circumscribed where *non-private investors* are concerned, but if the non-private investor upon whom a call is made turns out to be a 'small' business investor (and hence to be treated as a private customer in dealings with UK authorised persons) no business may be done.[3]

Deposit-taking

The Treasury has power under the Banking Act to regulate the making of unsolicited calls (whether by banks, building societies or overseas deposit-takers) with a view to procuring the making of deposits.[4] No regulations have in fact been made – presumably for the reasons discussed in the introduction to the section on unsolicited calls.[5]

---

[1] UCR 3.   [2] UCR 4.3, 4.4.b.   [3] UCR 1.2.

[4] Banking Act 1987, s.34: 'Unsolicited call' is defined as in s.56 of the Financial Services Act. But under the Banking Act the sanctions are criminal: s.34(3). Cf. FSA s.56(2).

[5] Above, pp. 314–15.

APPENDIX

The Principles stated by the Securities and Investments Board for the conduct and financial standing of persons authorised to carry on investment business.

1 Integrity

A firm should observe high standards of integrity and fair dealing.

2 Skill, Care and Diligence

A firm should act with due skill, care and diligence.

3 Market Practice

A firm should observe high standards of market conduct. It should also, to the extent endorsed for the purpose of this principle, comply with any code or standard as in force from time to time and as it applies to the firm either according to its terms or by rulings made under it.

4 Information about Customers

A firm should seek from customers it advises or for whom it exercises discretion any information about their circumstances and investment objectives which might reasonably be expected to be relevant in enabling it to fulfil its responsibilities to them.

5 Information for Customers

A firm should take reasonable steps to give a customer it advises, in a comprehensible and timely way, any information needed to enable him to make a balanced and informed decision. A firm should similarly be ready to provide a customer with a full and fair account of the fulfilment of its responsibilities to him.

6 Conflicts of Interest

A firm should either avoid any conflict of interest arising or, where conflicts arise, should ensure fair treatment to all its customers by disclosure, internal rules of confidentiality, declining to act, or otherwise. A firm should not unfairly place its interests above those of its customers and, where a properly informed customer would reasonably expect that the firm would place his interests above its own, the firm should live up to that expectation.

7 Customer Assets

Where a firm has control of or is otherwise responsible for assets belonging to a customer which it is required to safeguard, it should arrange proper protection for them, by way of segregation and identification of those assets or otherwise, in accordance with the responsibility it has accepted.

8 Financial Resources

A firm should ensure that it maintains adequate financial resources to meet its investment business commitments and to withstand the risks to which its business is subject.

9 Internal Organisation

A firm should organise and control its internal affairs in a responsible manner, keeping proper records, and where the firm employs staff or is responsible for the conduct of investment business by others, should have adequate arrangements to ensure that they are suitable, adequately trained and properly supervised and that it has well-defined compliance procedures.

10 Relations with Regulators

A firm should deal with its regulator in an open and cooperative manner and keep the regulator promptly informed of anything concerning the firm which might reasonably be expected to be disclosed to it.

ABBREVIATIONS

BA	Banking Act 1987
BSA	Building Societies Act 1986
Financial Services Act White Paper	*Financial Services in the United Kingdom: A New Framework for Investor Protection*, Cmnd. 9423 (1985)
FSA	Financial Services Act 1986
Gower, *Disc. Doc*	Gower, *Review of Investor Protection: A Discussion Document* (1982)
Gower, *Report*, Part I	Gower, *Review of Investor Protection. Report: Part I*, Cmnd. 9215 (1984)
Gower, *Report*, Part II	Gower, *Review of Investor Protection. Report: Part II* (1985)
ICA	Insurance Companies Act 1982
SSA	Social Security Act
SSPA	Social Security Pensions Act 1985
Wilson Report	*Report of the Committee to Review the Functioning of Financial Institutions*, Cmnd. 7937 (1980)

CASES

STATUTES

STATUTORY INSTRUMENTS

EUROPEAN COMMUNITY DIRECTIVES

RULES AND REGULATIONS OF THE SECURITIES AND INVESTMENTS BOARD (SIB)

INDEX